DREAM REPAIRMAN

DREAM REPAIRMAN

ADVENTURES IN FILM EDITING

ACADEMY AWARD WINNER
JIM CLARK
with John H. Myers

LANDMARC PRESS

For general information on our other products and services or for technical support, please contact LandMarc Press at (936) 544-5137, fax (936) 544-2270, or on the web at www.LandMarcPress.com.

ISBN 978-0-9797184-9-6

Printed in the United States of America.

10 9 8 7 6 5 4 3 2 1

CONTENTS

FOREWORD

I'VE BEEN A FILM EDITOR for more years than I care to remember. I've also tried my hand at directing and writing but it's in the cutting room that I've made my most substantial contributions to the films I've worked on. This book won't teach you much about film editing. I'm not certain you can learn such skills from a book. Editing film is really a combination of instinct and experience with a lot of experimentation thrown in.

On a movie, once all the actors and crew have left the payroll, everything is left in the hands of the director and the editor. Together they prune and trim and try things out and are, ultimately, the last people to work on a picture. If the relationship between them has been fruitful, the director will usually continue to work with the same editor on subsequent films as a kind of mental shorthand develops between them. There is also something of the confessional about an editing suite. Editors always hear the gossip about everyone. Indeed, if I were a less discreet person, this book could be a huge tabloid sensation but, sadly, should that be your inclination, it is not.

I don't really have a definite style. Each project brings with it a new set of challenges that must be met. Over the years I've learned to provide the director with as much choice as I can from the material I'm given, but so much does depend on that material. If you're handed a boring load of old tosh, it's rather difficult to weave it into a masterpiece, but often a fine film can be carved out of confusing footage. Having begun my career on the shop floor of Ealing Studios, my development has been slow and steady. I was able to work under and with some marvelous characters who have helped shape me into the editor I've become.

This book contains material about films you may never have heard of. The flops are given space along with the hits simply because their progress to the movie graveyard is memorable.

Film editors, as a rule, don't get too close to the stars, but you will find Cary Grant, Audrey Hepburn, Dustin Hoffman, Vincent Price, Robert De Niro, Glenn Close, Bill Cosby, Ralph Fiennes, Leonardo DiCaprio, and many others featuring in the stories I tell. There's no doubting the closeness between an editor and a director. In this regard I've worked closely with a great number of fine directors including John Schlesinger, Stanley Donen, Jack Clayton, Michael Caton-Jones, Roland Joffé, Michael Apted, and Mike Leigh. Another important player in the making of a movie is a strong producer and, again, I've had the good fortune to work with some of the best. David Puttnam, Robert Evans, Jerome Hellman, Joseph Janni, Art Linson, and Scott Rudin are just a few.

As long as I'm dropping names I might as well throw in some of the composers I've worked closely with: Henry Mancini, Elmer Bernstein, John Barry, Denis King, and Rachel Portman.

Most good film editors remain unknown to the public. This in no way diminishes the role they play in the success or failure of the finished product. We remember Alfred Hitchcock but not George Tomasini. We know Howard Hawks but not Christian Nyby and on it goes. In the film credits we are featured way down along with carpenters, but some of us have risen above our station.

Sometimes the editor finds himself in a dilemma about a major complaint. Do you voice it or merely keep quiet and cut the footage you've been given? It can make matters very awkward. I'm happy to say that I have never fallen out with a director by being outspoken, though these pages might destroy that happy state. What follows is not always kind, but it is truthful. Apologies to all who get slagged.

I should also mention here and now that I owe a very large debt to my wife and family. I have not always treated them well but they have continued to stick by me as the film industry has claimed my loyalty. Without them my life would have been a sad and dull affair and the following pages may attest that they have been wonderful, so it is to my family that this book is dedicated.

Thanks also are due to my film editing assistants over the years: Bryan Oates, Artie Schmidt, Gavin Buckley, Nick Moore, Simon Cozens, among others. I'm also indebted to writer Ken Levison for dredging up his memories of our collaborations and to Johnny Myers for helping me make this book a bit more readable than it might otherwise have been.

So turn the pages if you will and learn something of a life lived on the cutting room floor.

Jim Clark
London 2009

INTRODUCTION

VERY FEW FILM EDITORS OF Jim Clark's stature and renown have written the story of their working lives. Editors are, in a way, the unsung heroes and heroines of filmmaking, a fact that makes *The Dream Repairman* both a timely and remarkable book. Here, we have rare and firsthand testimony from the cutting room and, the editor's voice is always one to heed.

I first met Jim Clark in the early 1980s, over a quarter of a century ago, through his wife Laurence Méry-Clark, who was the editor of the first film I wrote, *Good and Bad at Games* (1983). After Laurence introduced us, the Boyds and the Clarks began to see each other socially from time to time. It turned out we had mutual acquaintances. Frederic Raphael and John Schlesinger, for example. Thus our friendship fortuitously began.

My professional association with Jim started a little later when my third film, *Stars and Bars* (1988), was produced at Columbia Pictures when David Puttnam was head of the studio. Jim had moved to Los Angeles with Puttnam to be a senior executive at Columbia, and I remember having lunch with Jim and Laurence at their rented house in Los Angeles while I was on a trip out there. I think Jim was gently shepherding *Stars and Bars* through Columbia though it was eventually released after David Puttnam's tenure and when the Los Angeles period of Jim's life was also over.

Our friendship continued back in London but we worked together again on the film of my first novel *A Good Man in Africa* (1994), with Jim editing, and with me as the writer/co-producer. Bruce Beresford was director but Bruce had to leave us early during post-production to shoot another film he had committed to and, consequently, Jim and I were thrust together to see the film through some of its post-production phases. I remember a particularly fraught afternoon in a Wembley sound studio supervising the recording of the score, Jim and I tentatively taking turns giving the composer our somewhat critical notes.

All this is by way of a preamble to explain why, when I eventually came to direct my first film, *The Trench* (1999), there was only one editor I could possibly choose as far as I was concerned. I asked Jim and, luckily for me, he said yes, with one caveat: He would have to leave almost immediately after the shoot and the first assembly of the film to go and cut the new James Bond movie, so someone else would have to take over for the rest of post-production. And who better than his wife, Laurence, who had edited the film of my first screenplay? Full circle, of a sort. So I claim this unique first: I am the only film director ever to have had his film cut by the husband-and-wife team of the Clarks. I was extremely fortunate, and I knew it.

When I first met Jim, I was aware of his reputation in the industry. The legendary "Doctor" Clark, the man who could make sick films healthy again. I knew about his lengthy career, his astonishing filmography, the great directors he had worked with, the films he had saved through his editorial finesse, the Oscars he had been nominated for, and the Oscar he had won. For a tyro film director like me, it was both an honour and, in many ways, an alarmingly daunting prospect to think of Jim in the editing suite waiting for the daily rushes of my film.

It turned out to be a fascinating adventure, and I wonder if my experience is common to the other directors he has worked with. Jim is a man renowned for his candour: he does not pull punches, he does not mince his words, he is fearlessly honest. Standing on the set of *The Trench* that first day, with Liz West, my script supervisor, I evolved a plan—not a plan of attack, more a plan of defence. Jim became a kind of admonitory ghostly presence on the set, as if he were hovering at our backs. We would shoot the scene in question and then Liz and I would go into a huddle and try to second-guess what the Clark analysis and response would be. "What would Jim think?" became our working mantra. Because we were shooting on a set at Bray Studios, the cutting room was only fifty yards away and Jim would wander over occasionally to see how we were getting on. He never said very much, but from time to time we would receive terse notes: "I need another closeup"; "This scene won't cut together"; "This shot goes on too long"; "I need a reverse on such-and-such a character" and so forth. From our point of view the aim was to go through a day without receiving any feedback from the cutting room, without one of these dreaded notes being delivered. We grew better and better. It was, I see now, a benign on-the-job learning curve for me, and I came to understand a huge amount about how to shoot a film professionally, properly and, equally importantly, I began to realise how a film is re-created in the cutting room.

The role of editor in the collective, collaborative process that is the making of any film is massively important but not one, I believe, that is generally recognised outside the small pond that is the filmmaking community. One of the great lessons of this wonderfully enjoyable memoir is that this point becomes steadily obvious, but it is made with subtlety, discretion, and modesty. It is also a potted history of the post-war film industry in England and America and, of course, an autobiography. The trouble with writing an autobiography is that you can't really say what a great guy you are, what fun you are to work with and hang out with, what insight and instinct you have about the art form of cinema, and how much and how many film directors are indebted to you. But I can, so now it is on the record. *The Dream Repairman* is a delight, a classic of its kind and so is its author.

William Boyd
London, April 2009

EARLY DAYS IN BOSTON, LINCS AND LONDON

'D ALWAYS WANTED TO BE in the movie business but the chances of that happening were remote. I come from Boston, Lincolnshire, which is on the east coast of England. That's where the American Boston got its name. But the buck stopped there and Boston, England, was a backwater.

I was born in 1931, the result, so they told me, of a Masonic dinner. My mother's family was in the seed business. I had two older siblings, Hazel and Dick. We all lived a stable, typically undisturbed, middle-class life. My father was managing director of the family printing concern, Fisher Clark, and I was supposed to be a printer when I'd finished my education at boarding school. That was my destiny.

Fisher Clark was a fairly big firm that employed around 700 people. It was the largest business in the area; its specialty was printing labels for any old thing, but mostly clothes. Every time you buy a bit of clothing, it has a label on it, which is thrown away by the purchaser. There was a lot of money to be made printing labels.

My father was also very interested in photography and cinematography, so, when I was ten, he gave me a silent movie projector. My grandfather was a major shareholder in a couple of cinemas in the town—The New Theatre and The Regal. When I was eleven, he gave me a special pass, which meant I could go any time for free with a friend. Many boys and girls, barely known to me, rapidly became my best friends.

So I became more and more interested in cinema and film and, as I got older, my interest intensified and I got involved with a group called the Federation of Film Societies. Everywhere you went in the forties and fifties, there were film societies because television didn't amount to much and you couldn't see foreign films easily.

People got together and ran 16 mm copies of the best French, German, Scandinavian, or Italian films. I started two film societies, one at Oundle School and another in Boston, and little by little I became more and more involved in these societies, which eventually brought me to London quite often for committee meetings, and the annual viewing sessions that would run for whole weekends. I met people who were in the business of actually making films.

Eventually, one of these people, who was working at a documentary house making industrial films, offered me a job as a trainee "gofer," doing bits and pieces of everything. The company was Industrial Colour Films, located in King's Cross. It was very small and had only five employees.

Having obtained a job in London, I was full of trepidation as I approached our house in Boston. I entered the living room where I found my parents listening to the radio. I came straight to the point. "Well," I said, "I've just come from London and I got myself a job." Horror! Although my mother was absolutely stunned that I'd done such a thing, my father actually gave me his blessing. I think, in the end, Father realised that I was doing what he'd always wanted to do and he was very supportive.

So I packed up the Rover car my father had given me for my eighteenth birthday and drove to London where I moved in with Dr. Booth and his family, good friends who were now living in Ealing. I occupied a flat in their house and worked as an assistant cameraman, editor, and general dogsbody for £3 a week. But after a year, Industrial Colour Films went bankrupt. Suddenly I had no job and didn't know what to do. I was twenty-one years old, had no film union membership, *de rigueur* in those days, and didn't know anybody in the business who could help me.

Good fortune, however, came to my rescue. Dr. Booth was the medical health officer for the Borough of Ealing and, seeing the predicament I was in, told me he had a doctor friend who occasionally went to Ealing Studios whenever somebody was injured or sick. "I'll ask him to put in a good word for you with the personnel manager," he said.

I was summoned to the office of Baynham Honri, who I presumed was the personnel manager. He was a short dark man with very thick glasses who had been in vaudeville before entering films and he asked me many questions about my ambitions, interests, and other aspects of my life, while cleaning his nails. I didn't leave there feeling I'd made a good impression, but I did tell him that my chief interest was in editing and left him with a piece of paper outlining my experience. We didn't call them CVs or resumes in those days. I left the studio without any certainty of ever entering it again.

Some weeks elapsed. My parents were worried about me. Finally the studio called. It was some sort of miracle. God and Bay Honri were smiling on me. This was a Friday afternoon, and I started work at Ealing on the following Monday morning as a trainee in the cutting room.

Ealing Studios

So much has been written about Ealing Studios but I have rarely read the truth of what it was like to work there. Contrary to glowing rumour, it was not always a cosy, maternal studio. It was suffused with pride for a start and, once there, you were expected not to leave, unless you had the misfortune of being told to do so.

Ealing was a microcosm of British society, reflected in the pictures they made. The celebrated Ealing comedies were mostly written and made by public schoolboys or university graduates, and major decisions were made at roundtable conferences chaired by Sir Michael Balcon, who was responsible for Ealing's rise and fall.

The studio was class ridden. You knew your station and stayed in it or incurred wrath in high places. It was such a small world that everyone knew everyone else's business. A big sign exhorted us to great effort, just like something you might have seen in China during the Cultural Revolution. It read "The Studio That Pulls Together" and was in big black letters up on the wall of Stage A.

I was in the cutting room with sound editors Mary Habberfield and Nick MacDonald. They were preparing tracks for *The Titfield Thunderbolt*, one of their lesser comedies that was directed by Charles Crichton. My duties were largely centered around the rewinder. I had to rewind the reels and also learned how to use the Bell & Howell foot joiner, a massive iron pedal-operated device. This was a machine you had to respect or it would have your fingers.

I was so thrilled at being there that I would willingly do anything but I soon learned not to give opinions or to be even faintly critical. I also learned to fear Mrs. Brown, the massive head of the "cuttin' room." Mrs. Brown never sounded a "g" in her many pronouncements. Her office was at the far end of the cutting block on the first floor, up a short flight of stairs. Her sister was in charge of the negative cutting room as Ealing always cut it's own negative.

Mrs. Brown bullied her sister dreadfully. In fact, she bullied everyone under her, while bowing and fawning to those above, particularly Sir Michael, whose rushes were always at 12 noon precisely. Mrs. Brown presided over the rushes (the first prints made of a movie after a period of shooting) and would not hold back her feelings if anything went amiss or, God forbid, any assistant was late delivering the material.

It was always an anxious time for us. Perhaps the labs had delivered late or the first assistant had problems syncing them up. Whatever the reason, there was usually a queue of frantic assistants waiting to leap onto the joining machine, dash through the reel, and hope that the joins would hold. Sometimes they flew apart and then there'd be the devil to pay and a trip up the stairs to Mrs. Brown's office.

This was before magnetic film. Optical sound was on a different spool, so action and sound were separate and kept in sync by the edge numbers that the assistant would put on every foot of film, using the Moy edge-numbering machine. These numbers, identical on action and sound, would allow the editor to keep the film in sync and to easily recognise what he was handling, since the edge number contained the slate number, the take number, and the footage. Occasionally the numbering block on the Moy would get stuck and, unless the assistant was very wide awake, this would go unnoticed, requiring you to then erase the incorrect numbers, using a solvent that would be banned today because it could give you a "high" and eat your lungs.

Ealing was fine if you'd been to boarding school. It was run on the same hierarchical lines. Sir Michael was the headmaster; the producers, directors, writers, and heads of departments were the senior staff; and everyone else were the students in varying degrees of seniority.

Being a trainee, I was at the bottom of the ladder but would gradually claw my way up. Working at the studio was pure heaven, and I met wonderful people there. It was the equivalent of today's film schools, though better since I had the incredible incentive of working on actual films for major cinema release.

Those not prepared to muck in weren't tolerated. I recall a university graduate entering the cutting room who didn't last long. He found the task of joining one piece of film to another tedious. Naturally he wanted to be a director and could not tolerate the notion of spending his days in that way, repetitive work requiring no intellect at all. My attitude, however, was somewhat different. Yes it was dull work, but it was a necessary part in the making of a picture. It taught me little or nothing about the editing of films, I learned that later, but I felt part of the team and I enjoyed the company.

I was soon moved onto the sound of *The Cruel Sea*, at that time the most ambitious of the Ealing pictures. Charles Frend was directing this epic naval story, based on a best-selling novel by Nicholas Monsarrat. Jack Hawkins was the lead actor, and the film editor, just up the corridor, was Peter Tanner. I worked under the sound editor Gordon Stone. I admired Gordon tremendously, not only because he was good at his job, but because he had a wonderful sense of humour that infected us all.

We all worked long hours getting *The Cruel Sea* ready for mixing. Ealing had its own sound department and the head mixer was Steven Dalby. In those days, the final mix of a film was an extremely tense affair, quite different from the systems we now use. Because magnetic film was not yet in common use, all of the sound was optical, so the dialogue tracks, normally three or four, were negative or neg cut. The negative cutting of a film is the final act of putting the scissors to the negative and assembling it to match the positive print that you've edited. A fine cut is the absolutely final version of the film that goes to neg cut. Once it was neg cut, it was cut for good.

The editor would cut the dialogue using the rushes and normally split this into two tracks in order to create sound overlaps. When the film was fine cut, these dialogue tracks would be neg cut, since they were shot on optical negative stock and returned for the mixing process. Any post-synched dialogue would be cut separately and we, therefore, ended up taking several dialogue tracks into the dubbing room.

We normally had two prints made up by the lab, using one print for rehearsals (it's not just actors and musicians who rehearse) and conserving the other for the actual final takes of the reel. Rehearsals were long and arduous since the intention was to iron out any problems and allow the mixers to learn the reel thoroughly before going for a take. If mistakes were made during final recording, the reel had to be restarted. Quite apart from the dialogue reels, the music tracks were also optical and given similar treatment. The sound effects were often laid up in reels or were looped, like a background of birdsong, running water, or light wind might be taken from a continuous loop of film, the join carefully "blooped" to avoid a click when it passed over the sound head. Blooping was a procedure that was an absolute pain for all of us assistants because the blooping ink used to go all over our clothes. It was, however, necessary in those days before magnetic. Every join, so that it should be soundless when it went over the sound head, had to be blooped. You would paint with opaque black ink, a triangular image on the positive optical track of the film itself. If you didn't bloop the join, it would make a popping noise.

Eventually when the mixers had balanced everything and the director had approved, they would go for a take and, at that moment, the tension increased. Mistakes were now costly. Being a sound mixer in those days was ulcerating, though, if a reel had been going well before errors were made, the good section could be saved and used, since it was possible to neg cut the final mix too.

One of my tasks as the junior assistant was to carry the spools of film over to the mixing room. This involved picking up perhaps ten spools of film, a heavy load. The editing rooms at Ealing were on the first floor and connected to the projection booths and the dubbing room by an iron gantry that was partially open to the elements. It was said that projectionists, if caught short, would piss over the side. Legend had it that one had once showered Sir Michael as he entered the theatre below.

One wet evening, we were mixing late and I was carrying a reel of tracks over to the mixing room, when I slipped, sending several spools of film falling over the gantry and into the muddy earth below. What a quandary! I raced down and gathered up what I could. The tin lids had mostly fallen off and the tracks were wrecked. I knew there were people waiting for them. There was nothing for it but to carry those sodden and ruined tracks back into the room and apologise. All work was abandoned on these reels until reprints could be rushed from the labs. Rather than give me a stern rebuke for wrecking things, those present, including Charlie Frend and Les Norman, the producer, simply accepted the situation and went home. I, however, felt terrible about it and never again was stupid enough to overburden myself with too heavy a load.

I had become friendly with another editor, Seth Holt, and, after I'd spent a whole year on a Bell & Howell foot joiner and several more months on a Moy numbering machine, I became his second assistant. Seth, unlike most of the editors, was an intellectual. He had started as an actor, and I don't recall how he rose in the ranks at Ealing, since he was still quite young. I suspect, however, that it was because Seth was related to Robert Hamer, the Ealing director who had made *Kind Hearts and Coronets*. Seth gave me my break as his second assistant on a now forgotten comedy *The Love Lottery* in which David Niven was directed by Charles Crichton.

☆　☆　☆

It was during the shooting of this picture that I met my first wife, Jessie Holling, who was Crichton's secretary. She was only twenty-four but already a widow with a child. Her husband, David Holling, had fallen into the Thames and drowned. Jessie originally became involved with David when he was a young scenic artist, working at Pinewood Studios. They had a fling, she became pregnant, and they married. She never spoke very much about him after he drowned. It was clear that nobody made an effort to rescue him, and I later gathered that he was a drunk and disliked by most people. Perhaps she felt relief that he had gone.

She now lived in Ealing with her elderly parents. Her mother, a Russian who never mastered English, looked after her son, Andrew, who was two. Her father, an Englishman, worked for the Inland Revenue. These were difficult times for her family, and Jessie and I, being co-workers, were often thrown together, mostly in the Queen Victoria Pub across the road.

At that time, all the younger cutting room people used to go out drinking together. One thing led to another and Jessie and I began an affair. It was my first, at twenty-one and, being a late starter, I soon discovered that movies were not the only route to happiness.

I was a regular at a special shop in Ealing that sold prophylactics. There were separate entrances for men and women. On entering I would be greeted by a man dressed in a spotless white lab coat. He would ask me what I required. "A dozen of the best," I would reply and he'd take from under the counter a cardboard box and a rigid piece of wood resembling an erect phallus. Then each condom would be rolled onto this device, a burst of air would inflate it, and the assistant would then wave the balloon over his face to test for leaks. He would go through the entire dozen in this manner no matter how many customers were waiting in line. I soon discovered that asking for twelve was always embarrassing.

I visited Jessie's parents frequently and became fond of her little boy, who was chatty and lively, but the relationship was riddled with friction. Jessie was given to tantrums, which I found very difficult to cope with. After six months, Jessie and I split up.

I went on to another film at Ealing and, although I saw Jessie almost every day, we rarely spoke. It was, therefore, a dreadful shock to learn from a third party that Jessie's mother had died and Andrew had been placed in a Catholic home in Brighton. I called Jessie directly and learned the whole story. It was not pleasant and she was deeply troubled by her situation—having to continue working to support herself and the child. She visited Andrew every Saturday. Having a car, I suggested I should drive her to Brighton the next weekend.

When I saw Andrew in the hall of the home where he'd been placed, I was very upset. This little boy who had formerly been active and chatty was now a thin, withdrawn figure who didn't utter a word when we took him out walking along the pier. I was confronted with a situation that I felt inadequate to address. Nothing had prepared me for this but I felt it was necessary to act. However irrationally, I knew I could not return Andrew to that home where he was, clearly, deeply unhappy and, yet, I did not have an alternative that made any sense. There was no real relationship between Jessie and myself. We had split months before and were not in love though we enjoyed one another's company. Jessie was often volatile, and I wouldn't have called her a good mother. Andrew was often screamed at and clouted on the head. She did love him, however, and she and Andrew were obviously suffering. I felt that I had to do something to help, so instead of driving them back to the home, I took them to Ealing where I deposited the child with his grandfather then took Jessie to dinner at a cafe on Richmond Bridge and proposed marriage.

Totally crazy though it was, it seemed the only way of keeping Andrew and his mother together. My parents were mystified and the Booths worried that I was making a major error.

Curiously I was not worried at all and even rather enjoyed this fuss. I arranged to move in with Jessie, Andrew, and her father and we all lived together in a small terraced house in Creighton Road, Ealing, while Jessie and I continued to work at the studio.

Because she was a Catholic, Jessie wanted to marry in a church of her choice. My mother, being staunch Church of England, was outraged. I asked my old Boston friend Chris Sharpe to be my best man.

The day of the wedding arrived. Jessie went into a funk and refused to get up and go to the church. Chris and I, with the aid of numerous tots of brandy, finally hauled her out of bed, got her into a dress and to the church where we had kept the guests waiting.

We had a reasonably happy life afterward, continuing much as before, though we could now afford to have Andrew cared for during the day. It wasn't long before Jessie was pregnant, and Kate was born in 1956. It was clear that the house was no longer large enough to hold us all, so I bought another home in Ealing on Warwick Road, which was nondescript but big.

Life with Jessie was seldom tranquil. She was not a natural mother, being subject to fits of temper that were often hard to accept. After she quit working to stay home and look after both children, she mellowed considerably. Having two children to attend to absorbed her, but it wasn't long before she was pregnant again.

☆ ☆ ☆

By this time I was gaining some ground at the studio, busy most of the year, rarely out of work and I had been made an "assistant" to Jack Harris, who would be crucial to my future career and development. Jack had started out in silent films. He'd had a long tenure at Twickenham Studios where he supervised film editing in the thirties. He had immense experience and he'd cut a lot of films for David Lean. As his assistant, I was very interested in his working methods. Jack was a terribly slow thinker. If you asked him a question, you had to wait at least five minutes for the answer.

Jack was both painstaking and non-intellectual. He was more interested in his garden than anything else. Very tall and thin, he smoked like a chimney. In fact, we used to worry that the ash would fall off his cigarette into the trim bin and set everything on fire. You weren't supposed to smoke in the cutting room at all because the film was so flammable. Jack never did actually cause a fire.

When Jack had a scene to cut, he would ponder the material endlessly. He would never begin thinking about the cuts until he had all the material to hand. He'd have the rushes on a spool-loading Moviola. There would be ten minutes of film on a reel that he would run backwards and forwards, backwards and forwards, incessantly for a day or so. It used to drive us all crazy because, it seemed to us, he was never going to cut the film. As an assistant, you'd be sitting there, just dying for him to stop the machine, take it off the Moviola, put it on the synchroniser, and actually make a cut. He would just keep spooling in a silence you could carve with a knife.

Jack was a very mild mannered man, but he did require that his assistants behave themselves. If there was too much noise, he would turn and say "Hey, Cocky! Be quiet!" One always knew when Jack was angry since the "Cocky" word was only uttered when he was disturbed. Normally, while concentrating on the rushes, he would not speak and nor would we.

Finally, after much cigarette smoke and silence, Jack would take his grease pencil and make a mark on the film. We'd all heave a collective sigh of relief, put the reel onto the synchroniser and he would cut the scene. He would then cut the scene very quickly, not joining the action and sound but attaching them with paper clips. The actual joining was done by the assistants on the finger-eating Bell & Howell joiner.

When the editor was cutting film in those days, the assistant would stand behind him, trim bin in hand, in order to hang up the discarded film on the correct peg, ready for filing. The filing of trims was one of our main jobs. We'd collect all the trims, action and sound, rubber banding them and winding them up into a single slate, then adding a label, which identified it. The slate was then put into a can with top and side labels. In theory this would prevent loss of material.

Some editors, while working alone at night, would be totally undisciplined and allow the trims to fall into the bin. The poor assistant might come in the next morning to find a chaos of trims, all of which had to be sorted out and filed, but Jack Harris was a very disciplined man and made life easy for his assistant by being scrupulous. I don't ever recall losing anything on a Harris picture.

The great value of Jack to a production, in spite of the time he spent contemplating the rushes, was that the rough cut was so expertly done that most directors wouldn't tamper with it. What I learned from Jack was patience—a trait that has served me well. Today a film editor has to be really patient. Not with the material, but with the producers and financiers, who, once the director presents his version are in the cutting room, arguing, stating their opinions, and making calls on their mobiles. It becomes a bedlam. Back in Jack Harris' day, nobody came near him.

✷ ✷ ✷

I was still an assistant at Ealing when I was called by Basil Wright, a great documentary filmmaker who I'd met briefly at the Edinburgh Film Festival. He was producing a feature for the Children's Film Foundation, *The Magic Marble* that was being directed by John Durst. His editor had suddenly been called away. Basil wondered if I might be interested in taking over the editing. This was an extraordinary suggestion. I had never cut a frame of film in my life, but it was a tempting idea and it only took a short time to make my decision.

The news was not received well at Ealing. Mrs. Brown more or less said I would never work there again.

Nervously I arrived at Rotherhithe studio and walked into the cutting room. The film was larded with special effects, the premise being that a small boy owned a marble that, when rubbed, would produce a genie and so things grew smaller or larger. I do recall that I was much helped with this magic by Vic Margutti who was a special effects wizard of the period.

The shoot lasted only about six weeks because the Children's Film Foundation did not make films with large budgets, and I do recall that we moved away from Rotherhithe and took a cutting room just off Kensington High Street. The film sound was mixed at Anvil by Ken Cameron and, although Basil Wright and I never had words, I got the feeling that he was disappointed in my work. We certainly never had any connection thereafter. I believe the film won some kind of award at a festival that year and was released under the title *One Wish Too Many.*

So there I was, a film editor without a film—nobody knew me so I had little chance of landing another job. Things got quite desperate for a time, and I eventually found work with the Disney company in London who had offices in Old Compton Street, Soho. This was followed by editing on two short documentaries that were directed in Cinemascope by Geoff Foot, himself an editor. One was about Scotland but it turned out to be a short job and then they had me cutting some puppet films featuring Sooty.

This was the lowest spot in my career. We worked in a basement room in Wardour Street with no windows. My assistant and I sweated over these wretched puppet films until I was about to cry with despair. There were moments when the idea of throwing in the towel and returning to Boston with my tail between my legs seemed attractive.

As a sort of desperate act, I called up Jack Harris and asked if he was doing anything and did he need an assistant? Jack must have realised how dreadful my plight was. It turned out he was about to start editing *The Prince and the Showgirl* for Laurence Olivier, but had already hired a first assistant, Desmond Saunders. Jack wondered if I might be interested in being the second assistant? Without hesitating, I accepted. I went directly from being a film editor back to a job as the joining boy. It was a move I've never regretted since it got me out of a rut and made me realise that life in the real world was hard and combative. I knew I would be happier in a more secure situation. I went, in one move, from Sooty to Marilyn Monroe.

☆ ☆ ☆

It was during this period that Jessie suddenly died. Bending down to tidy up after a children's party, she felt a searing pain in her chest. She was eight months pregnant.

When I arrived home, she was in the bath, hoping the heat would stifle the pain, but it seemed to increase rather than diminish. Since she was only a month away from completing her term, I thought it best to take her directly to the nursing home where she could deliver the child.

It was a short drive, during which she was doubled up with pain. I left her in the care of the doctors and returned home.

That night I had wild and vile dreams. I was awakened at around 6 AM by a phone call from the nursing home. At first I thought they were calling to tell me

Jessie had given birth. That was not the case. There was some sense of panic in the doctor's voice as he said, "Come at once." I dashed to her bedside. A priest was just leaving, having administered the last rites.

She was dead when I saw her. Just dead, still warm—I looked at her in complete disbelief.

The doctor tried to explain. An aneurism . . . the wall of the heart collapsed . . . blood into the lungs . . . terribly sorry . . . nothing could be done . . . have a brandy. I was so stunned I forgot to cry.

It was not until I walked into the hallway and saw the bag of clothes we had brought for the new child on the previous evening. I stopped, looking at the little bag—no longer needed—and then burst into tears.

Jessie's funeral was a sad affair and most of the friends who had attended our wedding were there, certainly all the old friends from Ealing Studios.

Andrew didn't come to the funeral. I thought it too soon to explain what had happened to his mother. It was some weeks before I told him his mother had died. He was five at the time and probably did not fully comprehend. Kate was not yet two so she had no way to comprehend what had happened. It was only a few weeks later that I adopted Andrew legally and Jessie's father came to live with us.

When you are young life seems limitless. I was twenty-eight when Jessie died. I had been married four years and had two young children to support. It was without reluctance that I went back to work. It seemed the best therapy.

FLASHBACK: *Nevill Holt Prep School*

Many parents sent their kids to prep schools when I was young. So when I was ten, my parents sent me off. Nevill Holt was the prep school for Uppingham Public School and lay between Uppingham and Market Harborough. It was entirely isolated and stood on top of a hill that overlooked a great valley. It is no longer a school, but at that time it was home to eighty boys.

On the big day my trunk was packed, my tuck-box filled with any extra rations my mother could spare, along with toys and other amusements. The box, made of soft white wood with black painted steel supports at the corners, had, on the top, my initials in bold, black letters. I arrived there in the Spring of 1941 clutching my gas mask and Mickey Mouse annual. My father had driven me to the school, using precious petrol coupons. I was introduced to the headmaster and his wife, a formidably large lady of French extraction. Then came introductions to the matron and a variety of teachers followed by tea in the headmaster's study. .

It was then time for farewells. No tears. Just a kiss from Mother and Father. The crunch of the tyres on gravel and in a flash they were gone. I was left to myself and my fate. That was the last time I saw my parents in the light of innocence; and though still a child, from that moment on, I had to learn the gentle art of self-preservation. In some sense my childhood had just ended. I was ten years old.

It was, in many ways, an enchanted place. The school had been constructed from a series of connected buildings, which had their origins in Elizabethan times and earlier. I recall King John's Tower. The buildings were joined to a small church, which was never used. Another series of buildings housed classrooms, a swimming pool, and a quadrangle for gymnastics and other communal gatherings. Small cottages were dotted about, used for staff quarters, and there was a farm attached. It was a completely self-contained domain, quite isolated from the rest of the world. The nearest village was a few miles off. A minor road lay outside the school, rarely used in those days.

I made many new friends very quickly. I played games. I learned to swim, read voraciously, and took up painting. My music lessons progressed beyond scales. The food was always good and the school farm kept us well supplied with fresh produce despite rationing.

My bed, in a dormitory shared with four other new boys, became a dark and secret room where I could become invincible. This was the time for homesickness to take hold. Other boys cried themselves to sleep. I don't remember being homesick at all. This new community life was too full and too exciting.

I had a torch through which I could project pictures onto the ceiling. I had a supply of slides for it and we made up stories to illustrate the pictures. It was the star of our dormitory. It was primitive movie making, for this was before I had really fallen for the cinema in any big way.

My real fascination lay in aeroplanes at that time. I had a copy of *Jane's All the World Aircraft*, which became my bible. It was a slim volume, hastily produced for aircraft spotters. All Allied and enemy planes were illustrated graphically. This, and the *Stanley Gibbons Stamp Catalogue* were my main reading for some years. Later I was to devour a new Edgar Wallace thriller every night.

Very soon I realised that I had to develop an inner life. My mind became a fortress. Generally I enjoyed school life, so unlike home life, which intruded when term was over and the holidays started. Before school, my natural habitat had been the nursery, which was my universe with Nanny Ada when I was small. Now it became my first home cinema.

The spin off from Father's home movies came with a Christmas gift of immense potential that he gave me in 1941. It was a 9.5 mm Pathé Ace projector, together with some short comedies and, best of all, a complete print of Alfred Hitchcock's *Blackmail*. From this, without any doubt, came my permanent and lifelong interest in film editing, for I hand cranked my way through many screenings of this silent classic. The sound was added later and was not necessary for an appreciation of the montage. Even at the early age of ten, I began, slowly, to understand something about the rhythm of the cuts. I couldn't have put it quite like that, but I was aware of the cuts and fascinated by the construction of the images into scenes that had suspense and tension. I remember my nursery with those images flickering on the wall.

The Pathé Ace must have been handed to many children of my age. A projector, however, has to be fed and Father allowed me to join a library operated by Wallace Heaton in London's Bond Street. He then, without complaint, began to pay for my habit, which quickly grew. The number of silent films available from Pathé at that time was huge. The catalogue was a treasure trove. I would comb through it for hours before deciding what to rent. Then would come the thrill of waiting. In those days Boston had a direct rail link with London. I would cycle to the station to await the arrival of those brown fibre boxes in which the films were dispatched, often disappointed when they failed to arrive. I could have the films for one day only, after which there was an extra charge.

Films were very important in those pre-television days. At the start of term, boys who lived in large cities would relate the entire plots of films they had seen during their holidays. The more extreme would even act them out, mostly in the dormitory before we all fell asleep or Matron called for "no further talking." One boy, I recall, had somehow been admitted to an H, for Horror, certificate picture, which was very rare indeed. He had to act out the really horrible bits many times for our "delectation and delight," a phrase I'd learned at Butlin's Skegness Holiday Camp. I think the picture was *The Bat*, maybe not, but I know it had Bela Lugosi in it. I rarely had to tell the plots of the films I had seen in Boston because they had been doing the rounds for months and were considered old hat by my more sophisticated friends.

The early interest I had from home movies with the Pathé Ace was fanned at Nevill Holt because the headmaster loved films himself and the school had a 16 mm Ampro sound projector, quite rare in those days, and a source of great interest to me. Films were shown on Sunday evenings during the winter terms, and this was when my interest was really kindled. The boys would sit on the polished wood floor of the Elizabethan ballroom that had a screen raised at one end and the projector stood at the other, operated by the headmaster. The loudspeaker and projector were permanent fixtures, the speaker high up in the ceiling, and the projector locked up in its case between the piano and the lectern. We also had church services in the ballroom, with the headmaster, officiating. Because the war was already underway, supplies for the Ampro were a matter of great concern to the boys, since the projection and the wonderfully worded "Exciter" lamps, essential to the sound, were prone to failure right in the middle of a movie. Spare lamps were at a premium, and we prayed they would last through the film. Later, when American soldiers and airmen were stationed nearby, the problem eased; it seemed their friendly PXs were well stocked with Ampro spares.

Excitement about the Sunday film would grow from mid-week when a small notice would go up announcing the title. It might have read:

Ask a Policeman

Will Hay, Moore Marriott,

Graham Moffatt. 8 reels.

It was that last bit of information that really got to me. I knew that a seven-reel film might not be too good, certainly not very long, whereas a ten-reeler would be the bee's knees. The headmaster always included a short, introducing me to *The Secrets of Nature* and the voice of E.V. H. Emmett as well as to the black and white Mickey Mouse and Popeye cartoons. How we boys laughed. Just like *Sullivan's Travels*.

It was the high point of our week, and the headmaster, well aware of this, used it as the ultimate punishment. Far more hurtful than any beating was that awful moment when he told you that you would retire to bed without supper instead of seeing the film. The dormitories were ranged around the Elizabethan ballroom, so the punished boy would lay in bed, in broad daylight, miserable, listening to a soundtrack, trying to imagine the pictures that accompanied it. I only suffered this once and made certain after that to follow the rules, so it may be that my passion for cinema taught me to be careful. Too careful, I sometimes think.

The films—mostly British—that we saw had been carefully vetted by the headmaster. He subscribed, I later realised, to the GeBescope library from which I also obtained films some years later. In fact the arrival of their annual catalogue was a real high spot. I never became a projectionist at Nevill Holt. Mr. Phillips, our headmaster, was far too possessive to allow that, but he did let me help rewind the big 1,600-foot reels that held forty minutes of each film. In many ways I owe a great debt of gratitude to him, for my first job at Ealing Studios many years later consisted of just that. Many of us in the cutting rooms began as rewind boys.

In the winter terms I longed for the Sunday film show. The weekly evenings seemed so long. After evening prep we were allowed two hours reading or playing table games before bedtime. Often, a few boys were invited to read in the Great Hall. This was a time I really enjoyed. The Hall had a magic atmosphere, exuding the ancient traditions that surrounded it. The lofty oak beams could reach the sky, or so it seemed. I often wondered how they changed the burned out lamps. Trapdoors in the roof was the answer. All around the panelled walls was a collection of spears, swords, muskets, shields, fox masks, and immense tapestries. In the centre of the long back wall was inlaid a great fireplace, on which huge logs lay smouldering for days. The chimney above it was so wide that two boys could climb it simultaneously. The wood smoke smell was unforgettable. It clung to the room even in midsummer. The jewel in the Hall's crown was the grand piano, maybe a Steinway, it was long and thin like the hands of a pianist. When my music teacher, Mr. Lindner played Chopin and Bach on it I was transported. Lying on my back, my imagination would soar beyond the roof and up into the stars. The Hall, the music, and the wood smoke were a potent mixture. When the music stopped, only vague shadows could be seen in the oak beams, and the creaking of hungry beetles.

Although parents were able to visit the school and take their boys out for lunch on a Sunday, that was a rare event for me. Petrol rationing had prevented that. One, however, had little time for parents in schooldays. In fact, a visit was sometimes simply resented, particularly if it involved missing a film.

My parents always encouraged me to bring a friend home, which was too embarrassing. On the few occasions I did this, I had reason to regret it. My mother was sure to say something that my "friend" would then spread around the school. Apart from writing the obligatory letter home every week, which was scrutinised by the teacher and heavily censored, I rarely thought of home. Others blubbered in their beds. Some had good reason for they had lost their fathers on active service. One boy in my dorm, named Barwell, lost his father early in the Battle of Britain and mourned him dreadfully. I think we understood and perhaps didn't tease him too badly.

We were, indeed, still at war and none of us could forget it. Perhaps because we were growing up we became more aware of events surrounding us. Dunkirk was now far behind, the Japanese were sinking most of the Royal Navy, and I had heard about the collapse of Italy during the summer holidays when we waited for a train at a country station. War news rarely reached us at Nevill Holt where no newspapers circulated and no radios were heard. The Blitz had not ended yet, and we knew our air-raid drill by heart.

Nobody seriously worried that Nevill Holt school might be bombed, but there was a large steel mill at Corby across the valley, which was regularly visited by bombers, and on these occasions we were forced to take shelter. Late one night, when I was asleep, we were awakened by rough hands, whisked into dressing gowns and slippers, and marshalled rapidly into the shelters in the garden. These had been standing idle since the early days of the war. They stood under the broad arms of three massive oak trees. Stumbling sleepily down the stony path, I lost one slipper and stubbed my toe. This woke me up. I reached the shelter and sat on the bench. Inside, the masters had lit oil lamps that gave off the sickly smell of paraffin. Not enjoying enclosed spaces, I began to feel ill. The Matron took pity on me and bound up my bleeding toe. The Headmaster urged us into a singsong, and soon the round "London's Burning" was going strong, an appropriate number for the occasion. Cocoa and biscuits were served. This was quite a party, a sort of midnight feast.

Presently, as we began to doze in our uncomfortable positions, the drone of engines was heard. It was the enemy. We all looked up and held our breath. Even the staff was quiet. It must have been quite a big raid. The engine drone coming through our ventilation shaft, pulsing, with an off-beat built into the tempo of the engine. The sound increased and some of us looked alarmed and pale under the weak lamplight. Nearer they came. Some of us prayed. I held my toe. I looked around at familiar faces. No laughing or singing now. The bombs had not yet started to fall. I glanced at the Headmaster, looking different in his dressing gown. He was nervously pacing in the centre of the shelter, moving his lips as if rehearsing a speech for Parents Day. Then came the dull thudding sounds that we'd been expecting. Corby was getting it tonight. We thought of the poor people on the other side of the valley. I think many of us were aware of our mortality for the first time. Some idiot master mentioned the fact that the bombers very often dropped the remains of their load as they turned to leave for Germany. That meant us. Or could. We'd be a nice little civilian target with our big old house and church high on a hill. The very thought of knocking off a church spire might seem fair game to a Nazi. For us, the worst part of the long night occurred when those planes turned for home, Matron busied herself with more cocoa. Another master led us in many choruses of "Ten Green Bottles," and eventually the threat died away. The engine sounds receded. We heard the all clear from the village and, relieved, wandered back to our beds through the damp dawn.

In the morning, we saw that the land was covered in thin strips of metal, dropped by the enemy planes to confuse our radar. Collecting these strips became a new hobby.

It was with some shock that I saw bombed buildings in Peterborough from the train that took me back home for the holidays. There were signs of prosperity at home. This seemed strange with a war going on, but the War Office had sent battalions of troops and squadrons of the RAF into the area. They spent much time marching the streets by day and drinking at night. Many men were billeted locally. At our house, the front room, which was normally unused, except at Christmas, had been turned over to two RAF sergeants. My father was always inviting strangers home for a drink so the house was never empty.

I went to the usual summer fetes, had tea on the lawn, played with friends, went for bike rides, and read my books. My chief interest, however, was in the cinema. The New Theatre was in effect, my real school. It's a Marks & Spencer now. The box office would have been just around where they place the knitwear at the front of the store. Mr. Howden's sister, with knitting in hand, presided. She knew me well, as I regularly arrived with my pass which read, "Please admit my grandson and friend." I used my pass regularly, twice a week at least, for years. Certainly between 1942 and 1951, when I finally left Boston, that little scrap of card was my passport to a world that existed solely between the solid walls of that theatre, which became my second home. When they pulled the theatre down and built a store over it, my childhood ceased. The Regal was newer and did not have the allure of The New.

There was a foyer with cane furniture and a potted palm, with framed portraits of the stars. Walking toward the stalls or up the stairs to the circle, you could usually hear a Victor Sylvester record, though sometimes it was Charlie Kunz, whom I hated. The auditorium is now the Food Hall. Before the place finally closed, I went backstage. It had been built as a theatre before cinema was invented, so the stage was deep enough to allow for pantomimes and travelling theatricals. Under the stage there were the very dusty relics of many productions and trapdoors for the demon kings. The two big Western Electric speakers straddled the stage behind the screen. It was said that the sound system was the finest in the county. When the lion roared, you were in for a good time at The New.

The projectors were first installed in the early days, when gramophone records reproduced the sound. We used to debate hotly whether the RCA or the Western Electric systems were best. Because MGM employed the Western Electric system and I thought of them as the last word in quality, there was little doubt in my mind. In any case I'd met the Western Electric district engineer, who regularly serviced the equipment, and I'd never seen anyone from RCA.

Under the stage, covered in many years of dust, stood three wooden packing cases. I'd been told about them by the projectionist, who often allowed me into his booth. He reckoned there might be some old films in those crates. I had no permission to trespass onto the stage, not from the owner and manager, Mr. Howden, who might not have been too happy with the idea of a filmstruck teenager wandering around under there. I was fairly nervous as I edged toward the packing cases. There was no light other than the flashlamp I carried. It was spooky, the place being empty and me trespassing, but once I saw the big boxes, I sensed that I might be onto something. Perhaps it was the sweetish smell that came from them. Or maybe it was the smell of the acetone we used in the factory. I saw the name "Howden" written on the boxes and realised that they had no lids. When I reached them and flashed the light inside, I was not too surprised to find them full of old rolls of 35 mm film, all highly combustible. Nitrate film stock had been the cause of many cinema fires and I had stumbled on the equivalent of a giant bomb that might as well have been a box full of nitroglycerine, though I didn't realise it then. Just as well I hadn't struck matches to light my way. The heat generated by torchlight might have been sufficient to set it off. I extinguished my lamp and stood in darkness, savouring the sweet, deadly smell. I suppose glue sniffers experience that kind of high. I made my way back to the stage door, knowing that I had to return with some help to retrieve the boxes. Having reported back to the projectionist, who was rumoured to increase the speed of his projectors on Saturday night in order to hit the pub before it closed, I gathered some chums and we lifted the boxes out of the theatre and into my car. Then, in the factory, I opened them very carefully and discarded all those films that had turned to jelly, keeping only those which that appeared not to be too far gone. Eventually I had several priceless reels that dated from the early 1900s and, after contacting the National Film Archive, I drove the films to their vaults for safekeeping. I guess they are still there, safe and sound.

YUL BRYNNER
OPENS A DOOR

The Prince and the Showgirl

The Prince and the Showgirl was made at Pinewood in 1956. Jack Harris had rooms in the old editing block where, years later, I would cut *The World Is Not Enough*. I shared it with him and Des Saunders.

I had a bench and a Robot joiner. This small device, unlike the Bell & Howell foot joiner, which I'd mastered at Ealing, could be placed almost anywhere. It scraped the emulsion from one side of the film and applied the film cement as the second part of the device was clamped to the first. Thus the film was scraped and joined. Not exactly a daunting task.

The Robot was the last of the cement, or hot, joiners. Soon it was replaced by the Italian tape joiner, which is still in use. It required no scraping, no cement, and lasted for years. The Italian joiner also avoided losing a frame when an edit was made, so it was goodbye to the "black buildup."

Working on this movie was fascinating from many points of view and has been well documented elsewhere, but being a junior member of the team, I could watch the egos at work.

In the beginning, Olivier and Monroe were great chums, but, going into the project, he must have been unaware of the influence that Marilyn's drama coach,

Paula Strasberg, had on her. This lady, the wife of Lee Strasberg of the Actors Studio, would sit on the set and watch every take with great attention. She was a formidable size and always dressed in black. When Olivier would call "cut," Marilyn would ask Paula for her comments, never the director.

After a couple of weeks of this, Olivier was beside himself with rage, but the Strasberg presence, would not be moved.

So, gradually, the wheels fell off the relationship between star and director. The rest of the film, at least nine weeks of it, was spent within this dreadful atmosphere.

Marilyn had only recently married Arthur Miller, who was with her more often than not. She had a dressing room on the stage and one of our jobs was to escort her, daily, to the projection room where she saw her rushes, very often with her husband and the film's producer, Milton Green.

So either Des or I would knock on her door about 5:30 and she'd walk with us down the long corridor at Pinewood, often clutching a copy of the collected poems of Dylan Thomas, which I never saw her open. She was very shortsighted and wore glasses until she was in front of the camera.

On the very last day of filming, Marilyn had reluctantly agreed to shoot some retakes that Olivier demanded. The crew sat around all morning waiting for her to arrive, which was not unusual, and when she did, she distributed champagne to everyone, which was fine, but caused even more delay and more frustration for Olivier, or 'Sir' as we called him.

She finally did appear in costume, ready for work, but was, by now, quite pickled. Olivier, out of spite, perhaps, printed everything they shot that afternoon, most of which was useless as Marilyn was bumping into the furniture and unable to act.

In the end, Jack Harris used about 6 feet out of 2,000. I have often pondered the lost opportunity to remove those rushes from the cutting room and secrete them in my garage for future use. Of course none of us knew the star would soon die, nor that she would become a screen idol and that these feeble rushes would have been worth a great deal.

Working on the post-production was good fun and, for me, quite important since Olivier had decided I should not be confined to the Robot joiner and elected to promote me to Footsteps Editor.

He had, I assume, discussed this with Jack. In those days, the recording of footsteps was an arduous task. Every sound of movement in the film had to be reproduced to separate it from the dialogue for foreign dubbed versions. We looped up the film into sections that could be endlessly repeated and a "virgin" magnetic loop of the same length was also cut to match.

In the recording studio, the footstep artist, normally the late Beryl Mortimer, would select a pair of shoes and a surface and then "walk" through the scene in sync with the actor on screen.

If other sounds were involved, such as a kiss or movement of props, they would be done on a second loop and, thus, the effects were built up. Dinner party scenes were dreaded. In America this procedure is called Foley, presumably after an inventor of that name.

When everything was recorded, the assistant would re-assemble the loops into their full-reel length so that the tracks could be used in the dubbing theatre.

This then was my task on the final stages of *The Prince and the Showgirl*. While Des Saunders concerned himself with finalising the film and dealing with the composer, I would be involved with the sound editors who were fitting all the effects and attending to the dialogue. Nowadays composers have their own music editors.

Olivier played a significant part in my career, though I never knew him well. Having promoted me on *The Prince and the Showgirl*, he gave me back some of the confidence I lost going from editor to second assistant and I would later edit two films he appeared in: *Term of Trial* (1961) and *Marathon Man* (1976).

Jack Harris, one of the most sought after editors of his day, was also a supreme influence. Olivier trusted Jack implicitly to cut his film.

Olivier himself was quite a distant man. He wasn't seen very much in the cutting room. Jack would run the film for him on a regular basis and they would recut it together. At these screenings, Olivier would give Jack his notes, though I suspect they were very few because Jack would cut the film perfectly well thus lifting a huge burden off the director's shoulders.

Indiscreet

After that experience, Jack took me on as his permanent first assistant for several years when Des Saunders moved on to direct episodes of *Thunderbirds*. It was during that period that we found ourselves at Elstree where Stanley Donen was directing *Indiscreet*. I knew of Donen from his musicals and was excited when Jack told me we'd be doing the picture. I was a huge fan, having sat through *On the Town* four times in the same day at the Empire, Leicester Square, including the stage show. Although *Indiscreet* was not a musical, it was a comedy with Cary Grant and Ingrid Bergman and bound to be stylish. In fact I barely got to know Stanley on that picture, since he rarely came into the cutting room. I only saw him at rushes, though I did sometimes sneak onto the set, but this was not encouraged. I had to wait until post-production before getting at all close to him. We often had lunch with Jack in the Grosevenor restaurant which was adjacent to the studio. Stanley was the first person I ever saw eating yogurt. He had just finished another film with Cary Grant prior to *Indiscreet,* and the two of them were now in a partnership.

It's curious now to think that Stanley was not much more than seven years older than I was. Having started directing early his experience was already huge, and he had an unmistakable aura of success hanging over him. Stanley exuded charm, and with his little southern boy accent was a pushover for people like me, always a sucker for a seductive voice. He was also impeccably attired, Savile Row style. In those days, directors didn't wear jeans and t-shirts. They wore elegant suits and expensive shoes and ties. They looked like businessmen. Stanley was never one to hang about the set. He would describe the next setup and retire to his office until called for rehearsal. He was very much into the business of films and was buying up real estate in Los Angeles. All this made sense in a business where anyone's future can be shaky.

Before filming began, I was told to call the production manager Al Streeter to make my deal. This was not a call I looked forward to because I was always nervous when discussing my pay. I asked for £25 a week—the top rate for an assistant editor. Jack Harris was a top editor and probably got £60 a week. There was silence on the other end and finally Streeter said, "And what makes you think you are worth that amount?" This rattled me and I stuttered some reply about being Jack's regular assistant and having a family to feed. After another interminable silence, Streeter said, "What you should have said is 'I'm worth it.' " He then agreed the price.

Indiscreet was shot at the ABPC Studio, and the second assistant editor was Terry Rawlings, who later became an ace sound editor and film editor. He and I waited for Jack to make his decisions which were, as usual, slow. The filming was almost entirely confined to the studio, though one big scene was shot at Greenwich and there were some romantic views of London on the Embankment.

I was appointed music editor and this was the first film to be scored by Richard Rodney Bennett. One evening I was instructed to run the film for him and Muir Mathieson at the old London Films building at Hyde Park.

Muir and I waited awhile and finally a breathless young man appeared, saying his plane from Paris had been delayed. Richard was only about twenty years old and still studying at the Sorbonne.

I have no idea how Stanley came to employ Richard, whose score was recorded at Elstree, but he turned down most of the music Richard had composed, except for one cue that involved a sort of mini piano concerto. When we were mixing the film, Stanley would call out "Jimmy! Bring on the blind pianist," which meant another reprise of this particular cue. In the end very little of the score was used but that blind pianist cue was perfect.

Because we shared a mutual interest in musicals, Stanley agreed to allow me to interview him for a magazine called *Films & Filming*, for which I occasionally wrote. I remember he was very gracious about this and, although he asked me to send him a typescript before I submitted it for publication, he didn't hold much back. He gave me a very detailed account of his early life, his desire to become a dancer, his start on Broadway, and his meeting with Gene Kelly, all of which I faithfully transcribed. The article was published at about the time that *Indiscreet* was released.

I never thought *Indiscreet* was a good movie. I found it a rather dull piece and very stagebound, but the public enjoyed it and it did well at the box office. For me, it wasn't easy to sit through many times without falling asleep.

Once More with Feeling and *Surprise Package*

After *Indiscreet,* Jack and I went our separate ways. A few years later, however, Jack Harris and Stanley Donen worked together again on *Once More with Feeling!,* a less than brilliant romantic comedy featuring Yul Brynner and Kay Kendall. Casting Brynner in a comedy was, perhaps, a bit rash of Stanley.

Jack had gone to Paris without me because this was a French production and he was required to have French assistants, but it was agreed that I could join the team when the shooting ended and they returned to England for the post-production work.

Because the film contained many classical music cues prerecorded in France, there was not much need for an additional score, but I was required to go to Paris with Muir Mathieson to look at the film.

We were at the bar in the Studio de Boulogne adjacent to the viewing room. It was near the end of the day and very busy. I met and chatted with a French girl who spoke reasonably good English. I arranged to meet her for a meal after the screening, but when the time came she had vanished and, sadly, stood me up.

Back in London, we were very close to mixing it when we heard that Kay Kendall had suddenly died. I had no idea she'd had leukemia throughout the shoot. It was kept amazingly quiet and we were all saddened. She was such a life force. Her death cast a pall over the whole enterprise.

Stanley and I became reacquainted when the film moved to London, though we saw very little of him at the time because he was already planning his next picture and courting his next wife. The picture was another Yul Brynner comedy, titled *Surprise Package*. Jack Harris found it impossible to contemplate such a thing. In fact, he became very depressed by the prospect of cutting another comedy with Brynner, whom he found totally unfunny. He was absolutely right.

So if Jack Harris wasn't going to cut *Surprise Package*, I wondered who Stanley would turn to. I suddenly decided that it could be my big chance. I asked Jack for his advice and permission to put myself forward. It was pushy, perhaps, but seemed appropriate at the time. Fortunately for me, and my future career, Stanley was quite happy with this arrangement, though I still had to prove I could do the editor's job to the satisfaction of one and all, including Columbia, who were footing the bill.

The picture was first shot on location in the Greek Islands and then at Shepperton Studios. It was in black and white, which was a pity since the locations were very attractive. Yul Brynner played a New York gangster who is drummed out of the mob and returned to his roots, where he becomes involved with Mitzi Gaynor and an exiled king, played by Noel Coward. It was based on a book by Art Buchwald, and the screenplay was by the legendary Harry Kurnitz.

I was so happy to be cutting a feature that I didn't pay more than scant attention to the script, even though in those days the editor usually didn't get involved with scripts, but simply sat back and cut the results.

In this case, as a novice, I was in double trouble since the film was being shot away from England and it was difficult to contact Stanley if I needed to discuss the rushes. So I just got on with it and put the thing together. I already had a fair inkling from *Once More with Feeling* that Yul Brynner was not God's gift to comedy. His approach was loud or fast and very often both at the same time. The material piled up and seemed to get even less amusing than the script, which was itself already a travesty of a rather witty original.

Stanley returned and the studio shoot commenced. We would meet at rushes and some wisecracks would flow between Stanley and the crew. He was always ready with a running joke that would carry through the whole shoot, and the crew would pick up on that.

The one bit of genuine amusement was having some dealings with the great Coward. Here was a legend that never failed to live up to it's reputation. He was genuinely witty and original. A hugely amusing man of style, charm, and taste. He never disappointed. Unfortunately his part in the movie singularly lacked the wit and style he displayed in life. He found trouble remembering lines and, in one scene with Brynner, went to an almost record breaking sixty-eight takes. He only stumbled through because Stanley finally broke the scene down to single lines.

Putting all that together in seamless style was quite a test for the young editor and I rather dreaded the moment when I had to show the film to Stanley.

I was rarely on the set and Stanley was even more rarely in the cutting room. I don't recall that he ever asked my opinion about anything and I don't suppose I ever suggested that the film was not amusing. I must have been satisfying his requirements because shortly before we finished shooting and were walking into rushes one lunch time he turned to me and said "Jimmy, I'm going to start another movie very soon and would you like to stay on and cut it?" This could be deemed rash since he hadn't yet seen too much of my work on his current picture. Of course I agreed without a thought, but we had a great deal to endure on the mis-titled *Surprise Package*. I handed the film over to the sound editor, Peter Musgrave, and began work on the next picture. We were in adjoining cutting rooms so I was able to keep an eye on both movies.

If *Surprise Package* had been my debut feature without a follow-up, I might have been dead in the water, but moving headlong into another film before the current one was even mixed, saved my bacon.

CARY GRANT, HOLLYWOOD, AND BROADWAY

The Grass Is Greener

Stanley's new film was *The Grass Is Greener,* and he was able to attract an impressive all-star cast. Cary Grant, Jean Simmons, Deborah Kerr, and Robert Mitchum were involved in the principal roles. There can't have been any other reason for making it since the material was thin and barely altered for the screen. It consisted of a lot of talk and was set in the aristocratic area of British life with lords, castles, and God knows what else, so it was certain to appeal to the American public. The editing phase of a Donen picture at that stage in his career was notable for the fact that you didn't see him too often. He was very busy preparing for his next picture or having some domestic upheaval. Stanley was a great one for tests. He would spend many days testing the clothes, makeup, hair, and stock. Chris Challis, who lit *The Grass Is Greener* would shoot stock tests on all the Kodak material available at that time.

During the post-production of *Surprise Package,* when Stanley did turn up, we would run the movie in the theatre and get some feedback for changes. I don't recall that we ran it too many times. There was a looping session with Yul Brynner, which I directed. He was Mister Speedy and broke Shepperton's record for the number of loops recorded in a session. None of this made him any funnier.

In fact, his dialogue was delivered so fast that it made him unintelligible. Stanley might have been influenced by Billy Wilder's direction of Jimmy Cagney in *One, Two, Three*. One day Noel Coward was in the room. He had very few loops and to flesh out the time I encouraged him to tell us about his wartime exploits, which I had been reading about in his autobiography. Having the real Coward in the room was exciting. He ended the session by inviting me to "Sit in the Rolls with your old Uncle." This brought me down to reality. Pity. Maybe it was one of life's lost opportunities.

Perhaps the director had given up on *Surprise Package*. It did, however, have to be completed, and I remember we ran a preview one evening in Slough, where we died by inches. Stanley had requested that a recording be made of the audience's laughter. This was a bad idea.

The Grass Is Greener was simple enough to edit since Stanley Donen shot it in a very straightforward manner leaving me few decisions to make. Like *Indiscreet*, it was an adapted stage play and he shot it like that. Frankly, it wasn't really very good and relied on its stellar cast to survive.

Cary Grant was co-producer and always a pleasure to work with and for. The picture was shot in Technirama, which was Technicolor's own Cinemascope, and I was cutting it on an old Acmade machine that had only a bull's-eye lens through which to see the tiny image. The machine made a terrible clattering noise too, so I was shattered after a day's editing, when we would wander into the old bar at Shepperton Studios to relax.

Maurice Binder, who had done special title sections on other Donen pictures, arranged a splendid tableau of babies for the credits, the babies representing the stars as infants, and an amusing morning was spent in the garden at Shepperton as Maurice directed these tots.

The film went together very easily and was almost fine cut when the shooting ended. Stanley took off for the south of France, leaving Cary Grant and I to supervise the music sessions that were held at Shepperton. A selection of Noel Coward's music was arranged by Douglas Gamley. It always struck me as odd that Cary was there, hanging around the music sessions and Stanley wasn't.

Stanley returned. We had to complete the sound mix early in order to preview the film in America, and I had to arrange for double sound crews to work day and night. I was in the dubbing room until five in the morning for a fortnight. I'd then drive home for a few hours sleep before returning again at eleven when Stanley would come to listen to the previous night's work. Very often he'd rubbish it and demand retakes. It was a trying time and perhaps not the best way to work. Stanley was always very fussy about the condition of the work print and, in this case, ordered that the entire thing be reprinted for preview, a job that was handled by my assistant, Mary Kessel. Mary managed to complete the job just as I was ready to board the plane for Los Angeles with the print.

This was heady stuff for me. I had never been to Hollywood and here I was travelling on a 707, albeit in economy, while Cary Grant was up in first class. We had to land somewhere in Canada to refuel, and I remember Cary came back to find me and we walked around on the tarmac for a while. Cary was instantly recognised by everyone and besieged for autographs. At that time, the British public were more respectful. They might have pointed and giggled but would never ask for an autograph.

In Hollywood I stayed with Stanley at the Beverly Hills Hotel, which was a paradise in those days. I was picked up every morning by Bill Hornbeck, a famous and accomplished editor who was then head of post-production at Universal. He had a Ford Thunderbird and I loved those sunny mornings as we drove over Coldwater Canyon with the hood down en route to Universal City.

There was no Universal Tour at this time, so the view of the San Gabriel Mountains was undisturbed. I was astonished by the size of the studio, where Cary had a permanent bungalow as his office. His assistant allowed me to use the bungalow as my headquarters since Cary was rarely there.

I was fascinated by the studio. The lot seemed to extend for miles, and I would walk all over, under a hot sun, looking at the standing sets or observing units at work. I would eat lunch in the commissary, discovering cottage cheese with fruit and yogurt, generally wondering that I was there at all.

One evening Bill suggested that I might like to attend a studio preview since I would have to endure our own shortly and should know the ropes. This was a preview for a new Doris Day movie, *Midnight Lace*, which Bill assured me I would enjoy as it was a thriller set in London, directed by David Miller.

A bus collected all the studio personnel and took them to a restaurant. On this occasion it was a dark and gloomy steakhouse, where we solemnly ploughed our way through a heavy meal before returning to the bus which then took off for the preview theatre which seemed a very long way off in the valley. It was a hot night and, on arrival, I was surprised to see young girls lining up wearing what appeared to be pyjamas. That could never happen in Slough.

We saw the movie, which I thought fairly bad. Afterward the studio executives, clearly proud of their film, asked for my opinion of the London setting. How did it compare to the real thing? Had their advisor done a good job? I told them, in no uncertain terms, that London buses no longer looked that way, and I never saw a film that was so studio bound. I then realised that this was a mistake since these men, who thus far had treated me very warmly, now hardened and turned away, leaving me alone in the foyer as they collected the preview cards, to be read and collated on the bus ride home. I should have kept my opinions to myself and praised their film, but I have never been good at hiding my true feelings and continue to this day to blurt out my blunt opinions instead of the platitudes more readily received. Too late I realised that all these men would be in attendance at our preview and would now not be disposed to act helpfully, so I felt I'd been stupid.

The journey back was a subdued affair. *Midnight Lace* had played okay, but the figures were not too good and I realised that being a pariah from England was no way to make friends and influence people.

When our turn came a few nights later and this whole tiresome ritual of eating and bussing was repeated, I was ready for anything, but I didn't foresee the technical trouble that would occur. The theatre was in Glendale and, travelling with us in the bus were both Cary and Stanley. At the theatre, to the fans' delight, were Robert Mitchum and Jean Simmons.

I sat next to Bill Hornbeck and started getting nervous, as I still do on these occasions, made all the more anxious when the film is unmarried and held together by Sellotape. The lights dimmed and *The Grass Is Greener* began. Maurice Binder's title sequence with the babies should have been accompanied by Noel Coward's music, but there was no sound at all. Not a note of music could be heard and the babies played in utter silence. I was out of my seat in a second, followed by Bill and Stanley. Our first problem was locating the booth. None of us knew where it was and rushed about searching for likely doors. By now reel one was well on its way and the only audible sound was the slow hand clapping of the audience. I finally found the door and burst into the booth, where two t-shirted projectionists were quite unaware of the problem. "There's no sound," I shrieked. "Stop the show!" They were not overly impressed by this and turned to inspect the sound head. Nothing seemed amiss. Bill and I cast our inexperienced eyes over the machinery while Stanley hovered and insisted they shut off the machines. Just then I noticed a switch marked "Optical/Magnetic," which had two positions. There was little doubt that we were still in the "Optical" mode. A quick flip of the switch and we had the sound, but we now had to wait for the reel to be rewound and relaced. At least we knew it would play and the audience settled down. The stars in the audience had been having a fine time with the autograph hounds. The film began again and near the end of reel one, I became aware of sounds that were not on the track. Minor explosive noises, which became more insistent as the reel reached its end. Stanley looked at me for some explanation, but I was just as puzzled as he. I went back to the booth and looked at the sound head as reel two progressed through it. Every so often a flash of light appeared to pass across the head, causing the "pop" I had been hearing and, as the core of the reel diminished, the flashes increased. I pointed this phenomenon out to the projectionists who remained steadfastly disinterested. They mumbled something about static charge and suggested I should touch the film as it went through, thus grounding it. So I spent the entire evening with my finger on the film, and every time I rested, the darned thing went pop right in my face. Fortunately only Stanley and I seemed at all concerned with this distraction, but I never went to a preview afterward without fully expecting a problem, and I am always a basket case afterward.

All these problems were lapped up by those executives to whom I'd played the arrogant British critic a few nights before. *Midnight Lace* had been a trouble-free preview, while ours was fraught with problems.

The card counting that took place on the bus produced quite a dismal result too and we retired, hurt, to Cary's bungalow, where everyone sat around looking glum. I had the temerity to suggest we open the bar since a drink seemed the best idea, but nobody seemed thirsty and a funny look from Cary made me realise I'd transgressed some unwritten bit of preview folklore. Actually, I think it was simply his built-in sense of thrift that prompted the reaction. Cary was very typical of those wealthy men who would give you a cheque for a thousand pounds without blinking if you asked nicely, but ask for a drink from his bar or the loan of a postage stamp, and he'd give you short shrift. For example, small transistor radios were the latest technological toy, and I was longing to get out and buy one to take to London. Cary was never keen to let me off the leash and when I told him what I wanted to purchase he said, "You mean like this?" and tossed over exactly what I wanted. "Keep it," he ordered. I thanked him and that was that. But when I suggested we all drink from his bar, it was a different story.

Finally Stanley and I retired to the Beverly Hills Hotel, where he confided that he never wanted to work in Hollywood again and told me how much he hated the system and the people. It was most unusual for Stanley to discuss his personal feelings with me. Up until then we'd never talked privately, only about the job in hand. It was quite a sad, melancholy end to a long evening. The picture hadn't played that badly. But I guess after the failure of *Surprise Package* he had been hoping for a more successful result. His sadness was not all business though. He told me that Elizabeth Taylor had been his girlfriend until she was grabbed by Conrad Hilton.

We had to fly to New York for further screenings and, once again, I was travelling with Cary. On the plane I sat next to another idol of mine, Charles

Walters, the director of *Easter Parade, If You Feel Like Singing,* and *The Belle of New York,* whose ear I bent for the entire trip. I think he was quite amazed when I told him I enjoyed *The Belle of New York,* which had been a big flop for him.

In New York we were housed at the Plaza Hotel, where Cary always stayed, and his fans were out in force as our limo arrived from the airport. I have no idea how they knew of his arrival because it was very late in the evening. It reminded me of Fred Astaire's fans meeting him at the start of *The Band Wagon.*

I was quartered in the room next to Cary's suite, and went about with him in the limo. The poor man couldn't set foot on the street without being instantly mobbed.

These were heady days indeed. Stanley asked me what shows I most wanted to see. *Gypsy* headed my list. "I'll phone Stephen," he said and there I was talking to Sondheim who let me have his house seats. But who to take? The only girl I knew in New York was busy, so she fixed me up with a blind date, which turned out to be a girl who couldn't stand Ethel Merman. This was a dreadful evening on the one hand and brilliant on the other. The show was fabulous and Merman was great, but I had no interest in my boring date.

The next show we attended was *Fiorello.* I had ditched the girl by now. The limo pulled up to the curb opposite the theatre, and I was sent ahead to signal to the car just before the curtain went up. Our seats were in the very front row of the stalls, which meant that a grand entrance was made, since Cary had to walk down the entire length of the aisle, followed by Stanley and myself. The audience recognised him at once and a standing ovation followed. It was extraordinary. The orchestra, already seated, waited until we had sat down. The remarks were often impertinent, or so I thought, calling out comments like, "Hey Cary, come on over, my wife would sure love to cook for you." The British would never have behaved like that. I thought it really embarrassing, but he took it with good humour, and soon the show started. This was another great evening, which flashed by in a haze of pleasure as one good number followed another. During the intermission, I went for lemonades while Cary was besieged again.

Afterward we crossed the street for dinner at Sardis. I really couldn't believe I was a part of all this. After the meal I left the restaurant and walked to Times Square, looking at the lights and gaudy displays. I thought to myself that it doesn't get better than this. I wondered where all this magic would lead to.

Where it led to was back to Shepperton. After all this fun, we still had a picture to finish and this time we did it correctly. Stanley ran the movie a few times, trimmed and locked it, then we remixed the entire thing.

My daughter Kate was about four at the time, and I brought her to the studio when there was nobody to babysit. Cary adored her and said if he ever had a daughter he would name her Kate. He had been much married but had never had a child. Later he had a daughter with Dyan Cannon and named her Kate.

I always considered that the American trip had been a sort of thank-you gift from Cary, who knew how hard I'd worked on the film. It gave me my first extended experience of Los Angeles, a city I was to return to many times. Cary Grant was always very pleasant. He was certainly considerate, very down-to-earth, and always chatty. That was the thing about Cary. He was exactly what you would expect him to be, off the screen and on.

The Grass Is Greener was not a great hit. Stanley would have to wait until our next movie for that.

FLASHBACK: *Oundle School*

My brother had already completed his time there and was in the RAF when I arrived at Oundle, just as the war in Europe was ending. This school was hard for a youngster of fourteen to grasp, after a somewhat cushioned existence at Nevill Holt. I was now one of eight hundred boys and on my first day, one of about fifty newcomers, all of whom were gathered together and indoctrinated into the school traditions that had to be strictly observed or punishments would result.

I entered the same house as my brother, New House, which, despite its name, was one of the oldest, being home to about eighty boys. The older ones slept in a dormitory across the street. When I arrived, the discipline in the house was rigidly observed by the prefects, a group of eighteen-year-old thugs who were into beatings in a big way.

The house was run by Mr. Burns and his wife, who were old and had come out of retirement for the duration, so it was not surprising that the prefects held sway and used bullying tactics to keep us new ticks in order. Mr. Burns was not into beating, but his senior boys were. These older boys, who imposed themselves on the younger set, would be off to the war as soon as they left the school, possibly to be killed, so there was some reason to feel sorry for them, cruel though they were.

To display an interest in art of any kind was, I quickly learned, taboo. I had unwisely packed a Pelican paperback of Arnold Haskell's *Ballet*. As soon as I was found reading that, it was snatched from my hand and thrown around the room amid cries of "Clark's a fairy!" This both surprised and hurt me. I did not know what a fairy was in this context and I disliked being teased. The book and I both got battered that day and it led directly to all kinds of innuendoes that I did not understand.

For starters there were constant allusions to sex. Since Oundle was an all-boys school, the relationships between boys sometimes blossomed into adolescent romances. The new boys such as myself were objects of interest to the older boys, acting as girl substitutes. Occasionally this might become physical but was largely contained in country walks and afternoons by the river. When liaisons were too obvious, the younger boys might get ragged and the older boy cautioned by his superiors.

The form sexual education took at Oundle was an embarrassment to all concerned. In my case I was invited into Mr. Burns' study during my first term and he rather awkwardly told me the basic rudiments of sex, but I could have told him more than he explained since my school friends had given far more graphic, if somewhat confusing, details on my very first day at Oundle.

There was also a local prostitute, rather uselessly pointed out as she passed the house en route to her place of work, which was the local graveyard. She had been given the sobriquet of "Fly-rip Kate." In those days trousers were not closed with a zipper but by buttons known as fly buttons. A favourite sport among the boys was to deftly grasp another boy's fly and rip it open, hence the term "fly-rip."

Life at Oundle was not all horror, in fact, there was much to commend the school and I never regretted the experience. It was, for me, liberating and taught me patience and perseverance at the possible expense of damaging my emotions.

One thing it taught me, from the very start, was to be able to defecate in public without shame. Taking a shit is one of the functions of life that most of us would prefer to do in private. In New House they were determined to teach us otherwise, so there were no doors on the toilets. After breakfast the whole house descended on the bogs and stood in line waiting their turn. Woe betide the boy with even the smallest touch of constipation. Nobody was going to hang around too long. It took me a few days to get used to this arrangement, but you can adjust to anything, and before long I realised the bogs were a sort of social club, a mere part of everyday life. I never, however, adjusted to the horror of the early morning cold bath. The boys were roused from sleep around seven and went directly to the bathroom, stripped off their pyjamas, and were then ceremonially dunked into a bath of cold water. A prefect was there to ensure complete immersion. This was their way of waking you up.

When the war ended, Mr. Burns and his wife retired once again. A new housemaster was appointed. But until he arrived, New House was a mess. The boys were leaderless and apathetic. They lost all their matches and performed badly in any communal activity. Being a New House boy was altogether the pits until the new housemaster was installed. C.A.B. (Arthur) Marshall had been a boy at the school and after University had returned to be a master, teaching French. The war came, he was drafted and finally became a major in the army. He was awarded the MBE, one of the finest honours. On the beaches of Dunkirk, as the soldiers were being strafed by German dive-bombers, Marshall was entertaining them with the wild and wacky exploits of Nurse Dugdale, a female character he had invented for the BBC. Arthur Marshall was most certainly homosexual which, in those days, was hardly a trait to be flaunted. Arthur was not only the possessor of a high-pitched voice, he was also very funny.

Arthur, whom we all called Cabby, became my housemaster and that was the turning point in my life at Oundle. For one thing he inspired us. He made us think, he made us proud, and above all he made us laugh. And he kicked out all those louts who had made our life a misery. No more beatings. A dressing-down from Arthur was far worse than any physical hurt. It is very sad to inherit a group of boys that has lost its spirit and we were ready for Arthur's magic touch. Though he had not been a housemaster before the war, he took to it directly. It must have been a difficult decision for Mr. Stainforth, the gruff and imperious headmaster, to appoint Arthur. Whether the parents were ever bothered by an obviously homosexual man being in charge of their boys I never knew. Certainly my parents were not outwardly concerned, though I doubt they knew what a real homosexual was, but Arthur was in no way interested in boys, except to attend to their welfare, which he did with enormous vigour and enthusiasm. Our position in the ratings started to rise. Before I left, New House was a positive hit and all due to Cabby.

When I arrived at the school, the projection equipment in the Great Hall was truly primitive. Two ancient machines dating from the silent period had been adapted by a science master who had attached sound heads. Picture and sound were both inadequate and frequently failed, but we did not care. Spending a couple of hours in fantasy land was enough and technical deficiencies were of no concern. I recall falling headlong for Jeanne Crain after *State Fair.* The senior boys were in charge of the gramophone records that played before the film, Harry James' "Trumpet Blues and Cantabile" being the favourites in 1945. We saw four films every term, the high spot at the end of school being Field Day, involving mock warfare in fields and villages around town when we put on our OTC uniforms and played at being soldiers.

After Cabby Marshall started booking films, the choices improved, but I was now sixteen and heavily influenced, like most of my generation of cineastes, by Roger Manvell's excellent Pelican book, *Film*, probably the first serious study of film appreciation to reach a wide public. It inspired many people to start film societies in their towns since there was now an interest in seeing films that could not easily be viewed outside of London. There had been film societies operating in larger cities for many years, the London Film Society began in the twenties, but the time was now ripe for expansion, and 16 mm projectors and prints were more easily obtained.

I decided to write, with generous cribs from Manvell, a manifesto that was directed toward the headmaster, to persuade him to allow me to start a film society within the school. It would be open only to senior boys and staff and be additional to the regular film shows. Arthur Marshall gave my somewhat fulsome piece to Mr. Stainforth who, much to my surprise, sanctioned the idea, provided a master was in charge and knew what films were to be shown, cautioning, "No smut please, so be cautious with the French films." During his period in Paris after the war, Arthur had met Francis Howard who was now in charge of an organisation within the British Film Institute called the Central Booking Agency. This provided a source of films for the societies to show. It was arranged that Mr. Howard would visit the school and inaugurate the first meeting when we ran the Swiss film *Marie-Louise*. This was a great moment for me and eventually led to my very first job in the film industry.

The second most important decision came with the scrapping of the ancient projectors and installation of two new 35 mm machines in a soundproof booth up in the gallery of the Great Hall. Now we had terrific screenings with the enthusiastic help of Mr. Pike, the projectionist. But not before I had run Fritz Lang's *Metropolis* and provided a musical accompaniment via a twin-turntable playing generous 78 rpm samplings of Vaughan Williams' Fourth Symphony and, of course, Arthur Bliss' *Things to Come*. This taught me something about film scoring that would blossom later.

The Oundle Film Society was a hit. This was 1947, and it is still active. My education was complete. Now I had to face a future in Boston, Lincolnshire, in a printing factory, while my school friends went off to University. This was not a good time. I was eighteen and trapped in a one-horse town. What to do? Start another film society of course.

Before this time, we'd been to America and back, which was very heady for a sixteen-year-old boy. The war had just ended when Alec Shennan, my father's business friend in Chicago, invited us over. We either went on the Queen Mary or the Queen Elizabeth—I don't recall which, but we took both boats there and back. I spent a lot of my time in the ship's cinema, while Mother took to her bed and stayed there, fearing sea sickness. As soon as we boarded at Southampton, rationing was off. We had grown so used to eating very little that our stomachs had shrunk. We couldn't look at the food without groaning.

In New York we were first diddled by a cab driver. Our hosts had booked us into the Drake Hotel. Our financial allowance was so pitiful that my sister Hazel and I spent most of our time in Radio City Music Hall, sitting through the stage show, and sometimes the movie, twice. Mother stayed in her hotel room. We visited the Shennan's in Chicago where our financial straits were somewhat relieved and I bought my first Biro pen. I also visited their daughter's school of 1,500 pupils. I was appalled by the standard of teaching and also by the pupils calling their teachers by their first names.

While there we saw both *Finian's Rainbow* and *Brigadoon* in their original stage versions. I lugged the record albums back home. I was already very pro-American. This trip only created a greater love, which was to last a very long time.

☆   ☆   ☆

Term of Trial

The production manager on *The Grass Is Greener* was James Ware, and during the course of the film we'd become friendly. We both loved popular music, and he made me laugh a lot. Jimmy had been in the air force during the war and was a live wire, extremely camp, and very funny. He had a wonderful sense of humour and, in those days, could make me laugh simply by the way he spoke. He played the piano like an angel, chain smoked, was obviously homosexual, and was wonderful at his job. He created a happy, relaxed atmosphere around him, and he was a character. The kind we don't seem to have these days.

After the film ended, he went off to prepare another picture and was instrumental in getting me an interview with its director, Peter Glenville. The film was *Term of Trial* and was to be shot in Ireland at the Ardmore Studio near Dublin.

Glenville was a theatre director who'd done a few films and had written the script of this one from a novel. It was financed by Warner Brothers and starred Laurence Olivier, Simone Signoret, and Sarah Miles.

This was the period of the "kitchen sink" pictures. *Room at the Top*, in which Signoret had excelled was already a big hit, and Jimmy Ware had worked on that one too, being a friend of its director Jack Clayton.

That winter I found myself in Bray, a seaside town near the Ardmore Studio, with my two children and my assistant David Campling. David's wife had agreed to join us to look after my children, though my stepson David was attending a preparatory school in England and would only be in Ireland for the Christmas holiday. He had also changed his name from Andrew to David—for reasons I never really understood. Kate attended a Catholic primary school in the town. Jimmy Ware and an assistant director joined us in the rented house.

It was something of an ordeal. The winter was cold, the house was damp, and we had a resident housekeeper who spent more time in church than looking after the tenants. The cooked breakfast she had agreed to make was always cold, sitting on top of a hot plate powered by two candles. Congealed eggs were her specialty.

Outside there were few compensations. The countryside was near and the views were fine, however, on a Sunday there was a marked lack of places to eat. At that time Ireland was not geared to tourism and unless one was a bona fide traveller, publicans were not allowed to serve alcohol.

Shooting the film was fairly simple, though the crew had no love for the director, whose lack of experience overshadowed all his endeavors. My old friend from Boston, Gerry O'Hara, was the first assistant director and delighted in watching Glenville get into a muddle with angles, more than once chuckling when the director painted himself into a corner.

The producer of the film, Jimmy Woolf, who'd also produced *Room at the Top*, was with us much of the time. Our cutting room was in the basement of the old house at Ardmore, next to the kitchens where cabbage seemed to be continually cooked. It was a really smelly place with the kitchen on one side and the Gents on the other.

All the principal players were staying at a nearby country hotel, once the home of John McCormack, the great Irish tenor. Once a week Jimmy Ware and I would dine there, escaping from the dampness of Bray.

One night Jimmy Woolf entered the dining room, clearly saw us, and vanished. "He'll be back" said Jimmy Ware and, sure enough, after a short pause, Woolf reappeared and invited us to his room for an after-dinner drink. It was no secret that Jimmy Woolf was homosexual, though just how active he was I never knew. He had a long liason with Laurence Harvey, now married, and was currently escorting Terence Stamp who was also in *Term of Trial*.

That evening in his apartment was a long and boozy night. He kept filling up the brandy glass, and it was clear he had no desire to retire to bed. We limped out of there in the small hours. A similar evening occurred on another occasion, though this time we were in Peter Glenville's room, along with his companion Bill Smith.

Sarah Miles made her debut in this film and was eighteen at the time. She was mostly seen with her parents, though it was rumoured that she had an affair with Olivier, recently married to Joan Plowright. This was perfectly possible, but then Olivier was often rumoured to be cavorting with ladies and sometimes with gents.

Although I'd worked with Olivier in a minor capacity on *The Prince and the Showgirl*, I was amazed that he remembered me. We spoke about Jack Harris, whom he admired, and of Tony Richardson and the "new wave" in Britain.

Olivier had been in the stage and screen versions of *The Entertainer* and was a big fan of modern cinema. I did not get to know Signoret at all, but our paths did cross again much later in our lives.

Glenville was not a difficult director to edit for. In fact, he hardly appeared after we had finished the director's cut. The finale of the film was a courtroom scene that he shot for several days and for which I had quite a mass of rushes. I assembled the material quickly in order to see if anything vital was missing before the set was demolished but this version of the scene hardly changed thereafter.

In the editing suite, Glenville was inclined to revert to baby talk and would say, "I think a little trimmy-poo here" and such comments, but he changed very little in the film after my first assembly, and it was completed rapidly at Elstree with a score by the French composer, Jean-Michel Damase, a friend of Glenville's.

Term of Trial was hardly a big hit, coming near the end of the kitchen sink period and not being considered a very fine example, certainly not in the same league as *Saturday Night and Sunday Morning* or *Room at the Top*. Seen now, however, it fares better though is a slightly manufactured slice of life.

Certainly Glenville had little knowledge of reality. The child of a famous pantomime couple, he thrived in a theatrical world, and the casting of Signoret and Olivier was weird. I could not fully understand their role as a couple—their mutual attraction. It was *Room at the Top* revisited, but not as satisfying.

However, for me, it led to a most worthwhile and important film. Through Jimmy Ware, I was introduced to Jack Clayton who subsequently asked me to edit *The Innocents*, a version of Henry James' celebrated ghost story *The Turn of the Screw*.

THE INNOCENTS
AND *CHARADE*

The Innocents

The shooting of *The Innocents* began on location at Sheffield Park, a country house near Brighton, which was doubling for Bly House. Deborah Kerr played the governess; Michael Redgrave, the childrens' uncle; Megs Jenkins, the housekeeper; and Peter Wyngarde the evil Quint.

It was a real pleasure to edit since Jack had a very certain approach to his material, having worked out everything beforehand. He was a perfectionist who left nothing to chance and was very precise in his approach to work. He was, in fact, a very complex personality. The iron fist in the velvet glove.

Jack had worked on a variety of films after war service. After John Huston's *Beat the Devil*, which was a Romulus film with the Woolf brothers, Jack wanted to try directing. He was given a long short film to direct, *The Bespoke Overcoat*, which was the story of a Jewish tailor and was sufficiently effective to allow Jack to move on to *Room at the Top*, which was a big hit for him and highly influential at the time. It was a landmark in British cinema though it did not actually start the kitchen sink wave, which had its real roots in the Free Cinema Movement started by Karel Reisz, Tony Richardson, and Lindsay Anderson. But *Room at the Top* was perhaps the first of its kind to get a large overseas distribution.

Jack was a big drinker who used to tipple quite frequently all day—mostly brandy—and he was a chain smoker. He mesmerized me, having a Svengali effect. He was absolutely revered by the crew, and I cannot deny falling under his spell. I've always been attracted to the voices of people, and Jack had a particularly mellifluous way of talking.

He'd been married a few times, and I remember Jimmy Ware telling me about when he was living in a London apartment just beneath Jack and his then wife, Christine Norden, who was a well-known actress. One night there was the most frightful noise above and this huge row was going on. He was hurling the furniture around, and they split up shortly after that. He later married Haya Harareet, an Israeli actress who was in William Wyler's *Ben Hur*. She gave up acting when she married Jack.

The script of *The Innocents* was based on William Archibald's play and was adapted by John Mortimer. The final version was given to Truman Capote, with whom Clayton had worked on *Beat the Devil*.

Truman was a character, and Toby Jones' take on him in the film *Infamous* is as near as any living person could get to that mixed up, mercurial, twisted, funny, camp person. I had a few lunches with Jack and Truman, who made me laugh so much I forgot how bad the Shepperton restaurant food was.

Truman had already written *In Cold Blood*, but he couldn't publish it yet. He would sit and fret about this. "I called the Sheriff last night," he'd say. "They won't swing yet. I can't publish until they swing." It was only later that I discovered he'd had a relationship with one of the killers; but from his anxiety, it seemed he couldn't wait for the man to go to the gallows.

Jack and I became good collaborators and eventually close friends away from the studio. This was partly because we lived near each other.

Jack, who was divorced at the time and living with his mother, had a house in Marlow, Buckinghamshire, while I had moved my children and housekeeper away from Ealing and into Bourne End, only a few miles away. My thinking then was that the country air and the local school would be better for them. I bought a pleasant house on an estate that had a large garden through which a stream ran. It was close by the Thames and quite idyllic. Later I discovered that Tom Stoppard was also living nearby with his first wife and the ex-Ealing editor Peter Bezencenet was also there. This was a close-knit community, prettily designed in the early twenties by a builder who had been to Venice.

Jack Clayton and I worked together very well on *The Innocents*, partly because we both enjoyed the material. He was meticulous, and he knew that I was too. His approach to editing was wildly different from Stanley Donen's. He would run the cut footage every night after shooting. It was a very relaxed routine. We would run the rushes at lunchtime with the crew, and every evening about seven, Jack would send his assistant, Jeanie Sims, to the bar for drinks, then we'd run the film as it stood. Obviously, each evening, it grew a bit. He didn't come into the cutting room all that much, but would give me his notes each evening, which I would then attend to during the following day, so it was a true collaboration.

This routine involved my assistant editor, Mary Kessel, picking up the rushes from the labs each morning. She'd then get to the studio quickly, collecting the sound transfers and synching them up so that they were ready for projection by eight. This was a hard task, but was very helpful to the director, particularly if he was in the middle of a scene.

This way of working left no time at all for a social life, but since neither Jack nor I were attached at that time and the summer evenings were pleasantly warm, we would repair to the bar, which faced the big garden at Shepperton, to continue drinking and talking about the picture. Often we would close the bar before driving home. We were both lucky not to get breathalysed. It was a very concentrated time. Jack had to be up early too. He had extraordinary stamina, especially in relation to booze and would often have a brandy and soda at his elbow.

During the shooting of the picture, Jack became fond of pigeons, which were used very often as prop birds fluttering around the garden set. I don't know if he was keen on these birds before, but after the film was shot, he had a large aviary built in his garden and soon became a national authority on certain species of pigeon. It was an odd hobby and he pursued it until he died.

The film was shot very well by Freddie Francis in black-and-white Cinemascope, with Pamela, his wife-to-be, on continuity. We soon got down to serious editing. Like Stanley, he preferred making judgments in the theatre rather than the cutting room. Mary Kessel reminded me that Jack would review everything he had shot after he had seen my rough cut. This meant that the assistant had to rejoin all the trims and spares into reels, since Jack viewed in the theatre. Nowadays I still encourage directors to do this, so they can be certain to have chosen the very best sections, but present day video techniques have, thankfully, rendered the need to join everything obsolete.

Jimmy Woolf was once again producer of the film, but it was really Jack's picture through and through.

After *Room at the Top*, there had been a long wait until he decided what he should do next. Jack was never one to make hasty decisions. He'd been highly influenced by John Huston and perhaps his sadistic sense of practical joking came from that period. Jeanie Sims, his personal assistant, was often the butt of these jokes. Jeanie had been Huston's personal assistant before that. She had been badly burned as a child, leaving her with scars on her hands and face. She was also, quite naturally, terrified of fire. So Jack, equally naturally, made it his business to try and set Jeanie alight as often as possible. He would go to enormous lengths, preparing bonfires that Jeanie would supposedly be put onto. Jack had a perverse sense of humour. Sometimes it was very funny and sometimes not, and I think he learned a lot of that from Huston. The creativity and time that Clayton and Huston would invest in elaborate practical jokes was almost certainly a product of boredom, because making movies can be terribly boring. Gradually the picture was completed in a spirit of total harmony. We all loved it and working with Jack was nothing but pleasure. It seems not to have been a very hard job, since we had worked on it during the shooting, but we had certain problems with effects. The scene in which Miss Giddens prowls the house at night was not easy to perfect, and Peter Quint's first appearance at the window was also hard. This was reshot a number of times. We were after the kind of shock effect that David Lean and Jack Harris had achieved in *Great Expectations* and I don't think we ever quite reached it, but the picture was a fascinating exercise in suspense and unspoken threats, all of which the editing assisted. At the time, we had no idea we were working on a classic, which is what *The Innocents* has become.

I was also able to indulge in some rather cunning dissolves, somewhat influenced by George Stevens' *A Place in the Sun*. These would not be simple mixes of equal length. A 4-foot mix is the norm, but these would last 15 or 20 feet, the images gradually merging. I referred to them as lopsided mixes since the overlaps were nonstandard and often there would be a third image in there too, so these mixes were like mini montages. I didn't always get them right the first time, and the optical house had its problems, but the results were very pleasing to Jack and myself.

We were also much helped by the music which Georges Auric wrote for the picture and a splendidly atmospheric effects track that sound editor Peter Musgrave created. He was one of the first to use electronic effects. We all thought these were inspired at the time, adding the necessary accompaniment to Miss Gidden's night prowl, but when heard now they sound oddly anachronistic, putting the film firmly into the late sixties, away from the Edwardian period that had been so carefully created.

I also recall that Twentieth Century Fox, who paid for the picture, seemed quite disinterested in it, much to Jack's annoyance. I don't think they ever previewed it. Maybe Jack's contract disallowed that. There was a lot of anguish over the end of the picture, when the boy Miles dies in Miss Gidden's arms. Jack was quite prone to agonising over scenes if he was uncertain of them, and we would run them over and over again, hardly changing a frame, until he felt reconciled to the sequence.

There were difficult days when I had become exhausted by the material, finally getting bored with trying to please Jack, and he was perhaps thinking that I didn't care enough. His mood became extremely dark, and he was hard to live with. One incident, haunted me for years: When the film was completed and was to be shown to the magazine critics at the Fox preview theatre in Soho Square, Jack was much too nervous to attend and sent me and Jeanie along to report back to him about the critics' reactions. The screening was held up for half an hour due to problems that a physically handicapped lady critic, Freda Bruce Lockhart, was having with her wheelchair. Since she was a much-respected figure, we delayed the screening until she arrived, thus making us late with our phone call to Jack, who was waiting at the studio. After the show, which was clearly successful, we went to the nearest pub with John and Penelope Mortimer, and Jeanie went to the phone to call Jack with the good news. She returned looking pale. Jack had been very unpleasant because she should have made the call at least thirty minutes earlier. He was going crazy, feeling like a prisoner in a condemned cell and gave her a terrible ticking off. We all commiserated with her and went our ways. The following day, Jack did not turn up at the studio as planned. Jeanie called me to his office, where a large-scale model of Bly house made of white plaster had sat for many months. It now lay in a mass of shattered pieces all over the office. Jack had smashed it to smithereens in his anger the previous night. When he did turn up, he refused to talk to either of us. The rift was healed gradually, but in some ways our relationship was never quite the same. I thought it was all frightfully unjust and became wary of him. I think I rather despised him for refusing to attend the screening, though he might have been right about that. Critics don't normally like the director to be around when they view his work. Perhaps it should have taught me a lesson. I had become too close to Jack and had, perhaps, transcended the boundary that should exist between director and editor. This is in some ways a master and slave relationship, and although I had never tried to impose my own will on his material, perhaps he felt he had, in some way, lost his own picture. His only way to protect himself was by lashing out, not at me, but at some object close at hand. In spite of this, he asked me to work on his next picture, *The Pumpkin Eater,* which was only two years down the pike. A surprisingly short gap for Jack.

Charade

It was during the final stages of *The Innocents* that Stanley Donen went into production on his next picture, a romantic comedy thriller, *Charade*. It had been written for London, but at the eleventh hour there were some tax problems concerning the principal actors and the whole thing was moved to the Studio de Boulogne in Paris.

Charade had Cary Grant and Audrey Hepburn in the lead roles and an excellent list of supporting actors. The screenplay was good and the actors well cast. Walter Matthau, James Coburn, and George Kennedy all went on to become leading Hollywood stars.

It was a film with a slender story but masses of style and Peter Stone, one of the two writers, was on set all the time to alter dialogue if Cary required it. Peter had previously written for television but had no film production experience and he wanted to learn how movies were made. He also helped keep the atmosphere light. There was great camaraderie on the set between Stanley, Peter, Cary, and Audrey. She had no faults at all. In fact, it was a very smooth production, largely due to Jimmy Ware's outstanding ability as an organiser in both languages.

Stanley had a very light touch as a director. He allowed the actors to do their thing and only interfered if it was vital. We never socialised with the actors unless they requested it. In France it was a ritual to throw a drinks party on the set every Friday after shooting, hosted by one of the actors. We celebrated Cary Grant's sixtieth birthday on the set. At the end of shooting, Cary and Audrey gave each crew member a small gift.

The editing would be done in Paris during shooting and then move on to London for completion, so it was necessary for me to leave Bourne End and my children and stay in a hotel on the Left Bank in Paris for the duration of the shoot.

Due to French crewing requirements, it was necessary to have a French editor on board, who wouldn't edit, but would act as my assistant. I was not against this, but I stipulated that a man who spoke tolerable English would be preferable to a woman, having recently had problems with Mary Kessel on *The Innocents*. Mary, who was a good few years older than I, was always attempting to mother me, which was extremely trying. It seemed as if I could do nothing unless she approved. She also hero worshipped both Stanley and Jack, which upset me, and one day I said something to her which was, perhaps, a bit rough. The next I knew, she was out the door, saying she'd arranged for a replacement. Shortly afterward Jack Clayton called and asked where she was so I told him the story. He then contacted her and persuaded her back, though it was hardly his business. She returned and Jack sent bouquets of flowers to the cutting room. I was mortified and our relationship, which had lasted for years, was now completely over. I decided a change would be necessary on the next film.

After a few attempts, the French production office failed to secure a male editor, but finally came up with a female, who they said spoke good English and would on no account try to mother me or take over the editing. So, without meeting her, I reluctantly told the office to offer her the job, figuring it would only be for the three-month shooting period.

I settled into the hotel over a weekend. It had been arranged that the French lady editor would pick me up and drive me out to the Studio de Boulogne, since I had no car and was unfamiliar with public transportation in Paris. I also spoke very little French. So on the Monday morning the editor was there waiting for me. I recognised her at once as the same girl who had stood me up some years before on *Once More with Feeling*. It was Laurence Méry. Of course she claimed not to remember the incident, but I was certain it was her. In fact Laurence says that when she first saw me descending the staircase of the Lennox she said to herself, "Thank heaven he's young!"

I started on the first day of photography, along with my crew. I had a Moviola shipped over from England since I did not want to edit on the French machine, the Mauritone, though it did have a great screen and we often used it for viewing rushes and cut scenes.

There was a sense of fun pervading the enterprise that made us all feel good. The hours were long for the editing staff because the picture was being shot according to French union rules. Shooting began at noon and continued without a break until eight in the evening, when the rushes were shown. The cutting room, however, would open up around ten in the morning, so that we were on hand should Stanley want to run material on the Mauritone. By the time our rushes had ended in the evening, it was around nine and we had just worked another eleven-hour day. But in Paris you can eat late and we were all younger then.

I soon became great friends with my French assistant, Laurence Méry, who had cut more films than I had. The editing routine in Paris meant many late evening meals in restaurants, and eventually we began a relationship, much to the growing curiosity of the unit who were dying to know whether we were an item or not. They half guessed it but never figured it out satisfactorily since we were quite distant with one another during working hours. In this case, my need not to be mothered hadn't quite worked. It was soon clear to me, however, that the long gap since losing Jessie was about to be filled.

The picture did not start shooting in the studio, but on location in the French Alps at Megève, where the unit, mainly French, were quartered in a newly built luxury ski hotel. The first day's shooting was achieved and everyone was happy but then fog descended making filming impossible for several days. The long-range forecast was poor. Not knowing when the weather would break forced the decision to pack-strike a set in Paris and load it onto *camions* for transport to Megève, a long and expensive haul.

Stanley also had me along with a Steenbeck flatbed editing table sent to location so that he could look at rushes. He rarely wanted to do this so I found myself walking about the slopes, in the fog, wondering what I was doing up there.

James Coburn was sent for, and they shot a scene in a garage with him. Stanley then thought we might also do the nightclub scene in Megève, but that required more parts of the set, which were in Paris. At great expense these were duly trucked up, but as the lorries arrived, the sun emerged from behind the clouds. The sets went directly back to Paris and we were back outside shooting the scene in which Cary first meets Audrey. Eagle-eyed viewers will see that all the closeups of the principals were done much later in the studio against plates that were shot in Megève.

Due to this week of hiatus, we all had a little holiday, walking, swimming, and relaxing. Just as well, since, after that, we hardly drew a breath for six months.

When the unit returned to Paris, Laurence and I took Walter Matthau out to dinner at La Coupole. He ordered some form of curry and they brought to the table, in advance of his meal, a dish of chili peppers that were extremely hot. Not seeming to care, Walter chomped his way greedily through the pile, talking about himself the while, and as he talked and chomped we watched his face grow redder and redder. He stopped talking, clutched his throat, and croaked "I'm dying!" He made a dive for the Gents. I followed him. Everyone around us realised something was up. In the toilet he vomited noisily into a basin, doused himself with water, drank some, vomited again, as the attendants watched, "Quel horreur" being the general tone. After a decent interval, Matthau, who was, at this point in his career, unknown to all the French who considered him just another crazy American, calmed down, bowed to all those who were still watching and making remarks that neither of us could understand, and together we marched back into the restaurant where Laurence was patiently waiting for us. By now he was well recovered. Walter sat down, a little puffed, but not phased, and proceeded to eat his curry.

James Coburn was a different sort of guy. With his wife, Beverly, in tow, Laurence entertained them in her bijou flat one evening, which was a tight squeeze. James was into a number of Californian fads at the time but had not, so far as I know, gone in for LSD, which Cary Grant had described to me one day on the set between takes. It was no secret that Grant had tried this drug under his psychiatrist's supervision. He had often floated away from his body, which he could see vanishing beneath him as he buzzed around above himself. His one fear was that he might lose sight of his body. He did not suggest that I should try this drug.

After the shoot, the editing continued at Shepperton. Stanley took a much closer interest in the cutting than he ever had before in my experience. He probably sensed that he had a popular picture that he should nurture. The construction of the script was very tight. There was little slack in it. We did not have the nasty length problem that had plagued a number of pictures recently. Stanley was his own producer, as was Jack Clayton, and it was in his best interest to watch the money and not waste it.

He shot *Charade* in a perfectly straightforward manner. The rushes were actually quite boring to sit through, especially the dialogue sequences since he covered entire scenes in long shot, medium shot, and closeup without moving the camera. These dialogue scenes were entirely made in the cutting room. It was simply a matter of looking at each take several times, picking line readings from the best, putting them together and then adjusting. We also line cut a good deal to reduce the scenes and make them sharper. I had, by now, developed some little tricks of my own. For example, I would never let a character shut a door, allowing them to start to move the door but having the sound of the closing off screen. Later on I developed this more, so that actions, once begun, were very rarely completed. Of course films were cut far slower in those days and scenes had time to breath. I am still averse to overcutting and deplore the pernicious influence of commercials and pop videos on feature films. There are exceptions, certainly in scenes of action, but when dialogue scenes are cut up into mini cuts, the rhythms go to hell and the acting stops, as does my interest. Stanley would never have been that crass. He always had the most elegant sense of balance within a scene, as befits a master of the musical. And, when it came to comic timing, Cary Grant was another master. His throwaway bits of shtick were always worth watching. We don't make them like that anymore. Today we don't have many actors who can create those seemingly effortless performances that make the editor's life easier.

Stanley Donen was much more relaxed during the whole of *Charade*, which had a lot to do with his home life. He had married the former Lady Beatty around the time of *Surprise Package* and was living the society life in London and in his country house in Buckinghamshire. He had a chauffeur and every other appurtenance of wealth and success.

He was also still very distant with the technicians. I had now cut three pictures for Donen, but barely knew him. Perhaps that was good, since getting too close to

Clayton had upset the balance. The relationship between directors and editors is a close one and often a long one. It is complex like a marriage.

I've often wondered whether film and book editors work in the same way. I am often curious if anyone has bothered to edit books at all or even read them. Like books, most movies can be helped or hindered by the editing. It is not just a matter of taking two pieces of film and splicing them together at an appropriate moment, though that is an important basic element. The technical aspect is only of so much importance. It is the approach to the material and the way the editor deals with the director that can be crucial to the outcome. Although the editor is not responsible for the final cut, he can help the director by guiding him. An editor can best make his point by skillfull demonstration. I have never believed in arguing with a director, which usually ends in bad feelings and hurts the film. But I do believe in cutting many versions of a scene to prove a point. Of course in the early sixties, the days of Donen and Clayton, this was rarely required. The paranoia that now surrounds post-production has made the whole procedure more nerve wracking and unsettling. There is much to be said for what now seems like a gentleman's club atmosphere in which we worked. Time has altered all of that. Pictures are often rushed through post-production in weeks when we had months. Sometimes these rapidly completed pictures succeed and make money, thereby causing the studios to decree that expensive, long post-production periods are no longer necessary. They also point to television series cut on video in next to no time. This is the direction the money providers would like film editing to go and they will doubtless get their way.

The films I cut for Clayton, Donen, and later for John Schlesinger and Roland Joffé, were done with a different spirit. It was the film that mattered, not the budget. We all tried to work within the budget, but we would not compromise. The pictures were made with love and that is now hard to find in the editing rooms of the film world. I am told that the same is true for books—a sorry state indeed.

The excellent score for *Charade* was composed and conducted by Henry Mancini, and Hank, as he was known, was one of the most charming men you could meet. On the first day of recording, we met at CTS in Kensington Garden Square. He was introduced to me, walked into the studio, greeted the orchestra, picked up his baton, and they sight-read the title music without a mistake. It was sheer magic. The *Charade* theme, later with lyrics by Johnny Mercer, was heard for the first time. "It's a standard," I said to Stanley, who nodded sagely. I was quite right. I know a good tune when I hear one. The session was interrupted by lunch at a pub and then we continued. Everything was wrapped up in a couple of days, and Hank was back on the plane.

Charade was put together rapidly. Stanley took it to Los Angeles to show to Universal. They previewed it and he returned. Some tweaking was required to the final scene involving trapdoors in a Paris theatre and that was that. It was probably one of the most successful pictures Stanley directed in that period.

☆   ☆   ☆

Having moved from Ealing to Bourne End during *The Innocents,* I now settled back into life on the Abbotsbrook estate. Although created by a spec builder who had fallen in love with Venice, the estate did not resemble Venice in any way, a stream with swans ran through it and the homes were rather mock Tudor in style.

I'd moved into Cornerways with a housekeeper, Mrs. Dring, a widow from Boston who my mother Florence had located for me. Mrs. Dring was charming and helpful. Kate went to school locally and my adopted son David was at a prep school near Newbury.

Laurence visited me in Bourne End after I returned from Paris. She soon christened it "Dead End," because Laurence perceived it as a commuter belt area where people were interested only in domestic matters. There was no culture.

In deference to Mrs. Dring, Laurence stayed in the guest room. This situation quickly became tiresome, and she moved into my bed. Neither of us considered what Mrs. Dring might think.

Shortly after Laurence had returned to Paris and before we decided to marry, I was driving my mother to David's sports day at prep school. Kate was in the backseat of the car. "Are you still sleeping with a board under your mattress?" my mother enquired. She was referring to a cure I had for backache. "No, he's not," Kate piped up, "Laurence didn't like it." Mother fell silent. She remained silent for the rest of the day, and we drove back to Boston without further reference to Kate's remark. The following morning Mother came into my bedroom, looking haggard and drawn. "I didn't sleep last night after what Kate said in the car." I grunted a little. I was, after all, well over thirty. "Did I understand that you and Laurence slept in the same bed *with Mrs. Dring in the house?*"

In fact, we must have been really active since Sybil was conceived around this time. My mother said, "I will come to the wedding, but I will not enjoy it."

Laurence and my mother tolerated one another, but I could not say they were close. Mother always said bad things about my wives. When I married Jessie, she described her as "attending the tin tabernacle," a reference to the fact that she was Catholic and had a Russian mother. Laurence was Jewish and French. My mother would have preferred a nice English girl, who was not pregnant.

One Saturday the marquee from Harrods went up at Cornerways, and Laurence and I were married at Little Marlow Church. Sybil was born shortly after while I was editing Clayton's next film, *The Pumpkin Eater.* Jack was a near neighbour and offended my mother by wearing casual clothes to our wedding and then compounding the felony by taking small children with him when he went to smoke in the back garden.

David and Kate were there and it was a family occasion. Laurence looked beautiful in her wedding finery, her family had come over from Paris and the sun shone all day. It was the start of a lifetime of happiness, though like all relationships it had its ups and downs.

FLASHBACK: *Photogravure*

My father had decided I should be apprenticed in the photogravure section of the factory that manufactured engraved cylinders from which the labels were printed. The department was under the strict rule of Mr. Booy, a small man with a big temper. Although I was the boss's son, he treated me exactly like anyone else.

I lived at home and tried to adjust to small-town life. I joined an amateur theatrical group, the Boston Playgoers, and rapidly became their juvenile lead. This occupied most of my leisure time and introduced me to a circle of local folk who had a nucleus of like interests. We would repair to a inn after rehearsals where we drank too much beer. On Saturday nights, a few of the male members of the cast could be found getting drunk in the "men only" bar of the White Hart hotel. Women were consigned to the adjoining room with its wicker furniture. I would consume too much beer and then retire to my bedroom. The room would revolve as soon as I lay down and just in time I would get up to throw up in the hand basin. When this became a regular Saturday routine, I knew it was time for a change.

I had made a few trips back to Oundle, often to discuss my future with Arthur Marshall. He never once encouraged me to drop out of the family business and engage in something to do with cinema. When he was my age, he had wanted nothing more than to become a professional comedian. His parents had talked him out of that and, as a result, he had abandoned his desires and become a teacher, which he never regretted. He felt it was sensible of my parents to steer me toward a secure future in the printing business. That I eventually spurned his advice always amused me. It was only a couple of years afterward that Arthur abandoned teaching, left Oundle, and became secretary to Lord Rothschild; then he became part of Binkie Beaumont's theatrical empire, and finally a television personality. He also never stopped writing humorous pieces for the *New Statesman* and the *Telegraph*. So much for his advice—which I never took.

The Boston Film Society had sprouted a production department. I had a 16 mm Bolex camera and with the help of Charles Whittaker and others, we made a short silent film that we called *Absconded*. I volunteered to play the lead. It was shot on the marshes around Boston and concerned a Borstal boy who had escaped from the camp and was chased to his death by drowning. My friends played the police, who determined that there would be no way out.

The film ran for ten minutes and was awarded a prize in the annual amateur film competition. It was awarded to us by Harry Watt, the celebrated documentarian who was now making features for Ealing.

This success inspired us, in 1951, to make a much more ambitious piece that we called *A Boston Story* featuring Charles Whittaker as an American returning to his native town in Festival Year.

Before this, however, my father had decided I should go to the London School of Printing for a year, to learn the art of photogravure away from the confines of the factory. He contacted their south England representative and asked him to find suitable accommodation. For reasons I now find odd, this man booked me into a guesthouse in Bromley, Kent, which involved me taking a train each day to Charing Cross, a needlessly expensive journey and one that required me to take the last train home. This curtailed any fun I might find in the city, since the last train left at eleven. I had to put up with the bizarre and repressive life that existed in the guesthouse run by the Carters, a grim and obsequious couple lately released from the RAF, who made my life a misery. They ran their prim and proper establishment as if it were something to be treasured and revered. They were house proud and had something like a dozen guests, of which I was by far the youngest. Most of the guests were middle aged and escaping from something like wives or taxes. Some were business reps who used the guesthouse as a cheap hotel once a week when on their rounds of the area. All in all, it was a motley bunch of misfits, mostly men, who met over breakfast and dinner in sullen silence. I kept as far away from them as possible. The atmosphere was pure Graham Greene, and the Carters were a rigid couple who fawned over the regular customers while treating me with disdain and overcharging for my room and board. I never felt so lonely. Once I contracted a bad flu and had to remain in my room. They rarely came to check on me. Somehow I felt that to be sick in their establishment was considered a slur. There was always a problem with food. We were still strictly rationed and they continued to cook and serve up food that might have just passed muster in the NAFFI. It was a grim time and I longed to leave. Salvation beckoned when

I contacted Dr. and Mrs. Booth. They invited me to a party and realised I was unhappy.

I was in the habit of returning to Boston on weekends during this period, largely to avoid a weekend in Bromley, but I had few friends in the town at that time since most of them were away doing their National Service. I had been rejected by the doctors on account of my eczema, an unpleasant skin condition that had plagued me since childhood. So, although I avoided two years of army life, I was feeling isolated and separated from my friends, who occasionally appeared on leave and complained about their wasted years during which their real lives were on hold.

At some point during this year in London, I made the conscious decision to leave Bromley, which had become unbearable, particularly after a nasty incident when I was stuck in a railway compartment with a drunk who lunged at me and attempted to remove my trousers, saying boozily, "You'd make a fine centre forward!" There were no corridors on these trains and I had to wait until the train stopped to make an escape. Fortunately the man did not pursue me as I dashed outside, but it was unnerving to say the least and put an end to Bromley.

The following week I moved into a bed-sit just off Cromwell Road. Now I was living alone, in a tiny room with a gas meter and a hot plate. It was, however, all mine and it was a more central location.

Back in Boston we set out to make *A Boston Story*. This was filmed in black and white, and we added a soundtrack with music and narration. It included a visit to London where Charles was seen wandering around the Festival Gardens, though his mind was still in Boston. To say that this amateur movie was poor is an understatement, but we ran it for a few evenings at the Assembly Rooms in Boston. It was favourably received and then we gave it a decent burial.

I had now been appointed the Publicity Officer for the Federation of Film Societies, despite being only nineteen, and was often in provincial cities for weekend meetings. I also attended the Edinburgh Film Festival and reported on films that members might rent for their societies.

One blissful year I was invited to Biarritz to a Festival of Films Maudit that was organised by Cocteau and his cronies. The invite came from the British Council. I met Ralph Glasser and Derek Griggs and we travelled to Biarritz by train, stopping at St. Jean de Luze. It was my first time in France and it was a very heady experience. I was, as yet, unexposed to much of life, particularly as led by bohemians in France. I was warned not to dip too heavily into bottles of Pernod, which might put me away.

On the opening night of the festival, I forgot those warnings and ended up with my friends in a hotel suite overlooking the Atlantic, the temporary home of Denis Price, the English actor who had been in *Kind Hearts and Coronets* and who was a guest of honour. He had not heeded the drink warning either and, drunk as a skunk, declaimed a speech Noel Coward had delivered in *In Which We Serve.* By this time we were chucking champagne into the ocean, and I eventually passed out on a *chaise longue,* from which I was rescued by Ralph Glasser just as Price was about to commit a rash act. They bundled me out of the apartment, and I remained in my room for two days, missing many films and wondering what had hit me.

It was shortly after this that I decided to leave home. I called Francis Howard, who was now with Industrial Colour Films. He got me the job that took me away from Boston. My parents, instead of being vindictive, were both supportive. But my new job, fun though it was, did not last. The company went bankrupt within the year. It was "I told you so" from the family, but I was not to be so easily brought back to Boston.

I was out of a job, not a union member, twenty-one, and totally unknown. In those days, it was of paramount importance to belong to the union and it was the hardest organisation to join. The catch-22 syndrome persisted—no experience, you couldn't join; not a member, you couldn't get experience.

Dr. Booth had a keen interest in my career, or lack of it, knowing that Father was now paying my rent. One day he casually mentioned that a doctor he knew in the Borough was called if any medical attention was required at Ealing Studio and wondered out loud if it might be a good idea to suggest he mention my name to the head of Personnel.

My interview with Baynham Honri was the outcome of this conversation.

ENTER SCHLESINGER

Senghenydd

While we were finishing work on *Charade*, an old school friend, David Morgan Rees, who lived in South Wales, suggested a subject for a short film to me, which involved a mining town, Senghenydd, which had suffered a disaster in the early part of the twentieth century. I visited the place and decided there was a film to be made there. So I bought the short ends of negative from *Charade* for next to nothing and, with my assistant, David Campling, returned to Senghenydd and shot the film myself with a 35 mm Arriflex. Laurence edited the eighteen-minute film, *Senghenydd: Portrait of a Mining Town,* that went on to win some awards.

Looking back, it seemed a very presumptuous move, to shoot a film without any real knowledge of lighting and in Eastmancolor. I waved my light metre around as if I knew what I was doing. Our local contact in Senghenydd was Bill Probert, a retired miner and now a photographer, who knew everyone in town. His sister, a massive and grand lady, was married to a miner, who was not breathing too well, and insisted on entertaining us with large fried meals after we had spent several hours in the local club with Bill.

We were staying in David Rees' house nearby, but would be sitting down at her kitchen table late at night with a plate of eggs and bacon. The finale of the film included a scene featuring the local male voice choir. I recorded them on my Ferrograph, filmed them to playback, and arranged to cut away to a rugby game when the choir drifted out of sync. I rented two lamps from Samuelsons to light the scene. It was a miracle that I obtained the correct exposure. The fact that the film did win a few awards must have meant that I did something right.

The Pumpkin Eater

Jack Clayton's inability to make a decision was legendary, which is the reason it took him so long to decide what his next film would be. He was a complex man— he drank too much, smoked too much, and was dangerously unpredictable. Jack was a barroom brawler who would, if provoked, attack people with his fists. He was also charming and seductive, which masked his many defects.

The Pumpkin Eater was the first film that Maggie Smith ever acted in, and we all agreed that she had a future in the business. It was also one of the earliest screenplays by Harold Pinter, based on a largely autobiographical novel by Penelope Mortimer. The story concerned the emotional traumas of an upper middle class wife with many children, whose writer husband is a philanderer. Penny's then husband, John Mortimer, was a writer and philanderer and Penny was left with many children, so it does seem that the novel was her way of getting back at him. Jack told me that she was very upset when Pinter was given the screen writing assignment rather than her.

The cast was strong. Anne Bancroft played the wife and Peter Finch was her writer husband. James Mason played the unsympathetic husband of one of Finch's conquests. The shoot seemed to go along well with no obvious hiccups. Although Peter Finch was a notorious drinker in those days, I don't believe he caused any trouble. My house in Bourne End was used as the home of Bancroft's parents. It was the first and last time I allowed a film crew into my house. Not that they did much damage and they did returf the lawn, but having a lot of strangers in the house did not sit well with me or my wife.

The filming of *The Pumpkin Eater* was a happy experience though I was not often on the set. Jack and I got on well and seemed to repeat the good times we'd shared on *The Innocents*.

One scene that had a creepy impact was when James Mason's character meets Anne Bancroft for tea at London Zoo and enthusiastically tells her of the affair his wife's been having with her husband. Totally thrown by this news, Bancroft becomes disoriented and begins focusing on Mason's teeth as he viciously recounts the details of their infidelity. We cut from the bewildered face of Bancroft to increasingly enlarged shots of Mason's teeth. This was my idea and was achieved by successively blowing up Mason's face optically until we got right into his teeth. Perhaps I overdid this, and it does stand out as being ridiculously modish now, but it was a good idea at the time and Jack seemed to like it.

One other scene that was seized on by critics is the slow pan from Bancroft in bed to the framed photograph of her father. It was originally shot beginning on the photo and panning to the bed but, in editing, Jack decided to reverse it. What none of us realised at the time, though I can't imagine why, was that she was smoking in bed with smoke coming from her nostrils. When reversed, the smoke appeared to enter her nose. I guess in the heat of the moment it seemed okay to us but later the critics hammered us for it.

The picture was released by Columbia in 1964 and was chosen as the British entry to the Cannes Festival that year. It was well received but the critics felt it was too long. By this time I was off the film but had gone to the festival anyway, and though my relationship with Jack seemed fine, after Cannes it deteriorated.

Jack came back from the festival determined to take five minutes out of the film, so I returned to Shepperton in an effort to help him achieve this. It soon became evident that he didn't know which five minutes he could lose. I came up with a few suggestions which recieved scant attention. He was in an agony of indecision and days went by as he tried this and that. I was rapidly losing patience with him and had private conversations with Jeanie Sims, confiding my feelings. Eventually it was the Harrods scene that took the bulk of the cuts. I had always liked this scene, which was pivotal to the film. The slow buildup to Anne Bancroft's breakdown was necessary to give the sequence its shape. But in the version that was released, Anne arrived at Harrods, had a short walkabout, and then had her breakdown. It all happened too fast.

Jeanie must have conveyed my feelings to Jack because our relationship never recovered from this disagreement. I believe to this day that he made a terrible error in cutting that scene. There were other scenes that could have been shortened.

Cannes was the closest thing to a test screening the picture had because the British didn't really preview films in those days, but if we had tested it, I believe Jack would not have attended. He was far too nervous for that ordeal.

My daughter Sybil was born while I was cutting *The Pumpkin Eater.* Laurence called me from Bourne End as she left the house for the maternity hospital in Beaconsfield. Her obstetric surgeon was called, appropriately, Mr. Butcher. Laurence had not had a child before, and she had no friends in England. It was therefore a difficult and challenging time. I drove from Shepperton Studios to Beaconsfield and went to her room. This was a Catholic nursing home, just the place for a good

Jewish girl, and the nuns did not encourage me to stay. "The baby will not come before morning." So I left and went home where I watched a television documentary about Marilyn Monroe. The phone rang at eleven. "You have a baby girl." I went directly to the nursing home, found an exhausted wife, and a charming little baby that Laurence had delivered really quickly, considering it was her first and only child. We named her Sybil Florence, after Laurence's mother and mine. Later Sybil confessed she hated her name, largely due to Basil Fawlty's wife being named Sybil, which caused much ragging at school.

Darling

I had met John Schlesinger socially many times in the restaurant at Shepperton while he was finishing *Billy Liar*, so when *Darling* came along, Gareth Wigan, who was the agent we both shared, suggested me for the job. John felt he needed to change editors for *Darling* and originally wanted to promote his sound editor Malcolm Cooke, but the financiers insisted on having an editor with a track record they could rely on. I had a meeting with John over lunch and we talked in general terms about films. I was fairly convinced that I'd not really impressed him very much. I remember going home and telling Laurence that it hadn't gone well. I didn't hear for a long time and was eventually surprised to learn I'd gotten the job.

Darling was a very interesting film to edit and working with John for the first time was also fascinating because he was a very charismatic man and we would, over the years, become good colleagues and friends. The thing I always remember about John is his sense of humour. He was outrageous, funny, and camp. He was a breath of fresh air and didn't behave like a serious filmmaker. John had an expansive gift for wit, and he could be colourfully scathing about other people.

Darling had been around for a while. It was written by Frederic Raphael but was actually based on other material. Godfrey Wynn had written an original treatment and then Fred Raphael, John, and producer Joe Janni rewrote it all. The concept was based on a girl they all knew, and it was a good year before anything happened because it was a difficult film to raise cash for. Originally financed by Nat Cohen, whose company was Anglo Amalgamated, *Darling* was designed as a vehicle for Julie Christie. Julie had taken over the female part in *Billy Liar* from another actress who had done all the location work in Bradford and then had a medical problem that caused her to swell up. They had to reshoot and Julie had been seen by Joe Janni in a small part in a Ken Annakin comedy, in which she shone through as an interesting personality. So she got the job on the reshoots of *Billy Liar* and became an instant celebrity. There was a famous scene in *Billy Liar* where she walks into the film to music composed by Richard Rodney Bennett. She seemed to become an immediate icon of the 1960s. *Darling*'s other two stars were Dirk Bogarde and Laurence Harvey.

The first week of work was all shot at Lords Cricket Ground. It was a huge scene of the test match and must have cost a fortune with all those extras. It was to be the film's opening where Dirk Bogarde meets Julie Christie, but when we put the film together, this scene was far too long and didn't work at all. Freddy Raphael didn't want to know about rewriting it, so weeks after we finished shooting, John and I sat down over a meal and thrashed out a new opening ourselves, very much shorter and to the point. There was a writer around named Troy Kennedy Martin who was doing *Z Cars* at the BBC, and John got him involved. He wrote the opening, following our ideas, and we got Dirk and Julie back and shot for another week at various places in London. These reshoots were expensive and the producer, Joe Janni, went to the States to raise more money by selling the American distribution rights to Joseph E. Levine, a big distributor at the time. John always claimed that Joe did a very bad deal and sold the rights rather more cheaply than he should have.

Joe Janni was a very mercurial Italian who John had christened the "Wily Milanese." Joe had been a student at Manchester University before the war where he was being trained for the dairy business. When the war came along, Joe, being an Italian, was arrested and was incarcerated for a while. He managed to get out and found a job in the film industry. Shortly after the war he was producing at Pinewood.

He was a very amusing, charismatic man and a great womaniser. He and John used to fight like mad. Of course they loved one another but they fought constantly. At screenings Joe and John used to argue a great deal, and we always had to stop the projection at some point while they argued over tiny points. In *Darling*, Joe claimed that because John was homosexual, he didn't understand women and therefore couldn't understand why Julie behaved the way she did. And then John would get personal about Joe, who was married, and complain about his "aunties." Joe, according to John, had many "aunties" in London. The whole thing would become a personal, venemous argument while my assistant and I would sit and wait for this row to subside so that we could get on with the projection.

☆ ☆ ☆

One night, leaving the screening room in South Audley Street after eleven and driving home to Bourne End on the recently completed M4, I was totally exhausted and collapsed in the bedroom, saying to Laurence that I had a job for her. Poor thing thought I had a job for her in the cutting room. No, I said, tomorrow you go out and find us a house in London. I can't stand these late screenings and then the drive back here. "It's not going to stop," I said. "So start looking." I knew she would not be unhappy since she had never settled in Bourne End and wanted our daughter Sybil educated at the French Lycée in Kensington. I gave Laurence a finite amount I could afford which was £18,000.

After a fruitless search for six months, she eventually told me she had seen a house "with a magnificent staircase." This was a sizeable house in Kensington Square. It had not been lived in for a while and had been an estate agent's office. I looked at it and, although the asking price was more than I had suggested, we bought it for £24,000. Some months later, having spent another ten thousand, it was ready for occupation.

Apart from the rows between Joe and John, there was no friction on the set of *Darling*. Before shooting began, John was terribly worried that he would find Laurence Harvey difficult but this proved not to be the case at all. He got along fine with Dirk and Julie. He was very concerned about Julie's welfare more than anything else. She was living alone in a flat in Baron's Court, and I guess she didn't have much money at the time. She used to turn up at the studio absolutely exhausted and was constantly falling asleep around the set. John became very concerned and soon learned that she was going home in the evenings after acting all day and was doing her washing, ironing, and cleaning, not getting enough sleep and being generally knackered. John was a very generous man and quickly arranged for her to have some home help.

John and I collaborated closely on *Darling*, which I always thought was a good film but slightly overlong, especially in the second half. I do remember that he shot a lot of footage in Italy at the wedding of Julie, when she married an Italian count, and he shot it in newsreel style. We were never quite sure what to do with it. One day I came up with the idea of turning it into a Pathé newsreel, so I cut the film and we got Bob Danvers Walker, who had been the voice of Pathé, to come in and read the commentary. I put library music with it and newsreel titles under the front and turned it into a Pathé newsreel.

John was never very happy with *Darling* and, when it opened, the critics were not kind. In fact it didn't do well in England, critically or financially. But when it opened in America, it was received with great acclaim and went on to win Oscars. Fred Raphael and Julie Christie both got Academy Awards, and John was nominated for one but didn't win.

I remember John calling me from New York after the premiere and saying, "Well dear, it's a hit. Don't ask me why, but they love it."

It wasn't, however, an easy film to cut. We had to work long hours on it, and one day at Shepperton, John took me out to lunch at a river pub. "You know, I think I've found the subject for my next movie," he pronounced. I asked what it was thinking I might be involved and he said, "Well, you know in *Darling*, we've got that boardroom scene with lots of people around the table? I'm having an affair with one of these men." So I asked which one and he told me I had to guess. I figured it wasn't Laurence Harvey and, there, over lunch, we went around the table but I couldn't guess who it was. He finally told me it was an extra. "The trouble is," said John, "That I never know whether he's going to be there when I get home at night because he's also having an affair with this woman in Hampstead." And that was the genesis of *Sunday, Bloody Sunday*. I told John it was a great idea for a movie, and he worked on that with Penelope Gilliat who wrote the screenplay. Other than this discussion, I was not involved with the movie.

It was while we were working on the dubbing stage with *Darling* that I received a letter from Jack Clayton that upset me greatly. In the letter he blamed me for the failure of *The Pumpkin Eater*. He claimed I'd never been behind the project, which was palpably untrue. It really was quite devastating for me, and I showed the letter to John who advised me to "burn it," which I did. I now regret that because I'm unable to recall most of the vitriol, but there were certain clues making me think that it was not from Jack at all. For one thing it was typed and Jack never used a typewriter. Also it was typed on Jeanie's machine. Of course Jack might have dictated it, but something always nagged me. Was it Jeanie getting her own back for some odd reason?

There was a definite coldness from Jack when my wife and I met him at that year's BAFTA dinner. "Laurence, come and sit with me. Not you, Jim." So I was clearly being ignored. Laurence told me later that Jack was drunk. We parted for many years until I met him again in Hollywood at Paramount at the time of *The Great Gatsby*. He'd upset everyone by hurling a chair through his office window. The office was on the first floor and the chair landed on some executive's parked Mercedes.

We met Jack Clayton again in Hollywood when he was preparing *Something Wicked This Way Comes* for Disney. He was perfectly pleasant and our past problem was never mentioned. Jack had had a stroke after *Gatsby* and had to be taught to speak again. If you look in his filmography, there is a big gap over this period. The stroke was kept very quiet.

☆   ☆   ☆

On *Darling*, I became friendly with Dirk Bogarde and, at this time, I very much wanted to direct. I'd come across a novel called *Lord Dismiss Us* by Michael Campbell, about a public school. I thought it might be a good vehicle for Dirk to play the master, so I suggested it to him one day and he said, "How strange. I've just read that book myself." He said that if we wanted to develop it, we should do it together, then I could direct it and he would appear in it as well as being producer. So we met the author and the two of us went into partnership, buying the rights and commissioning a script. We got Universal in London to pay for script development and we gave it to Hugh Leonard, the Irish dramatist to write. He was very late in delivery and wouldn't send us anything to read. By this time Dirk was off doing something else. The whole thing dribbled on and on to the point where we were about to lose the option and still didn't have a script. We eventually managed to get Hugh Leonard to deliver ninety pages of stuff but it was awful, absolutely not what we wanted at all. It was a very bad version of the book. We then had to go cap in hand to Universal saying we're terribly sorry, this script is no good, we've got to go to another writer. Also at this time Lindsay Anderson came out with *If*, which Paramount was releasing. So a combination of a script that was of no use to us and the huge success of Lindsay's *If*, set in a British public school, knocked our little project on the head. Dirk and I went no further with it but I did remain friendly with him until Tony became ill and came back to London. We corresponded regularly, and a letter from Dirk was a treat.

Dirk never came out though he lived with Tony for years. In his autobiography, he never hinted that he was homosexual. In the end, with Tony very sick, they moved back to England, and I saw Dirk from time to time, but eventually, after Tony's death, he became a recluse and died, alone in his Cadogan Square apartment. It was a sad end for a wonderful, witty, wise man.

Commercials and Documentaries

Darling seemed to propel my career in several directions. One of these was that Joe Janni invited me to go off and become part of his other company that was making commercials. It was run by a very nice lady named Connie Ingles who was a great trouper. So I began directing commercials. I was terribly ill suited to this work and didn't really enjoy it. I had no experience of that world or just how dreadful, sordid, and seedy it was. I did, however, enjoy doing the PG Tips chimps ads because it was a challenge getting those apes to work. They used to be shot at a zoo in Ashby-de-la-Zouch, which was run by two rather masculine ladies who were to train the chimps to do what the storyboards instructed. So if the storyboard said Mrs. Chimp gets up and walks over to the table or picks up a cup of tea, they were supposed to have trained the animals to do these moves. I don't think they ever really trained them to do anything because if the animals didn't do it right they just used to hit them on the head with a stick. Then the animals would scream and everyone on the crew would be horrified and then we'd have another go. We used to shoot hundreds of takes in order to get one that more or less worked.

One day we were shooting at the Drill Hall in the middle of town in Ashby-de-la-Zouch and the one thing the chimps wanted to do was escape, so everybody was told if ever they opened a door that led to the street they had to close it immediately. The chimps were all dressed in their special costumes, little dresses, suits, and ties. Some unfortunate person let a chink of light in through the door. The chimp that saw it made a B-line for it, dashing out into the street, dressed as a woman, and proceeded to run down the street, chased by everybody, including the public. It was straight out of an Ealing comedy, this chimp being chased by half the town. It was a wonderful scene. Eventually we managed to overpower the chimp and bring it back.

Nic Roeg had been lighting *Doctor Zhivago* for David Lean and got fired one Friday in Madrid, turning up in Ashby-de-la-Zouch on the next Monday to shoot the chimp commercials. It seems that Lean didn't like the fact that Julie Christie was paying more attention to Nic than to her director. I remember Nic kept taking a strip of 70 mm film out of his top pocket, which Zhivago was being shot on, and saying "It's come to this!" He, like most of the crew, was appalled at the way the ladies were hitting the chimps and left after a day or two.

I soldiered on with the chimps through quite a few of these commercials but thankfully, these women got fired and, by the last lot I did, they were looked after by some Swiss circus people. They never allowed these other people back. But they ran the PG Tips zoo for years, probably still do.

At the time *Darling* opened in London, John told me of an amusing little film he was about to shoot for the BBC television programme *That Was the Week That Was*, which Ned Sherrin was producing. It was to be a short satire on nudist films, and he had a good script by Ray Galton and Alan Simpson. Only a few days later he called me to explain that he'd had a change of heart and perhaps shouldn't be doing this cheap and cheerful stuff since *Darling* was such a success in America—

and would I like to take it over? This was a strange idea. I wanted to direct but had no actual experience directing actors and certainly not comedy. Ned Sherrin called and I agreed to this madness. Everything was prepared. All I had to do was show up and direct the thing over a three-day period. So I found myself at Woburn Abbey with some pleasant people to help me. I was out of my depth, but the final result pleased everyone at the BBC and they even repeated the segment. Seen now, it must be fairly awful. What did I know about acting or comedy or directing, come to that? But it was made and it was successful, so I guess at the time, I considered myself a director. I was, however, no substitute for Schlesinger who might have made a much better job of it.

Then Janni's commercials company was contracted to make a feature for the Children's Film Foundation (CFF), so I found myself directing *The Christmas Tree*. This was made for next to nothing around the leafy lanes of Bucks and was about a group of kids who were trying to get a Christmas tree to the local hospital. I had helped write the script. The children's efforts were hampered by all sorts of events, but they made it in the final reel. I had five weeks in which to shoot this and called in a number of chums to help. Anne Skinner was continuity, Peter Suschitzky lit the film, and Claude Watson was the assistant director. It was a happy experience that ended, rather drearily, in a World Premiere in Streatham on a wet Saturday morning. It has probably vanished forever, melted down for its silver. The CFF did not have long to live. Its core audience now preferred more exciting products.

Army Recruiting Film

It was due to the short film I had made, *Senghenydd*, that I came to the notice of James Archibald, a documentary producer who was about to make a film for the War Office. We made the film, which was never shown. It was shelved because it was perceived as "too real," but the act of shooting the film made the whole thing worthwhile, opening my eyes to the real world. Because of this experience I resolved to try and combine the real with the imagined in my future career.

James and I had decided to use, as our model regiment, the Royal Welsh Fuseliers, who were then based in Minden, Germany. We had no script. The core idea, which the War Office had agreed with, was to show a slice of life in the regimental day, so that recruiting officers could screen it for potential enlisters and their parents. The Welsh regiment was considered a model. Most of the recruits were eighteen and were coming from areas formerly connected to coal mining. The boys would, in the old days, have left school and gone into the pit. Now they were off into the army, so our assignment was to show what life was *really* like for them, which we worked toward, slowly, during our recce (reconnaissance) period in Minden, a town not too far away from Buchenwald.

Perhaps we should have realised that you should never show life as it *really* is, and certainly not in a government-funded documentary, but this did not occur to us at the time. We blithely watched, with some sense of mounting horror, as regimental life was put on parade.

We were quartered in the Officers' Mess, as befitted our status, and memories of public school life flooded back. The regiment was steeped in tradition and the officers were a mix of older regulars and young fresh-faced officer cadets from Sandhurst. The other ranks, however, were mostly young men with very little knowledge of the world. They were putty in the hands of the officers and the sergeant majors.

One of the prime problems facing the men when they were not actually out on manoeuvres was boredom. To cure this, the powers that be had decided that each hut, which housed a platoon, could have its own club—a basic bar—that would open every day at 5 PM.

The beer they served was German and strong. The average age of the soldiers was twenty. The result of this situation was that the men would get loaded in no time at all and would then get up to no good, either in the barracks or, worse, in the town. Rape, vandalism, and fights were regular events but nobody seemed to think the clubs should be stopped.

One night, while I was observing, a prank was played on a young recruit that appalled me. A newcomer of eighteen, clearly unused to drinking, was boasting he could karate chop a telephone directory in half.

I realised that the language in our film would need toning down—to hell with reality. "Whoaa," the others wailed. "Just show us, you fucking bleeder!" "Bet you can't, you fucking tosser!" "Yeah I can! I'll show you." So someone went off and found a directory of reasonable thickness into which he had placed a bayonet unbeknownst to the young recruit. Nobody stopped the poor young guy from attempting to demonstrate his karate prowess. This poor youth did a lot of huffing and puffing and working himself up and was urged on by all the drunken louts around him until he finally drove his hand into the manual. The bayonet did not quite cut his hand in two, though almost. It went in about two inches, and how those fellows laughed as the poor victim bled all over the room and was finally led away to be stitched up. This vile act had made their day, and I realised too late that I should have stepped in. I also realised I could never include this sort of thing in any movie. Our film would have to be "sanitised."

During the two weeks we were there, it became apparent that the film would not be possible without the use of actors, so we gradually constructed a scheme for the film as we enjoyed the hospitality of the Royal Welsh Fuseliers, whom we had come to dislike.

Back in London, I decided that the role of the sergeant major was the key. Having spent time with them, I felt they were like hardened criminals with a code. They acted as the hinge between officers and men and they maintained discipline through threats and shouting. I had met the actor Alan Lake at some point, probably on a commercial, and decided to talk to him about it. Alan was a bit of a rabble rouser—a gypsy and a drinker. Whether he had yet married Diana Dors or not, I don't recall, but he eventually did. After she died, Alan killed himself. He was always a dramatic person, and he became the first cast member for this documentary. The others were of less importance. We had our officer type and our recruit type and assembled a crew in London for a two-week shoot in Minden that would culminate in a sequence of our boys on maneouvres—the thing they enjoyed most.

The script now called for the wake up, reveille, breakfast, inspection, working day, relaxing after a working day, and maneouvres that would then lead to a singsong at night around a camp fire. We thought the finale would appeal to the mums and dads who were destined to be our audience. Nothing like a good old singalong to send them out happy.

Work began. We arranged for our actors to pair up with their real equivalents for a couple of days while we shot a variety of backgrounds and decided our schedule. Having Claude Watson along as production manager and assistant director was a great help.

Alan Lake soon endeared himself to the sergeant majors, rolling back to their barracks, dead drunk in the early hours. He seemed capable of shouting himself hoarse, which was good since our wake-up sequence required him to burst in on the recruits' hut and shout, "Wakey wakey!" This was somewhat toned down from the normal "Alright you fucking bleeders, let's 'ave your hands off cocks and on socks!" Throughout the film we insisted that the amount of shouting should be minimal, whereas in reality, it was a constant.

James Archibald, always a diplomat and a man of taste, kept himself busy, damping down any worries that the officers expressed about our activities. They were never exactly sure of what we were doing, but they were tolerant and James, an ex-military man himself, was a master of tact. In any case, as the producer, he was responsible to the War Office, who were paying for this exercise.

Everything appeared to go well most of the time but I sensed that there would be a breaking point before we were through. The actors were managing to mirror their partners when in front of the camera, but behind their backs the men were barely civil about them. "Bunch of poofs," being the kindest remark I overheard. Alan Lake was proving a bit of a problem too. Even the hardened sergeant majors were amazed at the amount of booze he could consume, and he had taken to insulting anyone who came within spitting distance. In front of the camera he delivered and continued to shout when directed to do so. He could improvise wildly, though not always considering the censorship that we would need to impose on his performance. "Don't stand there like the gypsy's whippet," we could get away with but the rest of the sentence, "All prick and rib," had to go.

It was with some relief that we left the camp and set out for the fields near Buchenwald where our boys would carry out their manoeuvres. They had all their gear with them. Tanks, personnel carriers, all sorts of arms and equipment, though they were to be fighting only with blanks. I forget who the enemy was on this occasion, though there were many other regiments dotted around Germany who could be called on to supply a cast.

We had planned to work for one last day in this location, so were able to film all the action required as our boys blew off their blanks. Their hours seemed to be the same as in camp. At 5 PM they stopped firing and went back to the barracks. But there were no clubs and, therefore, no beer and we still had our final singsong to shoot. We'd have to wait until nightfall since I had imagined the boys sitting in a circle around a camp fire, lit by the headlamps of their armored vehicles.

Our sparks (electricians) had already gone to the wooded area where this denouement would take place and were lighting it, so the selected recruits were driven down to the location in an already truculent mood. As the light began to fade, I sat them all in a ring. The fire was lit and they were ordered to sing. They refused. They would not sing at all, not a note. The real sergeant major did some shouting, an officer did some urging, James Archibald said, more or less, they were doing it for queen and country. It was Alan Lake who suggested "beer all round," which was received with enthusiasm. An assistant was despatched and came back with gallons of the stuff. The situation appeared saved, but it took them another hour before they were sufficiently oiled to agree to sing. Archibald then told me that our crew would be on double overtime if I didn't hurry up, and still the lads refused to cooperate properly, but were getting very drunk indeed. I had planned a nice crane shot, at huge expense, to end the film. Starting on a closeup of the crackling fire, we would pull back, up and up, past the singing soldiers until we were way above them, high in the sky, and the final fade out. We finally did get the shot, though I could not do more than a couple of takes because the men were now so drunk that they were standing up and lumbering off into the woods, no longer holding the boy scout pose that they had maintained for a very long time. Pissing was required. And so we abandoned the shot, and the sparks were told to douse their lights and go home. This is when the trouble really started because without our lamps the wood was, to all intents and purposes, pitch black and most of the soldiers were stumbling around in the dark, pissing and falling over and generally abandoning themselves to their urges. The officers present blamed us for this situation. The drunkeness was one thing, but these guys had to be fit and ready for manoeuvres the following day, and I knew I barely had a useable ending. Now some of the men were actually missing. Claude Watson, always helpful, began looking for the missing men. When he shone his torch in the back of the armored vehicles, he was horrified at some of the action he witnessed. Claude was a homosexual but even he was disturbed by these events that had taken on the atmosphere of a painting by Hieronymus Bosch and were as far removed from the requirements of our recruiting film as could be imagined. Gang bangs in the back of trucks were hardly our brief.

To top it all, Alan Lake got roaring drunk that night in the sergeants' quarters and attempted to kill one of them with a bayonet. It was just as well the crew were leaving the following day.

Back in London we edited the film and presented it to the War Office. It took them about ten minutes to decide they could not use it *in any form*. They decided *it* was just too real and would shock any parents who were thinking of enrolling their sons into army life. And there was far too much shouting.

Of course it was a very pale version of the reality we had witnessed. James Archibald and I were very upset. We liked the film. It wasn't shocking at all and it was a reasonable, if watered down, reflection of army life. Of course there was shouting. Army life is like that, but reality was, obviously, not what they wanted. I'd love to see that film again.

The Delivery Man and Far From the Madding Crowd

It was during this time that John proposed to make *Far From the Madding Crowd,* which had begun to germinate while we were mixing *Darling*. Because of my directing commitments, there was never a moment when I could edit *Far*. John was able, finally, to promote Malcolm Cooke into the editor's chair, having failed to get him promoted on *Darling*. I endorsed this notion, knowing that Malcolm was ready to edit. So John started shooting and a few months went by.

I was directing a documentary about an obstetric surgeon for Granada entitled *The Delivery Man*, and I received a phone call at this cheap hotel in Sheffield that Granada had us in. It was John and his message was to the point. If I didn't stop everything and rush to Shepperton Studios, Malcolm would get fired. It seemed that the then head of MGM had taken against the editing and Joe Janni had not supported Malcolm, who had fallen well behind in assembling the film. This put me on the spot. My producers at Granada were very supportive and allowed me to put my own film, which I had nearly finished shooting, on the shelf and disappear for three months. I was fortunate that my old assistant, David Campling, was free, and together we started work at Shepperton on the action scenes that Malcolm had no time to edit. I had no problems with Malcolm, who was relieved to keep his job and to have some help. David and I waded in. By this time, the shooting was almost over, but I asked John to leave me alone as we assembled the sequences. The film opens with Farmer Oak's sheep being driven over a cliff by a maverick dog. This was a scene that demanded a gradual build up, rising to a climax as the sheep are pushed over a cliff onto the beach below. Thousands of feet of film had been shot for this, and it took me several days to run and assemble. Gradually the scene took shape. I cut it silent, as I always do with action scenes that have no dialogue and then added some music. John viewed this sequence and was happy to see it coming together. Meanwhile Malcolm got on with the dialogue scenes. This is the way we worked for a few weeks. I tackled the action, which included a fire, barn dance, storm, and a scene between Bathsheba and Troy in which he demonstrated his swordsmanship. This last scene gave me the greatest problems. I experimented with opticals and superimpositions, which were not too easy to demonstrate on film. We gradually found the scene, though it didn't really come to life until Richard Rodney Bennet added his score. Then it worked. John was overjoyed and, as I recall, this was the last contribution I made to the film.

I know John had problems with Terence Stamp on *Far From the Madding Crowd*. He wasn't particularly keen on Terry's acting and their relationship wasn't good. He just could not drag the performance out of Stamp that he really wanted and it worried him terribly. He could be very cruel. He insisted that Stamp had to redo all his dialogue and that took a long time in the dubbing theatre at Shepperton. He would do it over and over again trying to get the accent he wanted. Terry's never been very strong in the voice department and the two of them sparred a lot.

John didn't really become successful until he was thirty. He didn't quite know what he wanted to do. When he was at Oxford, he'd made a silent film with Malcolm Cooke's brother, but after that, when he went out into the real world, he floundered for some time. As an actor he appears briefly in *Battle of the River Plate* as a Nazi sailor and was in some *Robin Hoods*. It wasn't until he got involved with television through *The Tonight Programme* that he began making these short documentary films. Then he was suddenly noticed by people, and it was *Terminus*, the film he did for British Transport at Waterloo Station that put him on the map and got the attention of Joe Janni for whom he made his first feature.

John was not really interested in politics but he was very pro-Israel. In fact when the war broke out in Israel, we were finishing off *Far From the Madding Crowd* and John was actually going to go there to help fight on the Israeli side. He even got himself measured for a uniform, which made us all laugh. Of course, being a Seven Day War, it was over before he had to go. John was Jewish, but he seemed somehow critical of Jewish people and he used to denigrate Jews quite frequently in his films. If he had a film producer character, he was always Jewish and he was always sent up. I don't think John's Jewishness was a big problem for him, in marked contrast to Freddy Raphael, who was constantly banging on about being pilloried as a Jew. I don't think John ever was. He may have been bullied a bit at school but I don't recall him ever saying so.

I remember his parents pretty well. They were quite dynamic. His father was a pediatrician and a very tough guy—small but tough. He was very assertive and a terrible driver. John was a very bad driver too. John could never really see what he was doing. He used to be called "speccy four eyes" by people because he couldn't see a thing without his glasses. I don't think he had accidents but he used to drive in a sort of lackadaisical way and talk a lot while he was driving. I went to Disney World with him at one point and it made me somewhat anxious because he never quite knew where to get on or off any of the exits. He would just sail on and say, "Oh, I think I missed the exit. Oh dear, oh dear."

John and I became friends for life but at this stage of my career I was off doing all these other things. It wouldn't be until 1968 when I would return to the cutting room and work once again with him.

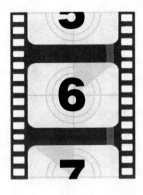

COWBOY, MADHOUSE, AND *LOCUST*

Every Home Should Have One

My career as a director was certainly frantic and, I must confess, more than a bit stressful because I never really felt confident. That others had great confidence in my abilities was, almost certainly, the reason I did it at all. One of these others was Ned Sherrin who, impressed by my little nudist film for *That Was the Week That Was*, now came knocking with a feature comedy about the advertising business. This was a subject that I should have, by now, known a great deal about with all the commercials I'd shot.

I was working for Joe Janni at the time, preparing a feature film that was meant to be my directing debut. It was quite a dramatic piece about unmarried mothers by Jeremy Sandford who'd written *Cathy Come Home* a celebrated television film that was directed by Ken Loach. Teddy Joseph was a very good production manager working for Joe, and he and I decided to shoot the picture in Birmingham. I had cast it already. Malcolm McDowell, who had only done *If,* was the actor I'd picked out of a crowd of young guys to play the lead, but as Teddy and I visited homes where young girls would go to have their babies, what we saw didn't ring true to the script. I began to feel the script was exaggerating the realities of the situation for dramatic reasons and I started to question all sorts of things in it. When I complained to Joe Janni about this, he pulled the plug on the project, partly, I think, because he had doubts himself and also because he was having trouble raising money for that particular subject.

I was still working at Joe's office in Bruton Street when I got the call from Ned Sherrin regarding *Every Home Should Have One*, which was a vehicle for Marty Feldman who was very big on television at this time. The screenplay had been written by Marty, Barry Took, and Denis Norden. I didn't know them but I knew their work. So I read the script and agreed to do it.

Ned was a madly enthusiastic person who never seemed to entertain negative thoughts. Whether something was good, bad, or indifferent, it was always "Wonderful!" He was also very big on casting and he used to cast by himself. I don't believe I cast a single part in that picture. Ned chose every actor we had. Apart from anything else, he knew everybody. Marty wanted to play the lead and, of course, he wanted to make a feature film. He'd already been a television comic and had written quite a lot of material including *Round the Horne* and, I think, he saw this as a step up.

For the American advertising executive, Ned had cast New York comic Shelley Berman, who I knew from LP discs. I got on very well with Shelley but he was not an easy person to direct and Marty was terribly suspicious of him because he always felt that Shelley got laughs at his expense. I remember doing a massage parlour sequence that I shot from above so we could see the two guys getting their massage, separated by a wall. I don't remember exactly what little business Shelly was doing to make the crew laugh but it upset Marty because he couldn't see what was going on.

Whether Marty ever made love to his co-star, Julie Ege, is a subject about which I know very little, and if I did know, I wouldn't tell. When we were at Frensham Ponds doing a parody of a Swedish nudist film, it was extremely cold, and Marty had to be seen emerging naked from the lake. He was blue with cold, so we bundled him into Julie's caravan with a bottle of brandy. They didn't come out for the longest time, but afterward, Marty seemed to have forgotten how cold it was and refused to wear a dressing gown. He was quite proud of his attachment and flashed it around the unit. I was constantly on the lookout for the Park Rangers who might not have understood.

Toward the end of production we were running out of time and money, but Marty was determined we would shoot all the stunts in the prop room, where the finale was set. Marty thought of himself as Buster Keaton reincarnated and did all the stunts himself, including standing still as flats, which were really heavy, almost fell onto him. He was always within an inch of getting brained, but he did it as a tribute to Keaton. I was told I had to complete the scene, but I knew we had at least three days of shooting left. Marty and I arranged an insurance scam, which I have never spoken about. We got together and Marty said on take 3 of the stunt, he would "injure" himself and have to be seen by a doctor. Take 3 came around and Marty suddenly yelled and cried out that he'd been hurt. He was rushed to the hospital and examined. Amazingly the doctor, who was not in on the act, found evidence of damage, probably old wounds that Marty had not bothered with. He was ordered to take three days off and we stopped shooting. The insurance money paid for those final days when Marty returned from the hospital. It was wrong, but it saved us from truncating the scene.

Marty was never really an actor. He was a character. Because of his protruding eyes, I suppose he was thought of as being a rather odd bird, which he was, but he was very funny and extremely bright. He was a wonderful writer and an excellent idea man. The partnership with Barry Took was interesting because Marty had the crazy ideas and Barry would marshall them into some sort of order and sense. Barry never liked *Every Home Should Have One* and blamed me for its lack of success, even though we became very good friends in the years after it was released.

Midnight Cowboy

John Schlesinger had initially asked me to edit *Midnight Cowboy* while I was busy in post-production on *Every Home Should Have One* so I couldn't do it. Because *Cowboy* would be a U.S. production shot in New York, John eventually went with an American editor that Arthur Penn had recommended, Hugh Robertson. When the dust began settling on *Every Home Should Have One*, I got a call from John, who was back from New York for a short holiday and he said he might be calling on me to come over to the United States to have a look at *Midnight Cowboy*. Basically, he wasn't getting on terribly well with Hugh and wanted me to take a look at things. It was actually a very tricky situation because Hugh owned the cutting room and had hired all the assistants. Also I didn't, at that time, have a union ticket in the United States, so the credit I did finally receive was as "creative consultant."

I flew to New York and saw the film, which I thought had terrific performances. I could see there were problems structurally, however. It was too long and the whole opening was a bit awkward. Getting the main character, Joe Buck, to New York was the main problem. John had asked me to give him some notes so I stayed for a couple of weeks and played around in the cutting room with this first sequence and then he prevailed upon me to come back to Manhattan after the Christmas holiday. Basically my job was recutting the fantasy scenes—the party and certainly the opening. Hugh did all the dialogue scenes. He had been cutting throughout the shoot but John had little time to look at the edited scenes because he was working long hours. Jerry Hellman, the producer, was probably viewing more material than John during the shooting. When I began working on the film, John would regularly come to me complaining about Hugh and saying, "You've got to take that reel away from him."

John was always more than generous about my contributions to *Midnight Cowboy*, claiming that I "saved his ass," but I didn't save the film because it didn't need saving. It was brilliant. It was a wonderful script that was beautifully acted and directed. We did, however, realise that it could be better.

Hugh, it must be said, was scornful of John's efforts, saying his view of New York was that of a tourist—an Englishman's view, not the real New York. I also suspect that they all thought that I was John's boyfriend because he and I were very close and spent a lot of time together out of the cutting room. This, however, was never the case. John was having an affair during this time with Michael Childers, whom he stayed with for the next forty years.

The party scene is the least effective bit of the film when seen now. It really dates the picture. John and I always thought it was too long and were constantly whittling it down but we never got it quite right.

Hugh's editing facility was a fascinating place to work. Some of the editorial assistants were on drugs, which I discovered later when they kept disappearing. I'd be saying, "Where have they gone? They can't all go the lavatory at once." Little by little, I realised what they were up to. It was at the height of drug taking, of which I was quite unaware. These assistants were an extremely strange bunch and very lax in their housekeeping. I kept finding developed film that hadn't been used under benches and in cupboards. I'd ask what it was for and be told, "Oh, some guy went out and shot that." But nobody had bothered to look at it. There was a lot of this going on and when, eventually, I was reconstructing the opening, I found myself using little bits and pieces of this material I'd found under benches. I had to reassemble all the material that had been used for the opening and start from scratch.

The writer Waldo Salt, who had adapted James Leo Herlihy's novel, was a wonderful man and a great character. Though not one of the Hollywood Ten, he was unable to get work because of his affiliations with left wing groups. The novel is very good and Waldo did a wonderful version of it but a tremendous amount of the dialogue between Joe Buck and Ratso Rizzo in the little space where they lived came out of improvisations by Dustin Hoffman and Jon Voight, which Waldo would record and then transcribe. John did a couple of weeks of this before they began shooting.

When we had pretty much got the cut right and John was reasonably happy, he decided to have a birthday party and show the movie to everybody beforehand. Dustin Hoffman came with his lawyers and Jon Voight was there. There were about sixty people and Dustin didn't come to the party afterward which upset John. It later transpired that Dustin was very upset when he saw the movie because he felt that Jon Voight had been favoured in the editing, which was entirely untrue. Of course he and John must have made it up because they worked together again on *Marathon Man.*

The other thing about *Midnight Cowboy* was that it had gone over budget and United Artists were concerned that it was costing a lot of money and that I'd been flown in to help out. They hadn't even seen the movie because the company's contract with Jerry Hellman stipulated that they didn't have to show it to United Artists until such time as they were happy with it. So we arranged the screening for the backers at ten o'clock in the morning at one of the labs in New York because, for political reasons, we didn't want to screen it on United Artists' territory. We invited all the bosses to come with their secretaries, as we wanted women there too. John and Jerry were very nervous before this make-or-break screening. I remember sitting just behind Arthur Krimm, the head of United Artists at the time, and David Picker, who'd been our big supporter, and these grown men were all in tears at the end. It was the most wonderful screening. We never changed a frame of it after that and United Artists never had a preview. The movie had that one screening and they said, "Great." They realised it was an X-rated film. It was the first X-rated commercial picture, so it was a huge gamble for them.

The Fred Neil song *Everybody's Talking,* which Harry Nilsson performed, was not written for the film. Curiously, Nilsson had been approached to write a song for *Midnight Cowboy* and while we were cutting it we needed some music to put over the beginning and Jerry Hellman sent over a batch of LPs that Nilsson had recorded, and on one of them there was this song, *Everybody's Talking.* One of us, and I don't remember whether it was me, Schlesinger, or Hugh Robertson, but one of us said, "Hey! That seems to work." We put it up against the movie and it never left. Not only did the music fit, but the words worked with the character. That was the extraordinary thing and I can well remember when we put it up against the film for the first time we all stood back and said: "Jesus, it's like it was written for the film." Nilsson did write a song that is used in the film, but it's in the background.

After recutting the film to everyone's satisfaction, I left before it was mixed. It opened to enormous success even though it was X-rated. It still lives, many years later, and was possibly the best film that Schlesinger directed. It was certainly one of the best credits I was ever given. Creative Consultant, it seems, was a more prestigious position than the humble Film Editor.

Teaching at London Film School

After *Midnight Cowboy*, I found myself teaching at the London Film School. This place still exists. A big banana warehouse in Covent Garden. It should not be confused with the National Film School out in Beaconsfield, which is altogether a more prestigious place. The London Film School was, at the time, full of rich kids from a variety of countries whose parents were very pleased to pay for them to go and study abroad. The Israeli students worked very hard, and the Arab students rarely appeared. There were something like four hundred students crammed into this crummy space with old teachers and even older equipment. It was run at that time by the Dunbars and staffed, very largely, by ex-Ealing directors who could not find work now that the studio was closed. Charlie Crichton and Michael Truman were there, as was Sid Cole.

As my time between commercials increased and I wanted to work, I became a course director for a few months. The staff also included Mike Leigh who had made one film, *Bleak Moments*, at that point and was teaching drama. I used to chat with him during coffee breaks. Mike is still one of the school's main supporters. It was not, so far as I was concerned, a very happy time. I didn't really like the place, which seemed like a graveyard for old Ealingites. I wasn't that old and, in any case, was hardly adequate to call myself a teacher. A fraud if ever there was one.

Zee & Co

It was time to return to the cutting room and the opportunity to do so was bizarre indeed. *Zee & Co*, sometimes known as *X,Y & Zee*, had as its selling point a sexual relationship between Elizabeth Taylor and Susannah York. This film was directed by Brian Hutton, an American, who normally made action pictures like *Where Eagles Dare*. *Zee & Co* had a dreary script by Edna O'Brien and contained situations and dialogue that now seem rich in humour. The lead actor was Michael Caine and, as I recall, he was married to Taylor's character and they bickered their way through a loveless marriage for several reels until, eventually, Elizabeth decided to sleep with Susannah York.

I once asked Brian why he wanted to make this nonsense and he explained that he made the decision when he read the line, "And what made you decide to become a nun?" The result was dire and I have not seen it since.

The film was produced by Elliott Kastner, who was always calling me from remote places to see if I was free. Normally he was in a bathroom, or at least, that's how it sounded.

Elliott had a chum who followed him around named George Papas. George was reputed to be a minder, employed to look after Elliott's wife who was fond of the grape. Elliott would run the rushes with George and myself at midday. He would arrive, give me a big kiss, then promptly fall asleep. George would ask me to nudge him when the rushes were almost over and would also close his eyes. Twenty minutes or so later, after we'd all been nodding off, I'd give George the cue and he'd promptly prod Elliott, who would snap out of his dream and declare, "Elizabeth is giving a fine performance in this picture!" This routine repeated itself throughout the shoot.

Zee & Co was well over schedule because Elizabeth and Richard Burton, to whom she was still married, were both working for Kastner. They would go into a hotel in Shepperton Village for lunch and roll out again at 3 PM, normally unfit for further work. In addition, Elizabeth was not always there in the morning, which was quite a headache for Brian Hutton, who spent much of his time playing ping-pong with the sparks.

Rentadick

We were mixing *Zee & Co* at Shepperton when I received a script out of the blue from Ned Sherrin called *Rentasleuth*, which I agreed to direct. On the first day of shooting, Ned came up to me and said, "Wonderful news, dear boy, wonderful news. The Rank Organisation love the new title." I then asked what the new title was and when he told me I was ready to resign on the spot. I said *Rentadick* was a terrible title. It sounded like a gay porno movie. Without a moment's hesitation, Ned declared, "No. It's commercial. It's wonderful. It's great. It's a terrific title. Don't worry about it. Just make the film."

It was originally written by John Cleese and Graham Chapman for Cleese to direct with Charles Crichton, a trick they eventually pulled off very well with *A Fish Called Wanda*. The script, however, was in the hands of David Frost who did not think that the Cleese/Crichton combo would work, so he sent it to Ned, who sent it to me. We then engaged John Wells and John Fortune to rewrite it. All this was more than a bit crazy. I don't remember the original script. In any case I wasn't going to flounce out of this since I was keen to return to directing and found most of the revamped film amusing. It was a reasonably cheap film, shot in six weeks in and around Elstree. Ned was able to cast it with good farceurs including Richard

Briers, Donald Sinden, and Ronnie Fraser, who when sober, was good value. Julie Ege, the Swedish bombshell from *Every Home Should Have One,* was again cast.

Our main location was a country house near to Elstree Studios. It has always been something of a mystery to me that I was seen as a director of comedy, but the legacy of the Will Hay and George Formby comedies hung over me. I had learned something from the directors, Marcel Varnel and Walter Forde, whose comedies were of the hit-and-miss variety. I still rank *Oh, Mr. Porter!* as one of the best comedy films made in the UK and in *Rentadick,* I tried to emulate the spirit of another Will Hay film, *Ask a Policeman.* Unfortunately I didn't have the trio of comics, Hay, Marriott, and Moffat, to work with. But despite the many problems and my almost total inability to pull it off, I enjoyed directing the film and did not think it too bad. It made me laugh and a test audience in Blackpool gave it a thumbs up.

Alas it was then slaughtered by the critics and nobody saw the film, which comes up regularly on late night television to embarrass me. Later I realised that there is a spectrum of comedy that is very narrow indeed and appeals to a minute audience. *Rentadick* fell neatly into that category. Of course the critics were quite right, as were John Cleese and Graham Chapman when they finally saw the film. They demanded all trace of their names be removed and we were lucky not to be sued. There was precious little of their work left anyway. If their script had formed the basis of the Cleese/Crichton partnership, *A Fish Called Wanda* might never have been made. So, in a roundabout way, we did them a service.

Visions of Eight

The idea of gathering a mixed bag of world-class directors and allowing them to make a short film of their choice around the 1972 Olympic Games was credited to the American producer David Wolper. There was a long history of feature-length films about the games, the most famous being the Leni Reifenstahl documentary made in 1936, which managed to be both a record of a sporting event and a political tract on behalf of the Nazi Party. The war then started before the next games could be held, after which there had been a lacklustre British effort by Castleton-Knight and an excellent Japanese record of the Tokyo games by Kon Ichikawa, who would be one of the directors working on *Visions of Eight.*

John Schlesinger was one of the eight directors who Wolper approached to make *Visions of Eight.* I was asked by John to edit his sequence, which would deal with the marathon, the last great event in the games.

The Olympic Village in Munich was still being constructed when we went across to reconnoiter the marathon route with our chief cameraman Arthur

Wooster and Michael Samuelson who was in charge of the many camera units that would cover the games. This was several months before the event and we took a couple of days to cover the course that led through the city, into the English Gardens, and back to the stadium.

John was very attracted to Munich, but we could never move too far before he would spot another bratwurst restaurant and dive into it for yet another sausage. John loved to eat and the sausages were delicious. The Gardens had quite a number of bierkellers and cafes and I reckoned we had sampled every one by the time we left.

Camera positions were laid out. John would say: "A low angle pov (point of view) here," and so it was noted that a hole should be dug in the park just where he wanted it. Similarly, high angles were decided upon and high-rise buildings were cased, to the astonishment of the occupants.

We arrived at one apartment, which was on the top floor of a tall block, and asked if we could possibly film from their living room. The owners agreed, for a fee.

No expense was spared. The route was twenty-two miles long and we decided to have thirty camera units. We also planned that each camera unit could occupy two positions during the race, making their move after the runners had passed them and thus giving us a total of sixty angles. One camera would be mounted on an electrical platform, designed especially by BMW so as not to release fumes. This mobile camera would always be in the lead. Arthur noted everything down and planned the operation in a thoroughly military manner.

After this we all went our separate ways until it was time to return to Munich for the actual event.

John's choice of the marathon involved a portrait of the British runner, Ron Hill, from the North country. We then had to film an interview with him. He lived in a small house on a council estate. The lights took up most of the available space and it was hot in there. Hill turned out to be a great runner who was a man of very few words indeed.

Frustrated, since he knew most of the material was uninteresting, John and I went into the road to try and figure out what we might do to liven things up. We were followed by local kids who were intrigued by our lighting trucks and the sight of 2K lamps in Ron's garden shining into his front room. Wherever we walked, the boys followed until John rounded on them. "Please don't follow us," he asked in his perfect English accent. "We weren't following you, speccy four eyes!" they shouted as they laughed and ran off. John was mortified. "Do they realise they are speaking to an Oscar-winning director?" Somehow this little incident lightened the atmosphere. We went back and John conducted a perfectly good interview, but he never warmed to Ron Hill, who remained solely interested in running.

I was sent ahead for a week's additional planning while John remained in London, not intending to make an appearance until the day before the actual race. He felt his work had been done at the planning stage since there was little he could do once the starter's pistol was fired. The camera people knew what was wanted. Arthur Wooster was already in Munich since he was, in effect, the chief cameraman of the entire shoot, under Michael Samuelson's command. The group of cameramen that Samuelson had gathered together were all hard drinkers and womanisers. I doubt they ever went to sleep throughout the games, but managed to keep most of the material in focus.

I was housed in the newly built Olympic village, in a high-rise block that was to become a hotel once the games were over. The Wolper office, a hive of activity, was in another block. Wolper himself was there along with his sidekick, Stan Margulies, who did most of the work.

The other seven directors were already in place—Milos Forman, Kon Ichikawa, Mai Zetterling, and Arthur Penn among them.

Arthur Wooster and I continued to plan, going over the ground several times, and also trying out the new electric platforms, built especially to film the race from the front and side without producing emissions that would bother the runners. The English cameraman Walter Lassally was to operate one of these cameras. I was astonished at the technical facilities available in the splendid new stadium, where thousands of media folk would be able to watch the activities on small television screens. In fact television was everywhere, which was why our film was made. It had become ever clearer that there was no public for a film of the games unless seen from a perspective that television did not cover. Hence the notion of involving feature film directors to convey their vision of the games.

Ichikawa decided to film the 100-metre race using several high-speed cameras, therefore stretching the one-minute race into a ten-minute film. Milos Forman was seeing the lighter side of Munich life during the games, though the lighter side was soon to be eclipsed.

One morning, after the games had begun, I walked over to the Wolper office and was told to call John in London. "I'm not coming," he announced. "You can tell Wolper it's all off after what's happened." Not knowing what had happened, I asked him. "Don't you know? You're right there!" I said no and it was true that, although my bedroom was only about a hundred yards from the Israeli compound, I had no idea that, during the night, the athletes had been overwhelmed by Arab terrorists and were being held hostage. John told me to get a unit together, go over there, and film whatever I could.

So I found myself, along with hundreds of other photographers and media people, spending most of the day with the scrum by the Israeli compound where a balaclavered terrorist would appear from time to time on the balcony. We had to jostle for a position from which we could film and spent most of the day there, waiting, rumours flying, with everyone filming the same shot of the gunman on the balcony. It was a day of high drama and great tension. The games had been suspended and nobody knew what would happen next nor whether they would start again. Many expected that the Israelis would send a hit squad to rescue their athletes, who were mainly weight lifters, and the authorities were constantly issuing conflicting news.

The Germans were horrified that this had ocurred on their soil, after their history regarding the treatment of the Jews. My German crew were noticeably subdued. We waited all day and then, as dusk descended, it was announced that the terrorists and their hostages would be bussed out of the village and taken to a military airport outside the city. Everyone was relieved. I invited my camera crew back to my hotel room and we opened up the mini bar. The helicopter that would fly the hostages to the airport was parked just below my twelfth-story room. We watched and cheered as they were taken from the bus to the helicopter, and waved to them as they rose up outside and vanished into the night, all safe, so we thought.

My German crew were delighted that all had ended happily and emptied the mini bar. We all went to the dining room where Michael Samuelson, confident as ever, was in constant touch with the authorities and gave us a running commentary. Everyone was in a happy mood when they went to bed that night.

The next morning, we awoke to the news that all the hostages had died when their helicopter was blown up. It was a sad, dark day. Everyone knew that the symbol of the Olympic Games had been tarnished forever.

John's first decision, that he would not attend the games or make his film of the marathon, was quickly overturned after he spoke to Wolper, who agreed that John could shoot more than the race and that the film would reflect the atrocity that had ocurred. It had been announced that there would be a memorial service in the stadium, which we would film, and we would include the closing ceremony in our segment.

After John arrived, we assembled our cameras for the memorial service, and even I was given an Arriflex to film whatever reactions I saw. There were plenty of those, but I failed to film most of what I saw simply because I felt I was intruding on the grief of thousands who were there and openly weeping. I did a bit, felt bad about it, and then retired. The event was too moving.

After this the energy seemed to go out of our enterprise. Rumours abounded and we were expecting more terrorist attacks. The marathon course could not be policed due to its length, so anything could happen. Nothing did, but we were constantly looking over our shoulders. Certainly the fun had gone from the games. Enthusiasm had noticeably fled from our crews who, when we saw the results of their filming, had let us down. Many of the sites planned by John and Arthur all those months ago, and religiously used by the crews, were useless on the day since the public were lining the route. The crews had been told to stay where they were. Some had moved when they saw the problems, others provided us with many minutes of the rear view of the crowd. This particularly applied to those who were down in the holes designated for low angles. They stayed in their holes and succeeded in filming nothing at all.

But for the many units that failed, there were others, mainly the Americans, who did great work and whose material saved the film. Naturally with any sporting event there are mishaps and dramas, most of which are unnoticed, but in the marathon it was, as ever, the losers who provided more drama than the winners. Ron Hill was seen but barely noticed in the final film. One of the cameramen captured the agony of a Kenyan runner who had developed cramps, others filmed runners who made it to the stadium and then collapsed.

When I began editing, I had about a hundred hours of film to reduce to seventeen minutes. Much of it chose itself and went directly to the trash can. Everything out of focus or blocked by bystanders was ruthlessly removed. I was finally left with at least ten hours of good material. It was, therefore, hard to choose the moments that would make it to the final. We edited the film at Michael Samuelson's base in Cricklewood. My first cut came in at thirty minutes and I whittled it down little by little.

Ken Levison, a writer who had helped Schlesinger on *Sunday, Bloody Sunday*, came in to create some narration for it. Once the race had started, I decided to cut it to music, choosing a part of Prokofiev's score for *Alexander Nevsky* and Debussy's *String Quartet* for a particularly sad moment when a runner was caught collapsing on the route. All the music I chose was eventually replaced since Henry Mancini was scoring the entire film. It was never quite as good, though Hank did follow my tempi.

After we sent our finished segment to the Wolper people in Los Angeles, it was out of our hands. Bob Lambert, a good American editor, was in overall command of the movie and had to see the eight films through to the finish. The final picture was a mixed bag. It referred to and was dedicated to the slaughtered athletes but had a very limited commercial run and was the last feature film built around the games. Once again television had killed off cinema and, although there are good things in the film, to have been there through the actual event is why I remember it.

Madhouse

The warm fire crackled, illuminating the portly American sitting in front of it, wearing a silk kimono and smoking an enormous cigar. His manner was friendly and we chatted amiably.

"The important thing, Jim," he said, taking another puff on his cigar, "is that we have to get those six clips into the shooting script. I don't care how you do it but we've got to see them." The gentleman in the kimono was Samuel Z. Arkoff, president of American International Pictures and the venue for our meeting was his sumptuous suite at the Savoy Hotel in London. I was summoned to meet Sam Arkoff because I'd been signed to direct a movie for him that starred Vincent Price. He'd never met me, never even heard of me, and, I suppose, he wanted to size me up before shooting began.

AIP was famous in the industry for shooting fast and cheap and, though I'd had experience with low budget pictures, I really had no idea about the nature of the beast I was dealing with.

The clips Arkoff was talking about were from six of the Edgar Allan Poe movies, which Vincent Price had made for AIP over the years, mostly directed by Roger Corman. I certainly didn't see any great problem about shoehorning them into our film.

Sam was a very good talker. Articulate and intelligent, but with his big belly, louche costume, and enormous cigar, he was a clichéd picture of a Hollywood vulgarian. When it seemed that we'd covered all the topics we needed to discuss, I got up to leave him luxuriating in front of his fire. As I reached the door, he turned to me and said, "Hey, Jim, remember. No Fellini shit."

The screenplay was titled *The Return of Doctor Death*, though it was later changed to *Madhouse* and it came to me through my agent from a man I knew named Milton Subotsky. Milton was an American producer whose company, Amicus, had an office at Twickenham Studios. I'd known Milton casually for years. We both had an interest in paperback fiction of a not terribly high quality and I recall that Milton's office shelves were lined with hundreds of these books—Ace paperbacks, Dell paperbacks. He was a voracious reader. I rather liked Milton, though having lunch with him could be a nightmare because he never stopped talking and his food always ended up on my lap. Milton was vulgar in many respects and yet quite cultured at the same time, being extremely interested in things English. His business partner, Max J. Rosenberg, was an intellectual, though you would never know it to look at the films they made over the years. Dreadful cheap rock-and-roll rubbish. Ghastly. But I never did work with him until this project came my way. I quite liked the idea of it and the fact that Vincent Price was attached made it appealing. It seems Vincent was trying to work out the remainder of his contract with American International Pictures because he was fed up with all the dreadful films they'd put him into over the years. He was constantly referring to Arkoff and his colleagues at American International Pictures as "Those cocksuckers!" I went to meet him at his rented flat in Chelsea. We got on well, though he did complain that the script was terrible. "We can't shoot this script," he said. "I've told Milton Subotsky that he's got to have a new script because it's just so bad."

The script was, indeed, very bad. The story was about a Hollywood actor, famous for playing a character called Doctor Death. The actor becomes involved in some mysterious murders and, as a result of the scandal, is unable to work again in America. Years later, however, an English television company brings him back to recreate the role in Britain and, as shooting gets under way, mysterious murders again occur and the prime suspect is our main character.

Before I'd had time to look around, pre-production had intensified. We were doing the costume and makeup tests and I was finding the locations when, about a week before shooting began, Vincent's voice came purring from the makeup chair, saying: "I haven't seen the rewrite yet." I replied, "Well, neither have I." I'd assumed that Milton had dealt with it. I immediately went to Milton who said, "I'll do the rewrite. I'm a great writer. I'll do it."

This threw me into something of a panic. I had little faith in Milton's ability to rewrite the script. Here we were, a week away from filming, with a poor script and a disgruntled actor. I, too, was becoming edgy.

I phoned Ken Levison and told him the mess I was in. He agreed to meet with Max, Milton, and myself at Milton's Mayfair flat on a Friday afternoon.

Ken Levison:

Jim Clark and I had worked together on John Schlesinger's segment of *Visions of Eight.* I had written some narration for him. One Friday afternoon he summoned me to a Mayfair flat to meet two tense American schlock merchants, Milton Subotsky and Max Rosenberg. They were about to make *The Revenge of Dr. Death,* as it was then called.

"Here's the script," Jim said brightly. "No construction, wooden characters, dreadful dialogue." The merchants squirmed. "The pink pages are the ones revised by Milton," he continued as Milton glowed. Max squirmed more. "We need a total rewrite. Studio and location dates are set in stone. So the script has to be rewritten in the order it's to be shot. Principal photography starts on Monday. It's a horror film."

I'll say, I thought.

"Can you do a new treatment tonight?" asked Jim. "We'll discuss it tomorrow and you can write Monday's stuff over the rest of the weekend."

On the way out I said, "Jim, I've never done a horror film."

"Nor have I," he said, cheerfully.

Well, I liked Jim and I was very broke.

We set to work frantically. There was very little time for rewrites, rehearsals, second thoughts, or breakfast. On the weekends, I would spend long hours at Jim's house, discussing the following week's work, with or without Milton, Max, and Peter Katz, the affable Head of American International Pictures–UK.

After my first rewrite, I asked Jim whether I had gone too far.

"You can't ever go too far," he answered. "Go further."

Peter Katz had intelligence and taste. Max Rosenberg was everybody's intermediary and friend, on everybody's side and behind everybody's back, including his partner's whom he eventually deserted.

Our real problem was Milton Subotsky, a cross between David O. Selznick and the Red Queen in Alice. David O. Selznick meddled endlessly with the script and everything else. The Red Queen screamed all day over the phone, involving us in a pointless waste of time and energy. Jim begged him to lay off me. I begged him to lay off Jim and to lower his voice to a scream, a catch phrase of the time. Milton would say: "What? What? Was that a joke? Was I shouting?" He scribbled all over my pages, taking out lines he didn't understand and restoring lines of his own which everyone hated. I was driven to justify every word. Max talked about "this Procrustean bed of logic you've built up," to show that, unlike Milton, he was literate.

I asked Ken if he could knock out a new treatment overnight and he said he could. "You've got to include six extracts from Vincent's previous films. You must use the locations and actors I've already chosen. All you can to do is rewrite the script." This he did. He produced a treatment that I showed to Vincent who approved it. Ken then started writing the scenes in detail.

We began shooting. Ken wrote during the day and night and would put the pages of script into my letter box each evening. When my car arrived in the morning, I'd pick the pages up and look at them on the way to location, sub-editing them if necessary. I'd then give the pages to the script girl who would type them up and distribute them to the actors. The actors would learn the lines while we were lighting the first set and then we'd shoot. That is how we got through this dreadful movie. We did that for the full six weeks and every day a more tired and ragged Ken would totter to my letter box. He did a wonderful job under very difficult circumstances.

Milton's script never materialised, but this didn't stop him meddling with the casting. I had already cast the film and then, just before shooting began, Milton phoned, saying, "They're too expensive. You can't have them." So in the end, supporting actors I'd never met, walked onto the set.

Ken Levison:

Mail order actors turned up, unequal to their parts. Their scenes had to be rewritten and reblocked to favour other actors. One of the *ingenues* arrived, not with her agent, but her protector. She had no talent whatever. "I'm sure she has," said Vincent, "But not in our field."

There were problems with gore. Jim duly beheaded the girl at her dressing table with maximum realism. The gore flowed.

"Oh dear, that's terrible, terrible!" Milton screamed. "We never have any gore in our pictures. We want a PG rating."

Jim reshot the scene. A goreless model head, bone dry, rolled onto a spotless floor, a housewife's dream.

It wasn't all bad. Vincent made intelligent suggestions in a modulated voice. Milton and Max made some good cuts and gave us some compliments. "Jim's a great director." "You guys have both been very civilised throughout this thing." And suddenly, after endless rewrites and rows over the party scene, Milton rang me. "I wanna tell ya," he cooed, "Everything's coming along fine. Jim shot both versions of the party scene. Yours and mine and yours is much better."

We also had Peter Katz on our side. He had taste, a sense of humour, and the last word. One day Milton, Max, and I were locked in a three-way battle fought with the strength developed over two thousand years of persecution. Peter said, "Why don't you Jews listen to me? My brother's a Jew, but I'm not." Milton said, "What? What, Peter? Whaddaya mean?"

Whenever Milton, Max, or Peter were going to reject an idea conclusively, they invoked Samuel Z. Arkoff. Peter was Sam's representative on earth.

"Dual role? No. Sam Arkoff would hate it. I'd lose my job," Milton said. "It's already been thrown out. Sam Arkoff would murder me."

Max said, "It would look so cheap. Sam Arkoff would kill us all."

Sam Arkoff was on his yacht somewhere in Polynesia recovering from shingles, no doubt brought on by *Dr. Death*. There were many offences for which he was ready to fire or kill. Top of the list, unexpectedly, was gaiety. Out of the blue and for no discernible reason, he issued a directive, "Tell the writer no faggy dialogue."

And late one night Jim got a call from Peter Katz in an uncharacteristically agitated state. "I want to talk to you seriously. This song. I'll lose my job if Sam Arkoff sees this song. It's camp. And Sam Arkoff hates camp."

Milton, who considered himself brilliant at all things, meddled in every department to such a degree that Vincent banned him from the set. "Tell that man to fuck off!" he'd bellow as Milton was fussing about. "Get him out of here!"

Yet in spite of the problems that Milton imposed on this film, we actually had a rather lighthearted time shooting it, mostly because Vincent was such outrageous fun. He was a wonderful laugher and there was certainly plenty in this movie to laugh about. Peter Cushing was also wonderful too, even though he had recently lost his adored wife. Everyone pitched in and we muddled through it.

Toward the end of the shoot, Milton made a series of cuts to Ken's script that absolutely threw our story out the window.

Ken Levison:

After four weeks, Milton, the Red Queen, went on the rampage, slashing and burning the script to ensure that Jim would finish within a fortnight, losing all character lines and many big scenes as well as striking sets. We were deluged with new pages, and the picture lost all sense.

Within hours, Vincent was on the phone.

"He sounded very huffy and puffy," Jim related happily, "As if he were on the job." This was before Vincent married Coral Browne. When he did, she announced to the world that their combined ages came to nearly two hundred.

Jim quoted Vincent as saying he'd been sitting in the flat watching television "and I began to brood. I want you to get that c**t Milton Subotsky on the set first thing tomorrow morning so I can ask him what the story is about."

Jim relayed the message and then sat back to let things take their course. The next morning the Red Queen cautiously appeared on the set to be met with a thirty-minute deluge of foul language from a fuming Vincent and his tempestuous co-star, Adrienne Corri.

Using some of the foulest language I've ever heard, Vincent told Milton he didn't know anything about character or construction and the entire crew were aghast at this display that went on for half an hour, after which Milton limped away like a whipped puppy and restored the scenes he'd cut from our script. Vincent actually apologised to the continuity girl for using such language in front of her.

The interesting thing was just how charming and friendly Vincent was with all of us in the face of his quite profoundly negative feelings toward Arkoff and Subotsky.

At this time, he hadn't yet met his future wife, Coral Browne. He and she were like a pair of perennial teenagers. She was incredibly witty and so was he. They never quoted others and when they were on form, they were brilliant. Vincent always said they met under the dryer because they were both in *Theater of Blood* and she played the critic who was incinerated under a hair dryer. I stayed friendly with Vincent right up until he died.

Madhouse was the last feature film I ever directed and as soon as the rough cut was finished, I was on a plane to Los Angeles to edit *The Day of the Locust* for John Schlesinger. If I'd stayed and fought for *Madhouse*, I suppose I might have prevented it from being a failure, but because I wasn't even on speaking terms with Milton, I decided to let it go. As soon as my back was turned, Milton recut the film and put the coffin lid on a movie that was stillborn.

As soon as I joined John in California for *Locust*, I felt I was returning to a world I understood. I preferred being an editor on good feature films to being a director of bad movies.

The Day of the Locust

I flew to Los Angeles with Laurence and my daughter Sybil, who was eight at the time. We had swapped houses with Jerry Hellman's friend, who was Julie Andrews' arranger and conductor. This house was in the Hollywood Hills and ideal for us. We could see the Hollywood sign in the distance and the fake 'H' that Richard MacDonald had built for our film.

We were in Los Angeles before shooting began. I was in John's office one afternoon when the actor playing Faye's father, an old vaudevillian, came into the room and said, "Well, I'm done for the day. I just died." He meant, of course, that the character had died and therefore he was not required for further rehearsal, but he actually died that night for real. That's how Burgess Meredith got the role.

All was not entirely smooth on the *Locust* set at Paramount. Bill Atherton nev-er became the star that we all thought he would. John had cast Bill in the lead and, after one week, began to feel that perhaps he wasn't up to it. He got terribly cold feet about Bill's performance, which was difficult for everybody, particularly Bill. The film was not shot in chronological order and most of the early scenes with Bill were subsequently cut from the picture. I recall John saying to me, "You've got to get everything together that he's in and we're going to run it for him at the studio on Sunday to confront him with his own performance." John had a meeting with Bill beforehand and laid it on the line. This was very difficult for a young actor. I put all the material together and we ran it. There was a discussion about it and things were resolved. Instead of making a change and recasting, they decided to carry on with Bill and he got through to the end but he always carried an air ticket to South America, just in case. John could be quite feisty and strong with the ac-tors when he felt he should be. He didn't mince his words. He was always tough in getting performances from people.

Donald Sutherland was fine. There were no problems on *The Day of the Locust* except, of course, that all of us, except for John, and presumably Jerry Hellman, who produced it, felt that Karen Black was miscast. We all kept saying to him, "She's too old and she looks like Bill Atherton's aunt." I don't know whether we were right or wrong when I look at it now. It wasn't the character that Nathanael West had written because his Faye Greener was seventeen, which made much more sense. The character that Bill Atherton played would fall in love with a sev-enteen-year-old girl. There were an awful lot of people after that role and Karen was very hot at the time because she'd done *Five Easy Pieces*. She was very well known and she was an excellent actress. Perhaps it makes sense that her character had never made it as an actress and was just a dress extra in the movie, whereas if she'd been a young and beautiful seventeen-year-old, you might think, "Why isn't she getting the parts?"

I had read *The Day of the Locust* long before we filmed it. I don't recall whether I thought it would make a good film. It probably never occurred to me. As it turned out, we managed to make a film that was longer than the book.

Because John Barry had done such good work on *Midnight Cowboy*, he was asked to score *The Day of the Locust*. He really wasn't the right man for the job. His music was okay but it never really matched up to the temporary score, the bulk of which was from a cassette I had of Max Steiner's soundtrack for the original *A Star Is Born*. It was from a poor quality acetate recording and I used it a lot in the original cutting copy which was a great hit with John and Jerry Hellman. I often thought this music worked in our favour because the reproduction was imperfect and it therefore had a period flavour. For one scene I used Kern's "Waltz in Swing Time" and Barry made a fair attempt at it. For the finale, John had used a piece by Penderecki that Barry also tried to equal but it's always hard for composers to match temporary scores and in many ways it's unfair of us to expect them to repeat the magic.

We made that movie at Paramount. I would drive to the studio, down Lookout Mountain Road, Laurel Canyon, and turn left onto Melrose. The studio was a short drive, maybe fifteen minutes. We were cutting in the old RKO block that was adjacent to Paramount. I think the studio wanted to keep me out of the way since I was not a member of the union and, though I was taking the film back to the UK, it would have been preferable if I was in the local union, which I later joined.

In those days, we still used the old studio gates and Nickodell's was there and open for business. Nickodell's was the darkest bar I had ever been to. Many Paramount editors could be found in there after lunch, tottering back to their cutting rooms in the late afternoon. I met both Sam O'Steen and Richard Sylbert who were, respectively, the editor and production designer on *Chinatown*, which was also shooting at Paramount the same time as us. We'd meet at parties but we never discussed work.

The Day of the Locust was a great film to work on and I still think it's one of the best things that John ever did and certainly one of the best things that I ever did. He gave me a lot of wonderful material, especially the ending of the film, which is terrific. It's a grossly underrated picture. Conrad Hall lit it with great brilliance and Richard McDonald's design made it wonderful to look at. It's a fascinating film about Hollywood. The Waterloo collapse of the hill took a week to shoot. It was a very complicated and difficult sequence because the set had to be cantilevered and was done in sections so that it would fall. Very tricky. A couple of stunt guys were badly injured on it.

We ran it for the students at Sundance in the eighties. Connie Hall was there with me and we decided to show it and most of these students had never seen or even heard of the movie and they were quite knocked out by it. It's an extraordinary piece of reconstruction and a very strong, sad and apocalyptic story. It's as current now as it was then.

The genesis of *The Day of the Locust* was the time when Nathanael West was a writer in Hollywood. He worked mainly on B pictures and never got any good credits. Waldo Salt, who wrote the script, was one of the group of writers who used to meet at Musso and Franks on Saturday mornings and they would talk about the horrors of working in Hollywood. West was working for Republic Pictures when he died and he had a very interesting take on the Hollywood of that period. You might say that the chief art director character, played by Richard Dysart, kind of represents people that might still exist, though even that kind of character is different now since they are not fully employed by studios. It's a much more hardheaded business now than it was, much more money oriented and committee based.

Not long after I arrived to cut *Locust,* Vincent Price invited us to lunch in his beach house near Malibu. He gave me instructions, but forgot to warn me that it was a long drive. We were to go along Mulholland Drive and turn off onto Sunset and find the Pacific Coast Highway, then drive until we saw a sign to Zuma Beach on the left. I drove too far on Mulholland which eventually petered out and became a dirt road, so I turned around and eventually found the highway, which I drove along for what seemed like forever until I found the turnoff. By this time we were late and had driven at least fifty miles.

Vincent was in this ramshackle wooden beach hut that was isolated in the dunes. It was a fully equipped weekend place and he was in his element in the kitchen, as jovial as ever. He was very much into cooking and into buying paintings. He was the art advisor to Sears and claimed that in the beach house he stored his Picassos, which I did not see. He told us that, sadly, the small community that lived on the beach on weekends would have to move since the city had decided to develop the site. That was the one and only time I saw the place because the bulldozers moved in shortly afterward.

Commercially *The Day of the Locust* was dead in the water and the critical response was not much better. John was very upset when *Locust* took a dive. He loved the film but I think he always knew that it was for a minority audience. I recall him saying, with glee and malice, that they would hate it in Los Angeles, and that the "sillies" would never get it. The "sillies" was John's way of referring to the general public.

There was no actual premiere for the film in England but John and I went to see it at the Empire, Leicester Square, on opening night and sat there a while. The audience clearly were not digging the film so, after a while we left and went for a good dinner instead, drinking to forget, but the film remains one of my favourites.

The Adventures of Sherlock Holmes' Smarter Brother

It was while we were cutting *The Day of the Locust* at Twickenham that Gene Wilder approached me to edit his film *The Adventures of Sherlock Holmes' Smarter Brother* in which Marty Feldman would play his second banana. Gene was coming to England to make his first film as a director.

Gene Wilder was a wonderful man to work with. He was appreciative, enthusiastic, funny, creative. He was everything you would want him to be. And he trusted me. We got on terribly well. I was able to give Gene a little advice if he needed it. The film itself was funny with a good script.

The only person I slightly fell out with was the American producer. I think he was jealous of my relationship with Gene toward the end. I believe he felt that I was closer to him than I should have been.

Of course directing a picture in which you're also starring is a difficult trick to pull off but Gene was much helped on the set by Gerry Fisher who was lighting it. Gerry would advise him quite wisely, where to put the camera and so on. Occasionally I was called in to help in terms of cover. But Gene knew. He'd been an actor long enough to know how to make a film. He was a good director.

He went on to direct several other films that my assistant cut. Chris Greenbury was my assistant on *The Adventures of Sherlock Holmes' Smarter Brother* and he and Gene got on very well. Chris went out on preview with me in America and never came back. He stayed in Los Angeles and made a career for himself, cutting several films for Gene and others. The booze, however, got him and he died at age fifty-five.

I always liked the film. I thought it was amusing. It was a spoof of Sherlock Holmes, of course. Gene was very funny in it. Madeline Kahn was excellent. Marty was wonderful. The whole thing was a great pleasure to do and we never had any problems. We had a lot of laughs and I got to know Gene very well and stayed friendly with him for a long, long time.

MARATHON MAN, AGATHA, AND YANKS

Marathon Man

Marathon Man was suggested to John Schlesinger by Robert Evans after he had seen *The Day of the Locust*, which he hadn't wanted Paramount to make at all but was overridden by the brass at Gulf & Western. Bob Evans had a rule of thumb that if he saw a film by a good director that wasn't working, perhaps the next one might work. So he used to leapfrog. He would get directors who had come off a flop and hope they would make a hit. After *The Day of the Locust* flopped, John was ready and Bob wanted him to do *Marathon Man*.

I remember meeting William Goldman when we were cutting *The Day of the Locust* at Twickenham and he was still writing the script. As soon as *Locust* finished dubbing, I went on to Gene Wilder's *The Adventures of Sherlock Holmes' Smarter Brother*. We previewed that in America and John had started shooting *Marathon Man* already. We overlapped because *Smarter Brother* went on a little longer than planned and it was six weeks before I was able to start cutting *Marathon Man*. John did, however, have a rough cut because Artie Schmidt was my assistant and he was able to supply cuts of whatever John needed to see.

Artie and I met over the phone. I was looking for an assistant to work with me on *Marathon Man* so I called the head of post-production at Paramount, Paul

Haggar. Paul knew Artie had been assisting Dede Allen on a film that Mike Nichols was directing with Robert De Niro called *Bogart Slept Here*. That film, however, collapsed after two weeks of shooting, leaving Dede Allen and everybody else looking for work. So Paul Haggar mentioned to Artie Schmidt that he had this limey editor coming over who was looking for an assistant and Artie phoned me. He didn't sound like an American; he sounded English. He was obviously very accomplished and had done many films as an assistant, so I hired him, which was a great stroke of luck for me and perhaps for him as well because our relationship on *Marathon Man* was very good. Artie's father had been a famous film editor and had cut *Some Like It Hot*. Sadly he died when he was in his fifties while working on a Jerry Lewis comedy at Paramount.

On *Marathon Man*, Artie did a lot of the editing himself because I realised he was capable of it. He cut the opening sequence of Dustin running around the reservoir. Then in the post-production phase when John and I were finalising the film, I gave Artie reels and sequences to recut with John.

After *Marathon Man* was finished, I gave Artie a very good screen credit as associate editor and that gave him more credibility. He then cut several, not very good films, until at some point he took over a television film that Michael Mann was directing called *The Jericho Mile*. He took it over because the original editor had not succeeded and it did very well. It certainly put Artie on the map and he never really faltered after that. He cut a lot of very good films. He began editing for Mike Nichols and Bob Zemeckis and has outstripped me totally in Oscar awards and goodness knows what. We're still great friends.

Artie Schmidt:

I first met Jim Clark over the phone from Paul Haggar's office at Paramount. Paul was the head of post-production and I needed a job. The film I had been working on as assistant/standby editor, *Bogart Slept Here,* had just been cancelled after two weeks of production. This was a severe blow to me and in desperation, I did something I had never done before. I opened *Daily Variety* and scanned the "Films in the Future" section. I zeroed in on *Marathon Man* when I saw an incredible lineup of talent. John Schlesinger, Robert Evans, Conrad Hall, William Goldman, Dustin Hoffman, Laurence Olivier, and Jim Clark. I remembered seeing *Day of the Locust* in Mike Nichols' screening room in Connecticut. At the end of the movie, Mike's first comment was "What a beautifully edited film that was." I agreed. Jim Clark was already an editor I had admired because I knew that he had come to the rescue of *Midnight Cowboy* and he had edited three of my favorite films, *Darling, The Pumpkin Eater,* and *The Innocents.*

I called Paul Haggar immediately. Paul had already assigned a female assistant to Jim but when Jim found out, he told Paul that the last time he had a female assistant he married her. So Paul made the call to Jim in London, put me on the phone, and, by the end of the phone call, I had the job. I was embarrassed that I was bumping somebody else that I knew out of a job but got over that quickly since it was Jim's decision and I wasn't about to talk him out of it.

I was on *Marathon Man,* getting dailies from Paris and New York for a month or so before Jim came on board. He was finishing Gene Wilder's *Sherlock Holmes' Smarter Brother* in London. I probably thought that with such a backlog of film on *Marathon Man* I might have an opportunity to edit, helping Jim catch up. At our first lunch together, however, Jim made a very un-Jim-like statement: "Nobody cuts on a Jim Clark film but Jim Clark." My heart sank. Not another nine months on a film without a chance to cut. He must have sensed my eagerness to get my hands on some film because I hadn't said a word or even hinted that my helping out might be a possibility. I had thought that, more realistically, he might hire a more experienced second editor to help out because of the tremendous backlog of film.

One day Jim asked me to come over to his Moviola and look at a cut that he wasn't quite sure about. It was the first time in my almost ten years as an assistant that an editor had invited me to look at a cut and give an opinion. Jim ran it for me, asked me what I thought, but, even though at best it was a bold cut and wasn't really all that great, I could not say that to Jim. He was Jim Clark, one the best in the business and who was I to criticize? Intimidated, I told him it looked okay to me. He probably suspected that I was lying because later on he changed it.

About a month passed and Jim worked feverishly to catch up. Then he asked if I would run scenes that he had cut and make changes in them. He wanted me to go through all the trims and do anything I thought would make them better. I was terrified. Improve the master's work—how intimidating and exciting and nerve wracking was that! I had complete freedom. Of course, this was in the days of film and there was only one copy of a cut scene, so unless a black-and-white duplicate copy of the scene was made, the minute I started making changes, Jim's version was history. The first scene I was given was where an Oriental man sneaks up behind Roy Scheider as he stands on the balcony of his Paris hotel room watching a street demonstration and tries to strangle him with a wire. I went through all the trims and made some changes. When I showed it to Jim, he said things like, "My God, where did you find that piece, that really works great." I couldn't believe how complimentary and generous he was. I thought I had just done some rather obvious things that Jim probably would have done once he had more time to sit and review the material. From then on all the Paris scenes became my domain.

One scene took place in a Paris flea market, involving a baby pram that had a doll, which was really a time bomb, in it. John had shot four angles on the doll in the pram. A wide shot, a medium, a closeup, and an extreme closeup. I knew that I was meant to use a different size each time I cut back to the doll from the other action taking place in the flea market, the extreme closeup being the last before the ticking doll/bomb blew up. I decided to try something a little different. Just before the bomb went off, I used all four shots in quick succession, starting with the wide and ending with the extreme closeup and then boom, the explosion. I thought it was quite effective, but Jim's comment when I showed it to him was very tactful. "Well, that's very interesting," he said. "But I don't think I would show it to John that way." And I didn't.

John, of course, quite rightly thought Jim could do no wrong, but wasn't so sure about me, the fledgling editor. I showed John the scene in the Paris hotel room and when we got to the part where the Oriental man comes out of the wardrobe closet, the door opened very slowly and when I cut to the reverse angle of the door opening, I had deliberately repeated a little bit of the action because I thought that was what was done in scenes where you are trying to build suspense. It was not an uncommon editorial convention, or so I thought. When I showed it to John, he screamed to Jim in the other room. "Jim! Jim! Come quick! There's a double action here. Quick. You've got to do something. You must fix it." So Jim took the scene away from me and went to his Moviola and made the trim to calm down the hysterical John.

Bob Evans was a great producer, one of the best I ever worked with because he was an intelligent man who chose wisely. At the time we did *Locust*, he was the studio head at Paramount. We were in competition with *Chinatown* at that point and I believe he picked up Polanski, after he too had had a flop. Bob was smart enough to hire the right people. He knew that John was the right director, he knew that Goldman could do it. He'd read the book and bought it. He knew he wanted Dustin Hoffman. He knew he wanted Olivier though I think John had a lot to do with that. Olivier hadn't worked for a long time because he was very ill and they couldn't get insurance for him. I came along because of my connection with John. Bob didn't know me. Connie Hall had lit *The Day of the Locust* so he was on board to light *Marathon Man* and Richard McDonald had designed both films so the team was similar.

John had already worked with Dustin Hoffman on *Midnight Cowboy* but their relationship was not particularly close. After *Cowboy* Dustin got the hump (got fed up) and didn't really speak to John but by the time it came to *Marathon Man* you wouldn't have known there was a rift at all. He was not combative and would take direction very well. It was a very happy shoot and Dustin was very protective of Olivier.

While we were working on *Marathon Man,* my eldest daughter Kate lived with us and I recall that she was involved in some jewelry-making classes with the male companion of Roddy McDowall, an actor I'd known for some time. Roddy invited us to his parties that were always crammed with famous faces. I remember sitting next to Rock Hudson at one of these shindigs and we were probably the only people there who didn't know he was gay. Roddy was very sociable and lived near Studio City opposite Gene Autry. He would give occasional poolside lunch parties as well as evening dinners, which were always catered. The food was not that good, but people attended for the quality of the guests. Roddy was a friend of John Schlesinger and perhaps they thought we did not get invited out too often because we weren't celebrities. It was always a gathering of the great and famous. Danny Kaye did a wonderful impersonation of Laurence's French accent, and Vincent Price, who had by this time met and fallen for Coral Browne, was often there with her. It was charming to see Vincent and Coral behaving like teenagers in love.

One of the great things about finding Artie Schmidt was that, athough he wasn't an editor yet, he was very capable and, when it came to the fine cutting, I could trust him to go off with John, take notes of what John wanted changed, and do it while I was cutting another scene and we'd leapfrog through the movie in that way. I did the scene with the old Jew chasing the old Nazi down the streets in their cars and smashing them up. The scene in New York's Diamond District was a combination of the two of us. That was shot in New York before I joined the film and I seem to recall that Artie put it together. I know I had a lot of trouble with the editing of that sequence, especially the lady who spots Olivier as Szell, the old Nazi. That was recut many, many times. John was never happy with the timing.

Because we were so pleased with the final result, we cut the negative before we went to preview, which was unheard of and daft. We'd mixed the film and cut the negative and we had a married print, which we took to San Jose. We did tremendously well with a great audience so we thought we were home free. The following night we ran exactly the same print up in San Francisco where we got a thumbs down and there was practically a riot because it was too violent. People were huddled in the manager's office. Hoffman, Bob Evans, and John were barricaded in by the security guards to prevent bloodshed. It was horrible.

Artie Schmidt:

We previewed the film in San Jose, California, one night and it was almost perfect. The audience loved it. We drove up the peninsula in limos to San Francisco the next day, confident that we had a big hit. Instead, the San Francisco screening was a disaster. People walked out, shaking their fists at Dustin Hoffman, who was sitting in the back of the cinema. They cursed him for being in such a violent film. At the meeting afterward in Bob Evans' penthouse at the Fairmont Hotel, it was decided that we should do everything possible to reduce the violence in the film. Jim and I went back and made at least seventy changes to trim blood and anything anyone deemed too graphic.

Without discussing it with me or Jim or John, the studio and the editors' union decided that I should have a shared editor credit with Jim at the beginning of the film. I, of course, was thrilled at the possibility of sharing a credit with Jim up front, but I didn't think I quite deserved it and I said so to Jim and John. Jim had, in the end, done most of the editing. They agreed and gave me a rather impressive solo "associate editor" credit, the first that came on the screen at the end of the movie.

After that the film was recut and we took out everything that was too graphic. We cut one dental scene out completely and if you look, you'll see that there's nothing visually that is at all upsetting. It's all on the soundtrack.

Marathon Man is remembered for that one scene, which has become infamous in dental circles and has probably unnerved many nervous patients when their next appointment is due. The astonishing thing about this scene is that it remains potently arresting while not being visually emphatic. Very little is actually shown. Since most of us are nervous in the hands of the dentist, the sequence carries a lot of anxiety from the audience and therefore it was not necessary to underline the action.

Originally there was another section that was much more graphic. I did suggest to Schlesinger that we should shoot some very close inserts of the drill touching the tooth. He did not think this was at all necessary but allowed me to shoot some material. I spent some time getting the special effects people to produce a whiff of smoke as the drill hit the tooth. I thought this was really good, which shows how insensitive I had become to the power of this sequence. The graphic inserts remained in the film for a long time and were there for that first preview without causing the audience to faint. However, the San Francisco audience reacted very strongly to the dental sequence, which caused Schlesinger and Robert Evans to reduce all the violence in the picture, which was probably just as well. So we shortened the dental scene considerably and took out all the graphic shots. My whiffs of smoke were the first to go.

The following breakdown shows that the scene relies mainly on sound effects to produce the tense result:

Breakdown: Babe has been returned to the hands of Szell who has already pushed a probe into a nerve so Babe (and the audience) knows what might occur next. (CS = close shot; MS = medium shot; VCS = very close shot; WS = wide shot)

1. MS: Szell takes an electric drill from a case and plugs it into a wall socket. (Szell has all the dialogue in this scene which is played over the following shots.)
2. CS: Plug inserted into socket.
3. CS: Szell.
4. CS: Babe looks off to see the drill.
5. CS : Szell moves away.
6. CS: His hands unravel electric cord—camera follows him—he tests the drill off camera and we hear the sound effect.
7. CS: Babe sweating.
8. MS: Babe. Henchman enters from behind. Babe ducks his head which is then forced up.
9. CS: Szell.
10. VCS: Rubber plugs in Szell's hand.
11. WS: Szell pushes plugs into Babe's mouth.
12. CS: Szell moves back and turns on drill.
13. CS: Zooming into Babe's eyes (intermittent drill sound effect off screen).
14. CS: Zooming into drill as it comes closer to camera and goes out of focus. As it does so, the image mixes to a zooming CS of Szell that swims

into focus and goes toward his eyes then the camera pans off to a white lamp, zooms into it, and the frame is filled with white light.

The sound effect of the drill was crucial to the effect we desired. As the drill came closer and began to go out of focus, we altered the pitch of the drill, as if it were boring into something hard. The sound continued until the camera panned to the white light when the drill stops and Babe's scream is heard. The out-of-focus image was created in the optical printer, as was the zoom into the white light.

When John decided to recut, he realised he could extend shots as well, but in those days we were cutting on film and if you extended a shot you lost two frames. So there are some jump cuts. There's one particularly bad one when Olivier as Szell, having killed the guy in the street with his blade, gets into a cab. I did an extension and therefore lost two frames.

John's was the main voice in the editing suite for *Marathon Man* and occasionally he would call up Bob Evans' office and say, "Bob, get your arse up here. I need your advice." And Bob would dutifully arrive, wearing his tiny little slippers, which Dustin Hoffman picked up on in *Wag the Dog*. And John used to say, "Oh, here she comes again in her funny little slippers, tripping along the corridor." He used to tease him regularly. He used to send all these people up. They were all gay as far as he was concerned. He would say, "Come out of the closet Bob, for God's sake." Bob, of course was a great one for the ladies. The head of Paramount after Bob Evans was Barry Diller. John used to send him up too. "Of course we all know about you Barry." The response of these powerful American executives to John's taunting was a kind of embarrassed confusion. That John had "come out" years before did nothing but make them uncomfortable.

Marathon Man was mostly shot in the studio at Paramount so I did see the actors from time to time. I'd worked with Olivier and Hoffman before. John wouldn't have the actors anywhere near him during the screening of rushes. That was an old rule that began on *Far From the Madding Crowd* when Peter Finch used to get pissed and make remarks out loud that offended John and he decided that he would ban all actors from rushes. However, on *Marathon Man*, I used to look up behind me at the projection booth and see Dustin looking through the window. John never knew that Dustin saw the rushes. He also came to all of the previews and I remember on the plane back from Dallas where we had our last preview, Dustin sat next to me and started to recut the ending—in his head at least. And he would say, "Why don't we do this? Maybe we could do that." And I, of course, listened and took notes dutifully and then showed them to John, who would say, "Oh don't do any of that. Don't take any notice. No, please."

The Last Remake of Beau Geste

I was friendly with Marty Feldman after *Every Home Should Have One*. When he directed his first film, *The Last Remake of Beau Geste*, which he shot in Madrid, he had a difficult time with his editor. He had picked an American editor who was quite well known, but after about a month of shooting, I had panic calls from Marty's wife Lauretta Feldman saying, "Mart's in real trouble. He doesn't like his editor and the guy's not doing a good job. Can you possibly come out and take a look at what we've got?"

So I flew to Madrid and looked at it. It was, indeed, very bad, but it wasn't the editing, it was the film itself. Marty's direction wasn't good at all. I read the riot act to Marty over breakfast one morning and said "You've got to pull your socks up. The script is good, but what I'm seeing on the screen isn't funny at all." He asked what he could do. He'd already fired the editor and the stuff was still being shot every day. I said the only thing I could suggest was that I take it over but I'd only do it if I could have Artie Schmidt work with me. Artie was on holiday in Italy at the time. I phoned Artie and asked if he could possibly come to Madrid and look at this material because I thought we should recut it and finish it together. So Artie came to Madrid, looked at the material with me and said, "This is terrible! Why do you want to get involved?" And I told him that Marty was an old friend and he was in trouble and I'd like to help him. Artie, because he was a friend of mine, and despite his better judgment, agreed to do it.

Artie Schmidt:

I was on vacation at my father-in-law's house in Italy, when I got a call from Jim telling me that he had just taken over the editing of Marty Feldman's *The Last Remake of Beau Geste*. The film was a mess, they'd fired the editor and would I come to Spain and help out? I said yes. I flew to Madrid and the next day Jim and I spent twelve hours looking at all the dailies that hadn't been cut. They weren't very good. The screening gave me a huge headache and I wondered if I had made the right decision.

So we clambered on board this very dodgy machine and we cut it at Twickenham while they were still shooting in Madrid. And every day we saw the rushes and every day there were no laughs. So Marty hadn't learnt any lessons at all from me. I used to call him and rage and scream and say, "But this isn't funny." "Don't matter, love. Don't matter, love. It's all right. It's all right. Don't worry," he would say. He eventually finished shooting and we still had this two-hour sprawl of unfunny film which he'd completely fucked up.

The next step of this sorry tale was that we had to take it to America, to Universal, who owned it. There were two producers, who were a nightmare because they thought Marty was a genius. They thought everything he did was crazily funny and it wasn't. One of them was Jerry Henshaw.

So we ended up in Universal City in Los Angeles one morning and we ran the assembly for the two producers and Marty. It was ghastly. The film had no laughs in it. However, Jerry Henshaw was busy writing on a yellow legal pad throughout the screening and I read it afterward, I just sort of glanced at what he'd been writing. In huge letters with a magic marker, he'd written: *Monster laugh, terrific laugh, great laugh*. So he obviously thought the film was a masterpiece.

Marty, however, had second thoughts about what he was looking at and he asked if I'd have lunch with him. So the two of us went off together to a steakhouse near Universal and over lunch I said, "It's not good, Mart. Let's face it. It's not a good film." And he said, "Can you make it good enough for me to get another film?" That was his only request. So I said I'd do what I could. We arranged to meet at his house in Los Angeles for dinner. I arrived at 7:30 and Lauretta said, "Where's Mart?" I said I hadn't seen him since lunch. "Oh, that's very odd," she said. "Because he never came home." He didn't come home for three days. They eventually found him dead drunk in a bar near the airport.

Marty did like a drop of alcohol but he also, because of his thyroid condition, had to take his pills. Whenever he forgot to take his pills, it was bad news.

We carried on cutting until Universal said, "We've got to look at this thing." The boss of Universal, Ned Tanen, and his number two, Verna Fields, who was an editor herself, looked at the film and pronounced it dead in the water. Marty then came up with fresh ideas. New ideas. Whole new scenes. A spoof of *Morocco*, the Foreign Legion movie with Gary Cooper that everybody thought was brilliant. So he was given permission to reshoot. That Foreign Legion spoof was probably the best thing in it. However, one day it was evident that, despite our best efforts, the film was still not funny.

Marty flew to London to do some additional dialogue with English actors and while he was away, Verna Fields coerced me to recut certain scenes. Marty looked at these when he came back. He was very angry about it. He now felt I was siding with the studio against him, so our relationship went sour at that point and it never recovered.

Artie Schmidt:

Verna Fields called Jim and me into her office and announced that Jim would work with her on the studio's version and I would work with

Marty on his version. With hardly any hesitation, I surprised myself, Jim, and Verna, by saying that I would not do Marty's version. When they asked why, I said that my friendship with Jim was too important to me and I was afraid that if we were to do dueling versions of the film, it might cause a rift in our friendship. To my surprise, they both said okay and decided that Jim and I would work together on the studio's version and our assistant editor could work with Marty on his version. And that's what we did.

Marty brought another editor on. Artie and I somehow managed to stay with it. We ended up previewing two versions of the film. Our version being the studio version. John Morris who was scoring had to compose two completely different films. We had to mix two different films and we previewed both versions and they both got identically bad marks which was interesting because the two versions were radically different though they contained identical material.

Finally Ned Tanen said, "Right. Somebody has to make a decision about what we release." I suggested that he be the arbitrator. We would all meet in Ned's office on Sunday morning and decide what was going to happen, what the order of events were going to be with the movie. Everybody was there, though not speaking. There was now a barrier between me and Marty that never healed.

We eventually decided that they would use my construction and their content, I think it went, or maybe the other way around. I don't remember exactly. So on the Monday morning we put both versions up on the machine and made them into one version by moving scenes from one version to another. The whole thing then became one version of the movie which was eventually released. Not, I would say, to great acclaim but it was, at least, released and it did get Marty another film, *In God We Trust*, which opened and closed more rapidly than his first. After that he never directed again.

I never really fell out with Marty's wife. I don't think she ever blamed me. Marty was not an easy man to deal with and he died shortly after this. He was working on a film as an actor and he forgot to take his pills. He died young which was very sad because Marty, before he'd directed his film, had become a bit of a star through Mel Brooks and Gene Wilder.

The Sorcerer aka The Wages of Fear

One of the strangest movies I ever got involved with was William Friedkin's *The Sorcerer*. Coming off the huge success of *The Exorcist*, Friedkin decided to remake one of his favourite films, Henri Clouzot's *The Wages of Fear*, which he mysteriously retitled *The Sorcerer*. Perhaps he thought the public might consider this to be another occult movie, whereas it was simply the brand name of a truck.

The production was to turn into an expensive nightmare for all concerned. The budget, which doubled or tripled along the way, was shared by Universal and Paramount, both of whom were to lose their shirts.

Friedkin was in his most megalomaniac stage, firing anyone who dared to confront him and was rumoured to be surrounded by minders who would attend to anyone whom Friedkin had crossed.

The lead actor in the film was Roy Scheider, who I knew from *Marathon Man*. Roy's wife at the time was Cynthia Scheider, an assistant film editor who worked on *The Sorcerer* with Friedkin's editor, Bud Smith.

On release the picture was greeted with disdain by critics and public alike. It was consigned to the shelf because there seemed no way to save this startlingly poor and wildly over produced film that barely resembled the suspenseful Clouzot original. Friedkin had taken a story he claimed to love and, with his writer Walon Green, turned it into a sprawling, over long tale that had zero suspense and was totally confusing. Funny how these movies ever get the green light, but I imagine they figured the first version was a hit in Europe and Friedkin had a track record. From what I'd heard, however, *The Exorcist* was hell for everyone and costly to make, which I guess they'd forgotten. Memories are short in Hollywood.

When Verna Fields, in her capacity as a Universal executive, asked me about a possible recut of *The Sorcerer* for foreign release, I was very hesitant to become involved. UIP, who handled the foreign territories for both studios, thought there might be some commercial life in the film if it could be restructured and shortened. Their London man, Jerry Lewis (not the comedian), was to be in charge. Verna told me I could have Cynthia Scheider with me in London to help, since she knew where all the material was in the Universal vaults. Roy Scheider was also keen to have the film recut and would cooperate.

Having heard about Friedkin, his temper, and his bodyguards, I did not agree to this work without some trepidation. Verna, however, was a friend and I wanted to help her out. She said that Friedkin had given his permission for the film to be altered in any way they desired, though I didn't altogether believe this. It didn't seem possible that a director of his eminence would let this film be changed without kicking and screaming. We already knew he did a lot of screaming.

I agreed to look at the film and see if I could come up with any suggestions. This was a dismaying experience and I could see why it had fared so badly at the box office. It was a very poorly structured version of the story. In the first place, Friedkin engaged a number of foreign actors and for the first twenty minutes, he indulged in scenes, expensively shot in different parts of the world to give the characters some background and explain why they had ended up in Mexico driving trucks filled with nitroglycerine. This device was both confusing and boring. It took ages before the story actually began. Then there was the question of clarity. Several of these foreign actors didn't speak understandable English and, unlike the original, this version had very little suspense and was dragged out to inordinate length. I really did not want to touch this movie but, finally, I agreed, as Verna was at her most persuasive.

Ned Tanen and Verna Fields were very tight. Ned wouldn't do anything without Verna's say so. Verna, known as "the Mother Cutter," was an incredible woman; she was the earth mother of Universal at that time. She'd been a sound editor originally, but after she'd cut *Jaws* and recut George Lucas' *American Graffiti*, she became an executive. She was promoted out of the cutting room into the front office and became very, very powerful. She was a physically big woman, who was very down to earth and everybody's friend. She was powerful because she had the ear of the throne—in this case, Ned Tanen.

I liked Ned a lot. He was intelligent, cultivated, and cultured. He would scream and shout as loudly as all the other monsters, but I always felt he was a benign shouter. He wasn't a bully.

At the same time the recut of *The Sorcerer* was being discussed, Verna was executive producing *Jaws 2* and the shoot had hit troubled waters. At some point they'd fired the original director and if they were not to shut down the production on Martha's Vineyard, they'd have to find somebody else to replace him.

Verna invited me to join her on a trip to Martha's Vineyard where we could discuss *The Sorcerer* with Roy. I accompanied her and for a brief time, Verna and I were going to take over the direction of *Jaws 2*. We were ultimately forbidden to do so by the Directors Guild, because she was an executive at Universal and you're not allowed, as a member of the Directors Guild, to be both an executive and a director. However, we had a nice visit with Roy, who flew me back to New York in his private plane. I was never so terrified. It was a tiny little plane, and as we hit air pockets and turbulence, it was banging and bumping and doing everything but turning over. Roy was very macho and took it all in stride, but I was extremely glad when it was over and we'd actually arrived alive.

Back in London I asked to have Ken Levison come aboard to help me with the restructure of *The Sorcerer* and to write dialogue that could be dubbed in. This was agreed and Cynthia Scheider was dispatched to London.

Taking advice from my agent, I asked a lawyer to prepare an indemnity that would prevent Freidkin from interfering in any way with either us or the work. After all the stories we had heard of Friedkin's behaviour, it seemed prudent.

So we started. Not knowing the material was our first problem. Cynthia was tremendously helpful. The amount of film that had been shot over six months was prodigious, so the volume of negative stashed in the Los Angeles vaults was huge, but Cynthia knew what it was and, more importantly, where it was.

We did have a script and could see where whole scenes had been deleted, some of which could be useful to us. So every day, when the studio opened in California, Cynthia would have a wish list of scenes that should be sent to London.

We didn't have a work print and the negative was, of course, already cut, so I worked with a combined print and a transfer of the existing soundtrack.

Ken and I decided to ditch all the scenes that opened the film. There was one in Israel, another in Paris, and so on. We decided to open the film with some spectacular aerial shots that had been used in the body of the film. Cynthia said there was miles of that in the vault so we got it sent over and used it for the credits which took us directly to the shanty town truck stop in the middle of Mexico where all the drivers, each a dropout for one reason or another, resided along with a variety of whores.

We tried every trick we could dream up to bring some semblance of continuity into the story from then on. I shoehorned parts of the original opening scenes into the narrative as flashbacks with new dialogue, which Ken had written, to explain how the men had arrived in Mexico. I was able to play some of these over the backs of heads and then revert to the original lines when sync was required. It was quite a puzzle and every day we would get another section of film from America.

We carried on like this, showing the film to Jerry Lewis from time to time. Eventually the new version was complete and had to be remixed. This was another problem because all of the sound elements had to be sent from America and recut to fit the new version.

Finally there was the vexing question of the title. Obviously *The Sorcerer* was out. Some bright spark at UIP decided to call it *The Wages of Fear* which I thought was a perfectly terrible idea. The film could hardly be compared to Clouzot's original, a classic of its kind, and our recut was, at best, passable, but that's how it ended up.

It was released and did no business. It occasionally appears on television in England and I wonder whether the exercise was in any way worthwhile. If we had left Friedkin's version alone, it would have had exactly the same fate.

I never met Friedkin nor his editor, Bud Smith, who I hope might now be forgiving.

Agatha

It must have been through my agent that I met Michael Apted for *Agatha*. It may have been David Puttnam who asked me to do it. I'd never worked with Puttnam and I do recall meeting him at Twickenham for lunch one day. David was producing *Agatha* and Michael Apted was directing.

We started shooting that picture, which was Dustin Hoffman's last film for a company called First Artists, which he and Barbra Streisand and various other actors had started. Their films were released by Warner Brothers and Dustin was working out his contract. He agreed, for reasons best known to himself, to play the small role of the reporter who tracks Agatha down and after about a week of shooting it was evident to everybody that Hoffman was inflating his role or trying to. His part was gradually enlarging and David saw all sorts of "Danger Ahead" signs, so after about two weeks, he defected off his own film leaving Michael Apted holding this can of worms.

The script had been written by Ken Tynan's widow Kathy. It wasn't a great script but Vanessa Redgrave and Dustin had agreed to play it and everything went sort of downhill from the beginning. Gavrik Losey, Joe Losey's son, was the production manager and he held the thing together while First Artists or Warner Brothers were sending over new producers from Hollywood. They were coming and going all the time. They would come for two weeks then disappear, so Michael had no effective producer. By the time the production had moved to Bath from Harrogate, Vanessa and Dustin weren't even speaking. Dustin had brought in Murray Schisgal, his own writer from New York, so Vanessa got her own writer, Arthur Hopcraft.

These two writers, who were not working together, would rewrite for their actor, so the scenes that Michael had to shoot, were being rewritten the day before and then collated by the script supervisor, Zelda Barron, who would take Murray Schisgal's lines for Hoffman and Arthur Hopcraft's lines for Redgrave then put them together and sub-edit them. The whole thing was a mix and match that must have been very difficult for the director. The real star of *Agatha* in the end, was the cameraman Vittorio Storaro, because it looks wonderful.

In the cutting room, however, we totally revised the construction of the movie. In the end, when we finished, there wasn't one single word of Kathy Tynan's script left. Nothing. The fact that the film worked at all was extraordinary.

This production had another strange and rather sad little story. Howard Blake had written an absolutely wonderful score for *Agatha*, which we recorded and mixed. It was very much in the Miklos Roza style and I thought it was great and so did Michael Apted. We ran the movie one night at BAFTA for an invited audience and, for some reason, Vanessa didn't like the music and she was instrumental in having First Artists dump Howard Blake's score and replace it with an American score by Johnny Mandel. It changed the nature of the movie because it became more sentimental.

What the fate of *Agatha* would been if David Puttnam had stayed is difficult to guess. Puttnam could see that Hoffman was going to create trouble and would try to take over the film and, rather than have a confrontation with him, David left. Michael Apted had trained as a lawyer before he became a filmmaker and I think it was this training that saw him through *Agatha* because he was able, using his legal skills, to fight a war of attrition between all these factors and keep his head above water, making sure that the film didn't suffer through all this nonsense. Michael was determined that it would be a good film and he used to say to me, quite rightly, that *Agatha* was his passport to Hollywood. And it was because afterward he went to Hollywood and made *Coal Miner's Daughter* and he never looked back.

Artie Schmidt:

One day Jim, who had just finished cutting *Agatha* for Michael Apted, called and said he was recommending me to Michael for a film about Loretta Lynn called *Coal Miner's Daughter.* Michael was coming to make his first film in the U.S. and was looking for an editor. An interview was set up and Michael gave me the job based solely on Jim's recommendation. I was just finishing up on a TV movie called *The Jericho Mile* with Michael Mann directing, for which I eventually won an Emmy and an Eddie, the American Cinema Editor's award. *Coal Miner's Daughter* brought me my first Academy Award nomination. Through Jim's generosity and friendship, he gave me opportunities that, over the years, kept opening doors for me and put my career on a trajectory that never would have happened if it hadn't been for that fateful phone call from Paul Haggar's office.

Yanks

John Schlesinger thought that Billy Devane was a wonderful actor and so had cast him in *Marathon Man* as the double agent. But then John put him into *Yanks* and there were many people who felt that Billy was miscast. Personally I've never thought that he was a bad actor but his career never really went anywhere in cinema. He has certainly had a long career on television.

Yanks came about while we were shooting *Marathon Man* in Hollywood. Colin Welland arrived one day to see Dustin Hoffman because they had worked together on *Straw Dogs* in England. He turned up peddling the idea of *Yanks* to Dustin, who he thought would be wonderful in it. Instead, Colin snared John as the director.

John read the script and said he'd love to do it, but he didn't want Dustin Hoffman. Joe Janni agreed to come on board and John worked on the script with Colin but, because the story was about American GIs in England, he wanted an American writer to be involved, so Walter Bernstein did a rewrite and shared the credit with Colin. Lester Persky, an American producer, also came in with Joe and the film was made shortly after we finished *Agatha*. In fact it was made at the same studios, Twickenham, with locations up north.

I remember them doing artist tests looking for the girl and John shot, I think, six girls. He shot the same scene with each one and I stuck them together while we were cutting *Agatha*. Michael Apted and I both looked at these screen tests and agreed on who should get the role. None of us realised that Lisa Eichhorn, who got the job, was American. Not that it mattered terribly but I never felt that her performance was exactly right as a North country girl.

Yanks was not a difficult film to put together. I know that John had met Richard Gere in Hollywood and decided he should play the young GI and I don't believe he had any great problems with the cast. John was quite ruthless with actors and if he wasn't getting the performance he wanted, he could be very cruel. If he loved them, he loved them to death and if he didn't love them, they were always suspect like Bill Atherton on *The Day of the Locust*.

On *Sunday, Bloody Sunday*, which I didn't cut, he was even more worried about the casting of Ian Bannen in the lead. And he'd been told by everybody that this was a bad idea but he wouldn't have it, he wouldn't take advice. But to his credit he realised, after two weeks of shooting, that Ian Bannen wasn't right and it was his great good fortune that Peter Finch, who had been considered and passed on it, was now available and was able to play the role as well as he did.

I don't recall any such battles of ego or actor problem on *Yanks*. He loved Billy Devane and he loved Vanessa Redgrave—both of whom were in the film.

John got terribly frustrated by the setting of the corner shop and the small cramped room that they basically lived in. He used to call me down to the set and say, "I don't know where to put the camera anymore. I've done scenes in this room too many times. You go with the actors to the corner store set and just rehearse them and see if you can find another angle on it." So I used to find myself with Lisa Eichhorn, Rachel Roberts, and Tony Melody, trying to work out some business in the corner shop that, perhaps, was original. He didn't like the camera man Dick Bush terribly and had a very poor relationship with him although he was his choice.

John, however, was very worried about the script and I remember on Keighley Station when we shot the finale of *Yanks*, I had a second unit, working alongside the first unit, picking up reactions because we had a big crowd. Colin Welland came over to me one morning and said, "I don't know what to do about John. He's just had a terrible row with me in front of everybody. What John doesn't understand is that I'm a celebrity around here. They all know me." Colin was a local lad from Yorkshire and had been in *Z Cars* and a number of other films, so he was better known to all these people who had turned up to be extras. It seems John was saying, "I need a line! I need a line for Richard here!" Surrounded by thousands of people, poor Colin was expected to come up with some line immediately and he couldn't or wouldn't. I wasn't around. I didn't witness this row, but Colin was terribly upset because John was screaming at him in front of all these people.

John would get terribly frustrated and became very angry in public. Michael Childers used to say, "Stop John. You'll have a stroke if you go on like that." And he did in the end. John's temper was something that he never bothered to keep in check, whereas other directors would take people aside for a discreet word, John would bellow at the top of his lungs in front of whoever happened to be listening. It didn't matter where he was. It happened on every film I ever did with John but he never once did it to me.

The next movie that John and I were about to embark upon would test our creative relationship in more ways than either of us could possibly imagine. Before we went into production, however, a letter from Dirk Bogarde arrived to cheer me up:

9th January, '80

My dear Jim,

Your Super-duper-Christmas-Number has just arrived today. Full of every kind of goodie, lacking only the Visit Of The Magie. I am swamped with pleasures.

I will deal with things as they come. Letter-wise that is. I am so afraid that you'll have gone back to that vile country before this gets to poor Laurence wandering round her kitchen wondering who she really is.

I AM sad about *Yanks.* Naturally everything that J. Schless does is vastly interesting to me. Annie Skinner was so overwhelmed when she saw a, I presume, rough-cut, that she wrote pages and they were stained with tears. So I knew that something might be wrong. I haven't, I must confess, met anyone who did like it so far . . . the middle-aged as well. Somebody said it was too "patronising" . . . and I know that Schless CAN give this erronious impression at times, but as I haven't seen it and, obviously, won't here in Cannes, I must keep my judgements alert and unbiased. But it does seem to me a dangerous era to make a film about. Not history, not nostalgia and overtaken anyway by events. I think that old Schless was much better with a luggage trolly in Waterloo.

The new idea sounds fun. Better by far than Ghandi which is my next door neighbour's dream-almost-coming-true. A cast of millions, a budget of the same proportions and a year's shooting in India. Can you believe it! And who will ever go to see *that.* I ask myself? My next door N. being Sir R. Attnbro, if you didn't know. The nearest I get to the movies these days. It's all being done by the evil J. Levine, naturally . . . and if it's at all like a Bridge Too Fucking Long, they'll be in the shit house. Not before time either. I really do like old Dickie but I cannot bear the films he makes or how he makes them. Already there are murmurs of Jane Fonda and Robert Redford. Who for I cry? Ghandi? No! . . . one for Margaret Burke White and the other for a "composite" reporter from UIP. . . . MUST have the Yankee names even for a "human documentary" on Ghandi . . . I shy away at looking at the script which is like two London Telephone books. But have made it perfectly clear that I am not in the market.

Delighted that you have at last pulled yourself together and taken out your license to Direct. With so many nitwits at work why not you? *You* have saved so much material in the past that you ought to know just how to put it all together for yourself. And you CAN do it . . . unless you have been totally corrupted in the last fifteen years, which would not surprise me in the least, only sadden me.

The names you dredge up from the bottom of the seive! Judy Scott Fox! Oozing with insincerity . . . and still alive, what's more. I imagine that she and Samantha Glick, otherwise known as Sue Menges, play backgammon together for Young Actor's. And G. Wigan! Goodness me. Days of yore . . . a fragile, it seemed, young fellow, pale and loitering by all kinds of lakes. And poor old. G. Brown . . . what will she take him for I wonder? I am terribly glad for Gareth though. I mean that he is with a powerful mob . . . I liked him greatly. I even really liked Ladd . . . If only they could do something other than Space Fiction which I simply detest. We have hours and hours of it on Telly here . . . and I simply won't sit in a movie house to pay for it. I hate mechanical people and rockets and bang! bang! to electronic music. Where has Irene Dunne gone for shits sake?

My life? Not that you asked really. But it goes well. I am hourly glad that I cleared off when I did. Eleven years here, can you believe it. I still can't speak French, but it seems not to matter dreadfully. I can manage with Doctors and Plumbers and the Tax Inspector, try that in any language, and I manage a Telly interview from time . . . by seeming to be to be to be shy, reticent, and very thoughtful. It works quite well. But I love France and the odious French . . . I went back to London in September to see my aged Mamma and fled to the Hovercraft without a backward look. When we reached Calais I got pissed in the station buffet with sheer joy.

But I'll probably be off to Germany again with my pet genius Fassbinder, in the fall . . . I know you don't care for his work. But just try working FOR him! Thats something other . . . Charlotte Rampling has just got back from NY aglow with joy for Woody Allen . . . it is the same relationship that I have with Fass. . . . Good at my age. Pushes you out a bit, strengthens the technique, forces you to try something new.

Losey for a day next week with a project. I said OK as long as it isn't about Space, Transvestites, or another Opera. Altough Don G. is simply terrific, if you like that sort of thing, and is a vast success over here. Predictably it was slaughtered in the U.S. "Losey's Communist Tract" said "New York." Oh dear. What are you to do with a nation which can't even get it's wars right?

I must go . . . I've taken up far too much of your time already. Unless you have left this bit lying on another flight somewhere . . . Love and a huge hug to Laurence . . . tell her not to despair too much. She decided to breed, so she's stuck with the result . . . now that they have fled the nest, or almost, she better have a very good think. Not that there is anything TO think about in British Movies . . . but why not Television for her? At least it's alive and well and sometimes kicking. . . .

Good luck with Honkey Tonkey Wonky . . . I hope everything goes smashing for you, really I do . . . it's about time after all.

With warmest affection,

Dirk

HONKY TONK
CAR CRASH

Honky Tonk Freeway

Honky Tonk Freeway started well. Perhaps too well. John came into the room when we were cutting *Yanks* and said that he may have found his next film. This was a script by an American, Ed Clinton, who was a friend of the English producer Don Boyd. Don sent it to John and so it got set up at EMI, who were making films at that time and trying to crack the American market.

The spectrum of comedy is broad, and within its breadth are some smaller bands that appeal to only about 150 people worldwide. After my experience on *Rentadick*, I should have perhaps recognised the dodgy area in which *Honky Tonk Freeway* resided. It appealed to John, Don, me, and, presumably, Ed Clinton. During production the signs were all around us that we were headed for a fall, because we all had such a good time, which often can prove fatal. It doesn't always hold, but many times if a movie sails through and everyone enjoys the experience, the end result fails to please anyone outside the circle.

In its defence, I must point out that there are now, years later, people out there who can be counted as fans. There's an old rule that if the crew laugh at the rushes, you'll have an unfunny movie and *Honky Tonk Freeway*, which John always referred to as "Wanky Wank Bumhole," was one of those. It was never

119

going to be cheap, but in the end it became scandalously expensive and was the subject of much ridicule. The critics reviewed the budget. The film was a huge flop and wrecked John's career for several years. It was also the last film on which we collaborated.

It did, however, begin with great hope and optimism when we all arrived in Los Angeles and set up shop at Warner-Hollywood. Don Boyd had a sumptuous office and began playing the Hollywood producer in a big way. John, being ever cautious, recruited Howard Koch Jr as co-producer, which rather blunted Don's style. John always needed secure backup and feared that Don, new to the game, would give in to studio demands. Howard had worked with us on *Marathon Man* and was, by now, an experienced producer. Ed Clinton was busy polishing the script. John was casting. I was on board as second unit director as well as editor, so I got my crew together for some pre-production shooting.

Having used William Devane on *Yanks* and *Marathon Man*, it was not surprising that he was cast as the Mayor of Ticlaw and owner of the Hotel and Safari Park. Many other old friends agreed to play in the film including Beau Bridges, Hume Cronyn, Jessica Tandy, and Paul Jabara. It became a very large cast.

The story concerned Ticlaw, a small town in Florida that had been denied a freeway exit. The inhabitants, led by the mayor, decide to create their own exit, and so a disparate collection of freeway travellers find themselves in this small town. Much of the script was dedicated to introducing and spending time with these various groups, intercut with the problems faced by the denizens of Ticlaw.

The freeway we could shoot on was a stretch of newly laid, but as yet unused road near the city of Sarasota in Florida. It was to be ready for our use in early spring. I was sent to the area to film the road under construction. For two days I buzzed around in a helicopter, shooting everything that looked faintly interesting, and then got out and did some staged shots, like orange trees felled by bulldozers and anything else that came to mind just in case it was useful. On my return to Los Angeles, John and the others looked at the rushes and thought they were really dull. True. Road construction shots usually are. It all looked like an Industrial documentary. But we figured there were enough bits to use in the credits.

Next, still in pre-production, a larger unit was sent to Salt Lake City. Here we filmed a rhino in a snowbound safari park being caught and shoved into a truck. This could have been fun, but the rhino, who normally lived in a zoo in Los Angeles, was driven up to snowy, chilly Salt Lake City. Here it was housed in a specially heated barn and chased around a field for two days. The animal was supposed to be angry and scary. In the script it did not want to go into the truck. The wranglers were expected to be scared too. In the event, our rhino was unsure of what might be expected and decided to play against character. It did not want to move or scare anyone. All sorts of methods were then employed by the crew to make it move. Cattle prods were brought out. Loud noises were made. But the animal was cold and scared and unused to snow. It sat immobile most of the time.

Meanwhile, the truck driver, played by Paul Jabara, sat in his cab making up songs and singing them, as scripted, and John shot that material while various methods of persuading the poor animal to move were considered. Jabara's material was the easy part to shoot. Getting the rhino into the truck was not, but, having used every resource around, the scene was completed in a general sort of way. I knew it would be necessary to involve some trick to get the beast inside and then for it to burst out again, which the script called for. In the end I resorted to jump cuts. As Ed said, "It was simple to write and hell to shoot." On the third night, the rhino died. Benjy Rosenberg, assistant director, reckoned this was a bad omen. He was right.

We returned to the studio in a somewhat depressed state. We had killed a young rhino for a movie. Ed Clinton was particularly upset.

Having buried the rhino, we then began shooting the movie which was, logistically, horrific. It called for four principal locations. Los Angeles, where we shot mainly in the studio, New York, and two separate locations in Florida.

Shooting got under way in Los Angeles and went smoothly, but the freeway construction was behind schedule, so the New York location would have to be shot first, in the winter. Most of the unit were moved to Manhattan where the weather was cold and wet. Stunts were attempted and failed. The budget began to escalate.

We all had high hopes and were enjoying the work. There was a strong feeling of camaraderie among the crew that I particularly enjoyed. The setting got me out of the cutting room and I felt part of the unit.

By the time we finished in New York, the freeway was still not ready, so our entire circus went to the first location, a small town in the centre of Florida called Mount Dora that had been chosen to be Ticlaw, where much of the film's action took place.

Mount Dora is a sleepy retirement town with an old-fashioned hotel and pool. It also had a lake where Bubbles, the water skiing elephant—another bright idea of Ed Clinton's—was already in training and had become a local tourist attraction. Bubbles was very important in our story and, thankfully, we did not kill her. Gift shops in Mount Dora had been quick to print t-shirts and mugs with Bubbles' picture, creating brisk sales. Bubbles was a star. The shopkeepers had also given permission for the entire Main Street to be painted pink.

John had put me in charge of the second unit, so I was cutting and directing, but the second unit was woefully under equipped. Arthur Wooster came out to join me as cameraman and was very helpful, but it always seemed that the first unit wanted equipment that we also required, and so it became somewhat frustrating.

Ed had written a little scene in which a rabbit was to come from its hole and onto the freeway. In order that the poor animal should not find the tarmac too hot, we were advised to film this at dawn. So a group of grown men were huddled on an unused freeway trying to coax one of many tame rabbits to come out of a manmade rabbit hole and totter onto the tarmac, but none of the rabbits would co-operate. Eventually we all packed up and went off for breakfast. After our experience with the rhino nobody wanted to cause the early demise of another animal.

One unfortunate aspect of being a second unit director is that, at rushes, everyone dumps on your work. It's never what the director would have done himself and so, in front of the whole unit, I would get bad reviews from John, as well as from John Bailey, the cameraman. Bailey would never like my work or the second unit cameraman's either. I decided, after that experience, to forego the pleasure of directing second unit, which some other sucker could handle.

My cutting room in Sarasota was in a dark theatre. We set up our equipment on the stage and also used the theatre to show rushes. I'd got behind in my editing because of always being hauled off to shoot something, such as the opening shot of the picture. Ed had described an idyllic skyline on which a palm tree stood, undisturbed, with only the sounds of the birds. Without warning there is a huge explosion and the tree disintegrates in slow motion. Someone had seen *Apocalypse Now*.

One cloud that hovered over the production period of *Honky Tonk Freeway* was the level of drug use by the crew. It was rumoured that the cocaine used to come in from Technicolor with the rushes, though I have no proof of this. There was, however, plenty of it around. The crew and the actors were not at all unfriendly toward this white powder. I remained blissfully unaware of all this, but have wondered ever since how much Hollywood invested in drugs throughout the sixties and seventies.

John's tantrums were another feature of the shoot. He'd have screaming rows if things weren't exactly as he wanted them. One morning he had a complete meltdown with the people doing the props. We were all there, waiting for a rehearsal. The knives and forks or the plates or some detail wasn't right and John went off like a rocket, screaming at the top of his voice. He was up a ladder looking down on all these people and he ranted for ten minutes solid. He was like that. Then he would settle down and everything would be normal again.

By now I had lost my British cameraman and was given a very capable and pleasant substitute from Miami who was young, with a wife and child. Two weeks after filming for me, he was tragically killed in a car wreck. It was as if the omens were stacking up around us. Shooting carried on as the production fell further behind schedule and the budget continued to soar. We all returned to Los Angeles and filmed the interiors.

The sets were designed by Ferdinando Scarfiotti who, apart from being Italian and brilliant, was also extremely expensive. You could have lived in the sets. Don Boyd, always an enthusiast, would watch rushes and announce that the movie would make $80 million. Such pronouncements by producers have always made me uneasy.

Perhaps I should have taken more notice of my American crew. When we were still shooting and they were looking at rushes, it was clear they found the film totally unfunny. I took this to be the difference between British and American humour. I would sit and giggle at a scene which left them staring, stony faced.

Lavish parties were also part of the fun and we seemed to find occasions for parties wherever we went, all of which I assume went onto the budget along with the recreational substances.

John and I didn't properly see the rough cut until we were back in London. We held a private screening at the Fox theatre in Soho Square. John had flown in from Los Angeles and my assistant, Bryan Oates, and I got set up in the screening room. We waited for what must have been almost an hour but there was no sign of John. Finally Bryan went off to the loo and returned a few minutes later to say he'd seen John and Howard Koch Jr in the lavatory, laughing their heads off. They came out and sat down and we ran the film. If I recall correctly, nobody laughed at anything except for John and Howard who laughed at everything, loudly, all through the film. It's Bryan's recollection that this was the first time we both realised that the film was in trouble.

Bryan Oates:

I realised early in my career that there were great editors and there were editors. I'd got Jim marked out as one of the great editors and, he became a target—if I could ever get near him, I would. One day I went to work as a fill in on *Agatha*. I took the job for a week and so got my first chance to get close to Jim but couldn't. He was too grand, too involved, for me to approach. He will say that's not true, that he's available to everyone, but

I didn't dare go into his room. The next thing that happened was that I made friends with Jim's sound editor and was taken onto the sound side for a little while on *Yanks.* During that time, I made friends with Jim's first assistant who I found out was going to leave Jim to work with Dede Allen on *Reds* and that there would be an opening. With that knowledge, I bided my time. Then I heard that Jim was making a film in America with John. All this time I was working as a first assistant editor on other pictures. I rang him and talked to him. He said, "Well, I've got your details. I know you." By then I had a reputation. We all get reputations. "I'll be honest with you," he said. "We're shooting the film in America. I'm taking an American assistant while I'm over there but call me in August when I'm back and I'll be very happy to use you." So August came and I made sure I was available. I rang his home again and got Laurence, his wife, who said, "Yes, I would like to see you because I'm a French editor and I'm coming back into the cutting rooms. I'm going to be Jim's first." That was a slight downer for me. "But," she said "You can be my second if we like each other, so come around to the house." That was the start of a friendship that has been deep and true for both Jim and Laurence with me and my family for a long, long time.

I thought, "I so want to work with this man, it's taken me so long, that I'll go and join his wife. I'll come down a peg and be the second on it." And that's what I did.

I worked with John Schlesinger in the cutting room. I got to know about his fantastic rages and his equally fantastic respect for Jim. I saw John rage to the point of being arrested if there'd been a policeman nearby, but he never lost his temper with Jim. And I can still see the two of them with Jim being taller than John, standing at the bench together with John looking up to him in more ways than physical. He'd be saying, "Well what are we going to do about this? This is terrible! It's not going to work!" And Jim saying, "John, it will work. Just give me a minute and I'll show you." John totally relied on Jim. He'd chosen Jim because he knew he would attend to his material and would understand it. And Jim did everything he could to keep *Honky Tonk Freeway* on its legs. But, sadly, it had its legs shot out from under it.

One day Jim said, "John, I'm fed up with you. I've got things to do here. You and Bryan go down to the end of the corridor and take those wretched LPs and listen to them and choose some music. I can't be bothered with you. You're getting in my way." I thought this was wonderful. I'm

with this famous director to help him choose music. Of course, I didn't.
I let John play them. I didn't dare open my mouth. When we got back to
the room I'd formed some sort of relationship with John and after that we
were able to talk to each other. I felt very at ease with him. One day we
were talking about his films in general in the cutting room. John was saying, "Oh, that was a disaster!" I asked what film he was talking about. He
said, *"Far From the Madding Crowd."* I said, "John, I think that's the best
film you've made to date." That put me straight to the back of the class
because John looked at me as if I didn't know what I was talking about or
where I'd come from. I haven't altered my opinion. That film wears. I don't
think anyone's gotten closer to Hardy than John with that piece.

It had always been planned that we would edit and mix *Honky Tonk* in London,
so we ended up at Cherrill's in Dean Street, edited the film, and then returned to
Los Angeles at some point to show the picture to various people and record Elmer
Bernstein's score.

Elmer was a very nice man. I first met him on *Midnight Cowboy* when his girlfriend was the production secretary and I used to go out with them in New York.
He affected a very British accent because his girlfriend was British and I think his
wife was too. He was a great fellow to have around. But I always felt, like all these
composers, that they had themes and scores and melodies in some bottom drawer
that they would bring out when required.

When I last worked with Elmer he said, "I need at least two weeks to look at
the film over and over again and then determine what I am going to write. I find
the themes and find the movie and sort of dig deep . . ." and he'd go on and on
about it. A terrible old act it was and I always felt that, behind all this bluff, as
soon as we'd left the room he'd say, "All right, we'll have theme number four that
I wrote in the fifties for another film and we never used it. So why don't we try
that one out?"

There would be this long silence from Elmer. Then finally he would say, "I've
found the film. I've found the theme. Why don't we go with this? Tell me what
you think?" And then he'd play it and it would be something wonderful. He knew
exactly how to play the game. Elmer was an extremely good actor. A bit of a ham
but an actor nevertheless.

However, Elmer had no trouble finding a theme for *Honky Tonk Freeway*. It was
a combination of score and some pop songs that were written for the film. Because
the movie has been so denigrated over the years, one has sort of forgotten it, but if
you listen to Elmer's opening march, it's terrific. It works. It's like a Sousa march.

At about this time, EMI began to appear rocky. Their films, apart from *The Deerhunter*, had not performed, and *Honky Tonk Freeway* was the latest potential financial disaster. The Los Angeles screening was the first to give us warning that perhaps it was not quite what we hoped. I began to wonder if my American crew had been right all along. Friends in Los Angeles who were normally excited and effusive over John's work were looking the other way. Some were wondering why he was making a movie like this, so the writing was on the wall. I guess we were oblivious because we took little notice of these signs and still thought it a good and amusing movie. Somehow we had contrived to make a film that only appealed to a tiny few.

Then EMI Films folded and all their product, still in the pipeline, was taken over, sight unseen, by Universal.

We were all feeling very self-assured about our movie, so much so that we'd actually cut negative. However, the late Gerry Humphreys, who had mixed all of John's films, was not amused. Our first screening for the film's new owners was one afternoon at the Hitchcock Theatre at Universal. All the heads of departments and the executives were there and they filled the theatre with secretaries and invited people. As soon as it started to roll, I realised that we were in trouble because the first scene that should get laughs got nothing. The second scene that should get laughs got nothing either. *They didn't laugh at a single thing.* This movie died in front of us and nobody quite knew what to say at the end. There was dead silence. There was no applause. The audience simply filed out. I was up in the circle. John was down below and the executives surrounded him. They accused him of making a film that was not only extremely unfunny but was also anti-American, which in our wildest dreams, we'd never imagined. It was, after all, written by an American. "How could you have that dead woman's ashes trampled into a shag carpet?"

Ned Tanen was a friend of John's and both he and Sid Sheinberg stood there attacking him vocally. Laurence and I could hear all this going on and we went to the front of the gallery. Looking down, all we could see was John's bald head, glistening with sweat and these people shouting at him in a very savage way. John was mute. The screening had been so unsuccessful that Laurence and I left without speaking to John.

The following night we were supposed to have a public preview and the studio disallowed this. The next morning we went to John's house and he said he'd decided to have a preview anyway. He thought he'd been very poorly treated and he was very angry indeed about the way they had reacted. They'd misunderstood the film and he didn't get a chance to defend himself. He did at that stage, rather unwisely, refer to Ned Tanen, who had been a friend, as "a fucking Nazi." The end of a beautiful friendship.

We took the film to Seattle the following day and, because it had been disallowed by Universal, we retitled it. Howard Koch called it *Stops Along the Way* and all the cans had to be renamed. We all flew to Seattle under pseudonyms because we didn't want anybody to know what we were doing and we ran the film that night in Seattle at the University cinema that was used by a lot of younger people and, although they didn't actively dislike the film, they obviously didn't like it well enough to give us a good report.

The following day Universal found out what we'd done, and they weren't terribly happy with that. Verna Fields, however, once again came to the rescue and suggested we should recut the film and take it out for preview properly. This meant getting all the sound, all the trims, everything from London over to Los Angeles and we worked on the film with John and with Verna.

Every weekend for six weeks we previewed again and we went down each time. You couldn't go on previewing a stiff film and, so, it ended up not as good as it had been in its original form. We were on film in those days. We weren't digital so we couldn't keep everything and, as a result, we could never get back to the original. Finally, after a last preview in Chicago, *Honky Tonk Freeway* was put to bed. It was now a shadow of its former self.

This film, sadly, was the last time John and I ever worked together. On a happier note, and years later, I have to say that *Honky Tonk Freeway*, despite being a ravaged film, still has its supporters and is available on DVD. Rent it from Netflix or LoveFilm or buy it from Amazon.

Privates on Parade

Privates on Parade was a film that came out of the blue. I knew Simon Relph who was producing it. Simon had been an assistant director and we'd worked together on *Yanks*. I had seen the play, which I'd enjoyed a lot, and the film was to be directed by the same man, Michael Blakemore. Michael was really a stage director and also was an actor and a writer. I was very happy to do the film because I liked the material. I enjoyed Peter Nichols' writing and I loved Denis King's songs.

The script was okay, but because of the financing of the film, they were unable to do any of the jungle material in an actual jungle. It all had to be done in England on the cheap and I fear it suffered from that low budget aspect.

Privates on Parade was produced by HandMade. Denis O'Brien was the boss of HandMade at the time and the money for it was largely George Harrison's. Denis

O'Brien was an American who had been a banker and was in love with English comedy films, specifically Ealing comedies, which he'd grown up with. He was also very enthusiastic about John Cleese and insisted on involving him in the film. John Cleese, however, had not been in the play.

Blakemore did a good workmanlike job on the film and was well advised by the people around him but, somehow or other, it was never quite as funny as it should have been and, in post-production, Denis O'Brien decided to inflate Cleese's role. So we did additional shooting. Possibly two or three days at Shepperton in order that Cleese should have more business to do. Denis even persuaded him into doing some silly walks which, he thought, foolishly, would make the film more commercial. This was all slightly over Blakemore's dead body. There were rows. The relationship between Blakemore and Denis O'Brien became very bad and Simon Relph was in the middle of it all as, indeed, was I.

Bryan Oates:

Jim asked me to be his main assistant on *Privates on Parade,* so off we went to Shepperton. I was concentrating on my work so I didn't get involved with the politics, but I do remember when we got a call saying that John Cleese was coming into the cutting room to make the film funny. One can imagine how well that went down with the director, who decided he wouldn't be there when John came in. Jim was not very pleased either. John did come in and there was an uncomfortable two hours on the Steenbeck. I think there was a frisson between Jim and John or one of them felt uneasy with the other. I suspect they both felt uneasy with each other. We went through the motions for the afternoon and Jim did John's notes but I don't think it made the film much funnier.

At the end they did a big Monty Python piece quite out of character with the film with John Cleese marching around and all the other characters falling over and doing silly things and showing bare bottoms.

They decided they'd split the screen. They had a union jack that would split into eight pieces and there would be live action going on to the music and they were singing to it. The film wasn't a big one so they said they'd only got so many thousand pounds for this optical. Once. It couldn't be made twice. We'd have to get it right. Jim threw it over his shoulder to me and said "Right. You can do that." And this was my test. I went, on my knees, to the labs, and told them my situation and they said, "Righto Bryan. We will all get together on this. We'll get it right for you." They did and it's in the film. My hands were sweating when it arrived in the cutting

room. The first and only print and negative of this optical. I think I would
not have been working with Jim again if they'd had to remake it.

We previewed in America, which was a nightmare for me and I'm sure for
Blakemore who had never been to Los Angeles and he'd never been to a preview
so he didn't quite know what he was in for. We were to preview in a shopping mall
somewhere near San Diego. I drove the film down myself along the Pacific Coast
Highway in the middle of the most horrific rainstorm. I could barely see where I
was driving.

I eventually arrived for a rehearsal entirely alone. I found the theatre and
went in. The projectionist asked what I was doing there and I said I have to rehearse this film as we're previewing it tonight. It was a married print, which is a
release print. It's a finished film, not double head which we very often previewed
with. With double head, the sound has not yet married up to the picture. Anyway,
he and I ran the film remorselessly.

When we'd finished, I sat in my car until about six thirty that evening, in the
rain and the cold, wondering what in the hell I was doing there and if anyone
would turn up for a preview on a night like this. I'd been recently asked to cut
Gorky Park for Michael Apted and I remember sitting in this car, waiting for a
break in the clouds and thinking about *Gorky Park*, which I had read by now and,
suddenly the heavens opened, the clouds parted and there was a shaft of light that
beamed down and seemed to clarify my predicament. I didn't ever want to be
back in a car park in America and therefore I didn't want to do *Gorky Park*. I felt
it was not God's intention that I should be anywhere near films in America at
that point.

Eventually, Michael turned up with Denis O'Brien, looking for an audience
that never arrived, so we abandoned the preview completely and went off to have
a meal. I'd been through all that for nothing. Obviously I'd seen the film a million
times by now. Eventually Denis O'Brien decided that we should preview in West-
wood, which is the University area of Los Angeles and he thought that, because
of John Cleese's name and the success of the Pythons, he'd get a good audience.
Well he got a packed house because it was a Saturday night, but they didn't really
respond to the film at all. It was a fairly miserable reaction that both bemused Michael Blakemore and depressed him. Of course he was already depressed anyway
by being in Los Angeles which he hated.

Denis O'Brien, who was about to make another film with a team of Canadian television comics, organised a party after the preview at his house and I drove
Michael there. At the party absolutely nobody spoke to Michael. No one came up

to him and said anything about the film. It was as if we were total pariahs. Our film was seen to have failed, so, after about half an hour of this unpleasantness, Michael said to me, "I can't bear it another minute. Please take me back to Chateau Marmont."

The film got fairly respectable reviews. It didn't do much business and when I look at it again I realise that, as a film, it didn't really quite work. As a stage production it had been stylised and worked well. Denis Quilley was wonderful in both the play and the film but in the play he'd been the lead and because of John Cleese, Quilley's part suffered. I also think that Denis O'Brien was disturbed by the homosexuality of Quilley's character.

Before I left Los Angeles, I called Verna Fields' office at Universal. She was not there. Her secretary told me that Verna was in the hospital. She had breast cancer and was not expected to live. "I'll tell her you called. Perhaps she'll talk to you." So I got to say goodbye to Verna, whose voice was weak but the humour and the outrage, which had pulled us through some bad times, was still there, intact. Verna was always a larger than life character, and remained so until she died. I still miss her.

These two films took a great deal out of me and I was saddened by the prospect of not working with John again. The immediate future, however, held a new professional relationship for me and this time it was with a producer rather than a director.

1951

Entered film industry as cutting room trainee at Ealing Studios. Became first assistant editor and worked on many Ealing pictures including, *The Cruel Sea, The Lady-killers,* and *Barnacle Bill.* After the closure of Ealing Studios went freelance and was assistant editor on various films including *Prince and the Showgirl* and *Indiscreet.*

Jim cutting *The Grass Is Greener.* Cribbing Eisenstein again? Photo, Peter Musgrave.

On the set of *The Grass Is Greener,* Stanley Donen, Deborah Kerr and Cary Grant watch a royal event on TV with the crew.

1960

Film editor, *Surprise Package* (Columbia) directed by Stanley Donen with Yul Brynner and Mitzi Gaynor.

Film editor, *The Grass Is Greener* (Universal) directed by Stanley Donen with Cary Grant, Deborah Kerr, Jean Simmons, and Robert Mitchum.

During the filming of *The Innocents,* one of the crew presents a gift to Deborah Kerr while director Jack Clayton and Jim Clark look on.

1961

Film editor, *The Innocents* (Fox) directed by Jack Clayton with Deborah Kerr.

Film editor, *Term of Trial* (Warner) directed by Peter Glenville with Laurence Olivier, Simone Signoret, and Sarah Miles.

1962

Film editor, *Charade* (Universal) directed by Stanley Donen with Audrey Hepburn and Cary Grant.

1963

Film editor, *The Pumpkin Eater* (Columbia) directed by Jack Clayton with James Mason, Anne Bancroft, and Peter Finch.

1964

Film editor, *Darling* (Anglo-Amalgamated) directed by John Schlesinger with Julie Christie, Dirk Bogarde, and Laurence Harvey.

1968

Editorial consultant, *Midnight Cowboy* (UA) directed by John Schlesinger with Dustin Hoffman and John Voight.

A naked Marty Feldman emerges from a lake while director Jim Clark confers during filming of *Every Home Should Have One*.

Jim Clark and John Schlesinger scout locations for *Darling*.

1970

Director, *Every Home Should Have One* (British Lion) produced by Ned Sherrin with Marty Feldman and Judy Cornwell.

Film editor, *Zee & Co.* (Columbia) directed by Brian Hutton with Elizabeth Taylor, Michael Caine, and Susannah York.

Jim Clark and Marty Feldman during filming of *Every Home Should Have One*.

1971

Director, *Rentadick* (Rank) produced by Ned Sherrin with James Booth, Richard Briers, and Julie Ege.

Jim Clark on set of *Rentadick,* which he directed.

John Schlesinger and Jim Clark viewing footage.

1972

Co-director and editor, *Visions of Eight* (The Marathon) co-directed with John Schlesinger and produced by David Wolper.

1973

Director, *Madhouse* (AIP) produced by Milton Subotsky and Max Rosenberg with Vincent Price and Peter Cushing.

1974

Film editor, *The Day of the Locust* (Paramount) directed by John Schlesinger with Donald Sutherland, William Atherton, Burgess Meredith, and Karen Black.

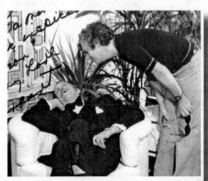

Director Jim Clark observes a sleeping Vincent Price on the set of *Madhouse.*

Guests around John Schlesinger's pool during the filming of *The Day Of The Locust.*

1975

Film editor, *The Adventures of Sherlock Holmes' Smarter Brother* (Fox) directed by Gene Wilder with Gene Wilder, Madeline Kahn, and Marty Feldman.

Gene Wilder and Jim Clark view rushes during the shooting of *Sherlock Holmes' Smarter Brother.*

1976

Film editor, *Marathon Man* (Paramount) directed by John Schlesinger with Dustin Hoffman, Laurence Olivier, Roy Scheider, William Devane, and Marthe Keller.

1977

Film editor, *The Last Remake of Beau Geste* (Universal) directed by Marty Feldman with Marty Feldman, Ann-Margret, Michael York, and Peter Ustinov.

1978

Film editor, *Agatha* (Warner) directed by Michael Apted with Vanessa Redgrave and Dustin Hoffman.

Film editor, *Yanks* (Universal) directed by John Schlesinger with Vanessa Redgrave and Richard Gere.

Jim Clark and John Schlesinger discussing the screenplay for *Yanks.*

1979

Film editor and second unit director, *Honky Tonk Freeway* (Universal) directed by John Schlesinger with William Devane, Beau Bridges, Beverly D'Angelo, Hume Cronyn, and Jessica Tandy.

John Schlesinger on the set of *Honky Tonk Freeway* the day the rhino was killed.

John Cleese and Denis King with unknown pianist.

1982

Film editor, *Privates on Parade* (HandMade) directed by Michael Blakemore with John Cleese and Denis Quilley.

1983

Film editor, *The Killing Fields* (Warner) directed by Roland Joffé with Sam Waterston, Haing Ngor, John Malcovich, and Julian Sands. (1984 Academy Award for Best Film Editing)

Jim Clark wakes up with his 1984 Oscar for *The Killing Fields* at the Schmidts' house.

The Killing Fields editing crew, Bryan Oates, Jim Clark, Ann Sopel (photo by Max Vadakul).

1984

Film editor, *The Frog Prince* (Warner) directed by Brian Gilbert with Jane Snowden and Alexandre Sterling.

Director Roland Joffé working with composer/conductor Ennio Morricone while recording the soundtrack for *The Mission*.

Jim shakes hands with Prince Charles at the premiere of *The Mission*.

1986-87

Senior Vice President, Production, Columbia Pictures, Burbank, California.

Jim Clark with Franco Zeffirelli in Positano during *The Young Toscanini*.

1985

Film editor, *The Mission* (Warner) directed by Roland Joffé with Robert De Niro and Jeremy Irons (American Academy Nomination and 1986 BAFTA winner for Film Editing).

Jim Clark at Columbia Pictures with one of the first digital editing machines—the Ediflex.

1988

Film editor with Bryan Oates, *The Young Toscanini* directed by Franco Zeffirelli with Elizabeth Taylor.

1989

Film editor, *The Memphis Belle* (Warner) directed by Michael Caton-Jones with Matthew Modine and Eric Stoltz (Guild of British Film Editors Award)

David Puttnam and Michael Caton Jones on the set of *Memphis Belle*.

1990

Film editor, *Meeting Venus* (Warner) directed by István Szabó with Glenn Close and Niels Arestrup.

Jim Clark and David Puttnam with editing crew of *Meeting Venus*.

1992

Film editor, *This Boy's Life* (Warner) directed by Michael Caton-Jones with Robert De Niro, Ellen Barkin, and Leonardo DiCaprio.

1993

Film editor, *Radio Inside* (MGM/Showtime) directed by Jeff Bell with William McNamara, Elisabeth Shue, and Dylan Walsh.

Film editor, *A Good Man in Africa* (Universal) directed by Bruce Beresford with Colin Friels and Sean Connery.

1994

Film editor, *Nell* (Fox/Polygram) directed by Michael Apted with Jodie Foster and Liam Neeson.

1995–96

Film editor with Alan Heim, *Copycat* (New Regency/Warner) directed by Jon Amiel with Sigourney Weaver and Holly Hunter.

Film editor, *Marvin's Room* (Miramax) directed by Jerry Zaks with Diane Keaton, Meryl Streep, Robert de Niro, and Leonardo DiCaprio.

Scott Rudin on the telephone in Jim Clark's editing suite on *Marvin's Room*.

1997

Film editor, *The Jackal* (Universal) directed by Michael Caton-Jones with Bruce Willlis and Richard Gere.

While on location shooting *The Jackal,* Jim's editing team took over a disused hairdressing salon and here's Jim under the drier.

1998

Film editor, *Onegin* directed by Martha Fiennes with Ralph Fiennes and Liv Tyler.

Film editor with Laurence Méry-Clark, *The Trench* directed by William Boyd with Paul Nicholls and Daniel Craig.

1999

Film editor, *The World Is Not Enough* (MGM/AU) directed by Michael Apted with Pierce Brosnan, Sophie Marceau, and Robert Carlyle.

Jim Clark editing *The World Is Not Enough* on the Avid at Pinewood.

2000

Film editor, *Kiss Kiss (Bang Bang)* directed by Stewart Sugg with Stellan Skarsgård, Martine McCutcheon, and Chris Penn.

2001

Film editor, *City by the Sea* (Warner) directed by Michael Caton-Jones with Robert De Niro and Frances McDormand.

2002–2003

Film editor, *The Gathering Storm* (HBO/BBC) directed by Richard Loncraine with Albert Finney and Vanessa Redgrave.

2003–2004

Film editor, *Vera Drake* (New Line/Fine Line) directed by Mike Leigh with Imelda Staunton and Phil Davis.

Film editor, *Opal Dream (*also known as *Pobby and Dingan)* directed by Peter Cattaneo.

The poster for *Vera Drake* at the Venice Film Festival.

Gavin Buckley and Mike Leigh during music recording of *Vera Drake.*

2005

Film editor, *Virgin Territory* (also known as *Decameron: Angels & Virgins)* directed by David Leland with Hayden Christensen and Mischa Barton.

Imelda Staunton, Phil Davis, and Mike Leigh meet the press in Venice for *Vera Drake.*

2007

Film editor, *Happy-Go-Lucky* (Momentum/Miramax) directed by Mike Leigh with Sally Hawkins and Eddie Marsan.

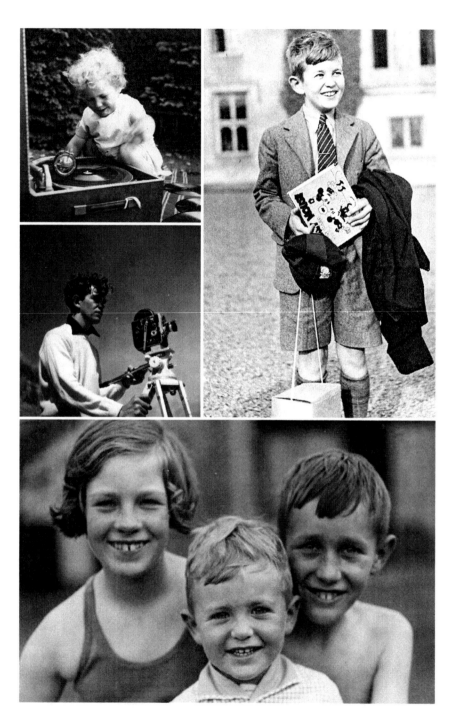

Clockwise from upper left: A very young Jim Clark with a windup gramophone; Young Jim Clark on his first day at Nevill Holt school; Sister Hazel, Jim Clark, and brother Dick in Boston, (ca.1935); A young Jim Clark shooting film in Ireland.

"While we were in Westchester—on a whim, mind you—Harold and I turned in to a drive-in movie and saw 'Honky Tonk Freeway.' It ruined our August."

Clockwise from top: A cartoon in *The New Yorker* about *Honky Tonk Freeway;* Stanley Donen from a ***Vanity Fair*** article; Bryan Oates and Jim Clark attack *The Killing Fields.*

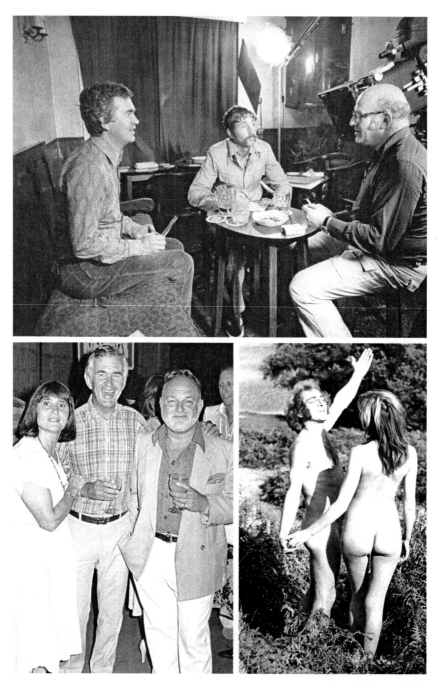

Clockwise from top: *Visions Of Eight*–Jim Clark and Schlesinger interview Ron Hill, marathon runner; Marty Feldman and Julie Ege during shooting of *Every Home Should Have One;* Jim with Laurence and John at one of the many *Honky Tonk Freeway* parties.

Clockwise from top left: David, Kate, and Jim with chimpanzee on PG Tips commercial; John Schlesinger on the set of *Yanks*; John Schlesinger and Jim Clark on the set of *Yanks*.

Clockwise from top left: Laurence Méry-Clark cutting film on *Honky Tonk Freeway;* At Jim and Laurence's wedding: Laurence Méry-Clark, Jim Clark, Jack Clayton; Ken Levison at the time of *Madhouse*.

Top: Jim Clark's daughter Sybil with Vincent Price during the filming of *Madhouse*. Bottom: Not long before John Schlesinger's death in Los Angeles. From left; Michael York, John Schlesinger, Jim Clark, and Michael Childers.

Back row (left to right): David Clark, Lucy Clark, Kate McNee, Jackson Caines. Front row (left to right): Jess Clark, Laurence Méry-Clark, Jim Clark, Dylan Caines, Sybil Caines, David Caines.

THE KILLING FIELDS AND THE MISSION

The Killing Fields

If an editor has a good working relationship with a director, he'll probably get involved in the pre-production of a film. Usually with John Schlesinger, I would be involved with the script early on and go through various versions with him but often what happens is that you're sent a script through the mail by your agent and asked to read with a view to cutting it. This happens to me a lot. Often I'm not interested in scripts and read them up to a point, then throw them aside. It's never wise to tackle a film if you don't like the script. If you read it and say yes, then you meet the director. If that meeting goes well and you feel you have a mutual understanding of the script and want to work together, then you may proceed. That happened to me on *The Killing Fields*. I only read it once and immediately knew that I wanted to get involved because I liked the script. I then met Roland Joffé who didn't know me at all. It was David Puttnam's suggestion that I should cut the film. Puttnam never actually called me himself. I had a call from Iain Smith who was the associate producer, asking me if I was interested. I knew Puttnam vaguely from *Agatha* but we had not been particularly close and I certainly hadn't seen much of him. I went to David's office for my meeting with Roland and we talked briefly about the script and about the film because he was about to go off to Bangkok to actually make it. So you could say I was imposed on him.

The script, by Bruce Robinson, was fascinating and written in an odd style that was not at all like a regular screenplay but more like an article written on speed. It was fuelled with passion and I could see straight away that, if it was well made, it would be an absolutely cracking, emotional film.

Before they left for Bangkok it was decided by David that the cutting room should be in London where the negative would be. So the film would be shot in Bangkok and Thailand posing for Cambodia but the rushes would be processed at Kay's in London.

David said that, since I would be the first person to actually see this material, I had to phone him in Bangkok as soon as I'd seen it and give him a report. "Be absolutely fearless," he told me. "Don't just say nice things to me. Whatever you feel you must say." So I did and the very first scene they shot was outside a cafe. Malkovich and Waterston are sitting, having a coffee and a bomb goes off. David phoned me after that and said, "Well, we did the first day and we nearly killed the actor," because the special effects people had got too close to Sam on take five and the fire had actually singed him. It was a very tricky moment for everybody and that was the take we finally used in the film.

I wasn't, however, concerned about the look, but more the way that Sam Waterston was playing the part. Bryan Oates was my assistant again and, while we were viewing the rushes, he said he wasn't convinced that this guy was a hardened war reporter. I didn't get that as quickly as Bryan, but I did say to Puttnam on the phone, as I'd been instructed, "Sam Waterston doesn't seem to be playing the role right. He seems to be too weak and soft." Naturally enough when Puttnam reported back to Roland Joffé that I had made these rather critical remarks, Roland wasn't very pleased because he didn't really know me and why should he take comments about the acting from the film editor? It's not something we editors normally do. We don't critique the acting, perhaps as much as we should, but this was a special case because we were some distance away from one another. I never spoke to Roland directly. I only spoke to David.

Things went on and after about a month of material coming in, Waterston's performance greatly improved. Whatever I had said and whatever Roland thought about my remarks, he did obviously communicate to Sam that he needed to be more convincing as a professional war reporter.

I thought the look of the material was very good but I was critical of Roland's interest in master shots and not in cover. The master shots were very well done but he failed to cover in closeups and various other angles, so I asked for more cover. Particularly with the evacuation of Phnomh Penh sequence. That was shot in a day using several thousand local people as extras. They'd walked them down a working railway line in Bangkok and as soon as the train appeared, they had to clear the tracks, so they only had time to do four takes during the day. This was covered by two cameras, so that I got quite a bit of material, though the light changed quite radically between each take. I put it all together and it was very long. Each take was a good ten minutes and we obviously couldn't have a sequence that long. So I told Puttnam I really needed close cover to make this work and to shorten it. Roland was, apparently, extremely unhappy about having to do additional shots because the editor had requested them and, although we never spoke, we seemed to be developing a dodgy kind of relationship.

The long-distance tension between Roland and me was only sharpened by a request from Warner Brothers and Puttnam that I should cut together a showreel of twenty minutes duration from the rushes I had and take it to Hollywood to show them. The studio was concerned about the cost and the quality of the film of which they hadn't seen anything. So I cut together as jazzy a showreel as I could to make it look big, noisy, and credible, then I flew from London to Los Angeles and showed it on a Sunday morning in Terry Semel's home. They'd gathered a lot of Warner Brothers people there and they thought it was wonderful. From there I went on to meet Puttnam in Hong Kong where we ran it for the Southeast Asian exhibitors. It went down remarkably well. They were very impressed by it and Puttnam was happy. Then it was on to Bangkok.

I was staying at the Oriental Hotel where Roland was. I arrived the day before they were due to shoot the additional cover I'd asked for, so I phoned Roland's room and I spoke to him, saying, "I'm here and I'll come out with you in the morning when you're shooting this stuff." He was very low key on the phone and I thought there was something wrong. He said if I wanted to come, he'd see me in the lobby at six o'clock the following morning, which was a Sunday. I went down to the lobby at six and he wasn't there. He never turned up. He'd obviously slipped through another entrance. I thought about this, then took a cab out to the location where Roland was directing pickup shots. At lunchtime everybody sat down outside to eat and Roland still didn't want to talk to me. One of the actors was having a party that night because he was leaving the film and I learned that Roland would be there, so I talked my way into this party and, because I'd had a few drinks, I had the temerity to go up to Roland. "Now look," I said. "You and I can't go on like this. We've got a film to make and we've got to get on. I'm doing my best and you're not talking to me." At which point, our relationship somehow changed. I don't know quite what happened but Roland suddenly decided I was all right and that I wasn't against him. I wasn't fighting him and that whatever I was requesting I was doing for a good reason. From that point on, our relationship was fine. We never had another problem and we actually got on extremely well. So well that we did a second film together.

Chris Menges, who was the cameraman on *The Killing Fields*, didn't seem to get on with Roland too well. They had quite a number of rows. Nothing was ever quite right for Chris. Roland's great good fortune was that he had a wonderful camera operator in Mike Roberts who sadly died young. Mike was a brilliant operator and, although Chris would light the scene, it was Joffé and Mike Roberts and Bill Westley, the foul-mouthed and brilliant first assistant director who created the action.

There was a lot of movement in the film in spite of the fact that we had long dialogue scenes between Sam and Haing Ngor. Haing wasn't an actor. He'd been through the Cambodian genocide and he'd lost his girlfriend in what became known, through the film, as the Killing Fields. They'd had a lot of problems trying to find somebody to play the role of Dith Pran. That had gone on a long time before I joined the film. Haing was finally found practising medicine in the Cambodian colony in San Diego and Roland was extremely lucky to find him. Rather than straightforward acting, Haing was reliving his life. His English started off being pretty bad and we looped his entire part with him more than once. Ian Fuller, who did a great job on the soundtrack, recorded every word that Haing said in post-sync so it was just understandable enough for the Western audience.

Someone who came into the Puttnam fold during the shooting period was an Italian, Uberto Pasolini. Uberto was not related to the famous director, but he went one better by being a Count who was related to Visconti. He had been a banker and wanted to go into movies and tried to get a job on *The Killing Fields*. He was interviewed by Puttnam who realised that Uberto was very keen but there was no opening for him, even as a runner, therefore he was rejected. Uberto, however, is a very persistent person and when Puttnam arrived in Bangkok, he presented himself on the set looking for work. He had paid his way there and was quite determined to work on the film. David was so impressed by Uberto's persistence and his tenacity that he took him on and Uberto became the unit runner and stayed with Puttnam for many films thereafter.

Puttnam had decided that the score for *The Killing Fields* should be written by Mike Oldfield. Mike wasn't a film composer, but he'd had a huge success with his album *Tubular Bells*. When we'd put the film together in its long form, we ran it for Mike and he was very impressed. He then requested a videotape, so we gave him one. This first cut was endlessly long, four hours at that point. Roland actually had additional shooting to do, so he went off to America and one day, about three or four weeks later, Mike Oldfield called saying the score was ready. Iain Smith and I were somewhat horrified to hear this because we realised that Mike had not spotted the film at all with Roland or me or anybody. He'd simply taken the tape of the long version, which we thought was simply for him to look at, and he'd scored it at home on his synthesiser. He invited Iain and me to his house in Denham. The film started. It was projected on the wall in his studio. This music began and it went on for four hours. He'd scored the entire film, albeit with a synthesiser, but nevertheless scored. When we told him the film was not actually fine cut yet and that, therefore his music wouldn't fit, he resigned from the movie. Puttnam was very anxious that this shouldn't happen. Richard Branson was the agent looking after Mike's professional life and somehow or other Mike was persuaded back onto the film. When Roland and I had completed the cut, we went through the proper hoops, which we always do, of running the film with the composer and stopping and deciding where the music sections should be and so on. In the end, I did manage to use quite a lot of his original score. It was electronic and very mixable. You could lay it up and play with it.

By the time of the final scoring, Mike had moved to Switzerland and we all went over there. We also involved another composer, David Bedford, because Mike didn't write music. He had no idea how to write anything down and Puttnam had decided that we needed, apart from the synthesised music, some additional score as well. David decided that the emptying of the city should be accompanied by choral music that he called *Requiem for a City* and that was written by David Bedford.

The editing of *The Killing Fields* took a while because the film was too long and the construction was difficult. Roland had shot the film extremely well but there was just too much material. He had to go back to Bangkok on two occasions with a small unit and Haing Ngor to shoot some patch-up stuff. Then he also went to America and Canada where they shot all the material of Schanberg back home which was the second half of the film. There was a tremendous amount of material of Schanberg visiting his father that was subsequently cut entirely from the film.

The sequence involving the evacuation of the city in big helicopters was shot half in Bangkok and the reverses were done in San Diego, which must have made life extremely difficult for everybody. When Haing Ngor is putting his wife and family on the helicopter, he's in Bangkok, but then when they go toward the helicopters which eventually take off, they are in San Diego. The unit couldn't have used the big helicopters in Bangkok because they weren't there. The marines had them in San Diego.

When we finally put the film together, the very last shoot of *The Killing Fields* was done at Beaconsfield at the National Film School. We'd decided that we needed another scene with Haing Ngor and Sam Waterston. This was months after we had completed the shoot and Sam had shaved off his beard. This was a problem for the makeup and hair artists because they had to recreate his beard. We did various pickups and all sorts of little shots in the countryside around Beaconsfield, which doubled for Cambodia quite effectively.

The first preview of the film was at Wimbledon and we lost a lot of the audience. They were walking out which was very unnerving for everybody, especially Roland, who had never been through a preview before. It was quite extraordinary that so many people left and we couldn't figure out quite why. Roland, David, and all the people involved, went off to have a meal at an Italian restaurant but I remained behind, packing the film up with Ian Fuller. We'd done quite an elaborate temp mix of the film and I was talking to Ian about why we'd lost so many people. Thinking it through, I decided that they left because they didn't know quite where they were nor what was happening. I think they mistook Cambodia for Vietnam and they were confused from the start. I joined the rest of the people at the restaurant and we talked about it. "I think we've confused them too soon," I said. "We know the film's too long, but that doesn't seem to be the root problem."

The following morning I went into the cutting room at Elstree and recorded a voiceover on a cassette machine as if it were from Sam Waterston, telling us who he was, where he was and who he was helped by. I then put it up against some shots that I got from various parts of the film and when Roland came in, he took a look at this and agreed that it made things clearer. Of course those words I wrote were rewritten by a number of people and recorded many times, but the idea remained and is still there. We never, in subsequent previews, lost the audience again. We had many other problems of length and compression that took a long time to fix but, happily, the critical response was very good.

David Puttnam came into the cutting room one morning, all huffing and puffing. "I've just had a stress test," he told me. "They have you on this standing bike for about fifteen minutes and then they can tell if you have any heart problems." I listened without too much concern since there was nothing wrong with my heart. Or so I thought. Some weeks later, while recovering from flu, I consulted my doctor and mentioned the stress test. "You want one?" he asked and, next morning, I had it. Nothing seemed wrong, but that night the doctor called me and said I'd better come and see him. I did and he sent me directly to a consultant, who, within days, gave me an angiogram. Sure enough, there was a problem. Three arteries were 75 percent blocked. I felt fine, but the next decision was easy to make, for if I did not undergo a bypass operation, I'd be a ripe candidate for a heart attack. I have always been grateful to Puttnam for suggesting the stress test.

I had the bypass and Bryan Oates looked after the film during my long recovery. I don't suggest a heart bypass if you want a good rest. It was a painful and slow recovery but it saved my life. It was more than thirty years ago, and I'm still here without having had a retread.

When I was fit again, the awards race regarding *The Killing Fields* was underway and several of those who worked on the picture were nominated for the BAFTA award. Having been nominated in the Best Editor capacity, I was invited to a nominee's lunch at BAFTA, which was a crowded event at which I met many old friends, including those nominated in the same category. I had never been connected with an awards ceremony before and this small event was to be the forerunner of a whole slew of luncheons and ceremonies, which peaked at the Oscar ceremony in Los Angeles. Prior to that, however, requests for photographs kept coming in, so I asked the stills man at Shepperton, who was working on *The Doctor and the Devils*, which Laurence was editing, to pop into the cutting room where Bryan and I posed stiffly for some snapshots, taken at the Steenbeck. These were mailed off to the Academy in America for their use in the Oscar brochure.

Visiting Shepperton was like going back to a decaying home. I had worked there steadily through the sixties on films like *The Innocents* and *Darling*. It was a great studio, which then fell prey to takeovers, mismanagement, and collective greed. It almost went under the hammer and much of its fabulous grounds is now covered in homes, an eventuality I had long since predicted. Part of the place, however, remained and the studio was then owned by the Lee Brothers, who were hoping to refurbish and restore it to its former glory. They couldn't, however, replace the backlot that once held the great *Oliver* set and the *Guns of Navarone*. They were gone for good. Much of the budget of *The Doctor and the Devils* had been spent on a large set, representing a Victorian street and pub. It looked great. Sadly the finished version of the film did not measure up to its set, but it kept Laurence busy until summer.

The BAFTA Craft Awards came around and for some reason, I was feeling nervous. Maybe it was the thought of possibly having to get an award from Princess Anne with the television cameras watching. Nobody had briefed us as to how we should behave if we won. Did you, for example, say anything to the assembled brothers or did you just take the pot and run? I was then told that the editing award would be second on the list, so I had little chance to operate by the example of others.

After a short preamble, Jim Cellan-Jones, the BAFTA president, introduced the Princess, who sat alone on one side of the stage. The first winner was announced. This chap accepted his pot from Cellan-Jones and was then introduced to the Princess, who shook his hand and had a short, inaudible, conversation before returning to his seat. I knew my category was next and began to perspire. Laurence gripped my hand. I hardly heard the names of the nominees. Then I heard my name and was up and down the steps without any trouble. The Princess shook my hand and quietly asked me, "How long did it take to make?" This was clearly one of her stock questions, to which I gave a quick reply and returned to my seat, clutching my prize.

After this, there was a flood of awards for *The Killing Fields*, which was most gratifying. The final one went to Chris Menges, who was the only recipient to grab the mike and actually thank his crew. I would have liked to do the same, but since nobody had told us the form, I was uncertain how I should behave. I suppose if everyone had given thanks the poor Princess would have been stuck on the stage for hours.

Afterward we all collected in the foyer for a buffet meal. Laurence and I were chatting with Ian Fuller and Bill Rowe, both award winners, when Alan Marshall sailed up and insisted that I should go and chat with the Princess. I suppose he thought I talked proper and would give no trouble. We found her sitting at a round table, with two empty seats to her left. Cellan-Jones was to her right. Laurence and I introduced ourselves and were seated. I realised we were supposed to eat our first course there and some panic ensued since I had no idea what to discuss with HRH. I ventured to give her some information about *The Killing Fields*, which she clearly hadn't seen, and then recalled that she was very active with the Save the Children Foundation, which seemed relevant. She talked very naturally and easily and I realised that the refugee camps used at the end of *The Killing Fields* would interest her. This evolved into talking about her experiences in India and that led me to ask if she had seen Lean's *Passage to India?* "No," she said. "But I am hoping to see it next week with my Mother." I wonder if she did. Someone once told me that *Rentadick* was the Queen's favourite film but I don't really believe that.

We ploughed our way through some more food as this conversation was held and it occurred to me, as our plates were swept away, that perhaps HRH would prefer to have her dessert with a different couple, since our small talk had worn thin and I didn't really want to return to the subject of *The Killing Fields*. I nudged Laurence and stood up, took my leave, and we retired, thankfully, to the bar. We had done apparently the right thing, for I then saw Marshall leading two other contenders into the ring. I felt rather sorry for the Princess, though goodness knows she must be accustomed to constantly meeting strangers. Then I realised she would be venturing forth again the following Tuesday for the bigger BAFTA evening at the Grosevenor House and all the time she might like to be tucked up at home with her husband and the kids, watching the telly.

Then the main BAFTA awards rolled around and we togged up again for an evening that seemed interminable. David Puttnam had invited us and we were seated at one of the Enigma tables. This year they had flown Kirk Douglas in for the event as well as Sam Waterston and Haing Ngor, who were there to represent *The Killing Fields*. Having already won my award, I felt far more relaxed and was prepared to enjoy the evening, but it was a touch marred by a group at the next table, who turned out to be involved with pop music and were totally disinterested in the film awards, so they talked loudly throughout. *The Killing Fields* did very well with awards until it came to the Best Director category. Wim Wenders received this, which had us all nonplussed and angry. Roland was passed over by the British jury. We were aware that *Paris-Texas* was a good film, but not really in the same league, so, when David went up to collect for Best Picture, he dragged Roland to the stage with him, insisting they should share the honour. Quite right too.

The Frog Prince

After we'd finished *The Killing Fields*, David Puttnam asked me if I would look after a film called *The Frog Prince*. This was shot between *The Killing Fields* and *The Mission*. Iain Smith and Uberto Pasolini produced the film that was directed by Brian Gilbert. It was shot in Paris with a largely French cast but I stayed in London. The film was very soft centered and rather pedestrian. It was never going to be a great movie and fit into the "Love Story" series that Puttnam was making at that time, mostly for television, where this picture really belonged.

Brian Gilbert was an amiable soul. Puttnam always maintained that Gilbert was his favourite director, but I could never really understand the mystique that surrounded him. He was certainly pleasant enough but not really a gifted director.

Bryan Oates assisted me again on this one and has memories of me being very impatient with young Mister Gilbert. Perhaps I was. He did have a tendency to use film school jargon rather than explain what he wanted in plain English.

The scoring of *The Frog Prince* was in itself a rather hard task, not for me, so much, but for the arranger, Richard Myhill, who had been called in at short notice to orchestrate for the Irish singer, Enya, who had composed the themes, but was quite unable to fit anything to the picture. The choice of composer had originally been made and imposed on Brian Gilbert and Iain Smith by David Puttnam. Enya had been with the group called Clannard, whom everyone but I had heard of, and came with her manager Nicky who clearly saw great riches lying ahead for both of them.

Through the good offices of George Martin, who did not want the job himself, Myhill was found just before Christmas 1984. Because he had never been involved in the scoring of a feature, being almost exclusively into jingles and library music, he was hungry for a credit and, therefore, set to work with a will. He saved our bacon in the process.

All of us met at Myhill's home near Amersham on Boxing Day to discuss the cues. We were right in the middle of all that while retakes were being shot at Lee Studios. Puttnam had decided that these were required to flesh out this rather limp romantic story. These new scenes involved flying the two boys in from abroad, putting up a couple of sets, and getting a crew together. Bryan and I attended with a Moviola, so that Brian Gilbert and the new cameraman Barry Noakes could see how to match the shots. Just why David Puttnam wanted to extend a film that was already a clear nonstarter was a bit of a mystery. We thought it a case of hurling good money after bad.

The scoring duly began and we found ourselves, on a very cold and snowy day, in a small studio called the Snake Ranch in Lots Road, Chelsea. The actual theatre was about big enough to seat a string quartet and the only musicians to turn up played drums and guitars. The control room was surrounded by synthesisers and Myhill was in his element. This all seemed a bit odd to me and I suddenly had that out-of-control feeling that had overcome me when I first set eyes on Mike Oldfield's rig at Denham. We had prepared a video of all the sections that were to be scored and so we started, by laying down, in their parlance, a "click" track. Then we recorded drums and guitars. All rhythm, no melody. Myhill seemed to be quite happy, but Gilbert and I were somewhat baffled and I was particularly concerned with the rigidity of the click, fearing that the music would end up in a straitjacket and would not be sufficiently romantic.

The sessions lumbered on, with Brian Gilbert becoming ever more anxious and, occasionally, daring to query something, mostly having to do with the emotional weight of the music. Invariably he received a quick blink from Myhill, who told him to stop worrying. You might as well tell the Thames to stop flowing, since Gilbert was born to worry and, certainly, I was unable to reassure him that all would be well. I was unused to this layer-by-layer method of recording that was obviously the thing in those days. It came much cheaper than hiring a band, so producers loved it.

The whole exercise was something akin to painting by numbers and I still don't like it, despite the obvious fact that it works and is relatively inexpensive. It has little heart and should not be allowed to take over the scoring stage. I was never more delighted to leave a session, having spent five days sitting there doing absolutely nothing until ten at night, except getting cold.

We started to mix *The Frog Prince* with Trevor Pyke at 142 Wardour Street. Somehow we all tottered through the next two weeks without mishap and finished the mix. We showed the film to David Puttnam on the very afternoon we were all due to leave the picture. Bryan Oates, Tony Tromp, and I were to work on *The Frog Prince*, on and off, for weeks. Although officially off the picture and unemployed, we were all back in the cutting room for the entire weekend, recutting for remixing, and we finally screened the movie to Puttnam again. I can't honestly recall what his opinion was, but I know that it was decided to put more cash into the venture and send Brian back to Paris to shoot a couple of new scenes and some inserts. I thought they were off their rockers, since I couldn't see the piece being radically improved by spending more money, but I often disagree with the profligate and ever-optimistic attitudes of producers, even those I admire, who don't seem too realistic when it comes to their own films. With other people's work, they are usually more pragmatic.

☆   ☆   ☆

For the moment, we were relieved of *The Frog Prince*. My next job, *The Mission* was some weeks away, but in the meantime there was the Oscar ceremony.

The nomination for the editing Oscar for *The Killing Fields* was, in itself, an honour and a surprise. Unhappily, Laurence was unable to leave her film for this ceremony, so when I arrived in Los Angeles, I invited my daughter Kate to fly down from San Francisco.

The lead-up to the Oscars is one of the film community's big bashes and almost everyone gives a party. The Academy kicked things off by hosting a reception for all the foreign nominees. As we entered, there stood David Lean, whom I had never met. He was the official host. As we shook hands, I wondered if he knew we were in competition for the Oscar. He seemed very young for his years but had this unnerving way of staring deep into your eyes when he spoke to you. This reception appeared to have dragged all the oldest members of the Academy from retirement, some, I thought, from their graves. There sat Rouben Mamoulian, looking amazingly well preserved, along with Cesar Romero and heaps of others leftover from a far more alluring age. There was a great deal of food and some speeches. If this was said to be the best event of the weekend, it was clearly going to disappoint. But we were only passing through, on our way to the American Cinema Editors (ACE) awards dinner, back at the Beverly Hilton.

ACE is an extremely prestigious group in Hollywood and I was so nervous that I kind of willed myself not to win. I was terrified that I would void my bladder on the way to the stage if I was asked to go up there and speak. I worried needlessly. The whole evening was so tacky, it made the British film editors' dinner look classy. We were seated with Bernard Gribble at his request. Bernard had moved to Los Angeles having once been the youngest film editor at Ealing. When it came to the awards, I was in such a state of nervous tension that I was actually relieved when I didn't win. *Amadeus* won, which was great for them. As we were leaving the event, I bumped into Michael Kahn, another well-known film editor and he said, "Don't worry about it, Jim. You'll win the Oscar tomorrow night. I voted for you." I said that I didn't win tonight so I'd no reason to suppose I'd win tomorrow night but he told me I shouldn't be too surprised if I did. Because David Puttnam had asked to be told the outcome of the ACE awards, we drove to the Bel Air Hotel to communicate my failure to him and to have a quiet drink.

I went to the Oscar ceremony with my daughter, having rehearsed a possible thank you just in case, but I really didn't expect to win, so I was very relaxed. I told Kate that we mustn't drink before the ceremony, even though the stretch limo was stocked with booze. We stayed with Artie Schmidt and his wife Susan in Sherman Oaks and the limo arrived about four o'clock. We'd put on our glad rags and off we went to the Music Center where we were seated next to the *Amadeus* editing crew. We went through the ceremony and I felt very relaxed, not at all like I was going to piss my pants because I was convinced that *Amadeus* were going to win. I simply sat back and enjoyed it until the editing award was given, then suddenly my name was called out and I thought "Oh, my God!" Of course the *Amadeus* people were terribly upset because they thought they were going to get it. I recall getting up to the stage and being told that we could only speak for thirty seconds or the lights would start flashing. I forgot everything that I'd rehearsed, but I did manage to thank everybody with the exception of my assistant Bryan Oates. To my dying day this is something that I will always find highly embarrassing. Bryan was the one person I should have thanked because he did an enormous amount for me on that film.

I was also very disturbed that Roland Joffé, without whom that film would not have existed, was not even nominated. I could not have cut that film and got an award if Roland hadn't given me fine material to do it with. I've always been concerned when editors get awards and directors don't. It seems wrong to me because without the material we can't do a thing. We are only interpreting what we're given. We are the dream repairmen. That's what we do. We repair other people's dreams.

The Mission

My first act on reading the script for *The Mission* was to make notes and consult with Roland Joffé. I read the script several times and attempted to note any problems I could foresee. This is always a difficult area. How much should the editor attempt to influence the director at script stage? Some would say that the editor should keep away from the script, but I presume that there is some merit in having comments from those who are about to work on a film, particularly if the director and editor have worked together before and have become reasonably intimate and candid.

I read through my notes while Roland took a succession of phone calls from New York. He was casting the film and had still not found a Cabeza character. He paid scant attention to my notes, most of which were expressing concern over the part in the story when Mendoza returns to the city and realises his girlfriend is carrying on with another man, who then turns out to be his brother. I was concerned that all this would prove too long and cumbersomely melodramatic. As it was connected with a fiesta that was going on in the town, I suggested that intercutting all this material would give the story thrust without becoming too heavy. Roland listened carefully to this and did very little to adjust the script. My notes also applied to the end of the picture, which I felt was lacking in dramatic believability. I thought, at the time, that the emotional impact of Mendoza's death would be strengthened if he was not killed on the site of the Mission, but was captured and put to death in the city, watched by his former girlfriend, who had, in some way, caused all this grief. Roland, however, didn't take to that and was certain that a quick death and finale would do the trick. At that time, the finale of the film was set inside the church, where the Indians and Gabriel would be immolated, which made sound dramatic sense. During shooting, however, it was decided to be too difficult and, so, the Indians were brought into the open air and became fair game for the soldiers who then massacred them. When I saw the rushes of this material, my heart sank since I didn't believe the story. In my view, the Indians would have run away as soon as they were fired on, but the thinking seemed to be along the lines of Jonestown. This was a theory I didn't and don't subscribe to. All this came back to me months later after many hours of brain wracking in the cutting room.

The Mission was a film that had been written by Robert Bolt before he had his stroke and his heart attacks and it had been sitting about for a few years. The rights were owned by Fernando Ghia, an Italian producer. After the success of *The Killing Fields,* Puttnam and Joffé were looking for another subject and decided that this unproduced script might be a way of getting Robert back into work, so it was picked up. Poor Robert was a bit of a forgotten man. He'd remarried Sarah Miles by now.

They got the script of *The Mission* and, of course, Fernando came along with it. Fernando Ghia was a very nice man but he and Puttnam didn't really get on. Fernando was ostracised. Although he remained with the film, he was rarely consulted.

The unit went off to Colombia to shoot the majority of the film and, as we'd done with *The Killing Fields,* the processing lab and the cutting room remained in London. Only this time Roland and I knew one another well and trusted each other so that whatever I said didn't upset him.

It was the same basic team as *The Killing Fields.* All the core people, except Stuart Craig who did the design for *The Mission.* The film was shot beautifully by Chris Menges, Mike Roberts again was operating. It was, however, a very different sort of film.

The basic problem was that Robert Bolt, who had recovered from his stroke and his heart trouble, wasn't really capable of writing anymore and his speech was terribly limited. He used to come to the rushes and all he could say was, "Fuuuuuuuuucking hell." That limitation aside, he was an absolute charmer. Bryan Oates and I absolutely fell in love with Robert, who I had known before his stroke and I remembered what he was like. It was sad to see that so much had been taken away from him.

The biggest problem with the film for me was the casting of Jeremy Irons and Robert De Niro. I never felt that Robert was the right person to play the slave trader and Jeremy was really too young for the priest. The priest role was originally conceived of by Robert for Alec Guinness. To have an old priest and a young slave trader would have made sense. I think the film suffered from the imbalance of the two principle characters.

We did everything we could to extract emotion from this story but it was clearly a film that wasn't quite working. And it never would. No matter how beautiful it looked and how grand it was. Somehow or other there was an element missing.

Again we had problems with preview. People not quite knowing where they were and perhaps not caring. The first preview we had was in Reading and it was premature. Roland had been told by Dickie Attenborough, who had seen either the whole film or part of it, that it was absolutely wonderful. He made all the right noises, so this inspired the director to preview the film before it was ready. Puttnam was never happy with this. I remember at the preview, people were walking out saying, "Oh, it ain't *Rambo*." I was out in the foyer because I couldn't stand the tension inside. The film had perhaps run half its length when I was amazed to see Puttnam walk in from the street, eating a hot dog. He asked how it was going and I replied not very well as they were walking out. He said, "Good. That's exactly the reaction I hoped for." It seemed very odd for a producer to be happy that his preview was not going well.

The following day, when Roland and I were in the cutting room, he said he didn't understand what had happened the night before. So I told him that the film was not ready to be previewed. It was the only time that he got waspish and difficult with me. He said, "Why didn't you tell me?" I told him he wouldn't have listened to me because Attenborough had said he'd made a masterpiece. "But David knew, and I knew, that it wasn't."

The film was quite heavily recut after that and certainly reduced but we didn't have Morricone's score yet. Having him was a master stroke. I never knew who decided on Morricone, whether it was Roland or David. Fernando was crucial to this decision, being Italian. I remember David saying to me at one point, "If he were still alive, I'd ask Benjamin Britten to write the score for this film." I'd used, in the temp score, *Sensemaya* by the Mexican composer Revualtas. I happened to have LPs of his music, so I used that for all the battles and also an English group of players called Incantation, who specialised in Andean flute music. Morricone first viewed the film with all the music that I had put in. He chucked out pretty much everything and started again but he did use the Andean flute group. He listened to them and got them in and they stayed in the film.

Morricone professed not to speak English so every time he came to London, which was infrequently, everything had to be translated for him by Uberto Pasolini. We had a piano put in the cutting room in Wardour Street. At his very first session, we began running the movie on the Steenbeck and we came to the first music section, which was Jeremy Irons playing the oboe in a forest. He was playing the Marcello *Oboe Concerto*, which he had learned. The finger work was perfect. I stopped the film at that point and said to Uberto, "Would you ask the maestro if he intends to use Marcello or whether he will replace the Marcello with a Morricone theme?" So Uberto translated this at which point Ennio went off like a rocket. This mild-mannered man, who looked like a bank clerk, suddenly went into a total rage and ranted, in Italian, for about five minutes. He was backing away toward the door and I thought we were going to lose him. Roland and I were looking at one another as though to say, "What have we done?" Eventually he stopped and Uberto said to me and Roland, "Ennio says if you engage Morricone you do not use Marcello." I said he could have told us that without all the raging. He had decided, well ahead of the game, that his theme would be played at that point. It would be heard for the first time so old Marcello and all of Jeremy Irons' hard learned fingering went out the window. The scene remains in the film but the music is different.

Recording Morricone's score cost a fortune. He recorded for two weeks at CTS, which cost £250,000, a lot of money just for the recording. We had the London Philharmonic for a week and all we ever heard from them was: "Zuuum zuuum, zuuum zuuum, zuuum zuuum." That's all they ever did, it seemed to me. There was no tune at all. We kept looking at one another wondering what we'd bought. Then, during the beginning of the second week, he brought in the smaller groups, the choirs and the other instruments and it became clear that he was layering everything. The London Philharmonic, which had seventy players, was merely supplying layer number one. Layer number two would be something else. So he would multilayer everything until, in the end, after two weeks of recording, we were able to actually hear the score that knocked our socks off because it was magnificent. In fact, the score has probably outlived the movie.

Robert De Niro, in my view, never really found the character of the slave trader. He didn't quite know how to play the role and I don't think De Niro, although he's a fine actor, is good in a period piece. Somehow or other, he's a contemporary actor and as soon as you put him into period clothes and take him back a couple of centuries, he's a bit lost. The character needed to have menace to begin with but then, he had to go through this metamorphosis after he'd killed his brother in a duel. The whole second half of the movie was about his conversion from a slave trader to a priest. The crux of the whole story centered around this conversion. How do you take a slave trader who is full of anger and rage and quickly, as it were, in movie terms, convert him to a priest? It was a very hard scene to play and neither Robert nor Roland really ever quite knew how to do it.

That scene was written and shot three times at three different locations. The first time was in Colombia and I had something like twenty reels. Each reel would run ten minutes and they always shot on A and B cameras so that one camera would be on Jeremy and the other would be on De Niro. The scene, no matter what I did in terms of editing, was not working. It was an impossible scene to actually write and play. They tried it again but the second time was not good either, and the third occasion was well after they'd shot the film, during post-production. It was at Dover Castle. Puttnam had put it out to all sorts of different writers— people like Tom Stoppard, John Mortimer, and various others. He'd given them all a crate of champagne to thank them for doing this instead of paying them, but in the end, Roland decided to do it himself. I remember receiving eighteen reels of rushes yet again for that sequence. I'd already had twenty reels initially, probably another twenty the second time, and now I had eighteen more and I was absolutely exhausted.

De Niro would stop in the middle of a take and go back to the start of the scene again. He would try all sorts of different voices, different deliveries, varying the whole thing somehow. Jeremy Irons, however, remained consistently the same. He would never vary whereas De Niro would try constantly to find the character. Roland obviously was unsure of Bob's performance. De Niro would start a scene, then either blow or dry or decide that he wasn't playing it right. He would then leave the set and make a second entry. This procedure would sometimes give me as many as sixty takes.

In the end we actually had to do post-synch on a lot of De Niro's part because his accent was all over the place, due to the different kinds of voices he experimented with. Roland always ran a thousand feet of film on both cameras. De Niro would probably, in the course of that reel, play the same scene between two and five times. To find and select the best reading of any line, I had to, physically cut out the lines and join them up so that he would have maybe forty or fifty readings of the same line, of which, we would only use one, but the director had to listen to everything yet again in order to try and find the right reading. With Jeremy it was dead easy because he was always the same. De Niro was different on every take.

We were well ahead with the finishing period of *The Mission*. We'd done our British preview at Reading and the film had been recut, but that was before the American previews, which were now upon us. Another temp mix was done by Ian Fuller and his team and we set off for Hollywood once again.

It was well below zero when we left London and I had heard of torrential rainstorms in Northern California, so went well prepared. Bryan and I flew Clipper Class on Pan Am, which was my favourite plane, involving most of the glories of first-class flying without the guilt. I clapped on my Walkman at Heathrow and sank into a Rossini opera, which took me halfway to Iceland. I did take off the phones for the meal, not wishing Bryan to think me too antisocial. They were screening *The Jagged Edge*, which looked too dire for words, so I eschewed that and moved on to Mahler.

We eventually arrived and normally I dread that moment when immigration look me up on their computer, thinking they will, one day, come across that parking fine I never paid and deny me entry but, because the plane had so few passengers, we were whisked through all the necessary departments and into a limo a block long, which took us to the Beverly Wilshire Hotel. The film, which travelled with us, was removed to Warner Brothers at Burbank for safe keeping over the weekend.

I did not need my winter clothing since the temperature was now about sixty and Los Angeles was looking its very best, having been cleansed by the rainstorms. Bryan was still wearing an overcoat, coming down to his ankles, which could have belonged to Bertie Wooster. I was not, however, destined for the hotel until after the weekend. I'd made arrangements to stay two nights with the Schmidts. Artie and Susan lived in a very pleasant house in Sherman Oaks, just beside a canyon on a sleepy road, quiet as the grave, except for the coyote calls in the middle of the night. The best thing about that area is that it is possible to take a walk. Imagine that in Los Angeles! Susan and I took a long one on the Saturday morning, by which time the thermometer had risen to ninety. We eventually found ourselves on Ventura Boulevard where Susan and I waited for Artie who was cutting *Ruthless People* and doing his obligatory six-day week. On his return, fortified with a pitcher of margaritas, we piled into a Thai restaurant for fun and noodles and then it was time for me to be ferried across to the hotel and the real world of Wilshire Boulevard. The Beverly Wilshire, which I had not entered previously, was no good to me. The place itself is okay, though rather poorly situated if you have to go to studios. I ordered up a hire car, a giant yacht of a vehicle that I found frightening at first but grew to love.

At the hotel I found there was an urgent message to call Barbra Streisand's assistant, about what, I couldn't imagine, but just prayed she wasn't about to ask me to cut *Yentyl 2*. It was to invite me to a dinner the following evening, which Barbra was giving at her Beverly Hills home for David Puttnam's forty-fifth birthday. I asked her assistant if Bryan was also invited and she called back to say yes. Bryan was thrilled.

Tuesday dawned. Bryan and I motored out to the studio at Burbank, where we were due to rehearse the film for an afternoon screening for the Warner top brass. There we met Roland, David, and Fernando Ghia. We waited for the gang to arrive and in trooped twelve suited gents and a few ladies. The top brass included Terry Semel and Bob Daley. The film ran through and very little comment was made. This looked sinister to me and they all muttered darkly that they would now return to their offices and air their thoughts. Roland smiled through all this, but David looked a bit concerned. I was *very* concerned. I asked David if he wanted the film to go to San Diego exactly in its current state, as we did have some alternate scenes with us, and he replied in the affirmative, so Bryan and I took the film off to a cutting room where we mounted it on 6,000-foot reels. For normal projection, we mount it on 2,000-foot reels, but it is easier to carry around if it's on larger reels. As the film was still in the work print stage, we had separate action and sound to reel up. All quite a labour. After accomplishing this, we stashed the whole thing in the car, which Fred Talmadge, head of post-production, would drive to San Diego very early the following morning.

Then we went shopping for a birthday gift for David, and found a wonderful book about the making of *Fantasia*. David was a Disney nut so this was perfect. I had it gift wrapped, wrote a card, and went up to my room to change, since we were due at Streisand's place in half an hour.

Arriving in my room, I saw that my message light was flashing. Then the phone rang and it was Barbra's assistant, in quite a state. "Where's the film?" she enquired hysterically. "What film?" I replied. "The Mission," she screamed. "It's being screened here at Barbra's home tonight, at seven thirty!" I explained that it couldn't be as it was on its way to San Diego. There was total panic on the other end as I remained quiet. "Please call Puttnam at the Bel Air Hotel and explain to him," she insisted, so I did and got an equally hysterical Patsy Puttnam, asking where the film was. I told Patsy the same thing and added, "If you wanted to show the film, you should have told me."

All the guests had been invited for seven thirty to see the movie and Barbra was rushing back from the Music Centre where she'd been presenting a special award to a very frail Mrs. Ira Gershwin at the Grammy Awards. So it was all a grand fuck up and I didn't feel in the least responsible. I had been with David all day and he never once mentioned this screening.

Bryan next called me to say he'd had Patsy Puttnam on the phone asking if "nothing could be done." Bryan said yes, but it would take at least three hours to fix as the film was in the back of Fred's car somewhere in Pacific Palisades. Then she said, according to Bryan, "You and Jim were only invited because we were showing the film." This made us both hopping mad and I then said to Bryan that we would go to this nonevent, give David his gift, and disappear. Well, we went and were the first to arrive. Our car got neatly boxed into the drive rendering escape impossible.

The house was in a dark road behind Sunset Boulevard, surrounded by impossibly high walls and a sort of portcullis, surveyed by TV cameras. We announced ourselves on the intercom and the iron gate rolled back, revealing a vast two-storied mansion, brightly lit from within and without. A small posse of feminine minions assaulted us with beakers of white wine. We stood about in a huge over-dressed room, about as cosy as a museum, until other guests percolated through the iron gates. I had pictured a rather large party, as befits the forty-fifth year of a celebrated producer, but I was wrong. There were nine of us around the dinner table and two of us were not really supposed to be there.

The guests were the Puttnams, Roland, Barbra, and her man of the moment, Richard Baskin. He was very big, with a mane of hair, cowboy boots, and a ranch in, I think he said, Dakota, though I didn't catch whether it was North or South. Then there were the Rosenbergs. Mark Rosenberg was with Warner Brothers when I last met him and was now associated with Sydney Pollack. Mark's wife, professionally known as Paula Weinstein, was a producer, and an Anglophile too. She was raised in London, her mother being Hannah Weinstein, who produced many television series such as *Robin Hood* with Richard Green. Paula asked me if I'd seen Barbra's Hopper. Yes, a real Edward Hopper, a really fine one too, which the boyfriend had sensibly removed from the clutter of Miss Streisand's museum and placed in his own study, a pine-clad place, quite peaceful under the circumstances. This painting is of a couple in a bare New York bedroom, the sun streaming through the open window. The man lies naked on the bed, his lady sits in front of him, carefully avoiding the exposing of his parts. It is a fine painting and cost the chanteuse a mere nine hundred thousand. Probably the best thing she ever bought. Well, after seeing that, nothing else really came up to scratch that evening. Certainly not the food, which was Hollywood pasta, tasteless and glutinous.

David received lavish gifts, making our book seem very cheap. He also made a sentimental speech, which I almost ruined by saying that, although he claimed to be forty-five, he really looked fifty-five. Once again, I was the oldest at the table, though trying not to be.

Finally we turned out into the now foggy night air, since we had to be picked up by Fred at seven. Bryan left, hugging Barbra and regretting he had not had time to really speak with her, but that, perhaps one day they might work together. Rather him than me.

At six thirty the next morning, there was no time for breakfast before we were off down the San Diego freeway in thick fog. We sailed along until my stomach made impolite noises and demanded fuel. We pulled into a Denny's, and devoured a quantity of rubbish food, as the traffic polluted the surroundings. We reached the shopping mall where our theatre was, the Grossmart or perhaps Grossman. Either way it was big, housing ten screens, and we were all set to rehearse our film during the morning. The sound engineer from Warner Brothers had already set up his machine and all that remained was to mount our 6,000-foot reels onto one huge reel. The picture was put onto a "cakestand" for continuous projection, thus more or less obviating the need for human projectionists, though three of the same, resided in the booth. The projectors lit their lamps at screentime, the curtains parted, the houselights dimmed, and the movie rolled. The projectionist had only to cast an occasional eye on the screen just to check focus and, when the film had unspooled, he had to rethread it ready for the next screening. It was not like this in the New Theatre, Boston, when I was a lad. We had to look at the screen, feed the arc, and changeover, flawlessly, every ten minutes. Now the guys are mere machine minders, and actually looked forward to previews, which took them into the real world of work.

Normally I am very nervous at previews, but these gung ho types really put me at ease. Dale, the chief, was around fifty and had just married a girl of twenty-three, whose picture he proudly displayed. She looked like his daughter. Dale had an infectious laugh and a full set of false teeth. All of the guys knew their days were numbered. The youngest, with three kids and a raggy beard, was studying to be a computer engineer while the others would play golf and screw young girls.

We went across to the Broiler House fish restaurant for lunch and had a large meal. The assistant sound engineer was an Argentinian, named, oddly I thought, Abdul. Having sat through the film, he claimed the Indians were not speaking Guarani. I thought Roland would be pleased to know that.

Bryan and I faced an afternoon filled with emptiness, since Fred had decided to check into a hotel. Being in a shopping mall, we went shopping and, boy, was that depressing. A Bullocks during the mid-week afternoon is a cathedral of consumerism, full of things for the home and clothes. No customers to speak of, but little clumps of lady clones waiting for customers, and seemingly very bored indeed. They couldn't wait to serve, but there was nothing we wanted, except to get out. The icy soulless state of these places seems to me to be the very heart of modern America—rigid, spotless, automated, and cold.

I thought of Bullocks as I watched our audience line up for the show and I knew we had nothing that they would buy. As the film started and I sat in the audience with a remote volume control, my heart started to pound again. In front of me, a couple were already in deep conversation and remained so for the entire show. It was as if they were by their gas fire at home. The opening sequence, in which the natives crucify and drown a priest, was greeted with laughter, especially when he was dumped in the river. Huge laugh. Well, they really want a laugh when they go out to the movies and who can blame them in that perfectly terrible society?

The show tottered on, sometimes I thought the audience engaged, other times they were walking in and out, with or without popcorn, enough to feed a large herd of goats. There were a number of walkouts, and the reception was fair, but not good enough, as the cards later testified. Our people stood about in the foyer, hardly recognising us. We were expecting to have another show in the same theatre the following night, but it got cancelled and we took a ride back to Los Angeles late at night, waving farewell to Dale and his cronies, who had done a good show entirely un-automated. Fred gave us a fifth of Scotch and put us into this long limousine that was driven through the foggy night by a giant named Bruce, who must have weighed almost as much as his limo, and was seen snacking throughout the three-hour journey on Frito Lays and other horrors.

The following morning we loaded up our car with the film once again and motored over to Burbank, where we had another screening, this time for CBS Records, who were expected to produce the disc of the film music. There were other people there too, notably the Rosenbergs, whom I had met at Barbra's party. They were very affected by the picture, Paula in floods of tears. Mark was exhausted looking and claimed to be more moved than at *The Killing Fields*. He begged me not to allow too much alteration. Well, you never know. They surely enjoyed it more than the crowd at San Diego or even dear old Reading.

But at a meeting that afternoon in Terry Semel's office, it was decided to continue changes, and to reshoot the cell scene, which had already been shot twice and never really worked. This was decided, finally, after some insistence on my part. My message to all of them was that no matter how much fixing we did, the film would never really work without that scene being correct, emotionally, for the audience. There was no argument.

I went off, happy to spend a final evening with the Schmidts. Bryan went off to run the movie at Barbra's home.

Bryan Oates:

I had been called and asked to take the movie to Barbra Streisand's house for a screening. I was to show the film and then join the Hollywood royalty at dinner. I asked Barbra's projectionist if I might come over the day before to check things over, as her projectors may have needed adjusting to take tape-joined film and sound. To project a film with tape joins, the gap the film passes through must be widened to allow for the thickness of the joining tape. "We run film here all the time," said the projjie. "There is no need for a check."

I waited a day and called again. "Look, it's only me worrying about this," I said. "May I just pop over for twenty minutes to put my mind at rest?"

"Bryan, believe me, it'll be fine. I've been projecting for many years now and know these projectors well."

So I had to forego my rehearsal.

The night came and my big black limo took me up the hills into the kingdom of the extremely successful. I was admitted through the palace gates and the film given over to the care of the projjie in chief.

I was shown into a sumptuous room filled with Tiffany glass suspended from ceilings and standing on all available pianos and furniture. I waited and waited. I walked over to the grand piano and sat at it, lost in the wonderment that is to sit at Barbra Streisand's piano.

A voice said "Do you have everything you require?"

Deep in the piano and not looking up, I said, "Yes, thank you." There was a pause during which I supposed that the maid had left the room. I looked up and there was the queen of popular contralto herself.

I leapt off the piano stool and immediately went into a sort of gush. "Oh forgive me, Miss Streisand," I blathered. "I was just lost in . . . sitting in front of a piano that you had sat and sang at." This went down okay and she was soon showing me the finer aspects of her fabulous collection of Tiffany.

The guests arrived. We all filed into a large room with a Hopper picture at one end. Miss S went over to a control and the Hopper slipped up into the ceiling leaving a projection screen in its place. I had voiced my concern about the projection to David Puttnam earlier and he said to Barbra, "May Bryan sit on the controls, Barbra?"

"Well, I like to do it myself," said she.

"But I want you to just relax," said David. "And let yourself into the movie."

"Fine," said she, slipping into the chair next to mine, by the controls.

"Please run the film," I said through the intercom linked to projection.

The opening moments of *The Mission* show a Jesuit priest being crucified and thrown into a river. We follow cross and man down river until they drop over the edge of a vast waterfall. At this point, Barbra gasped, "Oh My Gard!" she said. "It's Bobbie!"

I leant over and whispered, "Actually, De Niro doesn't appear for over fifteen minutes."

The first few minutes of the film had no dialogue, only Ennio Morricone's wonderful music.

After that all started going wrong. The voices sped up and then slowed down. David asked if I could do anything. I left the room and went to the projection booth. The projectionist could offer no advice and so I poked my head into the open side of the running projector and saw that the sound reel was rising up over the magnetic head. Ah. Here lay the problem. I asked the projjie for a pencil and pushed it over the soundtrack onto the magnetic head.

A minute later, a relieved David appeared in the booth saying, "I don't know what you're doing but, whatever it is, keep doing it. Everything is perfect now in the room." And he went.

I was left, holding a pencil in a projector with the full blast of the lamp playing onto my face and hand. Some minutes later, a uniformed maid came to my side. "Miss Streisand says that I should do anything you want me to."

"Well," I said, "I should like a drink."

She went and once more appeared by my side with a silver tray on which there was a Premier Cru White Batard Montrachet and a suitable glass.

"Would you kindly pour me a glass and then take over with the pencil for a moment while I drink it?" I said.

She did this and the changeover from glass and pencil went smoothly. The next two hours were spent happily by us alternately drinking and penciling. It was with relief and insobriety that I finally took the pencil off as the end titles rolled through.

By now, the maid and I were friends and this female Jeeves bobbed a curtsy, took the glass from me, and disappeared.

Barbra came back and said, "You will join us for dinner won't you?"

"Thank you, Barbra. I'll just put the movie in my car." I canned up the reels in two Goldbergs, hexagonal metal film travelling containers, and made my way through the front door, a Goldberg at the end of each hand.

The moment the door shut behind me, pandemonium was unleashed. Tearing towards me barking furiously, were two of the largest Rottweilers I had ever seen. When they were about five yards from me, I made a decision. Me or *The Mission*. It was *The Mission* and with all the strength I had in my arms, I raised the two Goldbergs and threw them as hard as I could at the death-threatening Rottweilers. The cans hit the tarmac, film reels dispensed themselves around Barbra's herbaceous borders and the dogs started howling louder than before. Searchlights went on, people poured from all corners of the estate, and above all this I could here the clear contralto of Miss Streisand, "Whart is going on! Will somebody tell me? Whart is happening?" I rushed in this direction and into the safety of Miss Streisand's house.

Unsurprisingly, after this, nothing I have had to do in the film industry has caused me a problem.

We still had much work to do on *The Mission.* The next stop was Cannes. *The Mission* was nominated that year for an editing Academy Award. Laurence came with me to the Oscar ceremony and this time I didn't win. Our friend Claire Simpson won it for *Platoon,* so I didn't have to go up and thank everybody yet again, though this time I probably would have remembered to thank Bryan Oates. I've never had the opportunity again to thank anyone since I've not been nominated for another Oscar.

One day, while I was cutting *The Mission* in Soho, David Puttnam came into the room and said, "How would you like to come to Hollywood and help me run the studio?" The studio in question was Columbia Pictures and in 1986, David was asked to run it.

Naturally it was a flattering question but I didn't know how to answer it immediately. I realised this was a long-term proposition and wondered if I wanted a job that would take me away from home for such a time. There was no way I could give him a quick answer. We still had to finish off *The Mission,* which was shown at Cannes that year on a double head. It was billed as a work in progress but it won the Palme D'Or. After it was completed and we left the film, David then went to America to begin his job with Columbia.

Back home this possibility was discussed endlessly. Laurence's feeling was not to be easily dismissed. Years in a city she loathed? What would she do there during the day? And there were the children to consider.

We both thought it might, with a bit of luck, go away. But go away it did not.

PUTTNAM'S COLUMBIA

AURENCE AND I DECIDED TO have a long rest that summer in Ars-En-Ré, following completion of *The Mission,* so we had left London in mid-June, not intending to return until early September. Laurence was to start a mini series for Central as soon as she got home, which would keep her busy until the early spring.

It was near the end of August when David Puttnam called me from the Bel Air Hotel in Los Angeles, to discuss the manner in which we could function together at Columbia. This was the climax to a few weeks of anguish and indecision. He had originally put his proposal to Tim Corrie, my agent, who had outlined it to me in late July, so the details of a new job with David in Los Angeles had come halfway through this holiday and had interrupted any relaxation we might both have enjoyed fully, since neither of us could look forward to returning to that city which we did not enjoy. This gloomy prospect was not enhanced by the vagueness of the offer, since it sounded like an administrative role, and the remuneration was not sufficiently staggering to make the move from London seem worthwhile.

Laurence, I felt sure, would have been happy had I declined. I was faced with a split, since part of me totally agreed and the other half naggingly considered that to refuse might just cut me out of a very special adventure, certainly never to be repeated in my career. It therefore seemed sensible to write to Puttnam to try and elicit some parameters, so that I could better consider what I would be letting myself in for.

In the meantime, Tim had discussed the proposed deal with me. I agreed to the salary and expenses, though both Laurence and Artie Schmidt told me it was too low on both counts. While realising they were probably correct, I decided not to push further, though allowing for an increase in salary should the contract run another year. I did, however, tell Tim to try and get a car out of Columbia's pool and asked for three return airfares. I also made it very plain that I would require an HI work permit and I felt it essential that I be enrolled in the Editor's Guild. All this was conveyed to David in a letter, to which there was no response. This lack of communication bothered me and I spent days in the sunshine fretting over it. Any good I got out of this long rest was rapidly eroding. Laurence looked on in quiet despair, always hoping I'd simply say to hell with it and get myself a film to cut in London so that our life could continue on its unruffled course.

My future seemed to be known by other people. Penelope Casadesus called from New York to tell me she'd dined with David who'd told her I was to be with him for three years as a Production Head. She thought I'd like to know. Three years had never been mentioned before. Then she called a second time to say that her friend Tony Scott, brother of Ridley and director of *Top Gun,* had also met David in Los Angeles, and had been told the same thing, though now it was Production Executive. I still had received no word from David himself, so I became neurotic and felt I was being heavily manipulated.

Tim Corrie did speak to David, however, since he required some response to the deal. This revealed that Puttnam had received my letter and found it contained much to discuss, but the job he envisaged for me would not leave me with sufficient time to edit anything and, therefore, there was no need for me to be enrolled in the Editor's Guild. Now I was getting *really* disturbed. Quite what he had in mind for me had not been revealed. I was terrified to be getting myself into something that would not be congenial. Tim advised me not to call David just yet, since he wanted a response to our requests before I started to question the nature of the job itself. I did write another letter to David anyway, simply to get things off my chest. Having slept on it, or rather, *not* slept on it, I decided not to send the letter, but to wait as advised and maybe call David when I was back in London the following week.

We were enjoying the last days of this long holiday. The sun was still very warm. The beach was by now almost deserted. We swam and sunbathed and talked endlessly of the future. If I started in Los Angeles in November and Laurence worked on her mini series until the next spring, we would be separated for about five months, then she could join me. But to do what? She loathed Los Angeles and the only way we could see our domestic life continuing in any kind of harmony would be if she too were working there. Her agent, Sandra Marsh, who lived in Los Angeles, had said she thought that prospects for nonunion work were good, but a work permit would be required. There seemed some slim chance that we could keep our marriage alive at least through the first year. Laurence looked around at the beauty of the beach and the calm of our life there and the happiness in London. "Do you want to lose all this?" she enquired. "Not at all," I replied, "But it's only for three years, and maybe less if it doesn't work out." In my heart I knew she was right. She usually is. Memories of previous lonely periods in Los Angeles when I was working on *The Last Remake of Beau Geste* and *Honky Tonk Freeway*, did nothing to cheer me. It is a dreadful place to be alone in and I had vowed I would never do it again. Now I was beginning to convince myself that it would be worthwhile. What was the secret of David's charm that he could unravel my life in such a way? Why didn't I simply say no now?

Later that day, I was reading a Raymond Carver story about lonely people on the slide, when the phone rang. It was David calling from Los Angeles. "Hello luv, having a good time? I got your letter and Tim's deal. It all looks good. You're going to be some sort of Production Executive. I don't know exactly, but I want you with me to work on all the projects as soon as they're green lit." He continued in his rapid-fire manner, charming and enthusiastic as ever. "If I had known you were on the phone in France I would have called before." I had given my French number to his secretary before leaving London. "Now listen. The world premiere of *The Mission* is in Madrid on September 30 and you are invited. I will prepare a dossier and we'll discuss our plans in Madrid. Okay? Then we'll start together in Hollywood on November 3."

I managed to give him some of my reasons for being uncertain about doing the job at all and that I absolutely could not function if I wasn't cutting, since that was my biggest asset. He did concede that it might be necessary, though felt we should both find our way step by step in the jungle. David said he wanted me to be there as an extension of his eyes and ears. He realised that he couldn't look at everything himself. In a major studio there was too much in the way of rushes, rough cuts, and fine cuts for the head of the studio to be looking at. He therefore asked me to go in as a sort of extension of himself. It seemed that I was hooked.

The Madrid experience was amusing. I had flown over with Robert Bolt, who was in his wheelchair. This gave rise to much hilarity and mirth since the handler could not get Robert out of the chair and into his seat. The process was repeated when we arrived in Madrid and when it was time to return to England. I rehearsed the screening in a huge old cinema that had been elected to be correct for a Royal Premiere. I sat alone, watching the film for the thousandth time and was aware of noise from behind. This came from a bar that was at the back of the gallery, and ran the entire width of the theatre. I hoped it would not be open during the Royal event, which was that evening. As the crowd was assembling, Puttnam breezed up and said, "The King and Queen have double dated themselves and have to leave after twenty minutes." This was not a good omen. The crowd stood as the Royals arrived and took their seats. The film began. Meanwhile I was up in the booth, to tell the projectionists to stop on a certain scene. Armed soldiers made certain I carried out these instructions. The scene arrived, the film was stopped, the house lights came up, everyone stood as the Royals left, and then the film continued. But the bar was not closed, and the noise from it echoed around the gallery. The drinkers were not interested in the film and I walked out of the theatre wondering whether the publicity was worthwhile. Robert when asked, merely shrugged and said, "Fuuuuuuuck it!"

Columbia Pictures

The Rites of Summer was a film made under the previous regime and I'd actually heard about it in London. Tom McCarthy, head of post-production at Columbia had warned me about it. The film was shot on location and had been found wanting and put on a very high shelf. It was about an outdoors adventure gone wrong. Kevin Bacon played a boys' camp leader who had taken his young charges into the wilderness, much like John Boorman's *Deliverance*, but for kids.

On my way to the coast, I had stopped in New York for the American premiere of *The Mission* and saw *The Rites of Summer*. I was seeing it alone, but was aware that, close to the finish, someone else entered the room. When the lights came on, I met the producer, Mark Tarlov. I did not think the film was that bad, but it had no satisfactory ending. I told Mark I would take it under my wing when I started at Columbia, for which he was most grateful. I didn't realise what a trap I was walking into.

Arriving at the studio in Burbank was just like my first day at Oundle school—new faces, new rules and regulations, new roads to tread. I must have been introduced to fifty people by noon, many of them the girls in the outer offices, who had names like Linda, Lou, and Karen. I rather wished they would advertise themselves with name tags like waitresses, since my memory for names is bad at best. But I first located Valerie and Betty, who were trying to sort out the shambles of David Puttnam's office.

Workmen were active all around us and furniture was not safe to sit on. I had been allocated Room 223 at the end of the "creative" corridor, opposite the men's room. This looked small but homey. It was reasonably sized with a desk, a television, a monitor, and a VHS machine.

I also had a lady named Jean Racko, who was English. Jean was my outer office girl who looked after me. Her job was to keep people away from me. Nobody could actually get into my office without her permission. When you're in that kind of position in Hollywood, all sorts of directors, producers, and writers will constantly try to come on strong to you with a project of their own, which they hope you will foster and support. At the pitch meetings we used to have, people would come in and pitch stories and you had to be polite to them and say nice things that they wanted to hear, but as soon as they were out the door, you forgot them.

In addition to her British accent, Jean had a motherly air. The school matron type, whom I knew would suit me admirably. She also knew the ropes and to some extent the politics and might help steer me through some of the trickier minefields. She did a perfectly good job of doing virtually nothing as far as I could see, but she was red hot on perks. Some of her suggestions seemed more like scams to me. Clearly the executives she'd worked for previously had been very active in getting all sorts of perks from the company. Whether it was dry cleaning or magazine subscriptions, she was always trotting out ways that I could get all these little extras, which I found slightly baffling as I was getting a reasonable salary and wasn't complaining about a shortage of money.

A meeting with John Feidler ensued. He was the head of production and exceedingly charming and smooth. He tried to put me at my ease directly. There was an element of the school head prefect about him. I'd been advised by others that Feidler could be a snake who bit, but my experience with him was fine. He was anxious for my verdict on *Rites of Summer*, on which he'd been a producer. I said, rather grandly, that I thought it could be fixed. He wondered if I could be correct. I met with the post-production crew and introduced myself. I should have realised from their reactions that I was going nowhere, as they all began laughing about how bad the movie was. I persevered and told Puttnam that with a new ending, the picture could be saved. Therefore, on my advice alone, he decided to invest a further $1 million in the film.

Tarlov was delighted that his movie was back off the shelf. We got Kevin Reynolds to write a new ending, which would take us and the actors to New Zealand's South Island, where there were good white water rapids, as demanded by the new script. I went along for the ride, the original director, Jeff Bleckner, was rehired and we spent a happy week shooting the rapids.

Back in Burbank, the original editor, David Ray, inserted the new footage. At the same time, we discussed the score. I thought it required a *Raiders of the Lost Ark* feel, so we hired a British composer to do a smart John Williams rip-off, which was recorded in Munich. We mixed the film and finally ran it on a Saturday evening for the studio bosses. They hated it. David Picker, who was second in command by now, particularly loathed it and demanded a new title as well as a new score that would have more appeal for youngsters. David Puttnam, who had sanctioned this work on my advice, never spoke of it again.

Mark and I filmed some sort of prologue with Sean Astin, who was still young enough to play one of the boys and we dumped the orchestral score in favour of some hip modern rock numbers. We retitled it *White Water Summer* and took it out to preview. We were sufficiently happy with the figures given by our core audience for the company to arrange a release in northern California. It did no business whatsoever and was never shown anywhere else.

Mark, to this day, insists that the film did well on cable as well as video and recouped Columbia's money but I've never seen any proof of this statement.

I failed miserably to save this film, only to learn that studio executives wield power and are not always correct in their judgments. Certainly the version we ended up with was a disappointment. My face was red and my stock went down.

Most people were surprised when Puttnam chose David Picker as his number two. A veteran American movie executive who had spent many years at United Artists, Picker was one of those who had championed John Schlesinger's *Midnight Cowboy* and *Sunday, Bloody Sunday*. I didn't dislike Picker, but I didn't always know where I stood with him. Something of an establishment figure, Picker was much liked by producers who he had helped in the past. He'd been a big supporter of *Bugsy Malone* and was responsible for financing *The Duellists,* so Puttnam probably felt indebted to him. He was, however, much younger in those days and, once he became a freelance producer himself, his track record was spotty. He was an instinctive man and I wasn't sure his instincts were always right.

After meeting John Fiedler on my first morning, he walked me around the place introducing me. I met Steve Norris, Puttnam's financial advisor from London. Steve was a bovine barrow-boy type, jolly and also probably fairly ruthless in the scrum. Another Columbia person was Sheldon Schrager, the boss of the production team. Shel had been production manager on *The Day of the Locust*. He and I got along quite well, but Shel was a very Hollywood type, super nervous, but relatively decent. Feidler walked me to an office he wanted me to have, bigger than that allocated. It had a grand view of a wall. I spurned it in favour of my view of the hills of Burbank. This may have been my first tactical error. The Columbia offices were being redecorated by David's wife Patsy and I decided to approach her with this task after she'd dealt with David's suite. It was a modern block, sort of a Bauhaus construction and she was doing it all in very good taste. The viewing room was all black leather and my office was just along the corridor.

One perk that Columbia Pictures didn't provide me with was a company car. I had to buy a car of my own, but they did give me a parking space that was very important. It's essential to have your own parking space wherever you go in Hollywood, otherwise you can't park at all.

There were two surprises waiting for me, one in the shape of Uberto Pasolini, who popped up looking fresh and bouncy. His exact role with Puttnam was, as yet, undefined. Then, lo and behold, Brian Gilbert's voice boomed over the phone. There he was in Room 207a, working on a movie which he would direct, *Vice Versa*, originally made by Peter Ustinov. David had put *Vice Versa* into production and it was to shoot in Chicago. I remember visiting the shoot at some point and having lunch with Ian Le Frenais and Dick Clement, who had written the script and were producing. The eventual studio preview, which I attended, went spectacularly well, with figures up in the nineties. Afterward we all went out to celebrate, but when the film opened it died at the box office, which made me leery of previews. You can never tell with pictures. Maybe the publicity was ineffective or the actors held little interest for the public. In this case, the most damning fact was that we came out after two other films that dealt with the same basic premise. Tom Hanks had already trawled this territory in *Big* and Dudley Moore had done so in *Like Father, Like Son*.

Everyone blanched when the weekend figures were read out on Monday morning. *Vice Versa* had tanked, yet the preview audience had loved it.

An activity that soon became routine for me was viewing the dailies and one of these was a sordid and rather poorly conceived sex scene for a movie called *The Arm*, which Ben Bolt was directing in Canada. This looked dismal and I borrowed the script to see how right I was. I'm afraid I was very right. This picture was produced by an old-time monster, Marty Ransohoff, and was already on its second director and second editor. I expected it to swim toward me quite shortly. The script had no magic at all and appeared to concern craps shooters.

Ransohoff had previously made two other films with a gambling theme, one being *The Cincinatti Kid*. Marty was an old, legendary Hollywood bull. He'd engaged the services of Harold Becker to direct *The Arm*, which had been green lit before we arrived. The film started shooting in Chicago and, after a week, Becker had slipped behind schedule and spent a disproportionate amount of his budget on a street set. Marty was apoplectic and went to Puttnam, who had a reputation for finding young, new directors, and asked him to find a replacement for Becker. Quickly, David told him of a young man living just up the road who could take over the next day. He was Ben Bolt, the son of Robert, who had come to Hollywood seeking work after making some television films in the UK. Believing that David always chose well, Marty rushed to the phone. He engaged Ben, then he fired Becker.

The production was moved to Canada, which was cheaper, and Ben began shooting.

Being part of the creative team, I had to attend the creative meetings on Monday mornings and one of the tyrannies of being an executive was that you had to read six scripts every weekend. These screenplays were, supposedly, the cream of the material submitted to the company. They had already been through the reading department and six were sorted out for all of us to read on Saturday and Sunday. To do this, I would set the alarm for 6 AM on Saturday, read the first script before breakfast, read the second before lunch, and the third before tea. This left me with the evening, which normally involved attending a preview of one of our films. On Sunday the ritual would be repeated. I found this routine oppressive and impossible. To concentrate on all these scripts was taking up the entire weekend, so I adopted a plan of reading maybe fifty pages and if it hadn't grabbed me by then I'd let it go. I was thus able to have reasonable time to myself over the weekend, but very quickly, it became evident at the Monday meetings that I wasn't reading them all the way through. I was castigated by the others but I continued not to read these wretched scripts because there just wasn't time to do it. Only one of the scripts I read ever made it into production.

One morning David Puttnam arrived, called me into his office, then marched me down the hall to the conference room for the weekly product meeting. Twenty to thirty people were in attendance and John Feidler chaired. It was the weekly resumé of all the product going through the system and was, therefore, attended by all heads of departments. I listened and understood about two-thirds of the dialogue, most of which was financial in nature, having to do with huge amounts of money. It was the financier's equivalent of Variety-speak as far as I could learn, so I sat back and let it all flow over me, thinking, "I'm creative, I don't understand

any of this. When can I go back to the cutting room, sir?" I was asked a few questions and Shel made reference to the rushes of *The Arm*, which we had viewed
the previous day, saying he thought the love scene might require TV protection
and what did I think? My answer was, "The love scene, if it could be so called,
seemed adequately covered and I'd get out of it as quick as possible." This was not
considered very droll. The meeting went incredibly fast. Everyone spoke double
speed, including Puttnam, who, if encouraged to speak fast, became unintelligible.
Feidler set the pace by rushing from one movie to the next as if driven. There was
no gap between movies so I didn't know quite when we'd finished one project and
moved to the next. Decisions involving millions of dollars seemed to be made
without thought. Perhaps this was part of the American way of doing business. I
knew they always considered us Brits very slow indeed, but I questioned the wis-
dom of rushing through agendas like they were all late for the airport.

Patsy was in my office before lunch and I finally asked her to give it the once
over when she had finished with the guvnor. We decided a sort of high-tech Japanese look might suit my office. She thought a Tatami carpet. She pictured me at
my desk dressed in a samurai outfit. I asked her to supply the ceremonial sword for
the eventual hari kari.

Stuart Baird called—another Brit on the lot. Columbia was now being called
"British Columbia."

I soon got very tired of watching rushes every day, then reporting to David
Puttnam on what was good and what was not so good. If I wasn't actually cutting
a film it was difficult for me to become interested in the rushes. When David took
over the studio, he was taking on, not only material he wanted to make himself,
but also material in the pipeline from the previous regime. So there were plenty of
films coming through in various stages of production that we had to finish.

Ishtar was ruled out of bounds. It was one of the conditions David made,
when he took over, that he would have nothing to do with that film because the
word was already out that it was a problem. After *Agatha*, when David had grief
with Dustin Hoffman, he didn't want to know about *Ishtar*, so none of us had to
deal with that picture.

I was denied physical access to the films, since the union did not allow executives to edit. This made me angry and was not what had been agreed. Seeing my
anguish, David Puttnam conceded that I could have a cutting room on the lot,
provided it was kept quiet. Tom McCarthy, head of post-production, took me
to see the far distant cutting room he thought I should have, since I had to edit
covertly. I didn't like what I saw and suggested a trailer. The only free trailers
were quite far off and looked abandoned, but I thought I would take one, have it

equipped and cleaned up, then use a bike to get to and from it. Well, it was an idea. It certainly would keep me away from all those other editors who might shop me to the union.

Tom was avuncular and, I suspect, a wee bit inefficient. I had told him my requirements weeks earlier and absolutely nothing had been done. He walked me about the lot with his arm around my shoulder, which I found unnerving. I guess he just liked to be liked. Somehow I thought it would take a long time for me to get a real cutting room going there. I missed Bryan's ability and persistence.

The first film David put into production was Ridley Scott's *Someone to Watch Over Me*. This picture had gone into turnaround at another studio so, in effect, David came to Ridley's rescue. I was called into Shel Schrager's office to discuss the post-production of the film, which they thought they might like to do in England. Tom McCarthy considered the budget to be too light on editor's staffing and overtime and it appeared he was correct. Michael Nathanson, who was in charge of the budget, was called down and did a big defensive number on Ridley Scott's behalf, since we had suggested the studio might regret allowing him to disappear to London with the film. I gathered this was a subject to steer clear of, but it would be silly to allow it. Ridley, for whom I had never worked, was known to be someone who could be difficult. There was talk of postponing the picture until January.

A film that had been put into production before we arrived was *Little Nikita* and it proved a difficult nut to crack. Directed by Richard Benjamin, the story suggested that an ordinary seeming family, living in San Diego, was actually an inactive Communist cell who, one morning, are horrified to learn that they have to carry out orders. It was a promising idea and well cast with River Phoenix as the teenage boy and Sidney Poitier as an FBI agent, but the script lacked suspense, in spite of the fact it was written by an Oscar winner. I would not have backed its production, but we were stuck with it.

Richard Benjamin was an exceedingly pleasant man with no guile and plenty of charm. He came to show his director's cut to Puttnam, Picker, and myself. When it was over, David, quite out of character, stood up in front of him and announced that *Little Nikita* was, perhaps, the worst film he'd ever seen. Picker was a bit less confrontational, but agreed with Puttnam and the two men walked out after uttering the new cliché, "Jim'll fix it."

I turned to Richard and his editor who were both ashen. We agreed to convene in their cutting room, go through the picture, and try plugging the holes. I knew it was no simple task, having read the script, but I was there to help them. We spooled through the film for a few days, making notes, and eventually decided that some scenes, particularly the end, required rewriting and reshooting. I didn't want to involve the original writer, so an SOS was put out to find someone who could fill our holes with something worthwhile. We eventually decided on a Yugo-slav writer, living locally, who had some credits and would not be too expensive. The reshoots involved all the major actors, some of whom were already engaged on other films and the new ending called for a location shoot on the bridge that divides the United States from Mexico. Not a cheap day's work, but Puttnam de-cided it was worth spending money to improve the goods and so a pre-production crew was engaged.

Around this time, the vice president for acquisitions, Bobby Newmeyer, asked me to look at two Japanese pictures that he thought they might buy and Ameri-canise, should I find a way to combine the two films. I did this and, much to my amazement, the result was good. The films were aimed at young people and were very big in Southeast Asia, but they both carried a rather pompous poetic com-mentary that we knew wouldn't work in America. We had named the new film *Milo & Otis,* one being a puppy and the other a kitten. We were unhappy about the scenes in which the litters came into the world because American kids shouldn't see too much and then there was the question of replacing the music. The original Japanese score was out of the question. We interviewed a number of composers, including Harry Nilsson, and ended up with Joe Raposo who had been involved with *Sesame Street* and was a friend of our writer, Mark Saltzman. I decided to fly to New York and talk to Joe who had his office in the Carnegie Hall building. I had no sooner arrived than David Picker called demanding to know why I was in New York when I should be in San Diego with the *Little Nikita* unit. I was unaware that they wanted me there to oversee the shoot, but there was no getting away from it. I abandoned my meeting with Joe and beetled back to Newark airport, luckily getting on board a red-eye to Los Angeles. I figured I could appear in San Diego at roughly the right time and contribute very little.

We shot all the new footage for *Little Nikita* and I wish I could report that the revamped version was a smash. It had cost at least another million dollars to fix, but the critics and public were indifferent to it. I'm happy to say that Richard Benjamin and I never had a cross word. He behaved like a trooper and did not complain about my efforts to make his film workable and commercially viable. I wish it had worked better.

In spite of my sophisticated title as a Columbia executive, my real job was stu-dio mortician. When I received these films they were dead and, though I couldn't bring them to life, I could touch up the corpse. That's what I was doing, touching them up so they would be releasable.

Joe Farrell attended one of our creative meetings. Joe ran NRG, a company that tested movies and made financial predictions on behalf of the companies. I'd last encountered him on *Honky Tonk Freeway* when, after each preview, Joe would come in with ever more dismal figures. Here he was making predictions about the upcoming movies for the Christmas period. After its opening in New York, despite the reviews, he declared that *The Mission* would do around forty-five million. It would be interesting to see where his predictions led. When Puttnam came into the meeting, he revealed that Warner Brothers believed they could do sixty million. This well-known cynic thought they were both on the high side.

This meeting differed from the big one the previous week inasmuch as it was a smaller group of people. Feidler was still in the chair, but the atmosphere was considerably lighter, with opinions exchanged of a generally unguarded nature. Two projects stood out for me. A script, *Providence*, which everyone had read, was a Dan Melnick development, based on a novel by Geoffrey Woolf. Most present thought it had not adapted too well. Some thought it pretentious, some objected to the development of the leading character. Puttnam allowed all present to give their considered views before weighing in with his, which was very positive. He had read it twice straight through and was very high on it. His idea, put crudely, was to cast it up and produce it down. Milos Forman or Bill Forsyth were mentioned as directors. The other subject, *Film Stars Don't Die in Liverpool*, was a new one to me. Feidler held up the book, a slim British novel, and declared that Schlesinger had expressed interest in it and had, in turn, suggested Alan Bennett to write it. Puttnam then threw this at me and told me to contact John and see what he really thought.

John was out at the theatre, seeing *Kafka's Dick* as it happened. I caught him later in the day. It seemed that Puttnam had the rights and approached John, who read the book on holiday and found it interesting. He would now ask Alan to read it. David had forgotten to tell me he had Shirley MacLaine in mind for the part of Gloria Grahame. So that's who it was about. A true story? I recalled seeing her in a play at a tiny theatre in Hampstead not long before she died. I had no idea she'd died in Liverpool. This sounded like a good project that could go somewhere.

First glimpse of the rushes on Bill Forsyth's *Housekeeping* were not very auspicious. Pretty scenery. Interesting looking acting. No way of judging plot or development. They had selected the takes for us, but most of them were disconnected. Tom McCarthy remarked that they seemed to walk a lot in the picture and complained about a lack of reverses. I could only assume they existed but they didn't want to bore us. Mike Ellis was cutting the show in Canada.

The latest batch of dailies on *The Arm*, now called *Big City*, were predictably dull. Tommy Lee Jones and Matt Dillon were doing their best but it was now obvious that Ben Bolt was not the right director for the job. For a start he did not understand the game of craps, around which the story revolved. Neither did I, for that matter and, it must be said that craps is the most nonvisual activity known to man.

Becoming alarmed after seeing rushes, Marty Ransohoff went back to David, who sent Uberto Pasolini to Toronto to find out what was going on. Uberto reported that Ben was behind but coping.

My agent had told David that I was uneasy in my role because it remained undefined. I had asked Tim not to mention this, but he did anyway. David told me later that neither of us would get a clear handle on the job until around February and that included him and Picker. I had no doubt he was absolutely correct.

At long last, the trailer in which I was going to work was ready and it had been equipped with a KEM. My Compeditor simply wouldn't work here, which was a real bore, since I now found it hard to edit without it. Seems they could transform the current okay, but it was the fifty cycles that bugged them. The machine ended up running 20 percent too fast. I was in deep conversation with the engineers, when, in the middle of all this, John Schlesinger called from London to say that Alan Bennett had expressed no interest in *Film Stars Don't Die in Liverpool* and that he was unsure who he should turn to. I suggested he speak to Linda Myles and talk writers. He was quite intrigued by David's idea of Shirley MacLaine and then wanted to go on and gossip, but I was stuck in the middle of this trailer with three people waiting for me, so I had to curtail him.

When David summoned me to his office to meet Marty Ransohoff, I knew why. He'd come to David with his problems about *The Big Town*, one of which concerned the editing of the picture. They simply had to get it assembled rapidly in order to see whether additional shots or retakes were required before they lost the cast. David threw me to this large wolf and I was given my marching orders to Toronto, leaving the following Sunday. As he led me to the door, David said, "And you were worried about not having enough to do."

My weekend was interestingly hectic. After a pleasant lunch at Roddy McDowall's home, I packed my gear, had a Thai meal with the Schmidts, then got an early night. At five something the following morning, a giant limo purred up to the door and deposited me at LAX, for a first-class flight to Toronto. During the flight, I gathered a few laughs from *The Money Pit* and read a bit more of Martin Amis' *Money*, all of which seemed strangely apt to me, though I didn't have half the fun or drink as much as his hero.

It was freezing in Toronto and, thankfully, Artie Schmidt had loaned me his Eddie Bauer parka, since my poor little Marks & Sparks coat was more like a wafer. I was met by yet another, even longer limo, which cruised me to the Sutton Palace Hotel. I was ten flights up on a windy corner, facing a building site and a big red crane that was right outside my window. The wind was howling and the temperature was around zero.

I called Laurence directly to tell her where I was. She was having dinner with John Schlesinger and Michael Childers. John told me of a number of good restaurants in Toronto and the name of a tailor. Just what I needed.

I called Stuart Pappé, the nominal editor of *The Big Town* and met him for a drink. Stuart was the third editor on this show and had only been there four days. He hadn't had much time to cut, since he'd been called to the set quite often. The studio and editing rooms were a forty-five minute drive from the hotel, just like Elstree. I was a bit surprised he wasn't working that day, since there was so much to catch up with. It occurred to me that Stuart may be an oddball. He told me that he had sat at the bar that afternoon, going over the material and cutting it in his head. I thought his eyes looked a little glassy and he did drink two bourbons while I was with him. He was known as a fixer and had recently fixed Hal Ashby's *8 Million Ways to Die*, though obviously not to any great effect, since the patient died. Most of the pictures he'd fixed had died. The good thing was that he understood the game of craps. We arranged to meet at nine the following morning.

I managed to track down Ben Bolt and met him in the bar. He was thin, about thirty-five with glasses and didn't look like his father at all. He also didn't look very much like a movie director. We arranged to meet for breakfast.

I returned to my room and finished reading the script, which didn't thrill me at all. It began as garbage and garbage it remained. I felt sorry for Ben, as it was his first feature and not one with which to make an auspicious debut. I wished someone could have stopped him, but I guess David thought he was doing him a favour.

Toronto International Studio turned out to be a couple of sound stages in the middle of a field, forty-five minutes outside the city. Stuart had the foresight to get one of the assistants to drive us, so we didn't have to learn the route.

My Compeditor had been sent in, so my room was very quickly organised. My first task was to cut together a sequence in which the villain shoots someone after stalking his victim through the street. This scene had become a bone of contention between Bolt and Ransohoff. Marty was displeased with the staging and had insisted on an additional night's work to beef up the action. Bolt had demurred at this, but I was asked to assemble Marty's longer version and send it back to him to evaluate. I realised Bolt was uneasy about all this, particularly as the movie was now over budget and schedule.

Before I got down to cutting the footage, and while my room was being fixed, I reviewed all the cut footage on the KEM in order to see how it was working out. I couldn't figure out why anyone had wanted to make the darn thing in the first place. Certainly, in the normal course of events, I would not have touched it, but here I was, in a position of some authority and having to service the producer who, presumably, liked this material. Reviewing the footage only depressed me further because the material, as shot, was no improvement on the script. If anything, it was worse. It was far too late to change the nature of the beast and I realised I could have little impact on its outcome.

I started to cut this chase and killing, the producer's way. My cutting room was directly opposite Stuart's and sometimes, when Marty called up, ranting, Stuart would put the phone on his bench and wander into my room as this disembodied voice raged on and on. Marty was, despite the bluster, correct to complain. The rushes were endless, often with two cameras running, and the results were lacklustre at best. Gradually, I got involved in the politics of the show, which were a little on the dirty side.

In essence I'd become a second editor on a poor movie, which was a bit rum after the first week of my appointment as a senior vice president with Columbia. Our working day was twelve hours for six days of the week. I hadn't worked such hours for years. As there was nothing else to do there, I figured I might as well pitch in and cut the bugger.

Bolt was another product of the National Film School and was clearly far too inexperienced to handle this material. He was, however, a cool customer. He was cultured, quiet, grateful, and stubborn. My influence on him was negligable. Even his DOP (Director of Photography), Ralf Bode, had given up making suggestions. They all knew they were on a bummer, flogging themselves through endless days of repetitive work.

We'd been seeing the rushes of the three crap games that are featured. These ran for hours and were very tedious to watch. I dreaded to think how we would manage to cut them together as they piled up in the room. Stuart would have to carry most of this burden, but in order to get the assembly completed rapidly, I took over part of the chore.

The saga of the alley killing scene continued. Marty had seen the version I'd cut at his request. He didn't like it and was determined to have it reshot. This would cost Columbia $300,000 dollars. Marty had used my opinion shamelessly to persuade Puttnam and Picker to reshoot, so there were many conflicting phone calls to find out precisely what I thought. My message was, briefly, that the shorter version as realised by Bolt would probably work, but a restaging would obviously produce a better scene. Whether that was worthwhile was debatable and I suggested we look at the scene in context, carefully, and without Marty's splenetic contribution. *The Big Town* was already about $2 million over budget.

Though all the production people at Columbia had been seeing the rushes for weeks, I still didn't think they really knew just how bad the film was. Somebody's head would roll over this one, maybe mine, since I was fearless enough to tell Puttnam that his protege was disappointing. Shortly afterward I had a call from Uberto, beseeching me to go easy on Ben. This advice, I figured, had come from David. If I had any function to perform here, it was, surely, to register my thoughts undisguised. That was why Puttnam hired me in the first place. The studios were riddled with politics and everyone had warned me I would soon become embroiled. I would probably get shafted eventually.

Marty had asked for a topshot of the craps game—the classic bird's-eye view. Stuart and I had urged Ben to shoot it to exclude the overhanging lights. This he failed to do, so we now had a shot, endlessly long, in which two Tiffany lamps predominated. Stuart told Ben that the shot was more or less useless. Ben said he couldn't cheat out the lamps. "Why ever not?" asked Stuart. "This is a movie." "I know it's a movie," rasped Ben waspishly. "I'm directing it!" I told Stuart he had missed his cue. "You should have retorted *mis*directing it," but he thought that would have been too rude in front of the unit.

I soldiered on with odds and sods, while Stuart got on with the interminable craps games. Fortunately, Marty had not been pestering me as he probably thought he'd got what he wanted out of me. He didn't yet know that I had advised Puttnam not to reshoot the alley scene. Marty still had a bug up his arse about it and would kick and scream if prevented from restaging it.

Eventually the shoot was over. Stuart and I had worked hard to have a version ready for Ben to view before he left Toronto. This involved a lot of overtime and anxiety. On the day Ben arrived with his wife and ran the movie, it was, of course, endlessly long and dull, but it was all there for the director to see and, instead of thanking us, he simply walked out of the projection room without a word. We were furious and I realised then that Ben had no idea how to count his blessings. Stuart, the Canadian crew, and I went out and got plastered.

Later, back in Hollywood, when I'd reverted to my real role and was no longer cutting *The Big Town*, I took Ben out to lunch and gave him a talking to about how to treat his crew. I said that he'd better loosen up if he wanted to direct movies.

Marty was often on the phone giving me his latest rant. He always called me "Lord Jim," doubtless a reference to the novel by Joseph Conrad, which I'd bet money he'd never read. Stuart continued editing and the film, when released, did poor business. As far as I know, Ben Bolt never made another picture.

Letter from John Schlesinger:

19th December, 1986

My Dear Jim,

Many thanks for your hysterically funny letter. I did warn you about the seven scripts per weekend, which would be my least favourite part of the job, I suspect.

Madame pines, as I am sure you know and I am popping around to see her before I leave for New York on Monday. I hope that your respective Christmases won't be too bleak.

I met with Iain Smith the other day and liked him quite a bit. He made all the right noises about Liverpool, as my agent insists on calling the project. We had lunch with Lynda Miles and Sheila Delaney, who Linda thinks should write the script. I am less certain as I am not sure whether she has any spark of humour and I hear that *Dance With A Stranger* was like pulling teeth from a director's point of view. Ian wants another meeting to see the whites of my eyes, as he put it and, I suppose, to judge my enthusiasm for the project. I have had to tell him that it is not at the top of my list, as there are other things I have been working on for some time.

Von Karajan has rung me from Saltzburg and asked me to go and do Boris there in 1988. Iain Smith didn't like the sound of all this at all, so I imagine "film stars may not be going to live or die in Liverpool." However, I quite like the idea, if we expand it from the book and make the boy gay or bisexual, which is what I think he is and won't admit in the book. I think that the relationship of two actors living in their fantasy worlds, from totally opposing experiences, coming together in the way they do, might spark off some very interesting results.

One or two interesting offers filter through, the latest from Disney, where their policy is to try and repeat the success of *Witness*. Take a mediocre script, get a good actor and director and voila, you have a hit. This time it is a mafia piece with Baryshnikov starring!

I shall probably arrive in L.A. around January 6th and hope you are there and we can see each other, particularly over the weekend of the 10th.

Your joint present has gone to Kensington Square.
Meanwhile, have a good Christmas with Kate and send her my love.

We all send ours—John

As soon as one mess was out of the way I encountered another. Fred Bernstein asked me to look at another unfinished film, *The Stranger,* formerly titled *Deadly.* I had heard about this one, made during the previous regime, which was already mixed and had received a dreadful reception after a studio preview. It was a real oddity. A film shot in Argentina but set in California. American actors were employed along with some other faces that looked anything but Californian. A mystery story starring Bonnie Bedelia and Peter Riegert, it was directed by an Argentinian and made for around $4 million.

I knew that David Puttnam had seen it and was aghast. Tom McCarthy had taken about fifteen minutes out of it after the disastrous screening, but claimed it was beyond salvation. They were now slating some retakes or additional scenes, though the original director was no longer involved, a situation that was becoming familiar.

After lunch I sat down with Tom and we viewed *The Stranger.* They say you get what you pay for in life and this was no exception to that rule. A total mishmash. Badly acted, badly shot, badly written, and badly directed. I couldn't follow it at all and kept wondering why it got so far without someone blowing the whistle. The film was about a woman who loses her memory in a car accident and has amnesia attacks in a hospital. For reasons best known to themselves, the filmmakers decided to show all the distorted flashbacks in colour while everything in the present was black and white. Or maybe it was the other way round. Whichever way, it was confusing.

Fred Bernstein was the production executive on it and told me that he had considered the director talented, based on previous work, and that the rushes seemed fine. This led me to suspect Fred's ability to read rushes. He was thirty-two, very personable, and came from the legal side. He was also deeply involved in *White Water Summer* with John Feidler, so I was beginning to suspect that these guys had little creative judgment. *The Stranger,* unlike *White Water Summer,* looked like a stiff to me. I couldn't see a way out for it. I reported all this to Fred, who asked me to look at the original cut that he had on tape. I did. Although it was just as awful as the shorter version, there were some scenes that should not have been deleted since they made some sense of the story. I then wrote a line-by-line description of each scene, each flashback, in its current order and then tried to figure a way in which this material could be reorganised to make some sense.

I tried to straighten it out so that it could be released at all, even directly to cable or cassette. I figured that additional shooting would be a total waste of money, but there might be a way to join up the flashbacks and superimpose a voiceover to tell some of the facts. There was a scene quite early on in which the doctor injects the girl with something so that she can try to recall what happened to her. I thought if we opened up this sequence, so that we saw the doctor asking more questions and the girl answering them, we could at least make the darn thing somehow more approachable.

One of the biggest faults of this mess was that it had absolutely no feeling of America and this was not because I knew it was shot abroad. The big gimmick of the story was that it was told backward, so that the audience didn't understand it until the very end. This must have seemed a cunning notion on paper, but on the screen, it was simply a confusion.

I had a meeting with Fred and Tom and told them they had two possibilities. First, they could clean up the existing version and release it. They could implement some of my ideas, though I would require the services of a writer, an editor, and some new scoring. The second course was that they could trash it. Fred looked relieved and suggested we implement course one without delay. In no time he was on the phone to the original writer, arranging for him to fly to Los Angeles to work with me. He also cancelled any plans for reshoots. He was excited by the prospect of being let off this particularly nasty little hook. I was flying by the seat of my pants and explained that all of this might be in vain. I could only improve the goods, perhaps 20 to 50 percent. Fred replied, "You'll improve it maybe 50 to 60 percent."

The Stranger was one of the first sickly movies to be wheeled into my new trailer. To be honest, I knew it was beyond salvation, but decided to tackle it anyway, which would allow me to touch film again. Withdrawl symptoms had been clear for some time. With Claire Simpson cutting *Someone to Watch Over Me* in the next trailer, I set about dissecting *The Stranger.*

First I tried to sort out the story by putting everything that was in colour into black and white and vice versa. Then we had a new music track written and recorded. Much revoicing was also done to try and make the entire venture more Californian. I cut out all the road signs that were not American. There was a good deal of time and additional money spent on this ill-conceived venture, so it was no longer a low-budget experiment.

It was tested again and it died again. Whether it was ever ultimately shown or went on a shelf is not known by me.

The next morning's creative meeting was about to start when David Picker walked in and said we should all leave for his office forthwith as the atmosphere would be cosier. It was then like a den meeting. Picker rattled through a number of items in his customary rush. There were a few that I had not encountered before, including Terry Gilliam's *Adventures of Baron Munchausen* and the script for Bill Cosby's *Leonard Part 6*. I was asked my opinion of the first two days of Ridley Scott's *Someone to Watch Over Me*. I gave it my high sign, and we all moved on.

A letter from Laurence arrived. She was angry with me for leaving her and our home and all that goes with it. I had anticipated this letter. Since I had accepted this job, our phone conversations had taken on a distinctly chilly feeling. Although we had been married for many years and our daughter Sybil was now in her late twenties, she felt I had acted rashly and cavalierly when I took this job at Columbia. Laurence, being French, had never been comfortable in Los Angeles. She came with me in 1973 for *The Day of the Locust* and again on *Marathon Man*, but she never really found anything to like about the place. It was an alien culture. On *Honky Tonk Freeway*, she was happier because she was involved, working on the film. But now that her career had restarted in London, I had left her again, for a long time and her letter was certainly expressive:

Dear Jim,

I hope you are enjoying your job, that it is worthwhile because you are causing me a lot of pain and anger. We had such a happy life, why disrupt it to such an extent at a later stage in our life? If you can leave all we have built over the years so easily, there must be something very wrong. But of course, I forgot, Work comes First, always, even though experience should have taught you better. You take these jobs without qualms because you think I am going to follow, I'm going to adjust. It's always me who has to make the effort. Not you. You think I am coming to L.A. and live in rented places which are not mine and not created by me. But I'm not so sure I can face it, that I can physically and mentally do it. When will you ever be back here in our real home or in the Île de Ré—our second real home? I wonder when. You seem so far away. It's still strange that we are separated for the first time in 22 years—and again you were asking me to come over—not you to come back. I just hope it's all worthwhile. Our "quality of life" was so perfect those past few years.

Written in desperation after one of those depressing phone calls when you are so near and so far. Maybe don't call me for a while, only when you need something like videos or medicine, when I can play my usual role of Housekeeper, provider. . . .

Anyway now you have all your machines installed in your office you must be the happiest man in town since we all know your love for machines. Each room here is full of those reminders. What about your love for Human Beings?

Love,

Laurence.

This was not the sort of letter one hopes to get from one's wife and I must have phoned her when I had read it and probably wrote a long letter trying to justify my actions. What really got to me, afterward, was a letter from Sybil:

January 17. 1987

Dear Dad,

Thanks to your wonderfully tactful letter, a major depression has been triggered off. Mum asked if I could read Dad's letter to her, not an unfair question, since I usually read yours to her, but I had to hum and ha in a not very convincing way until I was forced to admit that it would probably upset her very much, which alone, naturally, upset her very much. Well, how could I show her a letter which had written all over it, and *underlined too,* how boring she was becoming to her friends. It is all very well for you to make jokes about her nick-name, you are a million miles away and are trying to make light of a difficult situation by making flippant remarks. I know we sometimes joke about the fact she occasionally has "zee tahct of aan elephant." Well it's your turn to be in Jumbo's shoes now. Two days ago, mum came home and cried her eyes out for the first time in years a) because Ian had just died and she was feeling very emotional (which you might have considered), b) because it is extremely hurtful and humiliating to be told that people whom you have always considered close friends find you boring. What I find most shocking was your need to repeat this vexing piece of information, almost with glee, it seems. If

John and Michael cannot put up with one evening of mum complaining about her situation, they are obviously not the friends they claim to be.

Mum is genuinely upset by the situation she finds herself in and every time she resigns herself to it or forgets it for a while you come out with a real corker which throws her right back into the blues. Of course on the one hand, she is delighted that you are excited and fulfilled with your new job and we all agree that you had to try your hand at something other than editing in order not to stagnate. On that level, mum is very supportive and knows that you are right, but she cannot pretend to be happy with the fate you have created for her, which either means being lonely in the house she loves, or not lonely, but bored senseless in a place that she hates. You expressed in one of your letters a dubious wish, something to the tune of "had you been another kind of woman, you would have been happy to come and live here." Like it or not, you are a male-chauvinist at heart. You want a diplomat's wife, a woman who sacrifices her home and friends for the man she loves and who creates a cosy environment for him wherever he goes by ensuring the smooth running of the household, delicious meals and dinner parties etc. Well, mum is not Princess Di, or the Right Honourable Dick head's wife, and you should consider yourself lucky that Laurence is not a Stepford wife (i.e., a robot at your command). She played the perfect wife and willingly, for many years, leaving home and career to bring up your children and now suddenly she is fed up of making sacrifices without a murmur and angry at the fact it's always the woman who follows the man. What massive sacrifice have you ever made? If mum had a triple bypass, you would probably stay in the States with Puttnam and just pay for a nurse or visit for a couple of weeks. I fear I have now entered the boring clan, I hope I have not bored you to sleep but I do think you have become rather smug out there. You seem to think you are entitled to have your cake and eat it too as the rather strange expression goes and I'm not going to let you get away with it since I am the witness of the side effects of your behaviour and attitude and they are not always psychosomatic but have a real cause. I know we make jokes about La Frogesse and the way she repeats herself endlessly but when the joke starts becoming hurtful, it's no longer funny and it's time to stop. There, all this sounds terribly melodramatic and I'm not used to writing this kind of letter, especially to my daddy, but I think it needs to be said. What goes on between you two is not really my business, at least not directly, until you try to make me a partner in crime by trying to make me laugh at something that has hurt mum very much and which I have to bear the brunt of.

I'll stop laying into you now or you'll think I've stopped loving you, which is simply not true and I think that many misunderstandings are born from long distance communication. I hope that as soon as you are together, things will sort themselves out without bloodshed. In the meantime, take a few lessons in sensitivity.

Love, Sybil.

This letter really made me think I had done harm to my family by taking this dumb job and no amount of phoning would sort this out. Was I really that chauvinistic? I suppose I was. But what should I do? Resign and take the next plane home? I didn't know what to do to show Laurence that I cared about her and cared about us. We talked it over and I decided to stay, but whether I'd stay the full term was unclear. We seemed to have lived through that crisis, but "Work Comes First" was a phrase that Laurence repeated a lot over the course of time.

☆　☆　☆

I read the script of the Cosby film, *Leonard Part 6* and was disappointed, as it was not what I had expected for the current Cosby persona. This was an elaborate James Bond–style adventure movie, very expensive, full of action and jokes. I had thought it might be a rather calmer piece. It was a second draft and there was time to play with it, but obviously that was the style of picture they had conceived, and presumably what Cosby wanted.

The plot, having to do with crazed animal activists who were planning to feed a chemical to all the animals and birds so that they would turn against mankind, was quite ludicrous. In addition they wanted this film ready by Thanksgiving. It didn't complete principal photography until July and was stuffed with special effects. We'd see how it had gone down with the other troops at the next Monday morning meeting.

I then started to read Terry Gilliam's *Adventures of Baron Munchausen*, which made the Cosby show look very simple indeed. This script was a vast fantasy, based on the old German folk tales about the fabulous Baron. Being a Gilliam project, it was absolutely stuffed with visual jokes and effects and came out as a kind of giant Swiftian Alice in Wonderlandish saga. I had no idea how much this would cost, but it read very expensive indeed.

I knew that Puttnam and Picker had met with Gilliam about it and I thought that Puttnam had been connected with the project before, since it had been around for some years. Naturally it was a classy property and someone would have to decide whether it was at all practical. It certainly was the kind of subject only the cinema could do properly and that surely was the kind of thing we should be fostering.

Three films were in production at this point. *Punchline* with Tom Hanks, *Vibes* with Cindy Lauper, and *Me and Him* which was set in New York and directed by the German, Doris Dörrie.

And now *Munchausen*. It was not exactly unfilmable, but it was never going to cost twenty million as Columbia had been told—more like forty million. At the meeting I said my piece, that it would cost far too much. Nobody was prepared to heed the warning and it went into production. I can't exactly say what went wrong within the first month, but the cost had already soared and the bond people were muttering that Gilliam had to go. Richard Fleischer was mentioned as a replacement and Gareth Wigan was sent to the location to try and sort things out. Mercifully I was not to get embroiled in this disaster, but watched from the wings as the costs went up and up. Gilliam was not removed. The film would eventually cost about $45 million and do very little in the way of business.

Of course it looked good but it was a stodgy story at best and very few people really understood it. I'd love to hear Gareth Wigan's side of it. Gareth had been my agent in London during *Darling* and *Midnight Cowboy*, but had become a producer, eventually moving to Los Angeles, where he did not fare too well. Puttnam rescued him when he joined Columbia. Gareth is the only member of the Puttnam unit who continued with Sony when they bought Columbia, and he remained a highly respected studio guru to whom all their top directors and artists turn when they sense trouble.

★   ★   ★

Leonard Part 6 was a problem from the get-go because it had been green lit by the previous regime and was a script that none of us liked and nobody wanted to make. The story featured Bill Cosby as a private eye who comes out of retirement to save the world. It was kind of a Bond spoof and was well into pre-production when we arrived at Columbia. It should not be forgotten that Cosby was very big on television at the time, and studios were falling over themselves to obtain his services for cinema. Cosby wrote an outline, which was then fleshed out into a screenplay by Jonathan Reynolds. In addition to being the hottest thing on the box, Cosby was also very big with Coca-Cola, who had purchased Columbia in 1982, and even owned a bottling plant.

The film was without a director and because David still had a reputation for choosing up-and-coming directors, he picked Paul Weiland, a protege of Alan Parker. Bill Cosby would accept whoever Puttnam recommended, so Paul ended up directing it. Alan Marshall, who'd produced for Alan Parker, was brought on as producer and, for a variety of reasons, the wheels fell very badly off this film while they were shooting it up in San Francisco.

Paul Weiland had not directed a feature before. He'd done mostly commercials. The very first thing they shot was something called the "bird dance," all to do with animal rights, in which Cosby did not appear. There were many reels of rushes to sit through, none of which were amusing. I remarked to my companions that I didn't envy the poor editor in London who would be putting this together and reported back to David Picker, who was acting as executive on the film, but rarely had time to attend rushes. Nothing that I saw in the following weeks made me smile, and occasionally I dragged Picker to the rushes in order to confirm my findings.

In San Francisco there were other, more political, issues on the *Leonard* set. Alan Marshall, a brusque East Ender, not given to holding back his opinions, had been heard to make unflattering remarks about Cosby and his entourage. Cosby became upset by Alan's attitude toward the film and the people working on it. He called Puttnam, demanding that Marshall be replaced. As I remember it, Puttnam refused to accede to this request, so Cosby called his chums at Coca-Cola. I've always considered, rightly or wrongly, that this telephone call was the beginning of the end for Puttnam at Columbia, as Cosby carried a lot of weight with those people. You don't go against a guy who owns a bottling plant.

David might have survived longer had he produced some films that made money for them, but he flew directly in the face of Hollywood as we know it. For example, they'd made *Ghostbusters* at Columbia, which had made a lot of money, and *Ghostbusters 2* was supposed to be put into production, but David sat on it because the actors, he thought, were asking for too much money. His policy was to reduce budgets not inflate them. He tried to do a lot of things that were against the normal Hollywood way and got himself a bad reputation. He also made many enemies who, unfortunately, were all capable of bringing him down. It is, after all, a very dynastic business. Hollywood is run by a small group of people. Ray Stark had been a very successful Columbia producer and he and David didn't see eye-to-eye at all. Falling out with Stark was one of the first nails in David's coffin.

I was aware that David was fouling the nest because I would read his speeches in *Variety* and *The Hollywood Reporter* and think that he shouldn't be saying these things. He could say them privately, but not publically. I did often wonder whether he was doing it deliberately. He was a guest over there, somebody who had been brought in and invited to head up a studio. Normally it would have been an American. Here was an Englishman, with a reputation for doing good work like *Chariots of Fire* and *The Killing Fields*. He was known as a serious filmmaker, but David somehow never quite wanted to join the party. He was always outside of it.

I was in a very junior position but I was aware that we were making lots of mistakes. When you're part of a team like that, you do kind of get swept away. It takes over your life totally.

Laurence, in an attempt to smooth things over between us, came and went occasionally, but it was an uneasy time, because I was working, even on weekends. On Friday evening I'd fall through the door with my ghastly six scripts and then there were the equally ghastly previews, which were normally out of town. So I'd find myself on a plane to Seattle or Chicago or Dallas, leaving poor Laurence in a house in the hills, alone and lonely.

Leonard Part 6 carried on and shooting was finally completed. Paul Weiland returned to London and edited his film, which I forgot about until it was ready for us to see around September of that year.

With *Leonard* temporarily out of the way, we made other pictures. *Stars and Bars* was from a comic novel by William Boyd and shot in Texas by Pat O'Connor. This was produced by Puttnam's ex-partner Sandy Lieberson. I was seeing the rushes but had nothing else to do with the film, but, for a comedy, they did look rather dark and I told Puttnam about this. He suggested I call Sandy, which I did. I'm told that when O'Connor was informed that one of the executives described the rushes as too dark, he threatened to have that executive kneecapped. Not wishing to be lame for the remainder of my life, I kept quiet thereafter. I should add that when the film was shown to us, we all thought it not funny and too somber. Being the messenger is rarely rewarding and the recipients never listen to you.

At one of the Monday morning creative meetings, David Picker said in an awestruck voice, "This is the kind of script I joined this company to make." The script he was talking about was *Old Gringo,* a three-hundred page, unreadable load of tosh that Columbia subsequently made with Jane Fonda. Having hated it from the beginning, I managed to keep my distance from it and never actually saw the film in its entirety. I did eventually catch half an hour on television and found it turgid and boring.

One of our lesser messes, though it was a huge problem at the time, was *Rocket Gibraltar* with Burt Lancaster. This was to be directed by the script's writer, Amos Poe, who was known to Tom Rothman. Tom was one of our younger executives, brought in by Picker from New York. Tom subsequently became head of production at Fox, but back then he was a humble ex-lawyer who had done work with Amos on his previous film.

We all liked the script of *Rocket Gibraltar,* which was a family film to be shot on the Hamptons. It was not high budget. Burt Lancaster was the patriarch and his children and grandchildren were played by an ensemble cast that included Kevin Spacey and Sinead Cusack. Tom and I were appointed as executives.

I had agreed that Melody London should edit the film, having been impressed by her work with Jim Jarmusch. They started shooting and, within a week, Tom and I knew they were in trouble. Amos clearly had no idea how to direct so many people. His rushes would not cut. I spoke to Melody about it and she agreed with me and had already complained to Amos about the lack of cover.

Tom and I went to Puttnam and were on the next plane east. We needed to confront Amos with his first week's work and, if he did not agree with our findings, fire him from his own film. This was not easy for Tom, since he was a friend.

We flew into New York and Tom drove the two-hour drive to the Hamptons which is where the chic seaside homes of very rich New Yorkers are. They flock there in summer, turning Long Island into the world's largest car park. If it had the weather, the east coast of England could become a double for the Hamptons, which Fitzgerald used as the setting for *The Great Gatsby.* The homes are often quite exquisite, but a sudden rash of spec building was doing much to wreck the place, as the farmers sold off their land for more houses. The real estate developers preyed on these farmers and, as soon as there was the slightest sign of a need for cash to pay off a loan, these sharks were in there and another potato field would fall, never to return. Some of the new homes were pure fantasies. There was a repro French chateau adjacent to something like a small Sydney Opera House. Many of the leafier lanes, however, look like Berks or Bucks and were very beautiful.

We had arranged for a portable projector to be set up, and Melody came up from New York to help in the confrontation with Amos. It was a difficult scene, since Amos was so nice. It would be hard to knife him. After we'd all viewed the material, I, uncharacteristically, laid into him. The shots simply would not cut together and were, in any case, poorly staged. Melody agreed with me. That was on a Saturday night and, having looked at more rushes, I was inclined to fire Poe on the spot, sad though it would be for all concerned. We spent the whole of Sunday mulling over the situation and looking for any alternative that could keep things afloat. We had Poe to lunch and roasted him, to no avail. He smiled a lot while I told him how a director was supposed to suffer a bit now and then. The whole show was getting more political by the minute.

On Monday, the unit arranged to shoot in the Quogue Public Library, just up the road. I remembered that the wondrous Wodehouse had once conjoined with the even more wonderful Kern to write a ditty that they called "Bungalow in Quogue." I recalled that the great author lived out his life in the Hamptons and enquired of the librarian, who told me she had known him well and that he had often popped in to see how the latest novels were moving. She explained that he had lived up the road at Remsenburg. I spent a happy hour reading a biography of his life in America while Amos directed a simple two hander to which I could not contribute.

That night we viewed a week's rushes that lasted until midnight. We were all exhausted and I was getting tired of laying into the director and getting no kick back. The next day, we were up at seven on location in a cemetery, where Amos had to direct the entire cast without Lancaster who was being buried. I knew this would tax him, so leapt in and organised him so that the cast should not suss out that he was incapable at staging. I was rapidly making myself indispensable to the producer, which was a bad move, so I went back into my shell and observed from the wings.

I tottered back to Columbia, still uncertain as to the future of this venture, but knowing that we should have done the unthinkable and replaced the director. I ran the dailies for Picker, who did not react quite as violently as I had, and thought we should not be too draconian. His recipe for retaining the status quo was to send old Ronnie Neame, now seventy-five and quite hale, off to the location to act as a technical advisor. This was some form of solution, though hardly ideal. We stopped shooting for a day until Ronnie arrived. I'll not say he was, by now, a spent force, but he was hardly a dynamo.

The distress signals from the Hamptons finally forced us to fire Amos from his own film. We put out an SOS for a director, which was not easy. A good director is not usually sitting around waiting for a film to fix, but we did find Dan Petrie Sr, who was willing to come to our rescue and did so. Tom and I ran everything for him and the cameraman and a plan of attack emerged. We barely lost a day's work in this difficult time, but once we saw Dan's results we knew that we need not worry.

Instead of appearing angry at being replaced, Amos Poe seemed relieved, and headed home, leaving his young daughter, a cast member, behind.

Rocket Gibraltar is hardly remembered now, but it was not bad and gave the ensemble cast a good deal of exposure, resulting in a few long careers. It was, reluctantly, released by the regime that followed us.

☆   ☆   ☆

One of the pictures that Puttnam invested in was *Time of the Gypsies*, a film by Emir Kusturica. When Dawn Steel and her retinue replaced us, she read out the list of films we had bequeathed to them. Apparently there was much laughter when she came to *Time of the Gypsies*, which she announced was in Serbo-Croatian. This damnation nailed the coffin on other of our efforts, including *Rocket Gibraltar* which was hardly shown. They did, however, see *La Bamba*, which was the cause of some rejoicing when, on our Monday morning weekend review, it had come out on top. *La Bamba* was a buy in, so we had no real reason to celebrate. In fact, the biggest success of our regime was *The Last Emperor*, in which we had no creative input at all. *Hope and Glory* we had money in and did alter a little after American previews, but it was really John Boorman's film, not ours. As was Spike Lee's *School Daze* that was previewed to a largely black audience in New Jersey, a number of whom walked out. It was a movie that appealed to very few of any colour.

As an executive, I was able to support films that I thought should be made. Two of these were *The New Adventures of Pippi Longstocking*, which was directed by the retired Ken Annakin and *Earth Girls Are Easy*, which I have never seen. Largely due to my backing, both these films were made, specifically since I and our overseas buyer thought they would play in the Far East. I guess we weren't thinking straight by this time and I can't believe our reasons were justified. Both movies sank without a trace.

One of the better things to come out of my period at Columbia was, curiously, Steven Soderbergh. He was a penniless writer at that time and had not sold anything, but his old friend Bobby Newmyer, with whom I had worked on *Milo and Otis*, took pity on Steven and allowed him to use his office and his typewriter. Soderbergh had written a script that I liked and persuaded my group to read. Unfortunately they did not take to it, and so we passed on the script and on Steven who was to become a major talent in Hollywood. Bobby Newmyer produced Steven's *Sex, Lies, and Videotape*. Sadly, Bobby died suddenly in 2005.

Things were getting rough at Columbia. The only films that did any business were *Roxanne, The Big Easy,* and *The Last Emperor*—none of which we'd made. We had, however, made *Leonard Part 6* and that now came back to haunt us.

I had kept in touch with the *Leonard* cutting room in London and had been told all was well and that the director's cut would soon be ready for us to see. It was cut at Pinewood by Gerry Hambling who, like Weiland, specialised in commercials.

Paul Weiland would show it to Bill Cosby on their way to us in Los Angeles. We heard nothing but praise and so were not too surprised when Cosby called and said it was great, exactly what he'd hoped for.

Leonard Part 6 was to be Columbia's big release for that Christmas. We felt we had nothing to worry about, until a few days later when we saw it at the studio. It was terrible. A comedy without a single laugh. It was the only time that David Puttnam and I had the slightest friction between us. I went up to his office afterward and said, "I don't know what to do with it. That film is dreadful." It wasn't really surprising because I'd been reporting on the terrible rushes all along. He said to me, "I don't care what you think about it. You've got to fix it." He was in a bind and the only person he could think of who might perhaps breathe some life into it was me. He was off to China the following day to see Bertolucci. David Picker, whose movie this was, told me to recut the film so that it worked. I knew this to be an impossibility.

I told Gerry Hambling and Paul Weiland that a recut was required and that all the trims and spares should be sent directly from Pinewood to Los Angeles. I then went, cap in hand, to Tom McCarthy and told him I needed six new editors to recut the film. He sent out SOS messages and on the following Monday morning we had five. Gerry remained and I became editor number six. We were quartered down in the car park. Gerry was in one trailer and I was in the next. We divided the picture up and decided who should recut what. I then asked for the trims of each scene.

Gerry, though he'd been editing some very good films for years, was a bit less than thorough when it came to housekeeping and the trims were in a mess. All editors realise that it is essential to housekeep and that usually involved writing numbers on small trims that were under six frames and did not carry an identity. Gerry had cut a million commercials and was given to snipping off frames and dropping them, unidentified, into the bin. The assistant would then sweep them up and put them in a supermarket bag.

The state the trims were in caused a certain amount of consternation among our editors. One editor only lasted until lunchtime and was never seen again. Another was given the climax to recut and when he asked for the trims he was handed several bags of them. He went ballistic and charged up to Picker's office, interrupting a meeting. He then emptied the bags on Picker's desk. "Do you really expect me to recut this?" he bellowed. I don't know what Picker's response was, but the editor put all the bits back in the bags and swept out. He did recut the climax, under wretched cirumstances, but he couldn't save *Leonard*. Neither could I.

All the scenes were divided up among us; I was somehow given that ghastly bird dance I'd complained about back in rushes months before. The studio mortician and his henchmen all worked incredibly long hours trying to inject life into this particularly dead corpse. We worked seven-day weeks for a month and we were all exhausted, especially since the Elmer Bernstein score had to be recorded and a temp mix done for a public preview.

I went into Gerry Hambling's cutting room late one Saturday and found the producer, Alan Marshall, editing on a Moviola. I went wild, not my usual reaction. "But you're the producer!" I screamed. He explained that he used to be an editor, which was enough for me. I slammed the door and went home.

Leonard Part 6 was previewed in some unknown suburb of Los Angeles on a Sunday evening. Tom McCarthy drove me there for a morning rehearsal. It ran through, as awful as ever. When we came out of the theatre at 3 PM, it was very hot and the public were already lining up to see the film which would not be shown until 7:30 PM. That's how anxious they were to see Cosby. "Poor suckers," I remarked as we drove past. "They'll hate us." And they did. I can't say they threw rocks at the screen, but they walked out in hundreds and gave the film terrible marks on their scorecards. All the executives were there to witness this carnage. Cosby was not.

At the postmortem everyone was gloomy. What could we do in the time that was left? It was still our big Christmas movie. There was post-sync dialogue to be recorded in New York by Cosby who, by this time, was not speaking to anyone at Columbia. It seemed that, following a call with Picker, he had agreed to allow me to fly to New York and sit in the theatre with him. Picker had obviously sold him a bill of goods that I could save anything, so I went, with the list of loops and wild tracks we required. Cosby, who was never unpleasant to me, sat on a stool in the theatre, went through the list and refused to do most of the work, which he deemed unnecessary. But after two days, mostly spent listening to him philosophising, I had almost all of the requirements.

My job, however, was not yet over. Back in Hollywood someone had suggested a prologue might help the film, so I had to proceed directly to London, go to the Earl of Bedford's country pile, meet a crew in the kitchen, and watch another director put Tom Courtenay, who'd played the butler in the film, through a short prologue. "I can't begin to tell you what an honour it was to act as Leonard's butler. He was in retirement at the time. . . ." You know the sort of thing. It was only a day's shoot and I flew back to Burbank and cut it in. It made not a shred of difference and I never had to see *Leonard* again, but I had seen home and family for just a short time and was determined this situation would not last too long.

Leonard Part 6 opened to dire reviews and nobody went. It closed shortly after and it put the seal on our time at Columbia.

I had been house-sitting for a few different people during my stay in Los Angeles. I house sat for the Schmidts while Artie was over in London doing *Roger Rabbit* for Zemeckis, and eventually I rented my own place.

As the year ended I was thinking of buying a house in Los Angeles and did, in fact, find one. It had gone into escrow and my wife was not pleased by this prospect, since she had no desire to live there, but I was tired of house-sitting and renting. I finally wanted a place of my own since it looked as if I was to see this three-year contract out.

David Puttnam came to my office one night, a rare event in itself, and said, "I understand you're buying a house here. You know I don't think you should. I think you would be very wise to cancel it." So he was telling me that things were going to change and we weren't going to stay there. I cancelled the purchase of the house and about a week later David left Columbia.

On the night that Ridley Scott's *Someone to Watch Over Me* was shown to the studio employees, David made his announcement. Ironic that it should come at the screening of the very first film he put into production. I knew something was up as he'd asked for more video cameras than usual and the theatre seemed to be filled with people who would not normally be there.

David's announcement that he was leaving Columbia was received first in stunned silence and then with tears, mostly from the girls in the outer offices, who were all crying into their hankies. I noticed the extra cameras zooming in on them. David is a showman and he knew what a devastating effect his news would have. It is true that he had managed to endear himself to most of the employees, be they craftsmen or secretaries, by treating them as real human beings. Bothering to seek them out, talk to them, and make them feel a part of the Columbia fraternity. They'd all fallen in love with David. He was a god to them, so different was he from what they were used to. Then he spoke to them all and it was extremely moving. Everybody was in tears. When we all went back to our offices, the girls, particularly the secretaries and all those people that he'd enchanted, couldn't believe what they'd heard. It was, perhaps, sad that his magic did not work on those above him who required a return for their money.

Nobody had yet been appointed to succeed David and, until that occurred, there were lots of nervous executives sweating it out in the creative corridor, worried about their futures. I didn't give a damn one way or the other. In fact I was happy to leave. Labouring on *Leonard Part 6* had buried me temporarily so I was out of the loop. The one big joy of the current situation was that I no longer felt obliged to read six scripts each weekend. In fact I put them directly into the bin, which gave me enormous pleasure.

In spite of David's leaving, my contract was up for renewal and I signed it, realising I might not see the year out. There were soon rumours that our time was up and that David would be replaced by Dawn Steel and her own entourage.

The day came that Coca-Cola sent a lady lawyer from New York to fire us. She was put into Fred Bernstein's office, where a steady stream came and went throughout the day. I was not called. By six o'clock, I'd become worried that they might want to keep me. After all, I had gained an undeserved reputation as a film doctor. Perhaps Dawn Steel wanted me to stick around. I prayed not and that prayer was answered at six thirty when I was finally called, the last on the list. Fred Bernstein and I always enjoyed a laugh and a joke and he stood behind this well-dressed lady lawyer who, by now, must have been tired of trotting out the same message to the employees she'd been sent to fire. From the start of our interview, Fred made funny faces at me, willing me to giggle. I managed to hold a straight face until the lady said, in sonorous tones, "Mr. Clark, I have to tell you that you have been terminated." At this point I burst out laughing in a fit of giggles. I guess she never really understood why, as she was unaware of Fred's antics behind her back. I'd never been terminated before or since, but it was a fitting end to what had been a complete charade. I left her office saying "Thanks" and spluttering fit to bust.

One little bonus was that they would pay fifty cents on the dollar for the remainder of our contracts. Since I'd just renewed the contract, I ended up getting half my annual salary as I left, so I didn't do too badly and I was terribly relieved to be going home and leaving that job behind. And nobody was happier than Laurence. Our marriage had survived.

I realised, rather late in my career, that I was not good at keeping lots of projects in focus. I was best when attending to one item, and being a production executive had split me into endless bits, none of them really efficient.

I never returned to the so-called creative corridor. I returned to being a back-room boy in the cutting rooms, where I belonged.

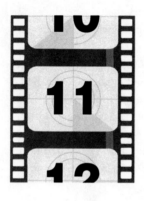

DAYS WITH FRANCO

The Young Toscanini

I was enjoying a quiet Sunday evening at home in London during the spring of 1988 when Richard Marden, a fellow film editor, called me. He'd been speaking to Franco Zeffirelli who, at that moment was lying in a hospital bed in Los Angeles, following a hip operation. Franco was also recovering from taking a look at the first cut of his latest film, *The Young Toscanini,* and was in a state of singular unhappiness. His regular editor, Peter Taylor, had sent a tape over and Franco hated what he'd seen. He was on the hunt for an editor to take the film over from Peter, sooner rather than later. Richard was not free to undertake this task and suggested I might talk to Franco as I was between jobs and had three free months before starting a new film.

A short stay in Rome was not an altogether unpleasant idea, so I called Franco, whom I had met briefly at John Schlesinger's Los Angeles home and we talked over the situation. I explained that I could give him three months but not a day longer and would want to involve my regular assistant, Bryan Oates, as second editor. All the Italian editing staff would be retained after Peter Taylor and his wife were relieved of their posts. Peter had cut many films for Franco without any previous problems but had been stumped by this one. I rang Bryan and he agreed to join me, Rome being one of his favourite places. I then called the producer and terms were agreed. Franco was delighted and lay back in his hospital bed, assuming his film was now in good hands.

At this stage you might be wondering why the title *The Young Toscanini* does not ring a bell. The film had a $20 million budget and starred Elizabeth Taylor. So far as I know, it never appeared anywhere apart from Italy and France.

The stupid thing is that I never asked to look at Peter Taylor's version before I left for Rome so that I could see what had upset Franco. I simply assumed that anything he directed would have merit of some sort and it never occured to me that I should give the goods the once over. After all those years in the cutting room, I should have known better.

When Bryan and I arrived in Rome, we went directly to the office of the producer, Fulvio Lucisano, and saw the film. This is when we should have taken the next plane home, but we didn't. Instead we started work on the recut long before Franco returned from Los Angeles. One day he appeared. The corridors at Cinecittà are built of marble. I heard Franco before I saw him. Like Miss Haversham in *Great Expectations*, his cane tapped out his return.

He invited us to lunch at the Villa Grande and the ageing, hobbled maestro was in fine form. His court bobbed and weaved around him. A genial host, Franco said to me, alarmingly, "I want to taste your flesh!" I never really found out, though I thought I knew, what this meant.

Laurence came over for a short visit, during which Franco kindly invited us all to lunch. All went well until we sat down at the dining table. Next to Franco was a high chair, such as you would have for a child, but Franco had no kids. He did, however, have Bambina who was a female Jack Russell of doubtful vintage, but with many teats. Franco spoke to her in a baby voice, "Bambina, Bambina, does my lovely girl like sitting next to her Franco?" This went on and he fed the dog who sat and ate the food that Franco gave her. Although Laurence did not outwardly react to this, everyone knew she was horrified. Later Franco said to me, "That woman is hard. She does not like dogs. She was offended by Bambina." Otherwise, it was a congenial visit.

The re-editing continued slowly as, daily, the whole thing became more and more unspeakable. Franco wanted to hang on to bad scenes, which he thought funny. He was all piss and Penhaligon. I was tempted to resign.

The other producer arrived. Tarak Ben Ammar, a wealthy young Tunisian. At a meeting that morning Franco had told me not to talk to Tarak, with whom he had been fighting, but Tarak sat down to lunch with us in the studio commissary, so there was no escape. Then he saw the first seven reels and came back saying it was all very much improved. I couldn't tell Franco I hated this movie. It's hard to be unkind with, or about, Franco, who was very thoughtful. I ran through three more reels. I felt nothing but contempt for this boring claptrap and yet had to appear interested.

For viewing the film we used a flatbed editing machine called a Prevost, a very strange, rather clunky contraption. Franco would never appear in the cutting room before four in the afternoon, by which time he was always a tiny bit sauced. Not drunk but not exactly sober. He would come in, sit down beside me and say, "Right Jeem. Show me what we did yesterday." So I'd put the scene up on the machine and we'd run it for a few moments and then he would say, "No, no, no, no!" He'd never get to the end of a scene, he'd just run a bit of it and then he would have a sort of explosion. He'd say, "No, no, no, no! This is not what we decided at all. I told you to do this. Why have you done it like that?" Then I would consult my notes, "Well, because yesterday you told me to do it this way. You said this is how you wanted it. You wanted to cut to the closeup here . . ."

"I never said anything of the sort," he'd splutter.

Then I'd say, "I'm sorry Franco, but that was what you told me yesterday and I'm only carrying out your instructions."

"Well eet was a stupid meestake! Eet was a stupid cut!"

So then he would simmer down and he'd run a bit more and then he'd stop, scream again and stab the screen with his finger, saying, "See? That ees a terrible cut! That ees a really bad cut! You should never do a cut like that!"

To which I would reply, "Well that was your idea not mine."

"Look," he'd say. "Remember. Whenever there's a problem, you cut to the beetch." And I, for awhile, didn't quite understand what he meant. I said, "Cut to the bitch? What do you mean by that?"

"You cut to Elizabeth. She ees the money. You cut to Elizabeth. Eef there's any problem at all, you cut to the beetch."

He was a devoted friend of Elizabeth, but he always referred to her as the bitch. I doubt that he ever called her this to her face. Bryan said it was harmless, vaguely amusing, and Franco's way of differentiating between the sexes. It was not in any way pejorative. To him, women were bitches and men were boys. "Now darling, go to the boy and then cut back to the bitch."

Bryan Oates:

Jim had slowly but irrevocably got more and more pissed off with being in Rome, working on a stillborn film for what he considered to be a partly inebriated director.

Franco had fallen in love with the zoom lens, something the Americans and British had got used to over the previous ten years. To Franco, however, it was a great new tool, allowing him to have any size shot he wished at will. The snag was that we editors often wanted a close shot when the zoom lens only offered a wide shot or vice versa. This infuriated Jim and his anger slowly burned until one day Franco berated him for not using the zoom in a shot. For Jim it was the last straw. I rarely saw him vent his anger but, boy, did he go for it that day.

"Look Franco," he exploded. "You can take your fucking zoom lens and throw it into the Tiber!" After an appalling pause, Franco turned to me and said, "I don't theenk Jeem likes the zoom lens very much." As ever, Franco got round the unpleasantness with this remark. We both laughed while anger spent, Jim, smiled.

Franco always had this little Gucci bag with him and he would, surreptitiously, pour a little bit from a bottle into a tiny paper cup that he would swallow, thinking I did not see him. What he never realised, however, was that on these machines, the screens would reflect and I could always see what he was doing by looking in the glass. I didn't have to look around, I knew. He was always knocking back these little quantities of Chivas Regal.

At a merry gathering at the Villa Grande, we met the Harwoods, Aprile Millo, who was Elizabeth's singing voice in the film, the agent Ed Lomato, who looked haggard, and Helena Bonham-Carter who looked young and pretty. Franco arrived at four and disrupted everything by inviting us to Positano for the weekend. I told him my daughter Sybil was coming to Rome with her boyfriend Eric. "Bring them too," was the reply. He wasn't taking no for an answer. I said we had to work on his movie, but that made no difference.

Bryan Oates:

Franco was ever keen that Jim and I should join him in Positano for the weekends. This, in my experience was only superb Italian hospitality, which I meet with from all in Italy when I worked there, something the Brits and Americans could learn from. Well, Jim, who wanted to be back in UK, avoided these invitations like the plague. "Why does Jeem not want to come to Positano?" asked Franco. "Don't worry, Franco, I'll bring him round. I should love to come." I went and persuaded Jim that, in the interest of peace in the cutting room, we should venture to Positano. I went back to Franco and told him he'd come. "Oh," said Franco. "That is wonderful news. You and he can pack your little bags and we all go to Positano!" And we did.

I remember Franco was determined to get all news of John Schlesinger from Jim. He had let the Positano estate to John some years back and it had clearly left its mark on Franco. He was full of questions. "Did John think this? Did John have such fine scenery? Did John have such marble, such pictures, such a chef, such fine clothes . . . ?" Endless comparison, to all of which Jim remained poker faced. This only served to confuse Franco in his relationship with Jim even more.

With Bryan, we took a train to Naples, then a local train to Metta, and finally a taxi to Positano. Franco was a terrific host in what must be one of the great houses of the world. It was on seven levels, gradually descending to the ocean. Franco was taken by Eric, my daughter Sybil's boyfriend, who was quite striking. Eric blushed. I explained, "Eric is a designer of houses and interiors." Eric was, at that point, a house painter, at which Franco showed even more interest. "You design homes? You are the new David Hicks?"

The rest of the weekend was given over to rest and relaxation. We dined on the terrace, Bryan got tight and asked Franco a string of highly personal questions. His answers were evasive, but entertaining.

The weekend ended as we journeyed to the mainland on a water taxi. Franco led us through the streets. It was like a royal procession. Everyone knew him and we dived into a variety of shops. We went to a ceramic shop, since Franco had ordered a dinner set that hadn't yet arrived. I saw a few pieces that I was interested in and showed them to Franco, who then whisked us all to another store specialising in hats. We went in hatless and came out sporting hats that Franco had given us.

There was, however, a darker side to the weekend. The Venice Festival had requested *Toscanini* and Franco was concerned. I had no idea how they could have it ready. I counselled him against showing it, finished or not. I knew it would get the bird.

One day Franco was in a weird mood and he seemed to be worried about the picture. He put me off my guard by announcing that a man of my experience should have no trouble fixing the narrative and constructional problems. The irony of this statement came home to me as I noticed that *Little Nikita* was playing at the local theatre. Just the sight of the title made my blood chill. How many wasted hours on that one? How many on this one?

The movie now ran for two hours, thirty minutes and we got it ready for a screening for more people than I thought healthy. We finally had everything ready by early evening and at the end, the crowd all simpered and gave Franco a big Bravo. He then beamed and hugged me. Was this his "flesh" moment?

Franco seemed quite unphased by the screening. A few people whose opinions he trusted had suggested that some scenes were, perhaps, a little long. We would make cuts. Hooray. I finally suggested the old voiceover routine. We ran the reels and Franco was quite merry, saying, "You girls can get on with your embroidery."

Franco rolled up at four the next afternoon. He ran several reels, decimating some scenes, then reached into his bag for his fifth of Scotch which he then sipped. His mantra of "Cut to the Bitch," was repeated. The rift between Franco and Tarak rumbled on.

Fulvio Lucisano, the real working producer, who employed us, called to say he was very unhappy being caught between Franco and Tarak. The negative was sitting in Paris. He asked if I would please call Tarak and have it released or he would have to give us all two-weeks notice. Yes, please, was all I could think to say.

Tarak came to town and it was arranged he'd see the movie. Franco heard about it from me, put a ban on the screening, and withdrew to his home with three reels of action, thus rendering a screening impossible. The screening for Tarak was cancelled and Franco pronounced he'd been defeated. We did, however, run it for Ronald Harwood, an English writer who was staying with Franco. He'd been hauled in to write voiceover for *Toscanini,* as well as a new script.

Lucisano called the next day to say he was with Franco's boyfriend Pipo and was a very unhappy man. Franco, he told us, was an impossible egoist who would never finish the picture. He then asked when I could supply a fine cut. I suggested July 6. It was either that or he would fire Franco and close down the picture. Furthermore, Pipo told me that Lucisano was going around town telling everyone that I thought the picture was lousy. I had once said that to him, weeks ago, in confidence. They came to the studio where we discussed the situation more calmly. Now I proposed to give them a fine cut just before I left on July 26. I then heard that our composer, Roman Vlad, had cancer.

More deviousness became apparent. When I'd left the previous night, I had reel eight wound down on my bench. The next morning it was still there but at a certain footage. Later, Lucisano called to inform me that he had run the film after we left. Nobody told us and the assistants had kept quiet. I was mad for a minute until I thought, "Fuck it. Why should I care about the way they carry on?" It simply confirmed that Lucisano was not to be trusted, and that saddened me.

We were all at the studio to watch when Elizabeth arrived for her retakes, but she did not appear though rumoured to be in her caravan beside the set. It seemed she was suffering from a bad back and unfit for work. Franco was looking distraught. This retake session had taken weeks to organise and was costing a fortune.

Liz finally turned up and I was introduced to her for the second time. She looked very strange in closeup. Her face had spread and become huge and her lips didn't move much. Her body seemed to be reverting to flab. She retreated to her caravan and didn't emerge for hours. When called, she didn't come and, it wasn't until eight that evening that she tottered on, to do a mute shot, complaining a good deal. Her acting was grotesque, the school of Gloria Swanson.

Bryan Oates:

After Ronnie Harwood had been summoned to Rome by Franco to sort out the film's ending, it was decided to call back Elizabeth to shoot a signing off scene with Toscanini's girlfriend, played out in the wings of a theatre with the two girls watching Toscanini conduct.

Elizabeth had put a lot of weight on since finishing filming six months earlier and Sophie Ward, the other actress, was six months pregnant.

Franco decided to shoot Sophie from the waist up, but was unsure how to film Elizabeth and shared his concern with the cameraman.

"Don't worry," said the cameraman. "I shoot her from the side with a lot of back light, that will take the weight out of her face."

So it was done.

When the rushes came in I told Jim that Elizabeth had an halation all over her face where the light had picked up her facial hair.

"Don't mention it to Franco," said Jim. "Just tell him the rushes are ready to screen."

Franco arrived with his retinue and there was a dreadful silence as Elizabeth's shots came up and her closeups revealed a soft haze all over her face. Franco stopped the machine and turned to Jim and I.

"We 'ave made 'er look like a Peeeeeach," he said, and then smiled.

The retinue smiled.

Everyone smiled. There was never a problem anymore.

Eventually we used very little of the reshoots, simply because Elizabeth had changed physically during the months since principal photgraphy. The cameraman almost walked away from his impossible task. To think anything would match was beyond belief. In the end, even Franco realised he could use little of this material and it had all cost the production a great deal of money. The only plus was that Elizabeth did most of her ADR (automated dialogue replacement) while in Rome. Franco seemed resigned, almost as if he'd finally lost interest.

At the end of the three months, when the time came to leave, Franco pronounced me a traitor. "You're leaving me! You teepical Eenglish! You traitor!" He didn't really say it maliciously but he did everything he could to keep me there. At the end of all this, Lucisano said that Franco wanted me to have a credit for cutting the film. I told him I didn't need a credit. I was neither keen on the film nor was I the original editor. He said that Franco wouldn't buy that and would insist on me having a credit, so I suggested he say the film was edited by Chivas Regal. In the end, Franco put my name and Bryan's all over it.

During our final meal, Franco presented us with gifts. I got the ceramic salad bowl I had pointed to in the Positano shop, so the devious old rogue had noted my interest. It was at that point that I felt sorry for him.

The problems I had with Franco on *The Young Toscanini* are not typical of my experiences as a film editor, but they bring into focus just how wrong things can go on a movie and the kinds of madness that everyone in this industry has to deal with.

Although I was away at Shepperton, cutting *Spooks* for Anthony Thomas, the tenacious and lovable old Italian had called in my absence, desperate to talk to me, and would call back. I knew what he was ringing about, having read some of the British notices of *Toscanini* after its Venice premiere. They were dreadful reviews and generally reflected my own opinions. The only hopeful sign was that both reviews wound up saying the film was "a classic of kitsch and camp," which I thought might be seen as a virtue in some circles. The picture had been received with catcalls, jeers, and boos every time Franco's name appeared, this being a kickback from the remarks he is supposed to have made about *The Last Temptation of Christ*.

I finally heard from him. He was in a state of semi despair, not because he'd been kicked at Venice, but because he wanted to make some vital final changes to the picture and had no one to turn to. He was begging me to drop everything and return to Rome. It was out of the question since I was employed and up to my neck. He was in such a plight, though, and I did have a soft spot for him so, in the end, I agreed to return for one day only and do what I could. I was to fly to Italy on the Sunday.

My sister rang on Saturday afternoon to tell me that Mother was very ill and not expected to live another twenty-four hours. I was prepared to drop everything and drive up to her deathbed, but my sister said that would be pointless as the old lady was heavily sedated and would barely know I was there.

I didn't go and Mother did pass away. My relationship with her had always been a problem and I can't say that I loved her until she became older and had lost her sting. She and my father had a troubled marriage and, if they had been together today, I doubt they would have remained a couple. But they never let anyone know. Only the children were aware that something was wrong. I sometimes would hear them rowing in their bedroom. Things were different then. My mother had hated classical music, which my father loved. "Not that old bugger Bach again?" she might say as he put a record on the Deccola, or "What's that? The tune the old cow died of?" Father did get his own back. One day he made a bonfire of all Mother's piano scores, including the complete *Our Miss Gibbs*, which she used to bang out, right foot permanently on the loud pedal. He once threw an old chocolate cake on the fire, which my brother Dick and I thought very funny, but angered Mother. "I shall go and put my head in the gas oven," she said.

The family set the funeral for the coming Thursday and I flew off to Italy and headed for the Villa Grande where I would stay.

Franco returned from Positano just after I arrived and we sat down to a meal with the "family." A young American, Bill Stadiem, had written the original script for the film and received sole credit. He was still in shock from having seen the film in Venice and was trying to persuade Franco to change lots of the lines. I don't know how he was to achieve this and Franco showed no interest in that aspect of things. I reported that the London critics had butchered the film, but liked the kitsch and camp and, therefore, he might consider capitalising on that aspect of the film. I thought he might like to restore some of the more purple passages that I had done my best to remove.

None of this interested him and he launched into an antipress tirade, saying he'd been totally misquoted over the *Last Temptation* affair, that he never referred to "Jewish scum" and that the Chief Rabbi had written to him removing all blame from his name. I asked why he didn't print that in *Variety* to help clear him and he was evasive. His American secretary, Julie Hoffman, also claimed he never said those things but she may have been toeing the party line, as she was fanatically loyal to Franco. Whatever the truth, the *Last Temptation* affair had damaged Franco's reputation and he'd find it hard to live down, along with the movie, which had not yet found an American release.

Having consumed much pasta, I retired to bed and slept badly. Franco emerged at ten and we went to the studio, where nothing had changed in the *Toscanini* cutting rooms. The assistants still stood by and the producer arrived looking very forlorn.

Franco, Bill the writer, and I ran the reels, which took us until lunch. I then had to get equipment into the room to recut a scene we had dumped months before and which, he now wished to reinstate. This was the beach scene, in which the feeble Arturo and his nun girlfriend first kiss. It was shot, hastily, in Tunisia and was dumped, due to bad lighting, bad acting, and bad dialogue. Now he wanted it all put back, but recut to make it really romantic, so I started in at three and by eight, had a version for him to view.

Meanwhile, he was in another room with the assistant and his Chivas Regal in attendance, recutting other scenes, which I didn't even want to look at. Every now and then he would appear, cup in hand to ask, " 'Ow's eet coming, dahrling? Are they going to fuck?" I did point out that in pictures of this kind the characters rarely fuck and I didn't think that C. Thomas Howell, known to us as Tea Towel, and Sophie Ward were quite up to that. "Ah yes, but the audience must theenk they are going to fuck."

The cutting room was quite small and was now full of equipment and film bins, so there was little room for the ever-expanding Maestro. I had to tell him to hop it if I was to finish in time. He became frustrated by the scene we ran, saying the dialogue was "sheet" and should be reduced to the bare minimum. He then wanted the entire thing restructured. Since it was already eight at night, I couldn't see how to manage it, so took a deep breath and waded into it again, calling him in to make instant decisions about the material I was using. He wanted to start the scene with dialogue taken from the middle, so I was into matching problems straight away. I then got into a muddle and lost a shot. This meant a search of all the bins, so we had a hiatus during which Franco ordered chicken sandwiches and wine to be brought while he continued telling me how bad the Scorsese film really was, and wondering how he was going to finish the picture without me. Finally the missing shot was found and we continued. By now he was at my side, slopping wine around, bumping into me, and winding the film through the machine himself. "Ees thees forwards or backwards?"

We both eventually became quite hysterical as we neared the climax of this dreadful scene. I was pulling the film around so that these two characters never spoke to one another, only looked, and all the dialogue went onto the floor.

At eleven thirty, we looked at this nonsense and he was relatively happy, saying he would "tidy it up" with Amedeo. But, and now my heart really did sink, because we were putting back this scene, we surely must put back another scene that occurred later in the story. What did I think? I thought we should pack up now or I'd drop dead and recalled what someone once said about Franco, "More is not enough." So we dragged this scene out of the tin and reviewed it. The dialogue was as dismal as ever and the thought of now settling down to recut it was too much for me and, I think, Franco, so we left it at that.

I said farewell to the assistants yet again and, limping out of Cinecittà at midnight, we went back to the Villa Grande. I thought I should retire at once, but no, there on the table was a meal, and the "family" had waited up for us, so, at around midnight, we waded into pasta and some hot meat dish that Franco told me was tripe. I ended up trying to sleep on that lot and barely caught a wink.

I dashed home in time to drive Laurence up to Stamford, where we would spend the night en route to Mother's funeral. I never really enjoy funerals at the best of times. My brother lived directly opposite a church in the house formerly occupied by my mother, who used to sit in the room overlooking the church and watch everyone coming and going. All we had to do was walk across the road, meet the undertakers, walk behind the coffin, sit through a commendably brief service, leave and drive to the crematorium for an even briefer service, and then retire to my sister's house for lunch. None of this was joyous. The church was full of mourners, most of whom I knew, but there was no opportunity to speak to them or thank them for coming. The parson's words, the hymns, and the psalms all seemed to be empty platitudes. I was standing next to the coffin for the service, and tried to think of her inside it, but even that image didn't really distract me and I found it quite impossible to summon up grief. My mind was still in Rome. Franco would have liked my mother. Her saving grace was a sense of the dramatic. She told vivid, colourful stories about people she had known and I guess some of my abilities come from that. I hope to Heaven that I am not that vicious.

I never regretted the experience of working with Franco on one of his more terrible films. I love the man for his excess and his wit, pain in the arse he might have been, but how we laughed. Years later I was working for Tarak Ben Ammar again and he introduced me to a friend as "the man who saved *Toscanini*." Some memories are short.

Some years later, I was watching late night TV in France and up came *The Young Toscanini* dubbed into French. It had been split into three parts. I watched it with fascination since I could not recall whether it was my version or the original. I don't think that we ever did get to the bitter end. It climaxed in some operatic scene and I don't recall ever cutting that.

It's a great pity that it wasn't shown wherever Elizabeth Taylor fans are because she was spectacularly awful in it. She played the mistress of the emperor of Brazil, an ex-diva who hadn't sung for years and the young Toscanini was sent from Milan to Brazil to do the opera and she had to get into blackface at one time, like Al Jolson, which was appalling.

The movie did, however, look fabulous. It was a very handsome film. It cost a lot of money, but it was a terrible script and Franco had managed to miscast it completely. Every part was miscast, including Elizabeth Taylor. Can anyone imagine her being a diva? The scenes where she was supposed to sing were excruciatingly awful. It wasn't her voice, of course, it was a proper opera singer's voice, but she could never get it into real synch.

Spooks

I had agreed before going to Rome, that I would cut *Spooks* for Anthony Thomas. It was a low budget spy movie for Vestron, an American company who had scored heavily with *Dirty Dancing*. I was attracted to the subject since the writer/director had made a number of interesting television documentaries. This was his first, and last, feature.

The unit were shooting in Sri Lanka while I was at Shepperton with my assistant, Nick Moore, who had climbed aboard as he wanted to work on the next Puttnam project, *Memphis Belle*, which we would start after this one.

Spooks went along smoothly but quite boringly. I realised I shouldn't get involved with low budget movies. They had the same sort of debilitating effect on me as the third world. I hated it when producers phoned and told me they couldn't afford something. The previous week I had to go to a video house to prepare some sections for use on the set in Sri Lanka. There was an element of rush required and the work cost £615, which I had to pay with a personal check, since they wouldn't release the material any other way. I just hoped I'd get repaid, since the producer then called to say it was too much. "Too Late," was my reply.

We had a visit from two Vestron execs, who made me feel very old indeed. A lady from their east coast office who can't have been much over thirty and a guy covered in leather and personal organisers from the West Coast. They sat dutifully through the forty minutes of cut footage and appeared to enjoy it, but then said they were worried about the pitch of Robert Loggia's performance. This had worried me from the start, but I hadn't made too much fuss about it. I could not imagine who would pay good money to see the new Robert Loggia movie.

During the editing of *Spooks*, we were invited to a party at John Schlesinger's to welcome Vincent Price and Coral Browne to London. The last time I had seen Vincent he was very doddery and his mind seemed to have taken a holiday. However, ancient though he was, he was still on his feet, though they gave him a lot of trouble. Coral, having had everything lifted, looked great. Her rasping Aussie accent was to be heard around the room, which was filled with a galaxy of talents including Alec Guinness, Alan Bennett, Alan Bates, and Dirk Bogarde. We felt very humble in the presence of this lot. In fact, it wasn't a very large group. John was there, getting prepared for a trip to the fat farm prior to the Venice premiere of *Madame Sousatzka*. He was also prepping an opera which Karajan would conduct in the next year.

Earlier in the day. I was driving down High Street and slowed down for a pedestrian crossing and found myself literally staring into Dustin Hoffman's face who was right there hailing a cab. I didn't have time to roll down the window to hail him. He was with his little girl, who was, I believe, at school in London. I knew Dustin had been fixing a house in the same street where John lived. John told me that Dustin never contacted him, though he had welcomed him to the street earlier that year.

At the party I gleaned that Alan Bennett had written two new plays. A two-part adaptation of *An Englishman Abroad* and the other, a new play about Anthony Blunt. Simon Callow would play the Alan Bates role and Prunella Scales would be Coral. Bennett himself would play Blunt. Coral was to be heard asking, "And what sort of fucking credit will I get, I'd like to know?' " It was Coral who orginally told the story of *Englishman* to Alan.

When I mentioned to Vincent that Coral was looking great, he remarked, "A triumph of makeup." The two aged ones were en route for Venice, where they would connect with a cruise boat, presumably filled with old yanks, all breathlessly awaiting a lecture from the Prices. Vincent could just about talk and Coral could be exceedingly witty and crude in a Bankheadian fashion, but what could she possibly lecture about? The use of the F-word in common speech? One had to applaud them, though, for actually getting themselves sufficiently together to do it at all.

Dirk had shrunk. I think he was suffering greatly from his partner Tony's death. He would, I hoped, totter round for dinner before he left the area. He was moving, he told me, since he didn't like Kensington. He was going to Cadogan Square. I thought, at the very least, he'd fetch up in Bucks or Berks. He sold the French house when it was clear that Tony was very sick.

Memphis Belle

We had all returned from our American adventure at Columbia Pictures, slightly tarnished, but David Puttnam decided to regroup at Pinewood, so Enigma, his production company, moved from the Kensington Mews, first to Shepperton Studios and later to an old stable block at Pinewood. The fact that Warner Brothers also had their offices there was probably the reason, since David had a deal with the company.

During our time at Columbia. Cathy Wyler had approached Puttnam with the idea of remaking her father's World War II documentary *Memphis Belle,* as a feature film. David had taken this idea as part of his severance from Coca-Cola (Columbia) so, the film was eventually made at Pinewood.

David had decided that *Memphis Belle* should be helmed by the hot young British director, Michael Caton-Jones, who had just made *Scandal,* which was well received. The crew was gathering. Stuart Craig was art director and David Watkin was director of photography.

There were massive logistical problems to overcome. The script had been written by an American, following the original documentary, but expanding it. It called for many B-17 bombers along with Messerschmitt fighters. Finding these was not easy, but, eventually, they amassed seven bombers, one of which was flown from America. An aerial unit was set up to shoot high in the sky. The flak that the planes flew through was also shot by a special unit, as were the models. It was a huge operation and very costly.

The crew of the Memphis Belle had to be young American actors, but we had a problem. Once they were airborne, they had to wear oxygen masks, which made them virtually unrecognisable. The start of the story, prior to takeoff, was opened up, so that the audience had a chance to recognise the characters after takeoff.

Up in the air, the plane was subjected to many attacks and, when it was over target, they had to drop their bombs, then make the perilous journey home. The Memphis Belle was badly hit and only just made it, something the original thirty-five minute documentary did not contain. In addition to this, we had masses of camera gun material in black and white from the Imperial War Museum. Nobody quite knew how this might be used.

A boot camp of sorts was set up and the actors were put through some rigorous training, designed to get them thinking like a trained crew. Shooting began and the weather was good. The location was an unused base in North Lincolnshire, but I remained at Pinewood until called to location.

Things went okay and we were on schedule. The actors were all well chosen, except for Billy Zane who Caton-Jones instantly disliked. I think Caton-Jones took against Zane because he never seemed entirely happy on set and was a bit of a loner. He didn't want to participate in the boot camp and, on the face of it, seemed more interested in his looks than his character. This was my first film with Caton-Jones and I didn't yet know that there was always one person on a Caton-Jones movie who incurred his wrath. So whether Zane was really miscast or simply didn't behave as Caton-Jones thought he should, remains unknown.

Once the location material was shot, using the planes plus models, the unit returned to the studio, where the interiors of the plane were filmed. These made up the bulk of the interior shots and hanging models were used, well out of focus, to show our plane was not alone up there.

By now, the planes were up each day, being filmed by the aerial unit. Every morning we looked at rushes and every morning Caton-Jones was complaining that the material was not good. "Too far away. Not graphic enough." They had perfect weather and each time they took off it cost a fortune. One day Caton-Jones was finally happy. Material of a fighter attack was partly ruined by a light leak. The loader had not fully closed the magazine, so the negative was mostly wrecked by red streaks. "That's it!" shouted Caton-Jones. "They finally got it right." Then I realised that the World War II aerial combat movies he knew, had all used poorly exposed or scratched negatives. They were imperfect, which was not what we were seeing normally. I, therefore, had 400 feet of material which the director liked, out of thousands that he disliked. Those 400 feet were used over and over again.

Cutting this material, which relied heavily on models and effects, was not easy. Caton-Jones decreed, correctly, that many of the shots would be improved if we added smoke and contrails. We were making this film just before CGI (computer generated imagery) became the norm, and our model shots, which looked ridiculous despite being dirtied down, were heavily criticised at preview, resulting in some expensive material being discarded. I recall trying to turn some black-and-white shots of bombs falling on their targets into colour shots. This took forever and was expensive, whereas now they would be easy and quick. We still had all the wonderfully graphic camera gun shots of planes literally disintegrating that I could never use, but we did have a scene in which the publicity officer, played by John Lithgow, reads letters from bereaved parents, so on a whim I played these moving words over the black-and-white shots and the idea worked, making the words even more poignant. This was perhaps my one truly creative passage in the film.

There are problems with this film, mostly technical, which would not be as difficult today. The characters were, perhaps, a little clichéd, but *Memphis Belle*'s heart was in the right place, and I went on to cut several films for Michael Caton-Jones.

Meeting Venus

I was nearing completion on *Memphis Belle* at Pinewood when David Puttnam asked me to edit *Meeting Venus*. István Szabó would direct it in English, in Budapest, with Glenn Close heading the cast. I knew about this film because it was originally submitted to us at Columbia and David had it as part of his severance deal. He would now make it for Warner Brothers.

The story was a satire based on István's experiences directing a production of *Tannhäuser* at the Paris Opera, which was beset with union problems. The original script had been rewritten into English by Michael Hirst. I was not entirely keen to cut this film. Three months in Budapest was hardly the tonic my marriage required after being too long in California. Also I did not know Szabó at all, though his reputation preceded him, and I had seen *Mephisto*, which I thought was wonderful. Puttnam was, however, persuasive and Laurence agreed to the time away, provided I could cut the film in London, once the shoot was completed. So I agreed and, with my assistant Nick Moore, set up in Budapest around the Spring of 1990.

The production was a real Europudding. There were a number of Brits and Americans involved, the cast coming from all over, and the entire film was to be shot in Budapest, along with some Paris locations. Puttnam was the credited producer, but the daily work was done by Uberto Pasolini and we had an accountant Gary Jones from Warner Brothers, as well as a publicist Ann Tasker. The majority of the crew were Hungarian, though Simon Kaye was sound recordist. Nick and I took on a local girl who spoke tolerable English and was able to help us out in the canteen and with our daily conversations with the labs.

We were based at MaFilm, the oldest studio in Budapest, built originally by the young Alexander Korda. Very little appeared to have changed since his time there, though a war and a revolution had occurred. Nobody had put so much as a lick of paint on the walls for a very long time. The small projection theatre where we viewed rushes was a dust trap that was never hoovered. Our cutting room, into which we had crammed our equipment, was hardly homey, with a hideous hanging lamp, containing three low-wattage bulbs, which reminded one of an interrogation room scene in a Hungarian war movie.

The studio was small with four stages and no backlot. I set out to explore it on my first day, which took about seven minutes. The feeling was cramped, dilapidated, and scruffy. Black-and-white stills of past productions, serious without smiles, decorated the corridors.

Having feared the worst when lunchtime came around, I was pleasantly surprised by the standard of food available and took a dish of excellent red cabbage soup, bread and a cucumber salad which cost me thirty-one florints, roughly thirty pence, or about a tenth the cost of a salad at Pinewood. Bovine ladies cooked and served this substantial fare and there was a coffee bar where you could sit in rather quaint areas, partitioned off like booths in a restaurant.

We were quartered in the Intercontinental Hotel on the Danube and my room had a view of the river and the National Gallery. There was absolutely nothing wrong with any of this and, surprisingly, everything worked. Even then, Hungary was in the vanguard of shaking off the Russian yoke and there was a feeling of prosperity just around the corner. Nick and I quickly grew to love the trams and the underground trains, which ran just beneath the wide boulevard. It was reputed to be the oldest in Europe. There was a whiff of pre-war Budapest, much of which was in a state of disrepair, and showed abundant signs of strife from the past years. Shrapnel wounds were all over the buildings and the war was never far away. The Russians had made the teaching of their language compulsory, but now they were changing over to English as the official second language. Tourism was growing and so, on our days off, Nick and I would often travel across the city, on trams, just to get the feel of it.

Most of the film was shot in the Opera House, a magnificent building, only a few minutes drive away. My initial meetings with István were cordial, but he was clearly suspicious of our working methods. Normally he would employ an editor only to stockpile and collate the rushes during shooting. He would never have anything cut during that time. Then, when shooting ended, he would sit in the projection room for a few days and review all the material, making choices and giving notes to the editor. After this he would cut the material himself, with help from the editor who would act, more or less, as an assistant. Having me around to edit his material did not sit well with István, though Puttnam had told him it was essential when dealing with a Hollywood-financed film.

Upon arrival at the Opera House on the first day of shooting, I was quite concerned when I spotted the clapper board, which appeared to have a set of numbers on it that bore no relation to the scene they were shooting. In the West, we generally have the scene number or the slate number inscribed at the head of each take, but here we had something altogether different. I casually asked the script girl, who was from Edinburgh, to ensure they used a numbering system we could understand. When this information was relayed to István, who was setting up the next shot in the orchestra pit, he went quite ballistic. He started to shout and rave in Hungarian and English that shooting would have to end then and there because the editor was unhappy with the Hungarian numbering system. He had used this method for twenty-five years and was not about to change now. I persisted. He was obdurate. I had succeeded in upsetting the director on day one. Something new. I outlined a possible compromise and kept a low tone as he began to boil over again. Eventually I decided to leave and discuss the situation with the script supervisor, Pat Rambaut, hereinafter known as Rambo. As we pulled away from the Opera House, we spotted the distraught director gesticulating to line producer Uberto Pasolini, who was now getting the full frontal assault.

Later, with Nick and David Puttnam, we devised a new clapper board, which would work for István's system and our own, so the problem went away.

After this, my relationship with István was strictly business. He always seemed dictatorial and insisted on getting his crew together each morning before shooting began, in order to tell them, in public, what mistakes they'd made the previous day. I only attended one of these sessions and was horrified, wondering why they put up with it. Since he had won an Oscar for *Mephisto*, István was treated like royalty in Hungary. He was a household name and whatever he said was sacred. I refused to become a part of this revisionism and therefore remained firmly in my cutting room, only meeting the maestro at rushes.

The film looked fine, being lit by István's regular cameraman, Lajos Koltai. Uberto had some control over things but was constantly harrassed by István's wilful ways. It was a hard film involving many actors from various countries. The material was promising, though hardly commercial. I wondered what Warner Brothers might do with such a film. In any case, they showed little interest in it and even Puttnam made only rare appearances.

Nick and I took ourselves to the famous Gellért baths, a large art nouveau building devoted to theraputic water cures. The method of ticketing and payment was arcane, requiring some ingenuity to work out. We enjoyed the indoor and outdoor swimming pool—a large, ornate pool, decorated with Doric columns and lions heads spouting water. We were informed it was required to wear bathing caps, available for an extra charge. We now had on two nasty plastic caps but realised we had no towels. Should have thought of that. There was some difficulty explaining this to the not-too-bright attendant, who did eventually understand when a tip was offered.

We then entered the massage area, where the sexes are segregated. We were required to discard our swimming trunks and put on an item not unlike a Masonic apron that kept slipping off. We were thrown onto metal tables by beefy gypsies who hosed us down and pummeled our bodies. After that we joined the others in two ornate heated pools. Thirty minutes of this puts you into a semi coma, so we retrieved our trunks, headed back to the cabin and thence to the outdoor pools. The cost for all this fun was exactly £2, not including the tip.

Glenn Close arrived partway through the shoot and it was rapidly evident that István was smitten. He had cast a Franco/Danish actor, Niels Arestrup, to play the lead role opposite Glenn. Her role was that of the star soprano who falls for the conductor of the opera. This love story was the central part of the film in the final version, though not in the original script, which leaned less heavily on romance and more on political satire.

David Puttnam invited me to join the nobs for dinner at the Marco Polo restaurant, probably the best around. I was sat opposite Glenn Close's dad, Bill, a genial old doctor who has been to the Île de Ré and spoke fluent French. He once operated on President Mobuto in Zaire, though he didn't tell me what the operation was. He also flew missions in World War II so was very interested in *Memphis Belle*. Patsy Pollock, the film's casting director, turned up and wanted to sit next to Bill and we all did a shuffle. I ended up opposite Glenn, who I hadn't seen too much of until then. She turned out to be very pleasant and far more attractive in life than on screen. She was also not at all stuffy. Pollock was being fairly outrageous and Glenn reacted well, though I think was a wee bit shocked. István was also quite larky, whereas on the set he is anything but. Glenn too can be quite difficult on set. She gave Rambo an earful one day, which quite pleased me. Uberto was present and the talk, inevitably, came around to who was bonking who on the unit, just like *Day for Night*. When Glenn started on the picture, she and Niels became very friendly but, after a few weeks, the friendship was over although the picture was not. They still had their parts to play. So we watched helplessly as the film began to totter and fall to pieces. István did not seem pleased about this relationship but whether it was jealousy or mere frustration, I didn't know.

There were certain stresses and strains on the film and relief came after hours when Ann Tasker would join us for a meal and, mercifully, a laugh. She had her problems too, but the profuse gigglings that occurred whenever we got together defused most of them since neither of us could take any of this seriously. Sadly, Ann died only a few years later from pancreatic cancer, at the early age of fifty, thus I lost a good friend and companion.

Puttnam would breeze in from New York for a couple of days here and there. On one visit I ran everything for him. He was reasonably content, while understanding my fear of excessive length and lack of cover. He sent yet another memo to István. Sometimes István would take notice of these memos, but often not.

I made a plea for the film to go direct from Paris to Technicolor, but we had no contact with the lab at all. Only the cameraman spoke to them and it soon became clear that I would not get any choices from István in Paris, so couldn't cut any of the material until he came to London.

I ran some rushes for Glenn, who I was getting to like. She was very natural and entirely unstarry, but she was affecting an odd accent in the film and, even though she was supposed to be Swedish, she came out like Julie Andrews at her most English. I wouldn't have dared tell her that. I was also highly amused to hear her telling me the details about her bollocking of Rambo.

As the autumn chill descended, my spirit also sank and there was little around to alleviate the general gloom. The movie was no help at all. Daily dollops of seriously unfunny rushes were dumped on me. My scissors flashed briefly. It didn't require great skill to cut this material.

We were at this time shooting all the two-handed scenes between Glenn Close and Niels Arestrup. All the other cast members had returned home and we missed their companionship. Our casting lady, Patsy Pollock, known by us as "Bollocks," was a case. Mainly cockney and quite loud with it, she was inclined to shout, "Up your bum!" when anyone upset her. She was by the pool one hot summer morning when a blousey lady took the next chair and moved very close to Patsy who said, "I'll thank you not to put your tired old tits in my lap," to which the lady responded in perfect English, "I beg your pardon." This didn't phase Patsy who undoubtedly added, "Up your bum!"

A letter from Schlesinger arrived telling me that his movie *Pacific Heights,* was opening in the states the next day. He expected mixed reviews. I hoped it would work for him this time. He reported that Coral Browne had her final dose of chemotherapy and, surely, wouldn't live much longer. Vincent, very thin, would sit on her bed all day combing her wigs. John thought Vincent was only hanging on by a thread himself. Very depressing.

I soon ran the assembly for István and Puttnam. They seemed delighted. I had to admit that, seen as an entity, it wasn't as dull as I'd feared and could turn out to be fairly stylish, though I did worry about the lead actor. Glenn was looking good and had a fair crack at singing the Wagner in sync with Dame Kiri. My main worry remained the sheer length of the piece. It would run at least two hours, forty-five minutes in its first cut, but it certainly looked very good.

Cheered by their reaction, I returned to the hotel, picked up my camera and went walkabout in the sunshine, which was an excellent, though solitary, way to spend the day. In the evening there was a huge party given by the company on a boat. Everyone came and consumed a huge amount of booze. The boat chugged up and down the Danube, occasionally returning to port, so that people could disembark if they wished. I lasted until around nine thirty, when they started bopping to a tinny disco and everyone seemed to be getting drunk, including István, who was knocking back an unwise amount of wine. Time, I thought, for this old body to leave. Unfortunately I chose to leave with our publicist Ann, who had organised the evening. She was both drunk and depressed. At breakfast the next morning, Ann was a mite sheepish, not to mention hungover.

I set out to get a haircut and walked straight into István, sitting in the next chair getting a trim. He was also hungover, and I was the last person he thought to see in a Budapest barber shop. As the day was vividly bright, I thought to spend it at the Gellért baths.

In the evening, looking very red faced from the sun, I dined with our writer, Michael Hirst, who was in from London. I had hoped he'd come to cut the script, but no joy. We were joined by Ann, who had got over her maudlin depression and was jolly once again. She was, evidently, a very unhappy lady under the banter.

We had started on the so-called romantic scenes, which would take up most of the next two weeks. Tortuous stuff. There was too much material, all of which would be pored over at great length by István, who is inclined toward torture.

Finally the company had moved to Paris while I stayed in Budapest. Ann Tasker kept me informed as to what was going on:

Dear Jim,

We had a night shoot and I wish you had been there. It was predestined for disaster. Sz was convinced the frogs wouldn't cope and, I think, deliberately chose the most difficult location he could find, in the middle of an enormous place which had at least eight roads emptying cars, buses, and taxis into it plus a viaduct with a train. It took forever to get the rain machines working and we were in an area, rich in drunks. One took to dancing in the middle of the road under the full power of the hosepipes until forcibly restrained by the police. We managed two takes before Sz threw a monumental tantrum, shouting and yelling at the French in French. He also gave Uberto the first of many bollockings.

Glenn and Niels stood around a corner dripping wet and unaware of what was happening. The drunk reappeared to dance in the road with a traffic cone on his head. Another drunk appeared and tried to interfere with Bollocks. I spent the next hour in the warmth of Glenn's caravan and emerged to find the drunk now was gaily directing the traffic.

It was now two am and my journalists had finally had enough. I told Sz I was going and he delivered a tirade about how awful the frogs were. You would have found Rambo irresistable. Apart from layers of very odd clothing, she was wearing the ultimate in boots, enormous and laced up the front to her knees. I don't think they had spikes in the bottom but she looked like a woman in search of a mountain.

Yours,

Ann

Filming finally ended in Paris and while some exteriors were shot, we moved back to London and set up our cutting room at Goldcrest in Soho. Ann had warned me that things were already being discussed behind my back:

Dear Jim,

I am recovering from a very strange evening organised by Rambo which involved thirty of us trekking across Paris to a Chinese restaurant. En route in a taxi with Sz and Simon we talked about "stage 2" of the film. Sz was very nervous because he says he has always edited his own films and now he has someone doing it for him. BUT he thinks you are a very nice person and that you have the same instincts as him and that 80–90% of the time you agree on the best takes. We did our best to reassure him that working with you would be a good experience. I did not say that you had no heart, only a worm eaten turnip where one should be.

Love,

Ann

It was clear from the start that István Szabó and I were not made for one another but, somehow, we managed to soldier through the film without rancour. It was a tedious and somewhat mirthless experience.

Being back in London after that three-month sentence was fine by me. I went into the cutting room every day. I was back in Dean Street with the winos and derelicts when Szabó joined me to start attacking the picture. I ran it twice for him and we both found its three-hour length quite interminable. Furthermore I just didn't see how to fix it. Taking a whole hour from a picture is never easy and should not, in my view, be necessary. If those concerned had listened to me when I told them, months earlier, we would have rewritten the script and not spent the money that I was now about to throw onto the floor.

I was saddened to see a gifted, serious-minded director like Szabó, corrupted by our system and I hoped he'd come to his senses before attempting another film. I came away from the last screening with the definite view that the love story between Glenn and Niels was, frankly, dull. I hoped Szabó had some good ideas about the editing, since I damn sure didn't. If we were to savage the love story in order to reduce the picture, we'd effectively take Glenn out of the show and that wouldn't please her or the money.

At some point we were obliged to show the film to Glenn or "Glennie," as István would gigglingly call her on the phone. The man was clearly nuts about her. She flew in and we ran it for her and Puttnam. This was a disaster. We retired to the Groucho Club for a chat after and it was evident that Glennie loathed the movie. Puttnam did what he could to soothe her and István was somewhat downcast. On leaving the Groucho, they bumped into a homeless man and both gave him money. Fumbling with change and Glenn not knowing the value of anything, I think the guy ended up with at least £10. Later on, when I walked past the Groucho, he was nowhere in sight and was presumably enjoying a decent meal and a glass of wine somewhere.

The following day we ran the movie again with Glenn who made many agreeable remarks, all critical but agreeable. We would write and shoot some new scenes in order to make more sense of the romance. This took a while to achieve and did not, in the end, make too much difference.

I had prayed nightly for a Scud missile to find its way to Technicolor, thus disposing of our fate, but God didn't smile. We had been through another baptism, this one directed by Glennie, who brought her own Scud to the situation. She produced a lot of anguish in high places and several phone bills soared. She scoured the rushes for unused gems and came up with a lot of notes, none of which were heeded. She went off to Budapest and shot a new scene with Niels. I wasn't on the set, but felt the tremors in Soho. They fought like alley cats. The scene was shot in my old room at the Central Hotel and looked like a Blackpool boarding house, though the lobby through which Niels rushed to reach her is the Radisson in Budapest. The new scene was mercifully short.

I returned to Budapest for three days with the musical arranger David Bedford. We were met at the airport by a little driver with the nice smile, moustache and Lada, who whisked us directly to MaFilms. In the looping theatre, we found Szabó, Simon Kaye, and assorted actors, as well as Uberto. Back at the Duna, almost deserted with not a tourist in sight, I watched the Gulf War unfold like an action movie on CNN.

This lemon was dry, but they still wanted changes and we started mixing the following Monday. I had been fighting this footage so long I was quite punch drunk. We finally got the footage into some kind of shape for previews in Pasadena, or whatever other neighbourhood was unfortunate enough to receive us. And so we winged out to sunny Burbank for a Warner screening plus a public preview.

I flew over on a Sunday, alone, and spent the evening with Artie and Susan Schmidt at a Mexican restaurant. The following morning I rented a car and drove to the studio where I encountered Michael Caton-Jones, who was looking great and seemed very happy. His film, *Doc Hollywood*, was being rushed out for July. I met his editor, a dishy lady, Priscilla Nedd-Friendly, who had cut *Pretty Woman*.

That night, through pouring rain, I drove over to the Schlesinger home for dinner. I hadn't been there since the days of *Honky Tonk Freeway* and had not seen John's new bathroom. It was the size of an average living room with a giant Jacuzzi and mirrors everywhere, though John confessed that he wasn't keen on the mirrors any longer.

John Schlesinger told me that Coral Browne was now on a morphine drip. He hadn't seen her in a while, but talked to her. She didn't want visitors. Last time they spoke she told him she was hungry. He asked her what she would like to eat. "A big cock," was her reply. Some old dames never change, which I find heartening. Vincent was getting thinner by the day and John said he was only waiting for Coral to die before he joined her. A very sad end for two charming old reprobates.

The preview in Pasadena was not a very happy evening. We had thirty-seven walkouts and the audience laughed in all the right and sometimes wrong places. It played better in America than London, but the cards were worse, which was really dire. Glenn turned up. She didn't say anything to me, though gave me a warm embrace. I guess she hated it all over again. István looked perplexed and ashen. The Warner brass seemed to be behaving in jolly manner, like they were attending a function on the Titanic. I kept my normal very low profile, skulking near the Gents with a British editor, Stuart Baird, who was then editorial advisor to Warner Brothers, not unlike my old job at Columbia. I told him he could take this turkey away from me any time he liked, the sooner the better, but he demurred. While agreeing with me that the film, as it stood, was virtually unshowable. Stuart suggested I should ask Szabó to go home for a couple of weeks and get out of my hair while I recut the picture but I told him frankly that I wouldn't know what to do with it. To end the evening, I got back in the car and went back to chez Schmidt with my burden.

The following morning I had to run the movie in the executive room for all the guys from Warner Brothers, very few of whom turned up, since they had already seen the film the night before. They clearly were nonplussed by the event and said little to Puttnam and Szabó. I skulked in the booth to avoid being questioned, but then went into a meeting with Semel, Daly, and all the Warner Brothers set, which constituted our postmortem. The figures from the previous night were now analysed.

Frankly, I found this meeting irritating, even though I am always fascinated by being a fly on the wall in the seat of power. Here we were in Terry Semel's posh office, the sun pouring in, the sky outside turned an unnatural dark blue by the filtered glass. A formal set of heavy cane chairs and sofas surrounded a vast glass-topped table. Semel's desk was very small and severe with little on it. There was a kitchenette in the corner and an outer office with two girls to guard it as well as an outer, outer office with one lonely girl to keep anyone out of the outer office. Everything was very quiet. We all sat around the table, me squeezed between Semel and Szabó. Lucy Fisher, our studio executive was next to Puttnam, and the market research guy Richard del Belso, whom I liked. That was the configuration. Semel, who is the tiny, Sicilianate boss, spoke quite a lot. He kept saying things like, "We think the picture is wonderful but," which really means: "We hate it and we don't have a clue how to sell it." Neither David nor István said much, but were also not prepared to admit that anything major was wrong, which annoyed me. I was in a militant mood and it was on the tip of my tongue to resign then and there, but I thought that was rather petty, so I duly took their notes and we left.

The film was what the studios refer to as an orphan. Nobody wanted it and it was never spoken about. It didn't really exist, only, unfortunately, it did and I had it.

Very little was learned except that we had problems. I took the movie back to the UK and arranged not to sit near Szabó on the plane since I knew he would want to talk about it.

We recut *Meeting Venus* yet again. Now they wanted to revoice various characters. How I wished the whole thing would evaporate and dribble down somebody's leg.

Puttnam was now quite disenchanted with Glennie, who had cornered Terry Semel at the Oscars and suggested they should reshoot the end of the picture yet again. It seemed she had made it plain that there would be no promotional co-operation from her if her demands were not met. A frustrated Puttnam told me he would now return to making male-oriented pictures.

I always liked the opening reels of the film since they described how this assortment of singers got together and it was only after the romantic story kicked in that the film became more commonplace. Not surprisingly, it didn't perform too well commercially.

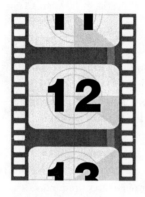

THIS BOY'S LIFE

A S FILM EDITORS WE ARE rewriters as well as cutters. I was called on to do some rewriting for the opening of *This Boy's Life*. The movie had an over-extended beginning and by the time the director, Michael Caton-Jones, and the producer, Art Linson, realised it, we were approximately one-third of the way through shooting and a million dollars over budget. Nobody was very happy about this.

Linson refused to drag screenwriter Bob Getchell, back into the fold to help us solve the problem, one manifestation of which was that our star, Robert De Niro, didn't appear until page twenty. So I was elected to have a go at rewriting the opening, probably because I was making the loudest noises of complaint, a situation I knew well. Explaining that I was no script writer, I devoted an entire week-end to rereading the novel and writing out a new version of the opening scenes. Since *Midnight Cowboy* was one of Caton-Jones' favourite movies, I shamelessly raided ideas from the opening reels to get Toby and his mother to Salt Lake City as quickly as possible. My main concern was an elaborate action scene in which a truck, out of control, careens past the heroine's car, crashes through a barrier, and disappears into a ravine. This had not yet been shot and seemed quite unnecessary and expensive, so I cut it. When I handed my rewrite to Caton-Jones and Linson, they complimented me on my efforts and proceeded to take absolutely no notice. I have often noted that the film editor's suggestions go unheeded although the messenger is first in line for the firing squad.

I first read the novel *This Boy's Life* by Tobias Wolff in 1988, not thinking it might become a film. It is a fairly bleak account of the author's teenage years with his abusive, bullying stepfather and hardly the material for a commercial Hollywood movie, so it was with some surprise that I heard from Tim Corrie, during the summer of 1991, that Caton-Jones was about to film it for Warner Brothers. The novel had been optioned by Warner Brothers through Peter Guber and Jon Peters and had sat around unmade for years until Art Linson discovered it, got De Niro interested and put together a package that enticed the studio enough to give it a green light. I told Tim to investigate the possibility of my cutting the picture. At this stage, I had only worked with Michael on *Memphis Belle* and he subsequently directed *Doc Hollywood* in 1990, which had been cut by Priscilla Nedd-Friendly, so I figured she would be doing the film but, as it turned out, she was unavailable and I got the job. I arrived in Vancouver during February 1992 to begin work.

The film was shot mostly on location in northern Vancouver, but we worked downtown in a cutting facility aptly named Pinewood, which was both pleasant and convenient, though nothing like our homegrown studio.

This was the second film I'd cut that starred Robert De Niro and unlike *The Mission,* he turned up knowing his lines. In fact, I think that Bob's performance in *This Boy's Life* is one of his best. I understand he did extensive research for the role of Dwight Hansen, which included quizzing Tobias Wolff about the tiniest details of his stepfather's behaviour. Both he and Caton-Jones were always aware of a certain humour that lay within the character of Dwight, despite the dark sides of his nature. He wanted to do right by the boy and straighten him out, though his methods were often brutal.

The boy was no saint either and his role required a young actor of considerable talent. During the casting, Bob flew to Los Angeles and read with the ten actors under consideration to play the stepson, choosing the young Leonardo DiCaprio from the others. I think there is something in Caton-Jones' psychological makeup that made him the right director for this film. He's not a great socialiser. He grew up in a rough part of Glasgow and keeps a lot of emotion bottled up and it was this, I think, that enabled him to understand Leonardo's character so well. He surely recognised some of the film's tougher scenes and he seemed to have an almost paternal relationship with the young DiCaprio. He was less happy with Ellen Barkin who played Leo's mother. He was certainly very keen to cut away from her as often as possible.

With Robert De Niro's work, you don't edit him, you mine him. You have to create the performance because it varies so much from take to take. On *The Mission,* this gave me editing problems of nightmare proportions, but with *This Boy's Life* things were different; here was an actor who was better prepared and playing a role he understood.

It was just before Easter when the unit packed up and left for the town of Concrete in Washington state, the actual setting described by Tobias Wolff. Here they shot exteriors and all the school material, returning to Vancouver for more interiors after Easter when De Niro wrapped his role. He was off to New York to direct his first picture, a coming-of-age saga set in the Bronx in the 1950s, in which he also appeared: *A Bronx Tale.*

It was around this time that Art Linson let us know we were over budget. Goodness knows how, although the unit had spent time and money shooting the truck crash that I had cut in my rewrite. It would have saved them money if they had trusted me since, after many versions, we decided to cut the scene anyway. The studio was unhappy. This was not the most commercial picture, dealing as it does in quite a lot of brutality or child abuse.

I kept telling my worried producer that you never can tell with pictures. We had some lovely scenes in themselves. I particularly enjoyed one where De Niro and Barkin danced a polka while the family watched *The Lawrence Welk Show* on television. But lovely scenes are sometimes not enough and, because it was shot in such discontinuity, none of us could see the bigger picture. String all these wonderful scenes together and you might have a movie. It could only work, however, if the audience cared enough about the boy's plight. That's hard to know until all the elements are in place. Out of all this we would, for sure, have something unlike most mainstream movies, but the video store could become its outlet. Those damn previews would determine its fate sometime in September.

I spent a long time looking at the rushes for the final scene, in which Dwight almost kills Tobias in the kitchen. Ellen Barkin's character comes in and whacks him with a baseball bat. He then goes half mad and mother and son decide to leave forever. De Niro continues to rage as they walk into the distance. I was not keen on the way it had been staged.

You can imagine what sort of meal De Niro made of all this. Miles of it, over and over again. Not easy for me, but I'm accustomed to bulky rushes. My real anxiety was for the scene itself, which was not too believable. While the father raved, mother and son were left standing around with egg on their faces before finally making up their minds to exit.

I knew, when I attacked it, that I just might make it work, but it didn't feel right. We were being asked to pity De Niro's character even though he was a bully and that was a hard trick to pull off.

I wanted Linson's input, since I thought we should be rewriting and reshooting the scene, not a popular thought when the actor has been signed off, and you are already over budget. I sent the film to Linson in Los Angeles, but it was no dice. Eventually we kept the scene more or less as shot and made every attempt to force it to work, but to my mind, it remained the one key moment that failed. I used to taunt Michael while we were cutting this for the umpteenth time, but it wasn't all his fault. Due to fading daylight, he'd had to keep away from all the windows, thus forcing the actors into a static position. I cynically referred to it as a Herbert Wilcox six shot, for anyone who understands that observation.

At this stage I was upset with Warner Brothers because I'd told them back in November that I wasn't a member of the Los Angeles Editor's Union. They said, "Don't worry, we'll take care of that" and I'd prodded them ever since. Finally they said, "Sorry old chum, you'll have to do it yourself," which I could have done months before. Suddenly the whole thing, which was neither automatic nor a pushover, had to be achieved in three weeks. So I told the studio that if I didn't get into the union, I'd stay in Vancouver and finish the picture there, which would be greatly preferable to returning to that crime-riddled, overcrowded, smoggy city.

While Laurence flew south to rent us a house, I returned to work on a sequence I'd been avoiding. A night car scene for which they'd shot about three hours of film. Literally hundreds of readings from De Niro. This stuff had been looking at me for weeks and I'd been saying, "Later, later," not wishing to tackle it. But we'd run the movie on the previous Saturday and Michael was concerned that this crucial scene was missing, so I was forced into it. The picture ran for one hundred and three minutes with five weeks to shoot, so the rough cut would be very long indeed.

As we continued to shoot, the film spread like a fungus. Now it ran two hours twenty minutes and we still had three weeks filming left. It would be mighty hard to compress, since nobody wanted anything over two hours.

David Watkin, the director of photography on the film, had also shot *Memphis Belle*. A crucial scene in which De Niro's character is first introduced to the boy and his mother appeared to be unsharp. As we were anamorphic, the focus was critical. I ran the rushes in many theatres in order to prove to myself, and anyone else who'd listen, that we had a focus problem that would show itself more clearly when edited with other scenes. Finally it was decided to reshoot the scene after Panavision engineers had been flown in to examine the lenses. Only then did David confess that he'd been shooting wide open which probably accounted for the problem. David Watkin had shot many fine films and was far from incompetent, but the reshot scene was, sadly, not as well acted as the original. Actors don't really like to return to old scenes.

☆ ☆ ☆

In Los Angeles, the Warner Hollywood studio hadn't changed at all since I was there in 1981 recutting *Honky Tonk Freeway*. Now I had a nice suite of rooms in what was formerly the Writers' Block, possibly the genesis of that dysfunction. This had formerly been the Goldwyn studio and was still redolent of that golden era. My two assistants, Peter and Eric were in the big room with a kitchenette and I was in the small room with the toilet. This was communal and so anyone using it had to pass through my room, do their business, and leave. So I was practically in the shithouse.

I turned sixty in May of 1992 and spent it entirely alone, moving into my new temporary home in the Hollywood Hills. Everything went smoothly. The owner's wife moved out at eleven, got on a plane, and went to her other home in the Hamptons. I packed up all my stuff and drove up there at noon and spent most of the day unpacking and sorting myself out. This place was quite small, but pleasant. It was an outdoorsy house, partway up Nichols Canyon and reasonably secluded. The main plus was that it was about ten minutes drive from the studio. We signed a six-month lease. Warner Brothers paid for it because "first-class hotel accommodation" was part of my contract.

Dede Allen, the renowned editor who had cut *Bonnie and Clyde*, was now an executive at Warner Brothers, and I would be showing her *This Boy's Life* in August.

I realised I had recut four reels in eight days and had only twenty-five days left before the first official screening. This included showing it to the producer and making a temporary mix with music and effects. Not a lot of time. Caton-Jones kept telling me not to fret since he wouldn't show the movie until he was happy with it, but I doubted he had the necessary clout to swing that one.

I went to a weekend party in Venice where Michael Childers, John Schlesinger's companion, was throwing a barbecue at his studio. A very LA sort of affair attended by mostly young gay men. The drinks were served by two almost nude male models wearing pearls and leather jock straps. Among the luminaries were Barry Diller, the previous boss of Fox and my old friend Jerry Hellman, recently divorced and not looking bad at sixty-three. Another guest was the singer songwriter, Paul Jabara, whom I had known since *The Day of the Locust;* sadly he was very sick with AIDS. He died only a few weeks later. Don Bachardy, partner of the late Chris Isherwood, was also present as were Richard and Ruth MacDonald, so we had a few friends to talk to. But it was a bizarre gathering. Jerry, Richard, and I were the only straight men in the room.

☆   ☆   ☆

Just as I was about to wrap for the holiday weekend, I hit the most difficult and time-consuming scene that I still hadn't confronted fully. Robert De Niro's character, drunk and deranged, drives the boy back to his new home in Concrete, hitting and killing a beaver en route. I had a notion to leave this pivotal scene until I'd completed everything else, though, perhaps that was putting off the evil day. It took Michael and me three whole days to recut that crucial scene. It appeared to be very simple and would not exactly stagger anyone, but it was a brute due to an excess of riches. Here was a sequence, shot with two cameras in one studio day, using the poor man's process in which the car, on hydraulics, is motionless on a sound stage. The actors pretend they are driving in a moving vehicle and the electricians move lights and shadows of trees around as the scene is shot to simulate movement. The sounds of the car engine are added later. This should not have presented too many problems, but De Niro was trying out different ways of playing it and cutting between takes was hard. Matching problems, pitch problems—lots of problems. Leonardo remained quite consistent throughout, while Bob went through myriad choices and a massive number of takes.

I ran all one hundred and fifty-six minutes of *This Boy's Life* for Caton-Jones, who was not suicidal. He just hated the wig that poor Leonardo had to wear. Not the best I ever saw. Curiously Tim Corrie, who had seen the film the previous week, also mentioned the wig. I couldn't do much about it at this stage and my real problem was the extreme length of the film. I simply had to find a way to reduce it. I decided to start with removing small chunks—ten minutes—not nearly sufficient.

I had to watch my tongue when I was invited to Richard Donner's. He had recently directed *Lethal Weapon 3* and Terry Semel, the boss of Warner Brothers, for whom I currently worked, would be present. I was not too keen to get close to Terry who would surely quiz me about *This Boy's Life*, which I'd been told he never really wanted to make. He actually merely asked me, "How is the movie coming along?" I said, "You'll be very proud of it," which seemed to be the right reply. I like and respect Semel. He had started life quite humbly and had risen spectacularly. A bright man who had held his position at Warner Brothers for about eight years at that time, in tandem with Bob Daley. I'd had to deal with Terry on all the Puttnam films since *Killing Fields* and he was always supportive. A sort of self-taught intellectual but not a bullshitter. I also liked him for his basic love of movies. He was responsible for a film compilation of the history of Warner Brothers, managing to get a lot of the old guys who worked at Burbank with the original Warner Brothers to talk about their experiences. He commissioned David Wolper to make the picture, which, he said, now existed in three lengths, starting at four hours.

The evening at the Donner's was typical of its kind and I don't mean to knock it. I didn't really feel I was there in person, more of a presence looking in on another kind of world, to which I had been invited by Shelly Hochron and her husband Ken Stewart, who were friends from the Columbia period. We went to this big, sprawling, one-story house above Sunset Boulevard, with guard dogs, an electric portcullis, TV monitoring of guests, and every other security device known to man. We entered the house through a revolving door as found in the old-style restaurants then into a hallway full of modern art and art deco furniture. We then moved into a horseshoe-shaped bar, where our host, a big benign bear of a man, was dispensing wine to a grizzled old party and a young lady with big bosoms. The old party turned out to be an ex-agent, Eddie Roth, who was somebody in his day and still seemed to be attracting the nubility. Everyone was informally dressed in jeans. After drinks and chitchat in an elegant room with a curious low ceiling covered in silver foil (which Donner said came from a San Francisco whorehouse) we went into the dining area. It was circular and overlooked the whole of Los Angeles, that fairyland of lights that was spread before us like a vast twinkling carpet. It was from this vantage point these "haves" must have seen all the fires set by the "have-nots" a few short weeks before during the riots, and wondered when the hordes would knock on the portcullis and demand entry.

The food was oddly undercooked. Vegetables like rocks. But the red wine was a Lalande Pichon '83, and they don't come better than that.

We moved out of the dining room and into the screening room, an addition to the house, outside in the garden. A room with sofas, tables, and a bar, as well as a studio projectionist on overtime in the booth. M&M's, chocolate drops, were guzzled as we watched *The Playboys,* extremely boring despite its Irish provenance. I nodded off a few times, so I was pleased when the picture limped to a close and somewhat bemused when Semel jumped up and declared it was a "lovely little film" and everyone appeared to instantly agree. I guessed that to be the form at private screenings.

As we emerged from the screening room and stood in groups discussing the movie, the sprinkler system suddenly opened up and sprayed our jeans and jerseys. Here I was in Hollywood driven inside by fake rain. Somehow it seemed just right.

☆   ☆   ☆

During one of her rare visits, Laurence and I celebrated twenty-nine years of married life. Some sort of record in the Hollywood Hills. Laurence was upset with me because I hadn't time to pick her up from the airport or buy flowers and didn't arrive home until 8:30 PM after a fiendishly active day. As an editor herself she realised we could not always have a simple private life.

We screened for Art Linson, who was full of praise and enthusiasm. "Magnificent," was his word, which made my blood run cold. There is nothing worse at that stage than producer's hyperbole, since they then run around town and call all their chums to say the picture is great. The film can't hope to match the hype and, therefore, when these guys, mostly the Warner Brothers executives, sit down to see the picture they are almost always disappointed. If Art Linson's "Magnificent" judgment was correct, we'd be okay.

The screenings of *This Boy's Life* were most instructive. Only our friendly executives attended the first show. They seemed to enjoy the picture, long though it was, and had very few notes. In the evening, however, we had two hundred people, mostly in the 20 to 30 age group, who had been recruited mostly from shopping malls and who were very attentive. They were involved with the picture for about the first fifty minutes, but when the De Niro character started to act ugly with the boy, they began to go off the picture and we had an uphill fight to keep their attention thereafter. The figures from the cards showed a high percentage of "fairs" and not sufficient "excellents." The general note was that it was too long and too violent, so we went back and reduced it by fifteen minutes and toned down Bob's performance so that he didn't peak too soon.

Our first public preview was almost upon us and I was busy making last minute changes. They were going crazy looking for a temp score. I had used a mixture of Erik Satie and Rachmaninoff, which went down like a lead balloon with the Warner Brothers' executives and my producer. They'd now settled for the schmaltzy score that Marvin Hamlisch composed for *Sophie's Choice*. Curiously, it seemed to fit the picture and might manipulate some people toward their Kleenex.

Tobias Wolff was to attend our preview, which excited me since I had been an admirer for some time. I wondered how he'd react to seeing his mother anally penetrated by dear old Bob. Not a scene he could have witnessed in life, nor was it in the book. In fact there was much about that chapter that did not merit deep scrutiny. His mother, incidentally, was still very much alive in Florida and perhaps he wished to protect her from this possible embarrassment.

The first public preview of *This Boy's Life* was held in Santa Monica at a new-ish complex on Third Street. Inside, my assistants had loaded the film onto the platter, or "cakestand" as we call them in the UK. The entire movie was joined up and sat, threaded, on the machine. The sound, separate, was on another machine, and the engineer from Warner Brothers, Jim Nord, whom I'd worked with since *Killing Fields* days, had everything ready for a rehearsal. Caton-Jones, despite my pleadings, had come along. It is really not necessary for directors to put themselves through these hoops. In this case it was now revealed that the house had not been used for previews before. We were the guinea pigs.

We didn't start the rehearsal until nearly one and then the trouble began. First the sound was distorted, which we fixed, but the picture was shuddering laterally, a very odd sensation that made one feel slightly sick. The focus was all over the place. Each join that went through the machine, and there were thousands, put the thing off focus. The projectionist, a youth in running shorts and thick glasses, fiddled with this and that, without any improvement. We then watched as they changed the lamp in the projector, quite a performance, requiring the close atten-tion of two engineers who handled the Xenon lamp as if it were a newborn child or, perhaps, a small atomic bomb. It was revealed that this lamp was at the end of its life and that accounted for the focus problem. The shuddering picture was cured by tightening up some loose nuts and bolts. We then repaired to a bistro and tried to get ourselves into the right mood for the preview.

I had been through many of these evenings, since *The Grass Is Greener,* but never failed to get nervous. There were now hundreds of people lining up around the theatre and snaking back into the car park. They looked like a more upscale crowd than usual and had been specially recruited as our target audience of regu-lar filmgoers and De Niro lovers. We all moved into the theatre. It was about fifteen minutes before the start and I saw a few familiar faces from the Warner Brothers' marketing department. I was chatting with them when a tall, balding guy appeared with the producer's assistant. This was Tobias Wolff.

I always find it very odd meeting the real person when I've lived with the im-personator for so long. I had this feeling with Sydney Schanberg, whom I couldn't separate from Sam Waterston in *The Killing Fields* for the longest time. So Wolff and I got to talking and made immediate friendly contact. I told Tobias this was going to be a very odd experience for him. He had, of course, read the script, but hadn't seen anything, save a few stills, and he had visited the set when they were filming in Concrete.

I spotted all the bigwigs from Warner Brothers taking their seats along with a frazzled looking Art Linson and a freshly shaved Caton-Jones with his wife, but they all sat away from me. My assistant, Peter Lonsdale, had a walkie-talkie in case he needed to communicate with the booth. I had the remote volume control. The show started. To say it played well would be an understatement. *It played very well indeed.* It might never play better. They laughed in all the right places, they cried at the end, they were suitably horrified by the violence. We pushed their buttons very well though I was aware of loss of attention during the last third. We lost seven people, all women, during the final fight between De Niro and Leonardo. Behind me, throughout, I felt the presence of Tobias Wolff, who was laughing heartily most of the time. I kept thinking to myself, "This isn't really a comedy. Why are they laughing so hard?" They started to laugh as soon as De Niro entered, as planned by us, and they stopped laughing when he violated Ellen Barkin. But not for good, just for a while when they realised this character wasn't just a buffoon, but a dangerous buffoon. There were times when I had to turn up the volume, they were laughing that loudly. At the very end they gave us a decent round of applause. Anyway, the point is that the film had been perceived to perform by the people that matter, the marketing department.

Naturally there was a lot of relief from our people. My main pleasure was having Tobias Wolff tell me how happy he was with the movie. It would have been depressing otherwise. The cards were filled in very carefully by the audience and proved useful. The projection, after all, was flawless. But imagine what it would have been like without our efforts to improve it.

Art Linson told us to meet him and Tobias at the Four Seasons Hotel for lunch the following day. Linson was in high form, specialising in invective and hatred for the studio. During the meal he worked himself into a lather about the studio suits. He told us exactly what they'd say about the movie and what their suggestions for improvements would be, correctly as it transpired, and slagged them all off. It reminded me of our reactions when I was a suit at Columbia. Wolff was rivetted by all this and I hoped he'd put it into his notebook for future use. Art liked me because I laughed at his remarks. He's a genuinely funny fellow, much influenced by his friend David Mamet, who immortalised him in the play *Speed-the-Plough.*

Dede Allen's remarks after the screening hadn't made too much sense to me. I thought it time she hung up her scissors. She was again in attendance when we drove over to the meeting at Burbank. Here we got the numbers and sat down with Bob Daley and Terry Semel. I had been through this ritual with Puttnam a number of times and it never varied. Richard Del Belso, the guy who had organised the preview, delivered his report. They looked at the numbers and the suits gave their views. It followed the script according to Art. "We love this movie and we think it's great but maybe a bit long here and there and maybe some points need clarifying." The main thing was that they liked the movie, which meant they'd promote it and nurture it.

The simple fact, however, was that they had no idea how to sell *This Boy's Life*. The studio were used to selling action pictures. This was an odd movie. Who was it for? Would we be cursed for displaying child abuse? Terry Semel said, "You need some voiceover like 'when I was a kid I got knocked about a whole lot by De Niro.'" He couldn't even get the character's name right. They kept on referring to Dwight as De Niro. Art was fit to be tied. Being at these meetings can sometimes be fun. You quickly realise the inmates really are running the asylum.

As the saga behind the scenes of this movie shows, you invest a great deal of time and emotion when cutting a film and it helps enormously if you actually believe in the artistic integrity of the project. As it happens, I still consider *This Boy's Life*, even with its flaws, to be a good and worthy film. That, however, means nothing in Hollywood as Art Linson describes in his book *What Just Happened?*:

> I was at the tail end of a contract at Warner Bros., where I had just put out the artistically interesting but dismally unsuccessful *This Boy's Life*. I remember that when it was first test screened in a Pasadena multiplex, Terry Semel, the then graceful but remote head of Warners, walked up to me at the concession stand, dressed in the newest Armani casual, looked me square in the eye, and slowly nodded.
>
> "It's a good movie and that's all that's important," he said in a calm and reassuring voice.
>
> "'Well, thanks so much, Terry, it is a good movie, isn't it?"
>
> "It's hard to make a good movie."
>
> "Very."
>
> At previews, everyone spoke euphemistically. I was fucked. I knew too well that at that very moment Terry's entire distribution staff was in the back alley throwing up on their shoes. You could almost hear them through the crack in the men's room door: "Oh, mother of Christ, De Niro is in this dining room kicking the living piss out of sweet little Leonardo DiCaprio . . . how the fuck are we going to sell this shit!" "I know! How 'bout selling it as *Father Knows Best* for the criminally insane?!" "Dead

beavers and paedophilia, what are they gonna let those disturbed assholes do next?!"

You get the picture. Good in Hollywood is a euphemism for "grease up, bite the belt, and try not to squeal too much when this baby comes out." Well, I tried not to squeal, but I can't say it bolstered my confidence any.

Despite good reviews, the promotion department at Warner Brothers failed to find an audience for *This Boy's Life*, which languished and expired at the few theatres in which it was shown. It was perceived as a film about child abuse, a topic that was seen as entirely uncommercial. After *Titanic* and the coming of Leonardo as a star, the subsequent video and DVD life might have cornered a few converts, but despite all our efforts it remains a film that few have seen.

AWAY FROM HOME: THE EDITING AND THE AGONY

Radio Inside

I cut most of *Radio Inside,* which I have lived to regret. It was a small film written and directed by a first timer. I only got involved because, in lieu of salary, producer Mark Tarlov promised me a half share in a Lightworks digital system. He also said the month of shooting in and around Miami Beach would be great fun. He was paying some per diem, but that was all.

I never thought the script was much good but it attracted a reasonable cast. Elisabeth Shue was the lead girl before she was discovered by Mike Figgis and the cast included Billy McNamara and Dylan Walsh.

I had a good local assistant, Gaston, who had come to help, though he was earning more on relief. The lure of South Beach with its art deco hotels and nubile girls was fine but the budget was so small that I was quartered in a less-than-ritzy hotel next to a rehab centre for drug addicts, who made a bit of a racket as they were weaned off their narcotics of choice. There seemed to be a large number of crazies around and I never felt safe there, but the events around me were nothing compared to our problems on set. The director evidently had little ability and Mark was on him like a ton of bricks. The atmosphere was frightful and the rushes were poor. All this on top of a script that was barely readable.

229

I was in despair most of the time but was asked to assemble a short five-minute showreel that would be exhibited at the American Film Market in Los Angeles. Gaston and I raked around the rushes, put some rock music over it and sent it off. To my horror this inspired MGM to buy it, sight unseen. I knew we couldn't possibly live up to this demo and, after a month of filming and being over schedule, Mark announced that the shooting was over, but, according to my script, it wasn't. We still had many pages to shoot and MGM expected to see a finished film. What could we do to fill the gaps?

I went back to England, leaving the film unfinished and in the hands of Gaston. As one brother in the story had an interest in fish, I suggested to Mark that the cameraman should seek out an aquarium and have a double for Billy McNamara look at the fish. That might fill one or two of the holes.

The cutting copy was sent to New York where it lay in Mark's attic while we got on with *A Good Man in Africa*, which was Mark's next film. This one had no money problems and a known director, Bruce Beresford, as well as a known actor, Sean Connery.

A Good Man in Africa

We made the film in Johannesburg, Pretoria, and various surrounding locations. William Boyd's novel was set in the fictional state of Kinjanja and the provincial city of Nkongsamba which were thinly disguised versions of Nigeria and the provincial capital Ibadan. According to Will, our locations looked just like a Nigerian city. I'd read this funny book before I ever became involved in the film and tried to buy the rights while attempting to re-animate my directing career after the Columbia episode. So, together with Jeremy Gibbs, who assisted me, I went off to what was considered to be the murder capital of the world.

In the lead role of Morgan, the bumbling British Embassy character, Bruce had cast an Australian actor, Colin Friels, which was mistake number one. After the first week of shooting, I went to see Mark and told him that his leading man had failed to make either me or my assistant laugh once and this was a comedy. I knew it was not going to work, but Mark was adamant that we continue, or risk a total shut down, so I kept quiet. I was, however, right.

Bruce seemed oblivious to the deficiencies of the film. He liked everything. Once again I was desperate and tried to make the movie as amusing as possible. William Boyd appeared at rushes one evening and afterward I asked him if Colin reflected his vision of Morgan and he replied that he did, so I kept my mouth shut again. After all, Will had written the book and the script. Years later, Will told me he'd tried to sell Mel Smith or Timothy Spall to the backers as he knew they were both keen to play the role.

Jeremy and I moved out of the modern hotel where everyone was staying. We didn't want to meet, eat, or drink with the crew every night despite entreaties that it was not safe outside in murder-happy Joburg. Jeremy and I found a house to rent in a suburb not more than twenty minutes drive from our cutting room.

I began to worry that we should, perhaps, have heeded the warnings. The house was surrounded by a wall with razor wire on top. There was a live-in maid, who stayed in an outside house and was rarely seen. The rooms were vast. The place might have been a country club and Jeremy and I were lost inside it. There were lockable gates top and bottom of the staircase. We were advised to always lock the gates at night in case of intruders. On the day we moved in, the owner, an elderly white farmer, handed me a Luger left over from World War I, saying ominously, "You may be needing this." Thankfully, I never needed it. Our stay in that house was perfectly fine. It was isolated and a bit lonely, but never seemed dangerous.

At work things were not always exactly amusing. Right next to the cutting room, which was in a modern building, was a patch of ground where odd characters could be seen lying under trees, wasting their days. This developed into a full-scale gambling hell on weekends, when women would arrive with cooking stoves and tend to the men, who would get drunk and fight. We always kept away on weekends, but one Monday morning we arrived to find a corpse on our front steps, left over from the night before.

I was very happy when the day came to leave Joburg and head home where we'd continue cutting at Twickenham. Not that I was happy with the picture. Despite Bruce being very optimistic, I knew we had another stinker on our hands. Meantime *Radio Inside* resurfaced and was removed from Mark's attic. MGM were concerned that they had not seen it.

A screening of *A Good Man in Africa* in London one evening confirmed my worst fears. The only laughs came from Sean Connery and his wife. To make matters more depressing, Bruce had decided that he'd found the right composer for the film. Georges Delerue had his fatal stroke on the podium while conducting his score for Bruce's previous movie so he was not available, but this composer was Mexican, had never worked on a film, and was mainly writing liturgical music. Just the sort of chap you needed to write music for a comedy. Mario Lavista arrived from Mexico City and was taken to the "Ship" at Twickenham as soon as he arrived. We thought a little culture shock would be good for him. We ran the movie that afternoon. Bruce talked to Mario about the music and within days the composer had gone back home. He came back about six weeks later and we recorded the music over a weekend in a church near the studio. The music Mario had written was almost entirely unsuitable and Mark and I both knew that another composer had to be found. Once again Bruce was quite happy with what he'd heard, but he too was on a plane since he was about to start shooting his next film in America. Mark and I were left holding the baby, and we eventually got John Du Prez to come to our rescue. He had written mainly for the Pythons so we figured he'd be okay. He did what he could. The movie didn't inspire any of us, but it had to be finished since Universal was breathing down our necks.

We mixed the film and took it over to Berkeley for preview. *Radio Inside* was being recut at the Saul Zaentz studio since Mark had to show it to MGM. I pitied the editor who had taken it over. Every inch of the fish material was used.

A Good Man in Africa died a miserable death in Berkeley that night. A very low score was all it managed. The publicity department had organised a meal in a restaurant after the screening. Colin Friels, who had flown over from Australia, drowned his sorrows at the bar. I sat next to Bruce, who, halfway through the meal turned to me. "Jim," he said, "I'm going to the Gents, but don't tell anyone, I'm not coming back." In fact he got on a plane and returned to Los Angeles, but he could not escape entirely since I had notes to take from him for final changes. I went to Los Angeles and ran the film with Bruce in his home. I took a few notes then returned to England. We mixed it at Twickenham and left fate to decide its end. A sad episode.

When it eventually opened, the film was poorly received. *Radio Inside*, however, was sold to Showtime, the cable company, and continues to be shown on television. It's also on DVD, and since it cost only about $600,000 must be making a profit by now. I'm still angry that I ever took it on and that my name is on it, but I did get to use the Lightworks after all.

After those jobs, neither of which had pleased me or my health, I realised that most of the films I had been associated with since *This Boy's Life* had been bad. I took a break and went on a walking holiday with Laurence. Forgetting films for a while was good for me, but there was always the allure and the prospect of something better just around the corner. Despite my reputation, I still courted trouble.

Nell

Michael Apted asked me to cut *Nell* for him. We had not worked together since *Agatha* so I was pleased to be available. There were two possible snags. The first was that it was to be shot and cut in America, so I would be away from home for nine months. The second was that it needed to be cut digitally on the Lightworks system, since Twentieth Century Fox had bought a number of these machines and they had to be used. I was happy to learn this machine, after all, I part owned one. I was given a week of training by a girl in Los Angeles before I returned to London. There were a few weeks to go before the film began shooting.

Nell was a film starring Jodie Foster, who was also one of the producers. She played a mountain girl, found in her mother's house after the old lady has died, speaking a language that nobody understood. Her case was taken up by a doctor, played by Liam Neeson. He became involved with her and together with a psychiatrist from the city, studied this wild child in her natural habitat before she was removed to a hospital. The script was based on a little-known play. It was an unusual subject and appealled to women. Jodie, speaking a nonsense language, gave a performance that worked. She was nominated for an Oscar that year. I often wondered how the subtitles were used abroad because it's hard to translate nonsense, though as the story progressed Nell's language was understood by Liam's character.

I headed for the location that was in the Smoky Mountains near Knoxville. I flew to Washington DC from London, then changed to a small commuter plane, fearing my luggage would never make it to the smaller terminal where the seven-seater prop plane was waiting. We boarded and took off on a thirty-minute flight. The pilot didn't look more than twenty-one. We didn't fly very high, but we got into turbulence and I could see we were approaching some extremely dark clouds. Suddenly the plane started to pitch and toss, lightning crossed our path as the pilot did his best to avoid the worst of the storm, eventually throwing the plane onto the runway. We were relieved to be on the ground, but I was soon to realise that my luggage had not made the plane. It would be sent on the following day.

The location, near Fontana Dam, was two hours away. The unit driver who picked me up said there were at least a hundred and fifty hairpin bends between the airport and the location and the rain was pouring down. The driver was quite correct in his calculations and, after an interminable journey, we finally arrived at the location. It was a camp, way up in the Smokies, as far from civilisation as anyone could wish. The nearest town, Robbinsville, was a half hour drive away. I was dumped, without my bags, in a small cabin on the edge of the camp. It was about 9 PM, very cold and there was no food or anything else to be had. I could not even brush my teeth. All I knew was that there was a production meeting at nine in the morning. I fell asleep, surrounded by silence.

The following day, I found my way to the administration office where about twenty production people seemed surprised to see me, but it was good to see the place in daylight. Clearly the next few weeks in Fontana were going to be interesting.

My assistant from Los Angeles, Eric Schusterman, with whom I'd worked on *This Boy's Life,* was already in Fontana. The settlement was comprised of about a hundred cabins and was originally built in the early forties to house the workers constructing the nearby dam, part of the Roosevelt TVA scheme. When they left, an entrepreneur purchased the site and converted it into a resort for hunters, fishermen, and walkers. It was very near the Appalachian Trail. The company making *Nell* had taken over the place and all those working on the film were housed there. The actual location where shooting would take place was about a mile away on the other side of a lake.

Our cutting room was in the Admininstration block and rushes would be viewed in a specially converted room. Eric and I decided to take a cabin that was different from the rather grand one allocated to me. Eric was in cabin 666, which we, naturally, called the Devil's cabin. I shared half of it. The cabins were wooden, a bit on the rickety side, and contained the basic requirements for weekend living. A living room, kitchen, bedroom, and bathroom. That was it. When it rained hard, mostly at night, the cabin would shake and every thunderclap sent it into a paroxysm of shudders. It was, however, our home for a while and I was very happy there.

It was also a wonderful place to learn the Lightworks machine. Processing was done in New York and the rushes were delivered to us. The poor unit drivers got very tired of their daily trek to the airports at Knoxville or Charlottesville. After we'd seen the rushes, they were flown to Fox in Los Angeles where they were viewed and digitised, so the turnaround period was at least a week. Fox kindly loaned me the rushes tapes of *Mrs. Doubtfire* on which to practice. I quickly learned to admire the editor who had managed to cut that film, which contained thousands of feet of Robin Williams improvising, on two cameras, no two takes being the same.

When the time came to cut my own material, I was well up to speed on the machine and soon appreciated the benefits of digital editing.

Filming *Nell* on location was good fun. Not only did I get to learn the machine, but our off time was spent hiking and visiting nearby towns, where we realised that much of rural America is still living in the past. The one black man on our unit was treated with great interest when he appeared in the supermarket at Robbinsville. The daughter of our costume lady went to a local school. When her date said he had to go home "to collect his uniform," she realised he was a sixteen-year-old Klan member and she quickly ran away. Our black man was lucky to leave the supermarket in one piece.

The real star of *Nell*, for me, was the location. A cabin was built on a piece of land that was on the lakeside and, to get to it, we had to be taken by motorboat. There was a feeling, while we were there, of being in an area of America that had been lost. It was beautiful, isolated, underpopulated, and two hours drive from Asheville, the nearest town of any size. Our time there was enchanted. We might not have made the greatest movie, but we had a great time shooting it.

Afterward we returned to Los Angeles, where we edited the film, but we mixed it back home at Twickenham since Ted Gagliano, the head of post at Fox was experimenting in order to find a cheaper route for sound dubbing. The negative was also sent to Deluxe in London and the initial prints were made there.

Copycat

After *Nell* had flown the nest, I decided not to work for a while and to take another walk abroad. This time to Portugal. Our peace, however, was again disturbed by Mark Tarlov. I had turned down the offer to edit *Copycat* for him since I had no desire to return, yet again, to America. Besides which, after I read it, I said that the script ended on page eighty, meaning that it was okay up to there and then fell apart. Evidently I wasn't wrong. The film had been shot in San Francisco with a good cast, directed by Jon Amiel but, after a screening, Mark and Jon had decided to dispose of the editor, hence the call to me. Being free at that moment, I reluctantly agreed to fly over to California in early March of 1995 and see what I could do.

Circumstances, however, prevented that because I came down with really bad stomach pains. I saw a gastroenterologist. Fortunately my presence was not immediately essential and Mark Tarlov was very understanding. This condition might not be life threatening, but it was certainly dragging me down. In addition to my poor stomach, I developed a chesty cough. I hated flying with a bad chest because the air conditioning always made it worse. An indicator of how low I'd sunk was that, in spite of wonderful weather, I couldn't drag myself out of the house. I just sat there reading all day. No harm in that, but it was so unlike me and fuelled my general air of depression. Normally I'd be dashing around a graveyard with my camera. I hated being in this condition and the thought of sitting on a plane for eleven hours was altogether alarming.

I had, however, made my mind up to leave and got to Santa Monica in one piece. My health held up, but I was aware, all the time, of my wretched stomach and, although a long day at work tended to take my mind off it, nevertheless, I lived on a knife edge, never knowing when I'd go off again. Also, in helping Mark out, I'd entered another hornet's nest.

The *Copycat* cutting room was above a restaurant in Santa Monica, very near the ocean. Mark had generously quartered me in a recently opened beach hotel, curiously called Shutters, from which I could walk to the cutting room. It soon became known as Shudders. I had an excellent seventh-floor room with a view of the pool and ocean beyond. It was very light and bright and painted white.

Copycat was fairly bad; the script was a mess to begin with and Jon Amiel, despite some nifty direction, had not been able to clean it up. A thriller-type movie in which Sigourney Weaver, wasted here, played a criminal psychologist specialising in the behaviour of serial killers. In the prologue she was menaced by one of these murderers, played by the weirdly miscast Harry Connick Jr. Here he was with a three-day growth and a badly blacked-out tooth, killing a cop in a toilet and stringing Sigourney up with a steel noose, from which she miraculously escaped. Fade to the present where we find our heroine living the life of an agoraphobic in her high-tech apartment surrounded by computers, through which she corresponds with the outside world via the Internet.

Meanwhile we are introduced to Holly Hunter, the shortest cop in the entire world. She was stalking a killer who was on the loose and eventually enlisted Ms. Weaver's help to track him down. It all ended up with little Holly being strung up in the same toilet and, seemingly, shot to death, but not by Connick Jr, whom they, perhaps, could not afford to keep throughout the entire movie. The killer then grabbed Sigourney and was about to knife her when he was shot and killed by, none other than, Holly, who had not been killed at all, since she had put on a bulletproof vest. Just how she slipped the metal noose is not revealed, much to the anger of the preview audience, who rightly picked on this hole. It was a ludicrous farrago, only made bearable by some smart camera work and set design.

That they fired the original editor, Alan Heim, was only a reflection on the paucity of the script. The man's work was, so far as I could tell, perfectly fine. I guess it was a case of "if it doesn't work, fire the editor," a common enough move in the motion picture business.

The first thing I did, having arrived in the cutting room, was to sit down in a nearby theatre and watch it. Not a happy afternoon. Returning to the room where Mark and Amiel were waiting for me, I was sad to announce that the film still ended on page eighty. Instead of slinging me out of the room and onto the next plane, they appeared to embrace the realisation that something had to be done. They had, after all, had public screenings with little luck.

So I set about recutting the film on the Lightworks with Paul Karasick assisting me. Paul was a real wizard with the machine and worked long and hard to help me. First I tackled the end reel, since this was considered overlong. I hacked away at it, taking out some excesses, but nobody could really fix it. It was far too late. I also recut a few other scenes and made some more cuts and Amiel was happy with this version that we were to preview again the following week.

There were, however, consolations. The crew were very pleasant and did not resent my presence, even though they'd all been loyal to Alan Heim, whose work I did not have to recut very much. I could walk to work, the job would not last too long, and it got me reacquainted with the Lightworks. Mark had also arranged a first-rate financial deal for me. All that was positive, but the film was a mess, which did very little to get me out from under the feeling of depression I'd had for weeks. That and the constant stomach trouble combined were not making me happy.

I had dinner with my friend Peter Boyle who was in town cutting *Waterworld,* the most expensive picture ever made at that time. Currently at $160 million, they were showing it to the studio the following week, at two hours forty minutes, obviously too long. Peter was not too enthused about the picture and I think he expected to get bumped off it. He'd also cut *Robin Hood* for Kevin Reynolds and Kevin Costner, amidst fearful rows, but who made it up and shook hands over *Rapa Nui,* which Peter also cut, last year's most expensive flop. Now it appeared they were due to fall out all over again.

The next preview of *Copycat* played even worse than before, despite our efforts. We recut the ending yet again, which was the main problem and contrived to make Holly Hunter shoot the killer. Formerly the SWAT team did the deed. We screened again but still no joy. Now the decision was made to rewrite and reshoot the ending, which involved three main actors. It was the only way out of this impasse, even though it would take time because everyone was busy and the scenes had to be written and sets constructed. We could see that the hiatus was going to last some time. Mark decided to move the cutting room to London and do the final editing there. Shipping the Lightworks back to the UK by air would cost a huge amount because it weighed over a ton.

I had not enjoyed much of this, since this picture was somewhat doomed and there really was very little I could do to help. Although Amiel was a perfectly pleasant and amusing person to spend time with, he was someone who needed to be in control and took ages fussing over changes. Also, he spent much of the day on the phone, leaving the assistants to work long hours to catch up. Despite these shortcomings, I liked him.

When I landed back in London it was almost as warm as Santa Monica. Even the police were in short sleeves. Everything was in bloom. The dull ride from the airport was unusually beautiful. People smiled. Even the driver told me London was looking good and so it remained through Good Friday, when the

British, beguiled by unseasonably warm weather, made for the seaside, thinking it was June. Poor fools. The clouds soon covered the sun and the thermometer plunged ten degrees. They said we might have snow.

I was soon approached by Neil Jordan about cutting his next film, *Michael Collins*, which was to star Liam Neeson in the title role. It was scheduled to shoot in Dublin and I agreed to it, provided I could edit it on the Lightworks and I had finished with *Copycat*.

I watched a documentary on *Michael Collins* made for Irish TV which I found interesting. I realised that Collins was an Irish hero and considered a great patriot, but he was also a murderer, responsible for the assassination of many British guys. I didn't honestly know why we were about to make this giant biopic, nor who would want to see it outside of Ireland and Boston, Massachusetts, or wherever Irish patriots were to be found. Then Neil told me they had Julia Roberts for four weeks, playing Kitty. They thought this was a casting coup, but in my view, it severely compromised the project for the sake of a marquee name. What were they thinking?

Copycat would not go away. I was endlessly recutting with Jon Amiel, who simply would not leave his film alone, picking at it like a scab. We endeavoured to lock some reels before Amiel and Tarlov returned to America. Not easy to do and we'd only managed to finalise six reels of twelve, which was hard on the sound editors and the composer who would have frantic last minute work once they had reshot. I decided to leave the show for a few weeks until the new material was in hand. No point in charging the company for all the downtime I foresaw. Better to spend it with the family instead of driving to the studio every day to sit and look at the walls.

I revisited the doctor and he put me on Prozac, so either I'd become Mr. Happy or Mr. Morose. This drug seemed to operate like that. I told him of my nasty depressions and he reached for the designer drug that was said to work miracles.

The *Michael Collins* saga continued. I was phoned by the producer, Steve Woolley, who explained that I could only use the Lightworks system if I agreed to get the picture completed before Christmas. This was the only way he could justify the expense to Warner Brothers, so I got hoisted by my own machine, which I insisted on using. Whether I could, in reality, achieve this aim was hard to say. It would give me a two and a half month finishing period, as opposed to the normal five months. In essence it meant that Neil had only sixteen days in which to complete his cut. Apted and I did the director's cut of *Nell* in seven days, but it was a much simpler project. This picture would probably run for fourteen reels, which meant we would have to finalise at a staggering rate of almost a reel each day and

I'd never faced that challenge before. It left no room for error and would mean working very late hours and a seven-day week. Was I being suckered into this? If they were to go over schedule in the shoot, it would all become impossible anyway. The only good aspect of this was that the picture would all be over and done by Christmas. I arranged to fly to Dublin to discuss the situation with Neil and Steve.

I was annoyed by Steve's plea of poverty. He said he and Neil had already forgone their normal fees to reduce the budget. Since I knew that Warner Brothers was putting $25 million into the picture, I guessed they were paying Julia Roberts a good whack in their mad, stupid casting. Steve also told me they were paying Chris Menges a huge fee to return to lighting, as his directing career had foundered, whereas they were underpaying me and drinking my blood too.

Maybe after my Dublin meeting I'd be off the picture altogether, which I would not cry over. It sounded like I'd entered another nightmare, which was perhaps not what I needed in my present state of health. My stomach was still misbehaving and now woke me every night around four with horrible pains, gurglings, and gas.

I had to fly to Dublin for the meeting with Neil and Steve, which turned into a trial, as I was clobbered again the night before with stomach problems. My journey to Ireland was marred by constant pain. Before departure, I had an attack of colic that wore me out and even the short plane ride was uncomfortable. Fortunately the pain diminished as I was driven into the city. I found the production office and was summoned to join the bosses at a restaurant on St. Stephen's Green, where I found ten people finishing off a lavish lunch, including Neil and Steve. They offered me food, but I couldn't look at anything without heaving.

Steve and I walked back to the office and discussed the accelerated postproduction schedule, which they estimated would cost Warner Brothers another $500,000. They submitted this schedule and budget and if it was accepted then I really had given myself an enormously hard task. In this case, my life would be easier if I cut on film in the normal time. At least they would not be rushing the picture out for Christmas. We had to get the picture right the first time, which would put enormous pressure on me and my crew. I didn't even know if it was manageable. If we previewed badly, and there was barely time for that gruelling exercise, then the entire enterprise was at risk. In that case, any overages had to be paid by the producer and director, who could catch a mighty bad cold.

In truth, the trip to Dublin was a huge waste of effort and achieved nothing that could not have been done by phone. The Prozac was bothering me. I had been told that two weeks was the period required for something to happen, but after five days, I felt much worse. My professional life was in a mess and although

I knew it would eventually sort itself out, for the moment it was not good. I was, by nature, an orderly person and I found messes difficult to manage.

The *Copycat* muddle got worse since they now could not shoot until June, which meant we need not have cancelled a holiday we'd booked. They were not simply redoing the end but lots of other things besides, which affected six reels, none of which could be mixed. On top of all the other woes, we were losing our sound editing team in June as they were contracted to go on to *Mission Impossible*. Just how to replace them was a real problem since they worked digitally and there were very few people skilled in that area at the time. I was planning to take the Lightworks to Ireland, but it would now have to remain in London with *Copycat* until that was entirely wrapped. So I had to go back to the *Michael Collins* people and get them to rent another machine. This meant I lost the rental for the whole show and the machine would gather dust in London. I was expected in Dublin on July 2 and would not have completed the recut on *Copycat* by then. That was one reason why I felt so disturbed. It was maddening to feel so ill. It sapped me of all energy, made me act irrational and hard to live with. Laurence was a saint and most understanding while not knowing how to help me. I just prayed the Prozac would kick in and help me out of the maze.

True to its reputation, the Prozac began to work after two weeks. I soon experienced the euphoria they claimed people feel as the drug kicks in. It might not last, of course, so I was not counting my chickens, but I found myself having a glorious Sunday full of pep and happy as can be.

After a good sleep without tummy problems, Laurence and I went to the Garden Centre to buy plants. Normally I felt faint and dizzy in those places and couldn't wait to leave, but now I felt fine. I cycled with my camera to Clapham Common, a good five miles, took snaps at the May Day rally, cycled back to have lunch at Khan's Indian restaurant in Westbourne Grove. I then returned home and washed the car, and took a long call from Tarlov regarding the future of *Copycat*. Even he now agreed it was a mess.

☆　☆　☆

I was on my own over the Easter break because Laurence was in France. My daughter Sybil and her son Jackson came to see me. The little chap was really a joy to have around and had just had his first real haircut, so looked like a regular boy. He also had proper shoes and talked a constant babble of mostly nonsense words, though Mama and Dada were clear. I think he said Grampa too, but maybe I was kidding myself.

Michael Caton-Jones' agent called me to check on my availabilty that summer because Caton-Jones might be doing a movie called *B Monkey*, with Hugh Grant, originally slated for next year. Perhaps I should move smartly over to that one.

I wrote a fax to Steve Woolley explaining why I might not be free to cut *Michael Collins* and begged him to find another editor if he felt so disposed. At least I'd warned him of the dangers and felt it prudent to have the details on paper in case they started to blame me for falling behind next November. I was covering myself, which turned out to be just as well. In the end, they decided that Lightworks was just too expensive. Redmond Morris called to tell me this news and my reply was simply, "If you don't have the Lightworks, you don't have me." I reckoned the whole thing was a ploy anyway. I was expensive, the gear was expensive, they would have to pay for my accommodation in Dublin and per diem on top of that.

So I remained on *Copycat* until the bitter end. It had been a poor year for me, creatively, and I was not looking forward to continuing with Jon Amiel and trying to make something out of the new material they would shoot in June. We then had to complete the movie before taking it back to America for a final preview. If it didn't play this time, I'd have to eat my hat.

About now there was an overture from Scott Rudin to edit *Marvin's Room* in New York. The script was sent and I read it with interest. Although we knew it would take me away from home again for at least nine months, Laurence and I agreed that it was not a job to reject, so I said I would do the film. It was to be directed by Jerry Zaks, a first timer who normally directed theatre. The cast was the main attraction: Meryl Streep, Leonardo DiCaprio, Diane Keaton, and Robert De Niro.

Neil Jordan called in a last ditch attempt to lure me back, but I told him it was now too late as I'd committed to finish *Copycat*. Neil was very pleasant on the phone and repeated that he really wanted to work with me. In the end *Michael Collins* was edited by Tony Lawson, who continued to cut for Neil Jordan for many years, so I actually did him a service. *Michael Collins* suffered with the critics and the casting of Julia Roberts was not treated well.

The reshoots on *Copycat* finally ended. Having Jon Amiel back in the room was a mixed blessing since he wanted everything recut in a jiffy. Time was of the essence, but he seemed untouched by it. I didn't care, since I would be off the movie before very long. I did have to make the trek to LA for the preview and then return home before going on to New York and *Marvin's Room*. I hoped my work permit was granted before then, since I hated to lie to immigration, particularly when I was obviously travelling with more luggage than the average tourist.

The reshoots of *Copycat* had taken time. Frank Darabont was induced to come on board for the writing and the rushes started to slowly come across from San Francisco. Some scenes were not too good and, on this occasion, the cameraman was Tony Pierce-Roberts, whom Tarlov was unhappy with. After one gruellling night shoot on a rooftop, Tarlov called me to enquire about the rushes, which he remembers me saying were shit. He did not go home happy. I had started cutting the new finale in which Sigourney Weaver was yet again strung up in a toilet by the killer and only saved in the nick of time from a messy end.

The *Marvin's Room* contract arrived for my approval. Mostly it was okay, but the sticking point was the matter of accommodation. I had asked for, as on *Nell*, first-class hotel accommodation. What they had come up with was: "Producer shall provide a one-bedroom apartment with maid service, which apartment shall be selected at Producer's sole discretion." I was very unhappy about the wording, which was a trap, so I called my American accountant, Dittany Lang, whom I now used as a kind of agent, and asked her to get on the case. She asked if I considered this a deal breaker and I said yes, so we'd see what happened when I called their bluff. I certainly wanted to do the picture, but not if they were intent on putting me into a flop house.

Caton-Jones called me. He had been very upset when he heard I'd jumped into *Marvin's Room*, since I'd not discussed it with him vis-a-vis *B Monkey*, which he claimed he wouldn't make without me, but the fact was he still had no idea when he would make it since he was dicking around with three other subjects. He did, however, ask me if I'd take it over after shooting, should he make it soon. In other words, let it all pile up and then move to Dublin with the Lightworks and cut it there with him. The idea of removing myself directly from New York to Dublin did not appeal to me or the family. Laurence would certainly find it hard to take, and so I hoped this situation would never occur. We couldn't do the work in London as Caton-Jones now lived in Dublin as a tax exile. Eventually he was fired by Harvey Weinstein over a casting issue. The film was directed by Michael Radford and was a disaster.

We had completed the cut of *Copycat* and were running it to make sure there were no further changes before preview. It now ran for two hours, which was, I thought, about five minutes too long. The assistants were running around like headless chickens, working half the night and getting the film conformed and the new music laid up for temp dubbing. Everything had to be completed for shipping to LA.

Another call from the *Marvin's Room* people revealed that they were sending a packet of apartments for me to choose from, so my ploy had paid off. I plumped directly for a place called City Spire, which was situated at 150 W. 56th Street. It was something like seventy stories high and had a health club and pool.

I was invited to a picnic lunch at the Puttnam Mill, so I decided to take a walk en route. I left home at 9:30, driving to Wantage where I parked, then did a three-hour walk up country lanes to the Ridgeway, through two lovely villages, Letcombe Regis and Letcombe Bottom, both stiff with thatched cottages and amazingly picturesque. Then I drove on to the Mill, where I found a smallish group of people. The day was very hot indeed, so it was pleasant to sit in the Puttnam garden, which is huge. His estate comprised forty-nine acres. We walked and talked together as he showed me how the arboretum had grown since my last visit. In the course of this he confirmed to me that he was going to retire from film production in two years time, when he believed the Labour government would be elected. He then intended to devote his life to politics. He'd certainly lost his passion for making movies, which was sad. He told me that he couldn't envisage himself as an old producer, trying to hawk his wares around the studios. After this I drove home, two hours on the M4 in sweltering heat, before joining Mark Tarlov and others for dinner at Bibendum, his favourite watering hole.

I returned to America for the final preview of *Copycat* which was a success, so I suppose all the bellyaching I'd done had been worthwhile. The reshoots had cost another million dollars, but the picture performed, not spectacularly, but enough to make some profit.

The film was expected to be mixed in Los Angeles or Berkeley, so I took my leave of it, once it had been approved, and made my way to New York for *Marvin's Room*.

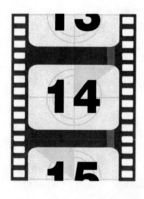

MARVIN'S ROOM, THE JACKAL, AND ONEGIN

Marvin's Room

I had originally met Scott Rudin briefly in Los Angeles in 1980 when he was working as assistant to Edgar Sherick. Scott was now considered something of a wunderkind, being still in his thirties. He had produced a number of films, including *Pacific Heights* which John Schlesinger had directed, and the two *Addams Family* movies. Apart from being a prolific producer, Scott was also well known for his temper. It was rumoured that thirty assistants had been fired the previous year. Scott made me laugh a lot with his big baby personality. He could be outrageous and rude. He would bully people and he had an amusing turn of phrase. He reminded me often of Schlesinger. I don't know that anyone else found him amusing. To me he was always genial and remained so throughout the production of *Marvin's Room*. I was one of the few who was unscathed, though there was a moment during the recut when he said something to me that sounded insulting. "Was that an insult, Scott?" I asked. "Did I just hear an insult?" That's the nearest we ever got to having a row, because he backpedalled very fast after that.

Scott's invective was mostly addressed to his director, Jerry Zaks. This was Jerry's first film. I had seen his theatre production of *Guys and Dolls* in 1993, so was aware of his talent. Jerry was in his late forties and had never been on a film set, so his experience with actors would be his strength. He could not complain about the quality of the cast who had been engaged presumably under some kind of deal since the movie was to be made for $14 million, which would not have accommodated their normal fees. Scott was also surrounding Jerry with highly capable technicians.

Marvin's Room had its origins in a play, written by a young American, Scott McPherson, who had sadly died from AIDS just before the play was produced. The play had been a success Off-Broadway in 1994 and the rights were purchased by De Niro's Tribeca company who had not succeeded in setting the film up. Eventually the rights lapsed and were picked up by Scott, who took it to Miramax for financing. Eventually, Scott joined forces with Tribeca and co-produced the film with Jane Rosenthal.

From the very start the picture was troubled and continued on a rocky path throughout production. It was my task, in the final analysis, to ensure the film survived the number of storms through which it passed without becoming overwhelmingly compromised. In addition, it was necessary to keep some kind of relationship alive between the parties concerned. I liked the movie and I felt it deserved protection.

Initial production began well enough. I first met Jerry at brunch with Scott the Sunday I arrived in New York. Jerry was a small man, with curly greying hair, a twinkle in his eye, and a smart New York sense of humour. We enjoyed one another directly. Scott too was in ebullient mood that day. The two had first met when Scott produced a play out of town that Jerry was directing. At that time they were functioning well together, though the play was in some trouble and never reached Broadway. Scott had hoped that Steve Zaillian would direct *Marvin's Room*, having previously directed *Searching for Bobbie Fischer* for him. Zaillian was unavailable so, in a moment of encouragement, Jerry Zaks got the job.

As soon as shooting began at the Astoria studio in New York, it was clear that Scott would be running the show. On the set, from first light, he made it clear to Jerry that everything he did would be scrutinised. He stood by the monitor all day and into the long evenings of overtime. Jane Rosenthal was very often there too. Jerry's longtime assistant, Lori Steinberg, was also on hand. Being a friend of Scott's helped her to build a bridge between the two, though her experience of film making was negligible. Somehow Jerry staggered through the first few days without mishap, though it was already clear to all concerned, including the actors, that he was floundering. His sense of fair play and humour saw him through those dark days, which were to become even cloudier.

I was editing away from the studio, in the Brill building at 1619 Broadway where, many years before, I had worked on *Midnight Cowboy*. My crew was first rate and we worked together in close harmony. My Lightworks assistant was Mitch Stanley and the film assistant was Debra Victoroff. We were all very happy to be working on a picture that looked like a quality product. The fine cast certainly helped to give that impression.

Rushes were run at Astoria during the lunch break, which meant taking them there in a car. To begin with there appeared to be no problem and, so far as I was concerned, the rushes cut together without problem, even if they appeared rather static. Jerry had not yet learned to move the camera and there was a clear danger of the whole enterprise looking like a TV movie with stars. Nevertheless, the performances were working. The early scenes with Diane Keaton, Gwen Verdon, and Hume Cronyn had us all laughing at dailies and the film had a good un-Hollywood look.

My first feeling of unease occurred early on when I was asked to attend an after-hours rehearsal of the first scene between Diane Keaton and Robert De Niro, a two hander in which Bessie first visits Dr. Wally. This was a difficult scene to play, involving a number of props and several pages of dialogue. De Niro greeted me characteristically with a smile and a "Hi, Jim" as he walked on. A man of few words, De Niro is an actor who comes alive in front of the camera when he fills the skin of a character. Otherwise he's taciturn and monosyllabic.

The set of Dr. Wally's office was tiny. It was hard to see where the camera and the lights might fit in, so very few changes of angle were possible. Rehearsal started and within moments we all realised De Niro had not yet learned the lines he had to know the following day. Not one. He read the script as he rehearsed. Keaton was word perfect. Jerry was very controlled, realising De Niro had not prepared, a situation that never occurs in the theatre.

When the rehearsal broke up, I could see, for the first time, that my director might need some support. We shared a ride and Jerry sat up front, saying nothing, just slumping mutely as we edged back into the city. He lived on Central Park West and I was nearby, so I suggested we go to his apartment to discuss the following day's work. He seemed to jump at the chance to evolve a plan so we went over the scene a number of times, charting possible ways to cover it. I don't reckon myself to be the brightest when it comes to such plans, though film editors are supposed to know how to cover everything and, I guess I've bluffed my way through any number of these situations. "Crossing the line" has always been a problem for me. I don't really care so long as it looks good, but I left Jerry that night with some battle plan and the vague hope that De Niro might have gone home to learn his lines. He didn't, and I was given something like 10,000 feet of film to find his performance. This is tiresome for the editor, though now that we're on digital systems it's easier. It's Bob's technique and it won't change. He's given so many great screen performances, especially for Scorsese, some of them containing long scenes without cuts. Presumably under those circumstances he does commit the lines to memory. I never plucked up the courage to ask him. Ironically I came to enjoy Bob's performance as the doctor very much. His physical business more than compensated for the lack of dialogue.

The production continued with a constant stream of problems. Scott had no faith in Jerry's ability to direct the film, but instead of replacing him, he decided to direct the movie himself, through Jerry. This gave rise to all sorts of friction and unhappiness on the set. Nobody knew whom to defer to. The actors were unhappy and the news soon leaked out onto the street. It was plain that *Marvin's Room* was troubled.

I had daily discussions with Scott, who asked me to urge Jerry into covering better and moving the camera from time to time. When I told Scott this was not my style, I was the editor and not there to bully the director, he said, "You English are so passive aggressive." "No," I replied. "Just passive passive." In fact I wasn't unhappy with the material, nor the performances. The tone of the piece would always prove a problem and the film was, perhaps, not suited to such a heavyweight cast. The play, after all, had worked well without them.

Scott, a bit like Jack Clayton, indulged in elaborate and cruel practical jokes to keep his boredom at bay. Between set ups, if he didn't wander away to make phone calls, he would mischievously pull all the plugs out of the sound recordist's equipment just to confuse him. He employed young men to act as phone minders and once he arranged for Phone Minder 1 to take a fake call from the White House saying that President Clinton needed to talk to Scott urgently. This was conveyed to Phone Minder 2 who nervously approached Scott on the set and gave him the message. "Tell him I'm busy!" Scott bellowed and PM2 crept away to relay the message to PM1, who insisted that Scott needed to talk to Clinton right away. PM2 returned to the set and was again bawled out. This charade went on a long time and whenever PM2 was screamed at, Scott would laugh and say, "I wonder how long we can keep this up?"

The film finally finished shooting in Florida around October 1995 and I had it together shortly afterward. Normally I wouldn't project the editor's cut, but use it as the foundation of the director's cut. I had done that on *Nell* and *Copycat*, but Scott and Jane Rosenthal wanted to project the editor's version, which we did one evening in November at Magno. Everything was in that version and it ran two hours thirty minutes. The projection was a disaster. It was technically impaired, the joins were all jumping across the screen, the focus was poor, and I became suddenly depressed. Seeing the picture on the screen for the first time, it seemed endless and unfunny. I was, it seemed, far more upset than anyone else, and having a drink afterward with Scott, Jane, and Jerry, I apologised to them for my misleading enthusiasm, adding that I felt ready to throw myself into the East River. This total reversal of my opinion was a puzzle to me. Here I was dumping on a movie that I had so far loved. Surely it was not just a poor projection that had so affected my judgment? In any case, it seemed we had problems and Jerry and I now settled down for a few weeks to create his version.

Jerry Zaks had never been through the editing process. Throughout the shoot, I'd prevailed on him and Lori Steinberg, to visit the cutting room on the weekend and view the cut scenes. Jerry always loved what he saw and rarely suggested changes.

We reviewed everything that had been shot and made changes accordingly, rebuilding the picture scene by scene and making substantial alterations. We also chopped out scenes that appeared redundant. The opening of the picture, as scripted, seemed to be a problem. Here, Leonardo DiCaprio was setting fire to the family home for reasons unknown. His mother, Meryl Streep, finds him arrested by the police. She is forced to move into a convent. None of this was funny. In the next scene, Diane Keaton visits Robert De Niro, playing the wacky doctor in his cockroach-infested office. This scene was expected to draw laughs. We tried a number of openings, finally moving the Keaton-De Niro scene up front. This at least set the tone we were after and was also repeating the way the play had begun.

The film script of *Marvin's Room* had been written by John Guare, who was around the set and cutting room frequently during production and attended several screenings. He was a great enthusiast and generally pleased with the results. However, as things progressed it became clear that neither Scott nor Jerry were particularly happy to have him around. Then they insisted to me that little or none of his script had been used. I was never able to verify this, but evidently John Guare sensed the atmosphere and stopped calling. I did meet him socially sometime afterward and he was vicious about the way he'd been treated.

After several small screenings in New York, none of which had been conclusive, the first public preview was held in Greenwich, Connecticut, in January 1996. The erratic tone of the piece and its sudden ending were apparent problems. The Greenwich audience appeared to enjoy the film until the end, when there was an audible gasp of astonishment at the sudden ending. The figures and the focus group produced two clear results. The ending was thought to be a sudden cop out and the part of Dr. Wally, as played by De Niro, was perceived as a problem. "Why," people queried, "Would Diane Keaton ever go back to that doctor?" It was hard to answer that, which in the theatre had never been questioned, but here we were in a realistic medium and the audience was not prepared to go along with it.

The preview was a real disappointment to our team and to Miramax. Scott Rudin, Jerry Zaks, and I drove back to New York wondering how we could fix it. Scott, as usual, came up with a number of ideas, all of which involved rewrites. In my opinion, the ending needed to be longer and more conclusive, possibly also more moving, but Scott felt the problems started much earlier in the picture.

Since John Guare was no longer part of the team, Scott asked another writer, Ron Nyswaner, to come aboard. This involved further screenings and discussions to determine exactly what was required. It was also necessary for Miramax to agree to pay for more work, which would probably involve the whole cast, some of whom were no longer available to us. Leonardo was in New Mexico making *Romeo + Juliet* and Diane Keaton was in the middle of *First Wives Club*, also produced by Scott Rudin. De Niro was making *The Fan* in Los Angeles.

Clearly this was a long-term problem, so I went off salary and returned to the UK for the whole of February. I returned to New York when we shot a new scene with De Niro and Meryl Streep over one weekend. Once again, De Niro had not learned a single line, and so Jerry shot many takes. After cutting this scene, I removed myself again and went on a holiday with Laurence to Guadeloupe.

Eventually I returned to *Marvin's Room* and became embroiled in the reshoots. This process went on and on, but sometime in July we all convened back at Astoria for a week. Conrad Hall was lighting, which was a pleasant reunion since we had not worked together since *Marathon Man*. The shooting was as fraught as ever, with Jerry Zak's work scrutinised minutely by Scott Rudin, who sat, Buddha-like, over the monitor and grumbled.

There was a new scene in which Meryl and Diane had to screech at one another in the kitchen while Leonardo watched. They rehearsed and blocked the scene over too long a period on a Friday morning and the result of this was that shooting finally came to a halt at 1:00 the following morning when Meryl finally lost her voice. Still it was unfinished. The Saturday had been allocated for a re-shoot of the Disney World scene, so we had to wrap, as the Disney scene would be an all-night shoot and the store was open for business during the day. We set up at six, Saturday evening, finally finishing at eight in the morning, by which time everyone was completely knackered.

My memories of the night are of Leonardo asleep on the floor, only waking for his scenes, Meryl, who'd worked most of the preceding night, being a solid trouper and never complaining, Scott falling asleep in his director's chair and, as we all flagged and wrapped, Connie Hall saying "Okay, what's the next set up?" He was, of course, the oldest member of the crew.

I cut the week's material together, mostly with Scott since Jerry was now directing the revival of *A Funny Thing Happened on the Way to the Forum*. Then I left the show before Rachel Portman scored it and before final previews. I had been away from home for a long time and decided enough was enough. In any case, the film was virtually locked, though I had not reckoned on the number of previews that would ensue. John Bloom came in to recut whatever was required whilst I joined the family in France, so this was the final cut for me. After many previews and endless discussions with Harvey Weinstein, it was decided that all the funny business with De Niro's Dr. Wally had to go. The preview audiences simply couldn't figure out why Diane Keaton would put herself into the hands of such an obvious nutcase. I was hauled over to New York once more to wield the knife. This hurt me more than it hurt him since I had always found the character amusing and believed De Niro had played it brilliantly, despite the fluffing and drying. But orders are orders, so I spent a day with Scott carving out the laughs.

What had worked on stage did not work on screen. The movie audience perceives the action as real whereas the theatre audience is accustomed to stylisation and can accept it. It made me weep to see this material savaged and I don't believe the film would have suffered if the humour had remained. This is the curse of the preview and the focus group atttitude to movie making that is so prevalent now. There are times when input from punters is valuable, but largely I don't agree with it. Many movies have been recut needlessly causing friction and bruised egos and great expense. Schlesinger used to say that if we'd had to preview *The Day of the Locust* we'd still be cutting it.

When finally released, *Marvin's Room* did very little business. It was, as I said right at the start, a television movie with stars and, as such, it has found a decent audience, helped by the fact that Leonardo became a big star in his following film, *Titanic*. When he told me he was doing a film with James Cameron I said, having heard of that director's aggressive behaviour, "Good luck. Don't allow him to drown you."

The Jackal

I turned the script for *The Jackal* down twice because it was really poor and I could see no point in remaking a story that had already been filmed as *The Day of the Jackal*. This version updated the story, but was badly constructed and overlong.

I didn't have a problem saying no to this one, but after a long interval and while I was on holiday in France, I took a call from Hollywood and was asked by Caton-Jones' assistant, Trish Owen, whom I knew from *This Boy's Life*, to reconsider doing it, "For Michael's sake." She caught me at the right time, after dinner when I was full of wine and good cheer. Despite my forebodings about the script, which Trish told me had been rewritten, I grudgingly agreed to cut the film. This was my first mistake, but all was not lost. Despite the material being poor, I always managed to enjoy myself on these movies and *The Jackal* was no exception.

The film was shot in America, on a variety of locations but the interiors were to be shot in London at Pinewood and the cast included Bruce Willis as The Jackal, Richard Gere as an Irish terrorist, and Sidney Poitier as a detective. It was also an expensive movie, so they'd pay me well. It was nice meeting Richard Gere again. He was kind enough to remember that we'd met briefly at a BAFTA awards evening. When we had made *Yanks* at Twickenham, the lady who ran the canteen had been a big fan so one day I took him there for a cup of tea which made her very happy. It was my impression from the beginning that everyone did *The Jackal* for the money rather than any higher motive.

I read the rewrite which seemed as bad as the first script, but I was on board. The initial cutting room was in Wilmington, North Carolina, and the Lightworks was shipped there from Dublin. Caton-Jones was living in Dublin at the time and the idea was that we would go there to complete the edit after Pinewood. However, Michael moved back to London and so that never happened.

When I arrived in Wilmington, where my team from Dublin were already assembled, plus Eric Schusterman from Los Angeles, it seemed to me that the cutting room they had set aside at the Screen Gems studio was small and inadequate. I suggested they looked elsewhere in the town for an empty space that could be converted. After numerous false starts they came across an empty hairdressing establishment, where the dryers and bowls were still in place. I took a look and decided it was just the place. It would be an open room that gave plenty of space for us to all work in. I had the Lightworks placed at the far end near the dryers and the film work was all done at the other end by the basins.

I was worried about security since we were in a bad area of town. Used shell cases and druggie's needles littered the pavement, but the owner of the hairdressing supplies store next to the building claimed that he'd fitted it with really safe security systems, the pass number being "1, 2, 3." I had that changed directly as there was a lot of valuable equipment inside. Another good thing about the room was that it took me five minutes on a bike to reach it from my designer hotel, which was in the old part of Wilmington near the river. The hotel was owned by devotees of musical theatre. Each room was named after a show, I had the *Music Man* suite complete with Robert Preston's costume. I was in that room until it flooded and they moved me to a split-level suite. There was no food laid on, so I cooked a little, but normally met my crew in a bar where we would play pool and drink whisky. My Irish assistant, Naimh Fagan, had a good rental flat in the old town, while Eric and his wife were in a very pleasant bed and breakfast nearby. We all had a good time and I never regretted Wilmington. It was like a really good holiday. The beach area had been badly hit by a hurricane shortly before I arrived, but six weeks later it was open for business. The beach was about six miles from the town and we all had bikes so it was good exercise to cycle there for lunch on weekends.

The unit shot material every day and eventually ended up in the studio. Being away from it, we didn't see too much of the director, nor of Jim Jacks, the producer, but whenever I did meet him to show scenes, he would always tell me what a great script it was. I was eventually openly disagreeing with him. He thought Chuck Pfarrer's script was brilliant. I did not and anyone who imagined this movie would not be three hours long in its first form was crazy.

Our idyllic time in Wilmington soon ended and we found ourselves on a plane to Gatwick to set up shop at Pinewood for the interiors. I carried on cutting. The film grew longer and eventually the shooting ended.

By this time, Caton-Jones had moved from Dublin to London, so we found premises in Golden Square and carried on editing. It was soon clear that the film was too long, and after a trip to Los Angeles to show it to the hierarchy at Universal, we came back to London where Caton-Jones decided, against orders, to preview. We went to Wimbledon, considered the graveyard of British cinema because so many films have previewed badly there. Toward the end of the film there is an extended visual effects sequence in a subway, which had not yet been received, so we previewed with the basic elements, which had the actors surrounded by physical gear such as lamps and fans, all of which would eventually be removed. The audience were warned about this, but when the shots appeared, all credibility was forgotten and they fell about laughing, guaranteeing poor marks.

Back in Hollywood, the company realised it was out of control and we were ordered to return, with all the film, so editing could continue in Los Angeles. The Lightworks and the crew were bundled back to Warner-Hollywood at great expense.

This time I had a rental that was huge, with a great view of the city, and Naimh had a tiny house near the Hollywood Bowl.

Caton-Jones and I carried on cutting. We were running three hours as I'd predicted, but the company needed to reduce that to two. We fiddled around for a while before it became clear that the hour could only be lost if an entire subplot was removed. This was done but now the story made little sense, so there was nothing for it but to have some short new scenes to replace the old, long ones. A meeting at Universal was convened and I finally met the genius writer who had created this wonderful script that had given me nothing but trouble for months. He was dressed from head to foot in black leather and barely made a coherent sound. I was determined he should not set about writing new scenes and made that plain to all in the room.

Meanwhile Carter Burwell was recording his score, though the film was not yet cut correctly. Carter and Caton-Jones had worked together before and were friends. Action movies are not Carter's forte. He was better off with the Coen Brothers and his score, so far, was all wrong. It had to be rescored and rerecorded later, but it did not improve. After we had mixed the film, Michael engaged some chap who had big drums called Tycho drums, and added them into the score, causing much wrath from Carter.

After additional shooting that involved Sidney Poitier and Richard Gere, we had a film of reasonable length, so we started temp mixing and previewing. We previewed three times in various shopping malls and each time we bombed. At the final preview after the film had been playing for ten minutes, three guys stood up, went in front of the screen and yelled, "Get out while you can!" and vanished. It was not a happy finish.

At our final meeting at Universal, Casey Silver, who was nominally in charge, said, "We'll say it cost eighty-nine million since I can't tell my friends it really cost ninety." When I told Stacey Snider, another one who was in charge, that I was leaving the film, she said, "For something good, I hope." "I'm leaving to go lie on a beach," which was not the reply she expected.

When the DVD of *The Jackal* appeared I bought it. Among the extras was that whole hour of film that we had removed, exactly as I'd left it, unmixed with all its Lightworks numbers prominently displayed. It was one way of not wasting the investment, but it was an embarrassment to me and, presumably, to Michael.

Twilight

I was asked by Scott Rudin to take a look at Robert Benton's *Twilight*, which had not previewed well and the editor Carol Littleton was due to start another film so could not continue. Having nothing better to do at the time I flew over to New York and viewed the picture. The actors were Paul Newman, Susan Sarandon, and Gene Hackman, but in spite of the fine cast, I realised it would never work well, though perhaps I could make it seem a bit better. Carol had done a good job and it would only be by looking through the rushes again that I might find a way to improve the goods.

I'd read this script while we were finishing *Marvin's Room* and hadn't liked it enough to take it on. Everyone thought I was crazy at the time since the script and the cast were so highly thought of, but I could see all sorts of problems. It was essentially a film noir set in Hollywood and I was not too surprised that what I saw that afternoon required serious surgery. Once again the main player entered the room as the projection neared its conclusion. When the lights went up I was not surprised to see Benton sitting at the back, asking me what I thought. "It doesn't work right now," I told him, "But let's take a look at the material."

I had given Scott Rudin three months of my time which took me up to Christmas and, as Carol was cutting on Lightworks, I had no problem digging in quickly since I knew the system. With the help of the two inherited assistants, Kent Blocher and Debra Victoroff, I started at the beginning, which I had thought strange. A quick read of the script made me realise that the original opening had been excised from the film. I asked if it was ever shot and Benton replied, "Oh yes, but we cut it out." I looked at the scene and at the rushes. The scene, as an opener, was too long and confused. I went back to the rushes and reconstructed a shorter version of the scene which I then showed to Benton. He had written the script as well as directed it and was delighted that the scene had been retained in a shorter version. I think this improvement deluded him into thinking I could fix everything, but it was not to be.

Scott Rudin was in Los Angeles producing another film. I called him. "Hey," he enquired. "Can you save my baby?" I said it was almost DOA but I'd try. That was the only time I spoke to Scott until I was packing up at the end of my three months.

We decided that some reshoots were required to try and beef up the drama and make the story more credible. Benton wrote lots of material and we narrowed our requirements down to two days of shooting, which would be done in Hollywood at Paramount.

The reshoots on *Twilight* seemed to go well but Benton had no idea who to ask to compose the score. We went through lists of names but the only one who struck a chord was Elmer Bernstein with whom I had worked on *Honky Tonk Freeway* as well as *Leonard Part 6*. We visited Elmer in Santa Barbara and got that ball rolling. He picked us up at Santa Barbara airport in his Rolls and took us up to his house where we found a whole crew of builders working on his new studio. I remember thinking that Elmer was being very optimistic since he was by now into his eighties and was starting over in a new and bigger studio. I had not been to Elmer's house before, but had walked past the wrought iron gates a number of times since my friends the Schmidts lived nearby. Elmer had looked at the movie a few times and, after lunch, he played us his themes. These were all good and acceptable.

Our test screenings of *Twilight* were still not performing. The story made more sense now but it was still uncompelling. I soldiered on and eventually the day of music recording arrived. We started with the title music. Benton, who was otherwise very savvy told me that he was "musically illiterate," which I think was an overstatement and, when a strange musical instrument was first heard, he turned to me and asked what it was. I'd recognised it as the ondes Martenot, a strange instrument that sounds not unlike a theremin. I realised that Elmer was playing homage to Miklos Rozsa, who had used the ondes in his score for Hitchcock's *Spellbound*. Eventually Benton met the English lady whom Elmer had imported to play the ondes since it seemed that very few people had mastered this odd instrument. We continued recording and, every time the ondes was heard, Benton turned to me and said, "I'm not sure I like that."

As the second day of recording began, Benton said, "I hope there's not too much of the ondes today," but soon it was evident that the main theme was being carried by it. Benton grew more and more disturbed and disgruntled.

Later that day I met a music editor who asked me who our composer was and when I told him it was Elmer, he said: "Is there a significant part for the ondes Martenot?" I asked how he guessed and he replied: "Elmer always tries to get his friend flown over to America."

It was almost Christmas and I was saying my farewells. I called Scott in Los Angeles. "Have you saved our baby?" he asked. "Well, that was a tall order," I replied. "You couldn't arrange for it to die?" That was the last I heard from him.

Benton and I got along very well. I liked him, though I would say that he is more skilled as a writer than a director. He was an art director on *Esquire* before he and his writing partner penned *Bonnie and Clyde* which they first tried to sell to François Truffaut. Benton wrote a number of scripts before he started directing.

After Christmas, without me, Benton hauled Elmer back to New York and had the score re-recorded without the ondes. The picture went on to do what the trade referred to as "lacklustre business" and while Carol Littleton's name was up there as editor, my contribution was mentioned among the many others who were thanked on the end roller, though there was barely a cut of Carol's left in the picture.

Onegin

Onegin was a film starring Ralph Fiennes that was directed by his sister Martha. The read through should have given me all the reasons in the world to desert the project before it began, but such a move would have been presumptuous, though in hindsight, sensible. Read throughs are rarely a true barometer of how a movie might eventually play. The actors tend to simply plough through the lines without attempting to act the parts and there is no real direction. In this case, the reading was lacklustre and, having a drink afterward, one of the many producers asked me, "Can you save it?" This is a question normally posed after the film has been shot and found wanting, not before the shooting begins.

It was clear, however, that the shooting script was not ready for the cameras and more changes were made before production began on location in St. Petersburg in March 1998.

When the unit returned, we ran all the rushes. Twice. An interminable day particularly as so much of the material was in slow motion. I was in the theatre for six hours. Martha and Ralph Fiennes were enraptured by everything they saw. The producers, who saw the rushes separately, were less than warm toward the director. The session was hilariously irreverent with many smart remarks from Ileen Maisel, an American producer living in London.

I realised the Fiennes were making what used to be called an art movie, whereas the producers and backers would prefer a more accessible crossover film. *The Piano* was always the inspiration. Ralph's read-through performance, which we had all considered a low-key effort, was being perfectly captured on film, and if Martha persisted in using slow motion the movie would run for hours. So far as we in the cutting rooms could see, the only merits lay in the look of the film, designer Jim Clay and cameraman Remi Adefarasin being the stars.

Ileen continued to come into my room and bellow like a bull about the material, particularly hating Ralph's performance. She raged in front of us, but did not, so far as I know, ever approach the actor himself.

As the days went by *Onegin,* known as "One Gin" by the labs, continued to give me pause for thought and we were already into the second week. I had major concerns, shared by the producers. Martha Fiennes was making an expensive art movie destined to curl up and die in front of any audience outside the major cities. She had a penchant for slow motion and brother Ralph appeared to be sleep walking through his role.

Martha was a high-strung lady and seemed to shut off and stop listening when anything that contradicted her vision was suggested. Having come from commercials and music videos, some of which I had seen, Martha told me that she was determined to make a modern-looking period film, as far from Merchant/Ivory as possible. She had some loony ideas, one being that the duel scene could be accompanied by an Iggy Pop track.

The producers decided to confront Martha with the error of her ways by screening all the edited material. They were all set to level with her and, more or less, tick her off and tell her to pull up her socks. We ran everything and the result was nothing short of a love-in. Nobody said boo. This was supposed to be the moment when Ileen and Simon Bosanquet would read the riot act to Ralph and Martha, but no. Nothing happened. Even Ileen, who had been fuelled on vitriol when raging in my room, was effusive, "Gee, Marty, it really looks great."

Shooting continued and the material flowed in, getting ever more problematic. We were in the midst of the ball scene. Many dancers doing a polonaise while Onegin spotted his lost love, Tatyana, among the crowd.

By now I had about ninety-eight minutes of the movie assembled and they had three more weeks to shoot, so I guessed we'd have a first cut of around two and a half hours. In addition, we'd prepared a thirty-minute selection of actual scenes and hoped the buyers at Cannes would not be put off by the length. The producers had been fighting the Fiennes over these three reels, and I was in the middle, as usual. I had the temerity to ask whom I should be listening to and Ralph took me aside and said, "You listen to Martha and me." Not easy when the producers are ordering changes. The hapless editor often gets between the creative talent and the money. Despite many screenings, nobody bought the film.

Shooting finally ended in May. The cut was running at a hundred and thirty minutes and would swell to a hundred and sixty by the time I had the rest of it assembled. At least we could then remove sixty minutes of excess, though I'd have a terrible tussle with les Fiennes, both of whom considered themselves above rebuke.

The first video screening of the film went tolerably well and I was asked out to lunch afterward to discuss the film with the Fiennes and the producers. This was less than exciting. Ileen Maisel was quizzed by Ralph. "Is there anything you don't like, Ileen?" he asked. She thought for two seconds, then replied, "Yes. Your performance," which, although truthful, was hardly polite. Ralph was disturbed and said her reply left little room for debate. Shortly afterward Ileen left the room claiming another appointment and I got out of there as fast as decently possible. She then went off to Los Angeles.

We moved out of Shepperton and went up the road to Twickenham where the film would be mixed in September. Ralph was now in Budapest working with

István Szabó and calling in for daily progress reports. He was regularly updated with videos of the film.

The tempo of work slowly dropped to a crawl. I could not to persuade Martha to cut anything out and the movie was still running at two hours, thirty minutes. The construction was still a problem. Martha told me that she consulted an oracle when things got rough and she had decisions to make. This person was consulted over the matter of the composer. The choice of composer fell between three possibles: Zbigniew Preisner, a Pole, who had been the late Kieslowski's composer; an English girl, Anne Dudley, who'd recently won an Oscar for *The Full Monty;* and Martha's brother Magnus who had not yet scored a feature. The oracle evidently gave thumbs up to Preisner, who visited. Flown in for a couple of hours from Warsaw, he was given a lavish lunch in the cutting room and consumed only two olives and a glass of water. My crew took most of the food home. The Pole was, I thought, producing a dandy stream of open options. "Everything is possible," punctuated by "You know," every other phrase. I was unimpressed and sensed anguish along the line. Also we needed a composer living down the street, not in Warsaw.

Things continued to totter along and the day of the director's cut loomed. The movie now ran two hours, eleven minutes. Being close to Martha for the past two months had given me more reason to feel sorry for her. She lived in a dream world, removed from any of the commercial aspects that film making demands. She had spent $14 million of someone else's money and seemed quite unconcerned about the backers or their opinions.

Martha had finally alighted on a composer, Ilona Schez, who was, I figured, about to be fed to the lions since the only composer Martha really wanted was her brother Magnus. This suggestion had been turned down by Rysher Entertainment who could not countenance another Fiennes on the show, but I just knew she would finally have her way even though Ralph had remarked that the film did not need a score at all. Ralph was calling from Budapest to speak to Martha every day. He had seen some tapes with changes and gave me his notes. I then dropped by the producer's office. Simon Bosanquet is a quiet, refined man, perhaps more suited to schoolmastering than producing. He was looking a little ashen since he'd just heard from Ileen that Rysher had seen the film on video and, more or less, washed their hands of it. They were now talking through lawyers. The man from Rysher, whom I met when the film was shooting, said he found the film quite uncommercial, arty, and pretentious, and that there was no sexual chemistry between Ralph and Liv Tyler. I was not too surprised to hear this verdict, nevertheless I did wonder whether they had ever read the script or watched the rushes. Just why did they feel disposed to shove money at it in the first place? This film had been arty and pretentious since day one.

That evening Martha called, in a state of hysteria to tell me the story—which I already knew. Poor girl. I was sympathetic. How could I not be after spending seven hours daily with her for twenty-two weeks. She was vulnerable at the best of times. This blow was very hard for someone making her first film. I'd expected the producers to move in after Martha showed her version, but they didn't. Simon tried but was rebuffed by Martha who, by communicating directly with Ralph, kept the producers at bay. Ralph had the whip hand here. He was the executive producer. His name raised the money.

I found myself, as usual, in a difficult position. While realising the film was hardly commercial and had its pretensions, nevertheless, I thought it had not yet been fairly tested. It might have an audience, and with some input, Martha and Ralph might be persuaded to reduce it. But, whatever surgery was performed, the film could not be changed into something it was not. I found myself in the peculiar position of defending Martha and her work, while thinking I should never have become involved. The fact is, I did, and must now face the consequences. Helping Martha and Ralph as much as possible before I either left the show, unfinished, or carried out the amputations which the producers, who paid me, demanded. The schedule problems were yet another issue. They could afford to continue for two further weeks, but with the version of the film forever changing, it was hard for the sound editors and the composer to keep on a prescribed path.

Previewing a film is an expensive business. The first preview was held at the Odeon, Wimbledon in early August. The English distributor, Nigel Green, was enthusiastic and felt that, with additional cuts, the film could cross over. But the results disproved his theory, and following some meetings, I reduced the film from two hours to ninety-eight minutes. So, although the reaction from the public was decidedly negative, it did at least move Martha in the right direction. She was shattered by the figures, which I was sworn not to divulge to anyone. Let's just say they did not read well. Apart from the overall slowness, the focus group did not really feel anything for the characters. I doubted we could ever fix that.

Martha, however, now seemed not to have realised she flopped badly in Wimbledon and was back picking at her movie like it was a masterpiece that should not be mauled by heathen producers advised by audiences. There were days when I figured she was either massaging her movie into life or torturing it to death.

I went a bit stir crazy trying to look after Martha and prepare the film for its second public screening. I looked ahead to the autumn when I would be joining Will Boyd on *The Trench*, instead of being a sort of extension of the Fiennes family. I felt rather like an old retainer who is tolerated and accepted because of his age. Frankly, in a long career, I'd never been through such torture for so little result. I kept explaining to Martha that she makes the changes but the movie remains the same. She was, once again, asking me to recut a scene. I asked her just why we were doing that and hinted I was losing my patience. She said she was trying to improve it. I told her the scene was pure salami, which upset her. As the saying goes, no matter how you cut it, it's still salami.

The second preview was madness and a big waste of money. The film may have been shorter than it was at the first preview, but it was basically the same animal and would, I predicted, play just as badly. What might happen after Wimbledon was anyone's guess since we only had two days remaining to make changes and then we had to lock the picture for mixing. Anyway, we did the second Wimbledon preview and it was the same dismal event as before.

After the show, the producers and I made for a restaurant across the street from the Odeon and ate a perfectly dismal meal while, for two hours, they grilled Martha and insisted that she make further changes. The gloves were well and truly off now. All the observations I'd been making for months, which had been ignored, now roared to the surface. They accused her and Ralph of making a vanity production and, furthermore, it now seemed plain that unless something drastic was done, the film would go direct to cable and a quick DVD release.

Martha was on the verge of a complete collapse and started, as ever, yakking off about her vision and the intention of the film. All rot, and I started to lose it again, finally announcing to the table that I would be quite pleased to resign. Unfortunately nobody was listening, though Duncan Heath did say, "Yes, we need a fresh pair of eyes," and I think he meant it.

As a result of this second preview, Ralph suggested a reconstruction of the film, which I thought workable and immediately implemented before anyone changed their minds. Now they managed to squeeze more money from the budget and extended the completion by three weeks which was to take me right up to my starting date for *The Trench*.

We ran the film for Ralph who was in London for the weekend, after which there was a discussion. The producers were present and the idea was to get Ralph to pass certain reels since he had final cut. All went quite nicely for a few minutes until we came to a certain cut in reel two, which Ralph claimed he no longer liked. It was, he said, "Clunky." I pointed out that this cut had existed for at least two months. Nevertheless, he wanted it extended. "Oh no," exclaimed Simon Bosanquet, "Not an extension!" Ralph went directly into a tailspin of hysteria. He didn't even work up to it. He just started yelling at the top of his voice, "This film is not too slow! I'm sick and tired of hearing it's too slow! I don't want to know what the people in Wimbledon think of this film! It's not too slow!" He continued to rant in this vein for a few minutes before subsiding. I could not look at him. I thought at any minute he might burst into tears and run from the room. He did, however, calm down and finally apologised for the outburst. He claimed that this picture had put him under great stress and that it could not be cut by committee. Also, as he saw it, the film was now beginning to move. At the risk of incurring further demonstration, I pointed out that we had to settle the cut by Friday, so it had better get moving quickly. He did not seem to appreciate the matter of dates and schedules. Ralph got on a plane and went back to Budapest, while Martha and I continued to struggle with the film, getting intermittent advice from Simon Bosanquet, who popped in and out and expanded, at length, on the editing.

We started scoring in late October and Magnus Fiennes was the composer. He did a very good job in a short time. It was not the sort of romantic score that I would have liked, but at least it had an interesting atmosphere. The sound editors had a mountain of work to achieve before the film could be mixed. Martha had recorded oodles of ADR lines and these had to be fitted and checked out by her. The fact was, nobody had the time for this, least of all Martha herself. It was all part of her need to control everything. The producers had given up fighting and Ralph was still away in Budapest, leaving Martha to play endlessly with her train set. I now got the impression that she considered she'd made a masterpiece and would no doubt complain bitterly if she was not given sufficient time to complete it.

My last day on *Onegin* was spent watching the tortuous dubbing process, with Martha controlling every decibel. She spent thirty minutes balancing three chords of music over the titles and the reel proceeded at a snail's pace. I pitied the mixer who had to try and complete the film in a week.

Martha did throw a small leaving party for me with champagne and a large bouquet of exotic blooms. I could never say I disliked her, but she knew I did not respect her and did not care for her film, which made life awkward between us. I was much relieved to leave the building.

After I left, more work was done and Kerry Kohler took over as editor for a few weeks. The mix continued and there were stories emerging about Martha's continued behaviour. The producers disallowed her to make any further cuts, and the assistants had been ordered to make certain she did not. However she apparently snipped a few frames off here and there and everyone wondered just why the reels were out of sync when they ran them with the cutting copy. One day, according to one assistant, she was so frustrated that she was throwing film cans around the room. After ten months of hardship, *Onegin* was finally finished.

I saw the final version at the London Film Festival that year. It wasn't at all bad. Much reconstruction had been done to the start of the picture after I'd left it. All good ideas which helped the film. I figured that Kerry Kohler had persuaded Martha into making changes. I have to admit that I had never thought of them. The second editor, having come fresh to the material and not having lived through the horrors of the past months was able to impose his ideas.

I was getting on with other work and was interested to read that *Onegin* had finally had a world premiere in St. Petersburg, part of a Pushkin festival, where it was received with very mixed feelings by the Russians, who felt their national classic had been defiled. Ralph and Martha conducted a press conference that seemed to have become quite a brawl. On their return home, they both declared the premiere had been a big success. Then things went quiet again, until we read in the press that *Onegin* would close both the San Sebastian and Toronto festivals in September. I have no idea how it came to be chosen as closing film by both of these bodies. Somebody must have pulled a string or two. The review that emerged in *Variety* after Toronto was positively glowing and both Martha and Ralph came out with high praise.

WILLIAM BOYD, JAMES BOND, AND WINSTON CHURCHILL

The Trench

William Boyd is a writer who had wanted to direct for some time. I first encountered him on *Good and Bad at Games,* a film for television that Laurence had edited, based on a short story. Then *Stars and Bars* was made by Columbia, and *A Good Man in Africa,* both of which were scripted by him and based on his own novels. Neither had turned out too well, which was not his fault. Despite the failures, Will's ambition to direct was reached with *The Trench,* a World War I story, which was an original script. Perhaps, like many other writers, Will preferred to direct his own material rather than entrust it to others.

We had a few meetings before we started shooting this low-budget film at Bray Studios, home of Hammer Horror. The studio was really on its last legs. Everything was peeling in that old house and it was winter, so cold and damp down Bray way. Tony Pierce-Roberts was the cameraman and Will had cast a good crowd of young actors to play the soldiers. Daniel Craig, who later became James Bond, played the sergeant and Paul Nicholls was the young soldier. The green room was next to the cutting room where Mags Arnold and I had set up the Lightworks, so the actors were always in and out to look at their scenes. Schlesinger would have frowned on this and their remarks. But actors are normally only interested in their own performances.

This was Will's first time as a director and the film was shot in the studio. I initially thought it was for budgetary reasons but Will told me it was a control issue. No weather problems, no aeroplanes overhead, no extraneous noise, and more freedom of camera movement. It was always good weather in the script, which is just as well since mud, which we associate with the trenches, was impossible to contain in the studio. Will maintained that research had proved that the trenches on the Somme in the summer of 1916 were dry as a bone and in immaculate condition. No-man's-land was a lush, unmown meadow full of wildlife without a puddle to be seen, and Will was determined to undermine the clichéd view of the trenches as knee deep in mud. The only time the action moved outside the studio was to a field in Bucks at the very end when the troops go over the top and are killed. Jim Clay, the film's art director had his hands full maintaining this vision.

Will wanted a *Das Boot* atmosphere, a feeling of claustrophobia. His direction of the actors, considering he'd not done it before, was good, but I was concerned about the lack of surprise in the story. I'd always considered Kubrick's *Paths of Glory* to be the model for films about World War I and was surprised to hear Will's somewhat scathing opinion of that movie. "It's a fantastical and utterly inauthentic representation of trench warfare," he said. "The film was wholly removed from reality as any military historian will tell you. You could drive an articulated lorry through Kubrick's trenches, they're like railway cuttings."

When it came to the music I was troubled that Will considered Evelyn Glennie as the composer. A well-known percussionist with a hearing problem who had little experience was not really the right choice, or so I thought.

As I soldiered on with *The Trench*, fate, in the shape of the next Bond movie, *The World Is Not Enough*, intervened. Michael Apted was directing this film and he asked me to edit it. I couldn't really turn it down. The thought of cutting a major action picture was too tempting. It would mean, however, that I could not take *The Trench* beyond its first cut. Fortunately Will agreed that my wife could take over as editor. Laurence had worked on the Lightworks, so she was able to cut the film with Will, without problems. In fact, this is the only film where we share a credit. Laurence took it over and did a very good job, but the picture received tepid notices and was not profitable.

The audience remained at home. Will was sad, went back to novel and script writing, while nursing his ambition to direct again. I stopped driving to Bray and went instead to Pinewood.

The World Is Not Enough

We started shooting *The World Is Not Enough* on January 11, 1999, for a worldwide release in November, so from the start of photography to delivery we had something like forty weeks, which left little room for error.

Somehow I never thought I'd end up editing a James Bond movie. To be frank, I had given up on them years before. I went to the video store and took out the previous Bond film, *Tomorrow Never Dies*. I realised how far these films had come since the days of Connery. Very polished, high-gloss techno yarns, with Pierce Brosnan now playing the hero.

The thought of attaching myself to such a venture was slightly awesome, inasmuch as the special effects and action scenes were far more complex than I recalled working with. I also worried about dealing with all that material, not being accustomed to editing action movies, but therein lay the fun.

After discussions with Michael and a vetting by the producers, I was on board. At least here was a film that had a finite completion date and a built-in audience. It would not meander along the slow and tedious preview route only to be scorned by critics and audiences as had happened to so many of the films I'd edited. In fact, there was to be only one preview of the Bond movie and that was only to see that the story held up.

The other good reason for accepting this job, quite apart from the fun quotient and working with Apted again, was that I would be using the latest Avid machines, which would be networked. Having not had experience on the Avid, I was anxious to get to it, since the future of the Lightworks system appeared to be in jeopardy. Avid, with its more powerful marketing and development had, temporarily, eclipsed the British machine, the ownership of which was currently up for grabs.

At first my courtship of the Avid was difficult, but after a short period and some instruction, I was able to forget the Lightworks and take the Avid to heart. It was not quite the pig I had named it on first acquaintance. Certainly this film could not have been achieved any other way since the one and only preview was to be via a digital projector.

The producers had gone this route with their previous movie, which had an even more accelerated post-production schedule. Since the visual effects could not be readied on film in time for preview, and a public screening with unfinished effects was not allowed, the digital route was necessary. Bond films, by their nature, rely heavily on action and, apart from *The Jackal*, I had limited experience in action films, but with Vic Armstrong directing the second unit, we were able to edit his scenes as they were shot, and this gave me confidence.

The primary problem was that every action scene was always too long and it was necessary to prune them quite viciously. No director likes to see his work butchered and, after a while, it is hard to know whether damage is being done. The danger occurs through familiarity. After many viewings, the scenes begin to seem slow and objectivity is hard to maintain.

I assumed the preview audience would tell us if we were still overlong. I was in the same cutting room where we did *The Prince and the Showgirl* in 1957. On that occasion, I was the second assistant and basically did the joining on a Robot splicer, a device now found only in film museums. The room and the studio had changed very little but everything else was utterly different. Not a Moviola nor a joiner in sight and no film at all. I was surrounded by high-tech equipment. Four Avids, all interlocked, and a giant plasma screen that turned the cutting room into a mini multiplex. All I had to do now was learn how to use it.

All this preparatory work resulted in very few errors indeed and enabled us and the sound editors to meet all our dates with time to spare. Having a director who was well prepared and producers who had been through the process many times was a considerable asset.

The previous Bond film had two editors sharing the burden and they were under the gun. In our case I managed alone.

This was the nineteenth Bond film and it was produced by Cubby Broccoli's daughter, Barbara and her half-brother Michael Wilson. Working for the family business was one of the more pleasant aspects of a production that was staffed by loyal subjects who had toiled on other Bond films. There was a routine built into the rhythm of the day-to-day pattern of work and the producers offered a subsidised lunch in a giant tent so the unit could eat together. I never worked on a film that fed so many. Some days four hundred people were catered since there were often three units working in the studio.

Bond movies have always been constructed around the action sequences and Vic Armstrong masterminded these beautifully. He was principally involved with the Thames boat chase, the skiing sequence, which he shot in the French Alps under difficult conditions, and much of the caviar factory section. Michael Apted controlled all the material that featured the actors. In addition, we had a model unit working under John Richardson. They started in the Bahamas with underwater submarine material, then moved back to Pinewood for other scenes.

While the second unit were in France doing the ski sequence, they were virtually snowed in and often unable to work. The forecast was poor. Avalanches were everywhere in the Chamonix area. Although we had storyboards for all the action, the producers were worried about the sequence, which was proving difficult to shoot and, perhaps, required further thoughts.

I worked with an excellent storyboard artist to plug the holes in the narrative. After discussions with Michael Wilson, these new images were spliced into the existing material so that Apted and Armstrong could see how Pierce Brosnan and Sophie Marceau would fit into the general scheme and, more or less, dictate how the shots could be achieved when the first unit finally made it to the slopes. This was good creative fun, but very time consuming since I was also cutting the rushes that came in every morning from two other units. First thing in the morning, I could be found cutting with one hand and eating my cereal with the other, which is just the way I like it. However, it is not so good for the digestion.

Since Pierce Brosnan did not ski, he had to be towed and it mostly looked like it. I cut him short and put on a bit of swishy ski noises and nobody noticed.

About midway through cutting the skiing scene, the producers requested a three-minute teaser trailer for screening in Portugal at an exhibitor's convention the following week. That was a tall order and I had just three days to deliver the goods. Fortunately, with all the digital gear, I was able to make a trailer in about thirty minutes that appeared to satisfy everyone. We then, however, had to manufacture the darn thing, scoring it, adding sound FX, reprinting the shots we had used, and marrying it up for projection. The promotional aspect of film making is something the editor has become increasingly involved in, though I have never claimed to be much good at inventing trailers. The final international and domestic trailers are normally manufactured by the distributors who employ specialists to work on them.

Other promotional material involving product placement was required and the assistants spent many hours making tapes for this purpose. We had product from BMW, Smirnoff Vodka, Bollinger Champagne, CAT tractors, and others to satisfy. Around the time of release, these companies would be using footage from our film in their commercials and print ads.

By June the crew were exhausted. They'd been shooting since January and ended up on a very complicated set. It was a submarine that turned turtle, went into a steep dive, and finished up nose down on the seabed. The set was on hydraulics and everything was played for real, which took ages to rig. Apted was going mad with frustration and everything was gradually slowing down. We now looked likely to exceed the deadline, thus eating even further into my finishing period, but no. . . . They did, finally, complete the principal photography on or around June 25.

The wrap party was a big and glittering affair. Like everything on these lavish productions, it was done with no expense spared. It was held in a disused factory opposite the semiconstructed Millennium Dome on waste ground and was thus a spectacular venue for a noisy party. The evening was cool and promised rain. The booze flowed like water. Bollinger Champagne was everywhere and about a thousand people turned up. They screened the eight-minute trailer I had prepped for the Cinexpo convention and the crowd whooped and hollered through it. Wandering around the rooms, I was amazed by the number of people I did not know or recognise. Did they all work on the show or were they liggers (gatecrashers)? I have often boycotted wrap parties since, for me, they are not wrap parties at all as my hard work is just beginning. However, this was too much fun to miss and I forgot, for a while, the travails ahead. This was on a Friday night.

On Monday I completed the cut and on Tuesday we ran it for all concerned. The editing crew were reasonably happy with the film, though I had to admit I was disappointed. I really believed there was little or no juice left in these stories which, no matter how much effort was poured into them, still seemed old fashioned and interminable.

The producers, however, were very pleased, saying the film was much better then *Tomorrow Never Dies*, though that one had been soured for them by lack of co-operation with the director. Here at least they had a team who were enjoying the experience. We realised *The World Is Not Enough* would please a lot of people and so now set about improving it.

The preview was set for August 3 at a modern multiplex just outside Reading. After that we'd know our fate. It was arranged that the day prior to the preview, we would set up and test the sound system that was installed especially for us. This was because the film did not exist in a combined form and the sound was running separately. All went well and I was satisfied with the standard of projection. The following morning we arranged to run the entire film before the public screening that evening. A core audience of about fifteen people had been invited to attend the rehearsal since I had reported all was well. We started the screening and there was no sound at all. Consternation. What had gone wrong? Several people were dispatched to the booth to examine the problem, but there seemed to be no solution. They even suggested that our track had been wiped by a giant magnet. That was rather unlikely, we thought. The chap who ran the sound had no idea what could have occurred and by now almost an hour had dragged by. Normally we had to leave the theatre by a certain time since they had a public performance of *Star Wars: The Phantom Menace*. Everyone was despondent and perplexed since the day before all had been fine. Quite without warning, the sound suddenly came on. It seems the sound guy had found a switch to press and so, we rewound the show and ran it, finally, without a hitch. Memories of *The Grass Is Greener* flooded back.

That evening we returned to the theatre for the preview. The skies were leaden with rain and three hundred people were lined up outside. They were allowed in early, but they had a further wait. The American execs from MGM arrived directly from Los Angeles and the guy from the research company made his usual announcement. The audience had been told that they would be seeing a new action movie, but not specifically Bond, so when it was announced they would be seeing the new James Bond movie you might have expected some reaction. Not a peep, so I knew we had a nerdy audience. That attitude persisted and, although we had no walkouts, we felt a distinct hostility. They filled in the cards and left. The focus group, quizzed afterward, were also unhelpful. I felt, overall, that it was a jaded lot. Eventually the figures were worked out and we scored around 78 percent. It was good, but somewhat lower than most Bond movies.

Apted and I were quite depressed after all this. We had perhaps expected the audience to be more receptive. In America they would have been much livelier. I suggested to Michael that we should take the print to New Jersey and have another screening, but he was not up for that. The producers would never have sanctioned it, not wishing to allow the MGM execs to have too much say in the final version of the film. This was one of the rare occasions when politics crept into the scene.

The film soon went off to Los Angeles and was viewed by the Ratings Board who slapped an R rating on it. Too much violence and too much sex. Really? There was very little sex in it. They demanded that the best line in the movie, "One last screw?" as Bond is garrotted by the villainess, be removed. Naturally this was fought over and won. I reckoned we'd be nibbling away at the gunplay until everyone got bored and gave us the rating we required. Since all those kids with guns had been holding weekly massacres in American schools and the movie makers had been blamed for the situation, the Motion Picture Association of America were now scrutinising every frame before passing a movie. They even asked us to remove blood from a shot where no blood was present. Now they were seeing things. After making the changes, the film was resubmitted and passed without problem Later when we discovered that it's not the same board members who see the film each time, I wondered how can they truly know what has been altered?

Later I saw *Casino Royale* in which Pierce had been replaced by Daniel Craig. In the six years that had passed, the ratings board must have undergone a change for, far from nitpicking about certain words and violence, they had gone overboard, allowing a nude torture scene and endless gunplay. The film was dirty and gritty and modern. They had awarded it a PG-13 certificate.

As the cut was more or less complete and, while the film was resubmitted to the ratings board, Apted and I were able to take a break. He had looping to attend to in America and I wanted to be with my family so we both took a couple of weeks off. When we started the show, I had never envisaged having a minute away from it and here I was with time to spare. Very odd. I kept thinking maybe I had not tried hard enough. Perhaps I should be worrying more over the film?

The only remaining imponderable was the score, which we now started to record. David Arnold had scored the previous Bond film, as well as *Independence Day* and *Godzilla* and was the only composer ever discussed. The producers liked him and that was that. He was obviously going to give us a very loud score. The sound editor, Martin Evans, had been upset by the scoring of *Tomorrow Never Dies* and had made it plain to everyone that there had to be more space given to sound effects, which had largely been drowned out by the heavy scoring. This time we all hoped that David would moderate things, especially during the action scenes. Michael had heard all the sketches and seemed happy with them. I already disliked the title song, which had been written by Arnold with lyrics by Don Black and performed by a group aptly called Garbage. Coming directly after a stunning river chase which put the movie into high gear, it was directly defused by this dire three-minute song that accompanied the titles. Well, what did I know? The kids would probably love it.

The music sessions were held at AIR Lyndhurst studios in Hampstead, a converted Anglican church much used by film composers. The music was, as predicted, very noisy. We were a long way from Rosza and Herrmann. The rather good boat chase was now dominated by the music and I feared the real mix would again be hard. Getting the balance between music and effects was difficult when both are going full blast. Everyone around me seemed to think the score was great. Then I saw the titles, a very complicated set, entirely made in the computer, and multilayered, with girls writhing around in oil. Very kitsch indeed. I didn't like to mention that word since the whole thing was treated with rapture by the producers and Apted and I guessed they cost plenty. Sometimes I think I am getting too old and too cynical for my own good. Bring back Maurice Binder, wherever he is.

Then we scored the finale, another thunderous wall of noise. I really despaired. Too much noise on the track makes the audience irritable. All this was partly due to so-called advances in recording systems that allow us to put far more information on the soundtrack which is a licence for already half deaf mixers to push the envelope even harder. There is a place in hell for Mr. Dolby.

On completion of the music recording which ended in a rousing new version of the famous Bond theme, the orchestra were treated to champagne by the producers, and they went away happy. Now we had reached the final stage of sound mixing. The premixes of dialogue, effects, and footsteps had been done at Pinewood while we were recording music and the negative of the film had been cut, so I was already looking at silent prints. The cameraman, the late Adrian Biddle, was in Nova Scotia shooting another film, so the print went off to Toronto for his notes after which final printing could begin when the sound negative was available.

We began the final mix that was completed in fourteen days. I named the mixers "Noise R Us" and kept urging them not to be overzealous. When a sound mixer gets hold of a reel full of explosions and helicopters overhead, all stops get pulled out and caution is thrown to the wind. The entire room shook when the big bangs occurred, but I had John Hayward's word that the film would not sound too loud in the Odeon Leicester Square. John had mixed many of the Bond films and does an excellent job, but I could not believe his hearing was not a tiny bit impaired after years on the desk.

After final mixing, we ran the film for a few people to see whether we needed to adjust any volumes. It all sounded too loud to me. A few days later we saw the final print and it looked and sounded okay so they started bulk printing. The lab in the UK made three thousand prints and the American lab churned out a further four thousand. Imagine the cost of all that.

It was some relief to realise we had actually finished the film on time as planned and with little fuss, but it was hard to break up. The end of a movie is like a *petit mort*, leaving a crew one has been with night and day for months, and may never meet again. I think we all felt saddened. The work had been hard, especially for the assistants who toiled long into the night after I had left the studio, but it had also been fun. Apted was a good leader and there was a distinct lack of tension, so everyone was happy. I know I was.

A few days afterward, I met the sound guys at the Odeon Leicester Square for a run through of the film, after which we had another last luncheon together. It was great to see it on one of the few remaining big screens and John had been quite correct in his assessment of the sound. It was loud, but bearable. I figured I did not have to look at it again until the cast and crew screening which was scheduled for a Sunday in November, but long before that, UIP had a big media screening which I was unaware of, and so, it was a surprise when the critic of the *London Evening Standard*, the late Alexander Walker published a grudging review, thus jumping the gun and annoying his fellow critics. This was not a kosher thing to do and could put us in jeopardy with the other critics.

On November 21, we had the cast and crew screenings of *The World Is Not Enough*. Virtually every screen on Leicester Square was used. Up to five thousand people attended. Apted introduced each screening. The film had already opened in America and Apted told each audience that the projected weekend take in America was $35 million which, if true, was excellent news. With Thanksgiving on the horizon, it might just have the legs to carry it over to Christmas, though there would be huge competition. He clearly hoped the film would make a fortune and, in some way legitimise him as a feature film director. Oddly, these guys are still insecure even when they been very successful.

The final scene was played out at the London premiere, a glittering and brilliant affair. I don't recall attending anything like it before. Lavish barely describes it. Someone had the bright idea of turning St. James' Square into a giant designer marquee for the party after the show. Imagine one of London's oldest squares turned into a place of fantasy for a night, with the whole space enclosed in some kind of black velvet, then adding lights, bars, and buffets plus a thirty-piece band playing up on a podium while about a thousand people in evening dress milled around drinking Bollinger.

Kiss Kiss (Bang Bang)

No, this was not the Hollywood film with Robert Downey Jr, nor was it Pauline Kael's collection of reviews. *Kiss Kiss (Bang Bang)* was one of the few films I have edited that never got a release. It didn't even go direct to video. It went nowhere at all, which is a pity. Well, it does turn up sometimes on cable tv, very late at night. We all love our orphan children, and *Kiss Kiss (Bang Bang)* was a true orphan.

It was conceived by Stewart Sugg who had previously written and directed an odd film titled *Fast Food*. I never saw that first film and might have thought twice about taking on *Kiss Kiss (Bang Bang)* if I had, but they sent me the script, I liked it and was keen to edit the film. I think they were all a bit surprised, particularly as I'd just come off a pricey Bond film. I liked the script because it was unusual and somewhat off the wall. I should have remembered liking *Honky Tonk Freeway* for the same reason.

The story was that of a middle-aged hit man, Stellan Skarsgård, who is doing his last job before retiring from the Hit Man Club, whose headquarters was under the Thames. The boss of the club claims that members cannot retire until death. However, our man, looking for honest work, takes on the task of caring for the retarded son of a gangster, played by the late Chris Penn, brother of Sean. This was a sort of faux gangster movie with a soft heart.

The shoot lasted seven weeks and the director of photography was fired after two days. Perhaps I should have realised something was amiss, but they took Tony Pierce-Roberts on as the new cameraman and we had worked together on *The Trench* so I figured he could get them out of trouble, though he had not been around to prep the film and one of the locations chosen was barely workable on their small budget. Had he been in on the prep, Tony would have talked them out of the folly of using that location which was to cost them plenty.

The film was so low budget that rushes were not printed. Because of this, we were unable to have proper previews and were confined to showing videos to small groups. This did nothing to help finish the film, which most people found confusing and unfunny. Stewart Sugg and I plugged away. I tried every trick in the book but nothing seemed to bring the film to life. Finding a composer was hard. Eventually John Dankworth was persuaded to write the score in his inimitable jazz style. We had not worked together since *Darling*.

The picture was mixed at Shepperton and I thought that was the end of the show, but no. They submitted it to Sundance and were rejected. The reason given was that the opening was confusing and the film did not know quite what it was. So I got called back to recut the opening and, while I was at it, they opened up the rest of the movie.

I have no idea where the money for all this came from. I waited for some information about the release but nothing came. Then I heard from Stewart that it was shown at the Taormina festival with great success and the foreign rights were sold to most territories, but not the UK, where, it seemed, nobody wanted it.

I never heard another word about *Kiss Kiss (Bang Bang)*. A sad story and a big waste of time and money, but I still like the movie and some French company must also have sniffed money since they marketed a DVD of the film, which I have a copy of, in English.

☆ ☆ ☆

I knew that John Schlesinger had not been well for a long time. That he was overweight was obvious, but when we discovered that his diabetes had gotten bad, it worried us. John did not walk too well. His extremeties were affected. He had difficulty with our stairs and had to inject himself with insulin in the stomach before meals. None of that deterred him from eating substantial meals, nor did his illness deter him from taking on work, sadly, because if he'd retired, the end of his life might not have been so difficult.

His last film was *The Next Best Thing* in which Madonna starred with Rupert Everett. Making this movie almost killed John, but he would not give up. I never saw the picture, but I do recall that our friend Ruth Myers was designing costumes for it. She could not, however, deal with Madonna and left the film. John was treated badly by his actors and, from what I understand, his several different producers. This in itself was sad for a man who needed a good solid producer who backed him.

When the shooting was finally over, he went to France for meetings with the film's composer, Gabriel Yared, but he was not well and collapsed on returning to his London home. He was rushed to a hospital nearby. I saw him there and he was making jokes about his state, but soon after, the doctors decided that John required a heart bypass. He was moved to another hospital and I visited him again. He was fretting about his film, which was then being mixed without him. All the advice in the world would not stop him worrying about this silly movie, but he cared about it as though it really mattered. John was professional to the end and Michael Childers, John's companion of many years, was adamant that he should not return to the film and urged John to drop all thoughts of it.

The one great advantage of the bypass was that John lost some weight and felt considerably better. He and Michael then returned to Los Angeles.

City by the Sea

I first read the script of *City by the Sea* when we were in France during the winter of 2000 just after the Christmas break. Michael Caton-Jones had spent a considerable time developing this subject for Al Pacino, who eventually passed on it. Michael's friendship with Robert De Niro had maintained over the years and Bob was interested in playing the lead. The script was based on a true story that had appeared in *Esquire* magazine concerning a policeman in New York whose father was electrocuted for murder and whose estranged son was then accused of a killing, which he didn't do. The script had been written originally by Frank Pierson, but this version was written by Caton-Jones himself.

While there was no immediate pressure to commit to this script which, frankly, needed work, I did express interest in it. Then the whole thing went very quiet for almost the whole of 2000, during which time I cut *Kiss Kiss (Bang Bang)* completing that in September. In the final stages, I received a variety of calls regarding my availability to edit further films. The one I really wanted to cut was *Harry Potter* and I was interviewed by Christ Columbus and David Heyman. Eventually they decided to employ an American editor, so that one went away. Then came *Posses-*

sion, which was based on a novel by A. S. Byatt and was to star Gwyneth Paltrow. Directed by the American, Neil LaBute, I found this script tedious and it was a quick and easy turndown, eventually being edited by Claire Simpson. Other approaches and turndowns included Tony Scott's *Spy Game,* Jodie Foster's *Flora Plum,* which was never made, Iain Softley's *K-PAX* Don Boyd's *My Kingdom* and Roger Michell's *Changing Lanes.* None of these films turned out to be great, so I'd made the right decision.

The family was not best pleased when I decided to stick with Caton-Jones, whose project was now green lit. This would involve living in New York for a lengthy period, which was not a happy thought. I enjoy the city but can get very isolated and lonely there. I felt it was time to stop being a gypsy and become a husband and grandfather again.

I began cutting *City by the Sea* in London at Twickenham when shooting began in November. I started a rough assembly as the material came in.

Early in the new year, I had an upsetting phone call from Michael Childers in California. John Schlesinger had had a stroke and was in hospital. I told Michael that I had to move the edit to New York and get things set up but would then fly out to see John. It seems that John hadn't been taking the antistroke medication he'd been prescribed after his heart surgery.

I arrived in New York later in January, working at Tools in Tribeca, most of which seemed to be owned by De Niro.

Once things got organised, I flew to California to see John. He was then at Cedars Sinai Hospital in Los Angeles. As I approached his room I saw, through the half opened door, a person in a bed. John's name was on the door, but I could not believe it was him. He was so thin and drawn. I asked the nurse who said it certainly was him. I knocked on the door, but there was no response. "You'll need to wake him up," the nurse instructed me. I tiptoed into the room. John, who had lost an enormous amount of weight, did not look up because he was asleep with a phone tucked under his chin. I dithered and wondered whether I should stay or leave. The nurse knew her patient. She gently shook him awake. "You have a visitor, Mr. Schlesinger," and John opened his eyes. I don't think he knew me directly. "I was on the phone with Betty Bacall," he muttered. I told him who I was. "Of course I know you," he said. For the next thirty minutes, John, when he was awake, slipped in and out of sense. For example, when his speech therapist came into the room, he said "This is Jim Clark who edited some of my films," but just before I left he told me, "From that window you can see the Music Centre," which was quite wrong, it being downtown. This first stroke had left him impaired physically and mentally. I left thinking I might never see him again.

City by the Sea finally wrapped in mid-February, amidst much anguish and torment because it had been taken over by the completion bond company who promptly fell into disfavour with Caton-Jones by firing his wife, Laura Vieder-man. Laura had kept the show afloat and was just going into hospital to have a baby when they did it. They also fired the line producer, Roger Paradiso, so we entered the post-production period without a producer, which is never a good idea. The post-production supervisor appointed by the bond company was Susan Lazarus, who held the purse strings and to whom we had been forbidden to speak by Caton-Jones since she belonged to the enemy. None of this made any sense. It is necessary to speak to these people who arrange all the events that have to occur during post. Relations between Michael and the production company, Franchise, were at a standstill.

Having had a couple of video screenings and reduced the film to a hundred and fourteen minutes, I figured we'd just about cracked it. With just four weeks before the screening of the director's cut, we had to push on. I also had to order optical sections, which meant talking to Susan Lazarus. Fortunately Caton-Jones had taken off for Toronto so I allowed Susan to come into the room to discuss the situation, though she had not been allowed to see the film.

Privately, I figured the film had deeper problems. The story seemed old fashioned and the central performance from De Niro was very low key. Michael's direction was lacklustre at best. I just couldn't imagine audiences paying money to see this film, which I also felt would be poorly received by the critics. I did not mention any of these fears to Michael since they were negative and unhelpful. In any case, he was obsessing about being ripped off by Franchise and I respected his attitude though I, in no way, condoned it. The Caton-Jones' vendetta against Franchise and the completion bond company got in the way of the reality of our situation and thus the completion of the picture was jeopardised.

We did go ahead and conform the film, so that we could run it and check focus and other possible problems that do not always show up on the monitors. While Michael went into the hospital for some surgery on his shoulder, I super-vised a rough mix. It was shortly afterward that he went to Los Angeles to show it to Warner Brothers, who would market it. The print, still with its holes where inserts had not been shot, was then sent on to Cannes where the suits from Fran-chise were attending the festival.

By this time, I had decided to leave the picture and the last meeting I had with Michael was mid-May 2001. My seventieth birthday was coming up on May 24 and I wanted to be home for that. Also I was tired of sitting in small airless rooms in New York waiting for something to happen on a film that seemed mired in inaction. Michael did not seem too unhappy with the prospect of losing me and rather fulsomely apologised for involving me in the mess.

So I left. I had a very pleasant final evening with my crew and got on the plane home. Fortunately I was able to involve Mitch Stanley, who had started the film in November as the Avid assistant, then subsequently was hired to edit some television shows in Los Angeles. These had failed and so he was again free. I felt that Mitch could cope with Michael and finish the show. Afterward I heard from him and Kathy via emails that the film was still on a "go slow" and that everything was taking forever to achieve. At least they now had a composer and the titles were finally in the works. I gathered that the blessed inserts would also get shot, but I never heard whether Franchise saw the film and had comments, nor whether De Niro had seen it. I figured the show would run until September, by which time I would have totally forgotten all about it.

However, in June, Franchise swooped down on this whole mess and had everything removed from the room over a weekend and sent to Los Angeles. When the crew arrived on the Monday morning everything had gone.

This was almost the final blow. Caton-Jones and Mitch were sent to Los Angeles to complete the film, thus missing the frightful September 11 terrorist attack that ocurred only a few blocks from the Tools editing facility in Tribeca.

When I got to Los Angeles in January 2002, working for HBO on *The Gathering Storm,* I was able to meet Mitch and Michael. Mitch was no longer on the payroll, having been bumped at Christmas, but Michael was still asking him to work. The music was being written by a composer from Liverpool who Michael had persuaded into the show. He was not too expensive for Franchise and the film was due to be mixed in February.

Michael and I had dinner, over which he told me that the three years he had been involved with the film were the most depressing of his career. He was exhausted by it and I knew from his behaviour that nothing had improved between him and Franchise. Though he claimed to be broke again, I urged him to forget Hollywood and the money aspect. I suggested he should return to his roots and also to involve a producer whom he trusted. It seemed to me that he had flourished when Art Linson was producing *This Boy's Life.* At least the two of them argued amicably and respected one another, whereas on *City by the Sea,* Michael was alone and forced onto the defensive every day, hitting back constantly and upsetting everyone, including himself. There is an ugly atmosphere when fuck is the most commonly used word.

When finally released, *City by the Sea* was hardly in theatres for more than a couple of weeks. Far more interesting was the breakup of Franchise. Under the leadership of Elie Samaha, who had started his career in dry cleaning, they had managed to make several losers and were then in court over some doubtful tax wangles.

The Gathering Storm

Returning home one evening, I had a call from a lady at HBO in Los Angeles enquiring about my availability to edit a film for them in the autumn. I recalled that John Bloom, who had edited *Wit* for HBO, had told me that he'd had a good experience with the company and urged me to accept anything they might offer. Shortly afterward I received another call from Julie Payne, who worked with Ridley Scott in London, also about the same project. This was to be a story about Winston Churchill in the thirties and was called *The Lonely Years*. Written by Hugh Whitemore, it was to be directed by Richard Loncraine and produced by Frank Doelger. I knew that Frank was a friend of John Bloom's and figured that John had been the number-one editor they had approached. I had met Frank when he was producing *Last of the Blonde Bombshells* which they had sent to me for comment. I had known Richard Loncraine for many years, since he had been hired by John Schlesinger to make sculptures for *Sunday, Bloody Sunday* while still a student. We had become friendly and he eventually did some second unit work for me on *Rentadick*, which I was certain he'd like to forget. Although he had pursued a career in features, Richard was basically known as a commercials director. That he had directed one episode of *Band of Brothers* for HBO was probably the reason they had given him *The Lonely Years*, later retitled *The Gathering Storm*.

I read the script, which I thought okay without being exactly great. It was good TV. Albert Finney was to play Churchill and Vanessa Redgrave was to be Clemmie. The airdate had been set for April 20, 2002, so whatever, we did had to be quick.

I cut this film at Shepperton which soon became tiresome because I was repeatedly stuck in traffic driving home. At least I got to hear the radio, but inching my way home after a hard day in front of the Avid was no fun. More and more I became determined to work only in the heart of London.

I spent one morning cutting a two hander between Finney and Redgrave. They were at the dinner table. He smoked his cigar and ate simultaneously, while she chatted and ate, finally losing her temper and throwing dishes at Winston. Neither of them could match anything. His cigar was always in the wrong place when you wanted to make a cut and Vanessa was doing different things on every take, picking up dishes and glasses in all the wrong moments. I found myself having to cut to get props to match instead of cutting for performance, which is never a good thing. It took a great deal of massaging.

Editing Winston's speeches in the House of Commons was quite laborious and I thought the results less than inspired. One night Vanessa got angry because she was not in the final shot of the movie, which made me wonder if she had read the script. The producer and director had to coax her back on set and had hastily written a new scene to appease her. Hugh Whitemore was dragged in to write it. This took a long time and so far as I could tell, when I left the studio, Vanessa had still not agreed to shoot the scene. Albert Finney was fine with it but it was Vanessa's last day on the film. She eventually agreed at the eleventh hour.

We finally wrapped the film on a Tuesday and there was a party held that night at the Irish Club in Eaton Square, a posh address, which was a good place for a party as there were two rooms, one of which was as a disco that did not impinge on the other. I had a long chat with Vanessa, whom I had not met during the shoot. She looked far better in life than she did on screen.

I had but one day to complete the edit before the producer saw it with the director, so I was somewhat up against it. At one hundred minutes in rough assembly, it ran quite well and they were both happy. I managed to slim it down to ninety-three minutes before prepping a tape to send to HBO in Los Angeles.

We were expecting to leave for Los Angeles in January for further work, though there wasn't that much they could alter unless they asked for additional scenes. Finney came out of the film quite well. Certainly his portrait of Churchill was consistent. It wasn't a fancy film, but a square old-fashioned piece, which should have pleased the older television audiences.

We finally moved out of Shepperton and into another cutting room in Barbly Road, Ladbroke Grove where I now faced a school playground, which was hardly quiet when the little terrors were out there slugging each other. It was a very ethnically mixed area, within striking distance of Portobello Road where there were good cafes. It was certainly far better than flogging out to Shepperton.

After Christmas we all packed up and went to Los Angeles where Gavin Buckley and I stayed at the Chateau Marmont on Sunset Boulevard. The living room became the editing suite with two Avids. Loncraine and his family were in the room above. Somehow the idea of rolling out of bed and moving directly to the Avid was oddly appealing to me. It certainly beat driving to Shepperton every day. On one occasion I was still in my pyjamas and dressing gown when Richard appeared. This was a first for me. I'd never edited in pyjamas before, but having everyone in the room, talking together or on cell phones or ordering room service, made it difficult to work. The room became bedlam. Richard likened it to a French farce.

LA, a city I'd never really liked, was fun this time. We worked hard and played hard. I saw many old friends in the evenings and was able to visit John Schlesinger who was still very sick after his stroke a year before. By that time Michael had decided they should move to Palm Springs, which would be much less stressful for John. It was there that they created their last home, but John's health did not improve. He had successive strokes, each of which returned him to the hospital, we kept thinking, for the last time. But John was made of very strong stock and, despite his frailty, he refused to die.

One Sunday my ex-assistant Nick Moore drove me to Palm Springs. It was January and the film festival was happening there. Michael asked us to lunch. Arriving at the house, we saw a whole slew of SUV's outside. Inside there were about a score of people. John was sitting in a wheelchair, covered by a blanket, looking gaunt and hollow, while everyone milled around him. He did not speak at all, but Alan Bates told me that he had spoken, he thought, the day before. It was sad to see John so changed. He was a mere shadow of the man I had known so long. What a cruel fate it was. I sat next to him at lunch. He ate nothing, but at some point, tried to talk to me. I never heard what he was trying to say. I left John's house that day with the knowledge I would never see him again.

☆   ☆   ☆

HBO arranged a small preview for fifty people. Hugh Whitemore attended. I met the fabled Colin Callender, a dapper fellow who had supported the film from the start, though Frank Doelger asserted he was basically only interested in its Emmy potential. The screening was technically fine, a miracle considering how it had been achieved. Changes were emailed to London and the online tape being altered accordingly. Sadly, the audience did not give the film the top marks we had expected. Always puzzling when they appear to be totally absorbed and then fail to give you their blessing. I was impressed by the laughter when the punters responded as planned. Though the figures were not great, HBO seemed pleased. Some new scenes were thought necessary and Hugh was sent off to write them. They were shot later in London over a couple of days, Finney being hauled back from Hawaii at great expense.

I had them all in the cutting room spotting music with the composer Trevor Jones. At the end, after hours of discussion, Jones announced that he might not have time to complete the score since he was engaged on a mammoth television series called *Dinotopia*. This set the cat among the pigeons.

In the midst of all this, Ridley Scott sat with us, smoking a big cigar and trying to redirect the show. The film was now, effectively, in the hands of the producers. Richard Loncraine and I were no longer calling the shots and I found myself surrounded by advisors who all had their ideas of improvements. The curse of the Avid had arrived. These machines which make work such a joy have a grave disadvantage. Anyone can use them and everyone can be an editor. Formerly there was always a waiting period when changes were requested and if a sequence required a recut it had to be sent to the labs overnight. Now you just press Apple D and the sequence is instantly available for changes.

It was at this point that an easy job suddenly became harder. I would not say it was unpleasant, just relentlessly difficult and something inside kept reminding me that this would never have occurred if we were cutting on film. The digital system was open to all. Particularly to Colin Callender. There was a scene involving several actors descending a staircase, which ended with a conversation between Linus Roache and an actor playing the German Ambassador. Linus is quite short and the other actor was tall, thus forcing Linus to look up at him. None of us considered this odd and for weeks this master shot remained unaltered. Then we suddenly had a request from Colin to arrange for Linus not to appear so short and not to look up at the German. We all considered this a potty idea and it would be almost impossible to achieve. Reshooting was out of the question. We consulted Angus, our visual effects man, who said it could be done digitally. Since the two actors moved away from the others when they reached the bottom of the stairs, Angus would gradually increase Linus' height so that by the time they faced one another they were level. What about Linus' eyeline? Wouldn't that mean he'd be looking over the top of the German's head? Not to worry. Angus'll fix it. Which he did. It cost about £25,000.

Finally it was back to England and whatever we did to the film now, had to be communicated directly to HBO and to Ridley Scott. Ridley was now touring the globe with *Black Hawk Down*, so Julie Payne sat in for him and the BBC were also sent tapes of the film for their notes.

The notes were flying but the movie remained much the same. Once again I felt like a masseur. I cut and recut and made more changes every day. On many occasions the executives sitting behind you were already having a second or third brilliant idea while the editor was still working on the first. Multiple versions abounded and it was sometimes hard to keep track of them. I might have HBO saying they liked version one of a scene, and Ridley saying, "No, no." Version two was much better, while the director wanted version three, and the BBC favoured version four. It became silly.

A simple little film had ended up being very difficult. A proliferation of opinions from a variety pack of producers both here and in the states meant that everyone had to be satisfied and I spent my days massaging every cut. At the time we were about to temp mix, the head honcho of HBO decided the movie was not yet ready for exposure to the magazines and demanded another recut. While waiting for his verdict, it became clear that if he delayed any longer we wouldn't meet our airdate.

My head had been in the trough for what seemed like weeks. We'd worked weekends and long into the night to satisfy everyone and I was heartily sick of it. The movie was fine. It was always going to be a minor television film, but now they saw it as a potential Emmy winner and therefore intellectualised every cut. Frank Doelger, a perfectly sweet man, was always polite but relentless in his pursuit of excellence. I hoped they had not massaged all life out of this film. The director's mind had gone on hold and he seemed to have usurped his position to Frank. The good thing was that they all got along without losing their tempers, though there were times when my fuse began to smoulder.

A message from our post-production person asked me to work on Sunday for a couple of hours. They must have thought we had no private lives. As it was, I had the kids over and was not readily available, but I ended up going in and messing around pointlessly for an hour or two. This company was constantly throwing curve balls at us. I was told by John Bloom that working for HBO was easy and pleasant. In this case, he was wrong.

For the next few weeks, we fiddled and diddled around with this movie for a variety of reasons. One screening was for the magazines to review before broadcast and Colin put us through many hoops, eventually leading us to a new composer.

Trevor Jones had been contracted to score the film and we had spotted with him in January. Now it was time to hear his samples. Before Richard left for Los Angeles to cast his next film, we visited Trevor's studio to hear some ideas, largely based on a Vaughan Williams piece that we'd used in the cutting copy. The section for the titles was first up and Richard was not happy. Though professing to be musically illiterate he was, nevertheless, able to describe what the music should be doing and what we heard was hardly promising. Trevor agreed to supply further samples. These arrived after Richard had gone. Frank heard them and was unimpressed, as were all the other members of the team. A rapid decision had to be made since time was running out. Frank decided to change composers before it was too late. He recalled meeting a composer named Howard Goodall, whom I had heard of but hardly in connection with serious work. I knew he had scored

Bean and other material featuring Rowan Atkinson, but whether he was up to this I wasn't certain. There was, however, no time to waver. Howard was engaged and produced samples quickly, all of which were sent to HBO in LA for their approval. Our new composer was put on the right track by Richard and Frank and, in the end, supplied a score that worked well, considering the time constraints.

While Howard was writing, we were mixing with John Hayward at Pinewood. The premixes were already made and, as Graham Sutton provided the music, it was mixed in. Finally I was given permission to cut the negative or we would not make the airdate. Normally cutting the negative is the end of the affair, but this is no longer the case because negative can now be recut without losing frames.

We finally completed the mix at midnight on a Wednesday and I left the film the following day. As I left, Frank Doelger proposed I should edit another film for HBO in September. Not likely, I thought.

Having left the film, we were in Ars-en-Ré when Cory McCrum-Abdo, our tough post-production person called to say that the mix had not been received too well in Los Angeles. They hated the music and were unhappy with the semi-animated titles and a freeze frame at the end of the film. Also, while we were at it, please remove the drool seen to be dripping from little Charley's mouth in one shot. We had all been staring at this scene that we had watched two thousand times without spotting the drool and now, at the eleventh hour, some wiseacre at HBO sees it and wants it removed.

So John Hayward, the sound mixer from Pinewood; Chris Ackland, the effects editor; and Graham Sutton, music editor, were despatched to Los Angeles where they would remix the film under Ridley Scott's instruction. I did wonder where Richard Loncraine was in all this and, if they disliked the music, how they intended to fix it without the composer. I had got out just in time.

This nightmare, however, fulfilled its function. The film did win Emmys, thus justifying all Colin Callender's requests. It was also a success with the critics and the viewers.

I now began a period of rather comfortable unemployment that stretched on for many months, largely due to the quality of the scripts that flopped through the letter box. My next film, however, wouldn't even have a script.

MIKE LEIGH AND SLOW FADE TO BLACK

Vera Drake

In September 2003, Gavin Buckley and I visited the rooms on Wardour Street where we'd edit the Mike Leigh film, *Vera Drake*. The rooms were new and therefore empty. The gear would be installed the following Wednesday and we'd start shooting on the 30th, which was the day I'd have to make my speech at John Schlesinger's memorial.

John had died in late July. Thankfully I was first on the bill so I didn't have to follow Alan Bates and Alan Bennett. This sad event was held at the St. Johns Road synagogue, where John, it was said, used to worship. His big memorial had taken place already in Los Angeles and the British equivalent was nothing like as lavish. John's brother had arranged it. I could not help but think that John's memorial should have been held in a gay bar. This religious venue seemed all wrong. Alan Bates spoke in what turned out to be his last appearance in public because he sadly died shortly afterward. He was very brave to turn up at all. Many didn't recognise him. Alan's memorial was held at the Royal Court Theatre which was a far more fitting place than a North London synagogue. John would have loved it.

I had known Mike Leigh since I was a member of the teaching staff at the London Film School in the seventies. We met only during breaks and, over the succeeding years, as he made more films and became known for his improvisational techniques, we met only occasionally. Mike had just watched his *All or Nothing* collapse at the box office and was very unhappy. We saw the film, which we liked, but there was evidently a small audience for it and it had fared badly in America. Evidently the public no longer wanted to see bickering families in a high rise.

So it was surprising to receive a call from Tim Corrie in the early months of 2003 regarding Mike's new film, which he was interested in having me edit. I was surprised because Lesley Walker had cut *All or Nothing* so I expected her to be involved in the new one. As it happened she was busy with Terry Gilliam on *The Brothers Grimm* so was not available. I had a meeting with Mike and his producer, Simon Channing Williams, and they offered me the job. Mike would say little about the subject, save that it involved abortion. "Are you scared of blood?" He had already started work with the actors, a process that would take six months. Shooting was due to begin in October.

I went to France that summer with the knowledge that I had a good job to start afterward. In fact it was more than a good job since I was exposed to Mike and his technique, which was a blessing. For once there was no script. I did not have to make notes about something that didn't exist.

A week before shooting Mike gathered all the technical staff together and talked us through the story. There was even a sort of breakdown that passed for a script. It consisted of headings only. At least we now knew that the period was 1950 and that a working class family was involved. The leading actress was Imelda Staunton, whom I had seen only in musicals. She was to play the mother, a cleaning lady, and backstreet abortionist.

Mike was very adamant about secrecy, not just because of the possibility that someone would blab to the press. He wanted to allow the cast to perform without knowing what was really going on. It's a director's trick of course, but when it works, there is clearly spontaneity that he would like to preserve.

We left the room with the knowledge that this could be an interesting ride. Shooting was to start the following week at locations around London. Mike had Dick Pope, his usual cameraman, and the intention was to shoot on Super 16, tests of which had already taken place. It blew up to 35 mm via the digital route to everyone's satisfaction.

The shooting went as planned. Everything was thoroughly rehearsed. I was happy not knowing exactly what the rushes would bring. I had most of them cut by lunchtime, then Gavin and I had to find something to do until the rushes, which normally happened on a television monitor on the top of a bus or at the location in North London. At these sessions, knowing what I'd chosen and edited during the day, I was interested to hear what Mike chose. Normally the same take. After I'd muttered, "That was the take I used," several times, Dick Pope suggested they should make a t-shirt with that rubric.

Mike did not shoot a lot and it was all very easy to edit. One simply went for performance and tone. He made few choices at rushes. Clearly we'd be raking through everything when he joined me. He worked entirely on intuition and so far the material was very typical Leigh. The working class characters were dear to his heart and the upper classes were seriously lampooned.

After shooting ended, I had a rough cut of two hours, thirty minutes. We completed the shoot on a Friday and I ran the cut for Mike on the Monday morning. After lunch we returned to the cutting room and carved out the unwanted material. We worked together for two weeks and then the film was locked. It was just about the quickest job I'd ever done, simply because Mike and I were in sync. He rarely looked at other takes, having trusted his editor, and *there was nobody else to please.* It was a very happy experience. Not only did I like Mike and his films, but working without a script was a real release. I knew this was a film I admired and wasn't surprised at its eventual success. I always thought, however, that it was a little long and told Mike several times, but he didn't want to hear, so I shut up. "If I'd edited *Topsy-Turvey,*" I said. "It would not have been three hours long." This remark got a look from Mike that implied I shouldn't continue with that idea.

We now had three very important screenings. On a Monday we were off to Paris at the crack of dawn to show the film to Alain Sarde and his gang who had backed the show. We left on the 8:10 Eurostar, arrived in Paris at 11:30, and were met by a young man in a small car, who took us directly to the Club Marboeuf, a screening room that turned out to be quite good. They sat through the movie and then waxed ecstatic. Their praise was a bit too fulsome for my taste. They said it would surely be entered for Cannes and was quite wonderful, at which point the flunky drove us back to the Gare du Nord and we boarded the 5:10 to London.

Then on the Tuesday we had two screenings for the British backers. First for the Film Council in the morning and the other investors in the afternoon. You can imagine how sick we were becoming of viewing this piece. Both screenings were met with complete silence, which I hoped did not denote disinterest. I was convinced we were five minutes too long at two hours, but Mike didn't agree. Now we had to press on to prepare for the Cannes selection committee.

It was late February when Mike finally decided that the title of the film would be *Vera Drake.* I was beginning to worry that it might go to the Cannes selection board as *Untitled 03*. I looked at the tape that was going to Paris and hoped that the selection board would accept the film because, if they didn't, it would throw poor Mike into a decline.

We started final mixing of *Vera Drake,* while the saga of getting into Cannes continued. Nigel Stone, our sound editor had done wonders with the dialogue tracks. The police station was shot in a location that was on the flight path of City Airport and poor Imelda's big scenes were often overlaid with jet engines that were not in general use in Vera's day, so they had to be removed. Nigel had cleaned the tracks up, spending many exacting nights doing so. In the end, Imelda had no loops at all. Nigel had saved the originals.

Mike Leigh and Simon Channing Williams heard from Paris that our inclusion in the competition was unlikely. Mike and Simon decided that to be rejected by Cannes would look very bad. Luckily, Simon had the wit to send a courier to Rome. The man who ran the Venice Film Festival saw the tape directly and called up to say he wanted the film for his festival in September, so things looked better.

☆   ☆   ☆

It's not every day that one has a film in competition at the Venice Film Festival, so I was interested in listening to the world's press and participating in the discussions. It's always fun to be in Venice, even for forty-eight hours, so, despite the fact that Studio Canal wouldn't pay for my flight or hotel, I decided to go and pay for myself.

I left London on Sunday afternoon, flying with Imelda Staunton, her actor husband Jim Carter, and Phil Davis, who played Imelda's husband in the film. We were met by Festival officials and decanted into a water taxi that took us to the Excelsior Hotel on the Lido, which has a jetty and is clearly where most stars appear since there were hundreds of photographers and fans around. A car then took me to the Hungaria Hotel which was five minutes walk from the Hotel des Bains where most of the luminaries stayed. I walked about in the broiling heat and acquainted myself with the place. Our group met back at the Excelsior for a trip to the mainland where we had booked space in a restaurant. By this time Mike was with us. We were hosted by the publicists for the film and heard tales of how disorganised the screenings had become. *Neverland* had been billed to screen at midnight and eventually got shown at two in the morning. The punters remained in their seats, partly because they knew Johnny Depp was coming.

We turned out at eight thirty the next morning for the critics screening, which was packed with about a thousand journalists. We sat through about thirty minutes to check that all was well, then returned to the Hotel des Bains for breakfast on the terrace, where we bumped into Harvey Weinstein, who actually appeared to have lost weight. "I edited myself," he told me with a wry smile.

We then attended the press conference and sat at a long table with microphones. The press asked questions that were translated and most were addressed to either Mike or Imelda. None came my way. Then we were back to the Hotel des Bains for a buffet lunch in their exquisite garden. I bumped into Helen Mirren and Taylor Hackford. She was on the Jury that was headed by John Boorman. The premiere was a very grand affair. It was on time and the audience was most attentive. The projection was excellent and the audience gave a big round of applause when the film ended.

The film won two major awards: Best Actress and Best Film. Mike rang me later in France with the good news. There are few prizes at Venice and we copped the best. I think even Mike was taken by surprise and was somewhat fearful that the media hype might lead people to expect more than the film could deliver, but the main thing was to get the film into theatres in the first place. As it was only the beginning of the awards season, we'd done well.

The fallout from the success of *Vera Drake* had been considerable already and the next manifestation of this was the opening night of the London Film Festival. The night before I did a rehearsal and it was amazing to think that this film, which started on Super 16, was able to be projected on one of the largest screens in the country without appearing soft or grainy. Dick Pope, the cameraman, remarked that he never thought he'd see a Mike Leigh movie in the Odeon in front of a black tie audience. *Vera Drake* took three awards in London and, almost immediately after, Mike Leigh flew to New York to receive a Gotham Lifetime Achievement Award.

Opal Dream aka Pobby and Dingam

This movie gave me many headaches. It was based on a book about a small girl living in the opal mining area of Australia. Her dad was a miner and she had a slightly older brother. She also had two imaginary friends named Pobby and Dingam who disappear. The brother then discovers them, dead, in dad's mine. The girl languishes and eventually dies.

It was directed by Peter Cattaneo, who had helmed *The Full Monty.* At an early meeting, before they left for the Antipodes, I had queried whether the American distributors knew the girl died. "Of course they know," said Cattaneo. "It was the only reason I wanted to make the film." These were words that he eventually had to eat.

The film began as low budget and was shot in Australia. I was in London with Gavin. I should not have touched this movie and my feelings were confirmed as the first rushes featured the little girl, who was not a natural actress and lacked charm. She should have been replaced, but wasn't, and the film died despite all our efforts to save it.

There were so many producers and writers that one got dizzy wondering who would walk into the room. The boy, who was a good actor, recorded a voiceover for the movie and was constantly asked to rerecord it. The music was scored by Dario Marianelli, who developed a cunning and original sound for the invisible and non-existent creatures, Pobby and Dingam. Sadly, all this became mangled in the many opinions that floated round the cutting room. Poor Nigel Stone, whom we had brought on as sound editor was driven crazy by the constant changes.

I eventually left the film, which was shown that year in the marketplace at Cannes. The very first thing the American distributor insisted on was that the little girl should not die. They would foot the bill for a recut and a remix. This was done by Nic Gaster, whom I met one day in the street, imparting the news. He wanted a shared credit, which I was pleased to give him. I'd have been happy to remove my name entirely. He'd recut the opening and closing scenes, but had left most of the internal editing alone.

I forgot about *Opal Dream* until one night when it turned up late on BBC2. I looked at it. Thank God the BBC, who had money in the film, had decided not to cut the ending. In the version I saw, the little girl died as before. But why did they try to bury it so late at night? It would have made perfectly good family viewing. The only person I knew who saw it was my daughter Sybil, who watched it with her son Dylan, who was then nine. She found it quite moving.

The Decameron: Angels and Virgins
aka *Virgin Territory* aka *Medieval Pie*

You can guess what happened to this film by the number of titles it has had. Dino De Laurentiis produced it with his wife Martha and Tarak Ben Ammar, who had battled with Franco on *The Young Toscanini*. Dino had contracted to make three movies in 2006 and was already in his late eighties. These were the films: *Hannibal Rising, The Last Legion,* and *The Decameron*. All three tanked. Harvey Weinstein, who had recently left Miramax and had formed the Weinstein Company took all three films. It was rumoured that Tarak had invested heavily in Harvey's company so Weinstein was unable to decline. We thought he might have smelled money in *Hannibal Rising*, which dealt with Hannibal Lecter's early life and he must have been disappointed when the viewers did not run to the box office. Each film cost something like $30 million.

The Decameron was shot in Italy, so Gavin and I were set up in cutting rooms at Cinecittà, where years before I had worked with Zeffirelli. Shooting had begun in Tuscany, under David Leland's direction. The lead actress was Mischa Barton whose character had the hots for Hayden Christensen's character—the male lead. Sadly Ms. Barton's performance did not come across well. She had come from a television series and the relationship between her and Christensen seemed non-existent. She never looked happy. After mulling this situation over for a couple of days, I decided to call the director and level with him.

I made the call on the weekend. Leland agreed with me. "I've tried very hard to get a performance out of her," he said. "She is not co-operative, but Hayden is good. Don't you think?" I didn't think he was so good either, but I didn't tell David.

We soldiered on. Dino and Martha dropped into the cutting room and said they were pleased, but Dino had a bee in his bonnet about the "Cart Pusher" scene in which David Walliams had a cameo. I had this recut many times. As we left Rome, Gavin turned to me and said, "The good times are over." He was quite right.

Nothing is worse than warring producers. The editor finds himself simply there as protector of the film. Dino and Tarak installed themselves in my very small cutting room in Soho. Dino sat near the monitor to my right, speaking mostly in Italian. This was translated by Lorenzo, a young assistant from Italy and Los Angeles, who sat near David Leland. David was like the umpire who was constantly shouted down. On my left sat Tarak, speaking loudly in French. Occasionally they would all speak at once in a mixture of languages. I would sit with my back to them, doing nothing. Then I would turn slowly to face the bedlam. "How can I work with all this noise? Would you please be quiet and tell me what you want." All would stop and silence fell on the room for about thirty seconds. Then it started again. This scenario continued until preview.

David Leland, inspired by Boccaccio, had decided that a prologue was required to help condition the audience. He had been poring over books of explicit engravings of vaginas and penises that he had put into the scene over which Michael Palin gave a cod lecture. This would have normally put us into an X-certificate territory. Rampant cocks generally do. This was the copy we unleashed on an unsuspecting audience in New Jersey, who were stupified. Did they expect more of the same in the body of the film? If so, they were in for a disappointment. The preview, attended by Harvey, Dino, Tarak, Lorenzo, and David, was a disaster and the film never recovered from this screening.

At a postmortem meeting, Harvey suggested we should, "Monty Python the film up," and had we seen *Spamalot?* We saw it that night and could not see how we could achieve this suggestion.

Back in London, the prologue was the first thing to go and voiceover was added soon after. We mixed the film, which was then given over to the Weinstein Company, retitled *Virgin Territory* and consigned to a very high shelf, unshown in theatres and DVD, until the summer of 2008 when it appeared briefly in Paris under the title *Medieval Pie*. It was not a good experience.

When a film starts by being miscast, there is no saving it. To inject life into a dead film is hard, some might say impossible. The experience of working on *Virgin Territory* did nothing for me, except to illustrate that I was now too old for this game, which had changed. There were just too many cooks around spoiling whatever they touched. I decided not to accept any old script that plopped into the letter box. I would wait for Mike Leigh to make his next.

Happy-Go-Lucky

I wanted to work with Mike for years. There is no script. It's a bit of a gamble, but it's fun and putting my trust in the filmmaker is important. At least you cannot blame yourself for being involved. I felt lucky that someone still had faith in me. At the preliminary meeting, Mike introduced me to the cast as the oldest member of the unit. He was probably the second oldest. Afterward, as he found the film with the actors, I waited six months for shooting to begin which was April 2007.

Again, working with Mike was a happy experience, though not without its days of worry and concern. There were a few periods when I had no idea where the story would go. Was Poppy a lesbian? Would Scott, the driving instructor, kill her? I was not sure about this film. So much so that I called Mike and told him I was worried. "So am I," was his reply. He told me to stop worrying. So I did. The shooting continued and I did notice that Mike would stop shooting for several days and work with the actors. Was it my imagination or was he stopping shooting more often than usual? Presumably, he was finding the film, which was proving elusive.

We sat in the production van in Finchley Park on a very wet night and saw the rushes of a night shoot in what's left of Battersea Power Station. In the scene, Poppy encounters a tramp and listens while he talks a stream of what might be sense or nonsense. I didn't believe the scene. What was she doing there in the first place and why did she go to investigate the tramp? I was concerned that this scene would topple the film over into gross fantasy and asked Mike what the point was.

He defended the scene, which seemed to have strayed from another script, and it stayed in the film, though I would have cut it out.

Apart from that, the movie fell together easily, though the driving scenes were hard to edit, especially those, improvised on camera. The sequences were experimental. They were shot on HD, using four small lipstick cameras. Two on him and two on her, with a film camera, and Dick Pope, in the back, shooting forward.

Directors, when running tape instead of film, tend to allow the scenes to go on and on. I received many hours of material and the transfer of tape to Beta/SP cost a bundle. It had been budgeted at eight grand and ended up costing more than double that. Also I had no idea what Mike might use. He was ruthless with the material and hours were reduced to minutes.

The unit went to Southend-on-Sea, one of my favourite day trips, where Poppy's sister lived. They spent days hanging around as Mike "found" the scenes, which were set in a back garden that could have been shot anywhere. These two scenes were shot in single takes with no cover. The interiors were shot in the studio. So apart from a scene-setting shot and an end section with Poppy and her family on the seafront, Southend was barely seen.

Happy-Go-Lucky took Mike and me three weeks to cut and lock. I had not beaten my own record. I used to tell producers that I wasn't good but fast. Mike then worked with Gary Yershon on the music. Gary was writing his first score for a film and he did a great job. His score was spare and melodic.

We finished the film and mixed it at De Lane Lea during November and it was entered for the Berlin Festival in early 2008. On our first night there, a dinner was thrown by the production company at the Paris Bar, where the service was deadly slow. I got quite sauced and did not get to bed until one. I was up again at five to run a rehearsal of the film in the massive theatre. Mike stuck with me. We ran the whole film because I'd asked for it to be plattered, otherwise we would not have run the whole thing. We limped out of there, had some breakfast, and then Mike went off to do endless interviews. By now the two actors, Sally Hawkins and Eddie Marsan, had arrived.

The film was not yet sold to America, though Gail Egan, our executive producer was trying to do a deal with Miramax. She finally succeeded at three in the morning.

The press had seen the film that morning. This would be the first intimation of reactions. There were hundreds of world press there and many cameramen. Mike and the actors answered lots of quite good questions, and it became evident that the film had played much better than I'd expected. After a drinks party, we all went off to the premiere in the huge theatre that had been completely empty at

5 AM. The theatre was now packed. The film played very well. The audience were really with it, laughed in the right places, and enjoyed themselves. At the end, they gave us a great ovation. Mike and the actors went on stage and he called me up to represent the crew, making a very flattering speech.

Then we read the first reviews in *Variety*, *The Hollywood Reporter*, and *The London Evening Standard*. All were very positive. The only so-so review was by Bradshaw of the *Guardian*, but even he gave us three stars.

There were many awards showered on it after that. I was pleased that Sally Hawkins was recognised by the Berlin jury and got her Silver Bear. After the British premiere in Camden, it opened in the UK to great reviews. It subsequently played in many festivals and Mike was on hand in America and elsewhere to do Q&A sessions.

It was at a screening of Sean Penn's *Into the Wild* that I bumped into Art Linson again. The film, under Penn's direction, had been a little long but had its heart in the right place and I saw, in the credits, that Art was the producer. As we moved from the theatre to the party, I mentioned to Laurence that I would have easily made the film thirty minutes shorter. We went into a crowded room for drinks, not realising that Art was present, but he saw me and, though we hadn't met since *This Boy's Life*, he rushed over and gave me a big hug. "I want you to meet Sean," he said with enthusiasm. He called to him and Sean Penn left the group he was with and came over to us. "Sean," said Art. "I want you to meet the greatest film editor in Europe." Sean said, "What did you make of the film?" Instead of saying good things and praising the director, which is normal on such occasions, I simply said, "It's too long." Penn turned on his heels and walked away. Art made a face and said, "That didn't make him happy." Perhaps I shouldn't have been honest.

Nine

Mike was away with *Happy-Go-Lucky* when I went on to edit *Nine*. Finally, I was to cut a musical film, a very rare event in the British film industry, and this was a big one with a starry cast. I had not been too well for months with balance problems, which became so severe that I stopped driving. However, when the agents asked me if I was interested in editing *Nine*, I put aside my ailments and went to the interview with Rob Marshall, director of the film version of *Chicago*, which I had loved.

I had seen the stage version of *Nine* some years before at the Donmar. It was never one of my favourites, being concerned with Fellini, here called Guido, trying to find his story that eventually turned into *8½*. When I told Rob I no longer drove a car, he said a limo and a driver could be at my disposal. The production team also agreed that Gavin could be my assistant. Rob told me he had used the services of a young editor in New York, Wyatt Smith, who had cut a television special for him and asked if I'd mind having him on board. I was happy to accommodate him. Rob then explained that the post-production would be done in New York for fourteen weeks. After some delay, during which other editors were interviewed, I got the job and was jubilant. Rob had agreed to everything. The film was to be shot at Shepperton, where I had spent most of the sixties.

Back home, Laurence wasn't so sure. "You are seventy-seven years old," she said. "You have a balance problem and you should not be going to New York for months in the middle of winter."

I went to work on *Nine* and things hotted up straight away. The film looked terrific, but Rob's technique for the production numbers was exhausting. He shot an average of eight hours film for a five-minute number and it all looked fabulous. This was his way and I could see why Wyatt Smith was on hand. In fact, Wyatt taught me a lot. Using his system, it wasn't difficult to get through the vast quantity of material. It was actually fun. What to do then was the problem. In post, you could go on cutting these numbers forever and they'd look good every time. How to decide? A plethora of choice would face anyone who tried to edit this stuff.

One of Rob's orders was that Harvey Weinstein, who was the money, was not to see any of the rushes. "Don't show him anything," said Rob. After we'd been rolling a couple of weeks, Harvey arrived in the cutting room at Shepperton Studios. "I got you this job," was his first remark. "What are you going to show me?"

"Nothing," I replied.

"Who said that?" asked Harvey.

"The boss," I answered.

"But I'm the boss."

"No," I said. "In this case, the director is boss."

He thought about this for a minute then, without seeing a frame, ordered that a promo reel should be made which would go out with *The Reader*, his current release. I said I would make that, and I did, though the bulk of it was cut by Wyatt Smith.

"Remember," Harvey said as he left. "I'm the boss."

Rob was pleased that Harvey had not seen anything, but I felt bad about it. After all, the money had come from him.

The production numbers continued to flow in with titanic regularity. Of course there were dialogue scenes as well, but despite the luxury of being driven to the studio every day, I began to feel even odder and out of it. So much so that I consulted a neurologist who asked for various tests. He quickly discerned that I was suffering from apraxia and, in no way, should be editing a stressful film. He also said that I certainly could not travel to America. The doctor showed me my brain scan. He pointed to white blobs that had no business being there. How to disperse them and what they indicated was less clear. What was clear was that I wasn't well.

So, after five weeks, I resigned from *Nine*, which was hard. I hated letting everyone down, but I knew it was the right thing to do. I went on the set to say farewell to everyone. Rob was high up on a rostrum. Climbing it, I found Harvey up there too, so I said goodbye to him as well and told him not to contract apraxia, which had messed with my head. Everybody was extremely pleasant to this old film editor who had let them down badly.

They did not replace me for a few weeks, but then Claire Simpson came on board. Claire had cut *The Reader* and was a good choice. I felt relieved that they had her. She was, however, taking on a major headache in the Hamptons, where *Nine* would be fine cut for an opening sometime in late 2009 to qualify for Oscars, while I faded slowly into the sunset, now facing retirement. In my case, let's make it a long fade. But not before I have made some observations about the future of film editing.

The Future of Film Editing

Prophecies are always dangerous, but here goes. Already we are seeing changes—crewing is down to a minimum, and salaries have not increased—if anything, they've gone down. So, with an almost solo experience and more and more producers advising him, no *telling* him, what to do, the editor has little or no autonomy any longer. So perhaps the film editor will work on the Internet. Already we are seeing the rise of the laptop editor on lower-budget pictures. The larger movies will stay in the cutting rooms for a while and computer generated imagery (CGI) will be used more and more. Crews will get smaller and storage will increase. Even today, with films like *Watchmen* and *Transformers* cut really fast, there is scant need for structure or sense. None of this will make much difference to the finished result. Audiences will not say, "This was cut at home by a lonely editor on a Final Cut Pro." No, they might be observing that the film had been edited by a team in different houses, even in different countries, and that not one editor had anything to do with it. Obscurity will be considered a necessary requirement. In fact, the longer the movie and the less understandable, the more it might be revered. I exaggerate of course.

But films should still tell a story, which requires a writer, a cast, and a crew who can bring it to a screen. Nothing can be achieved without those elements, whether the story is shot on a chip, recorded on a paperclip, or cut in a back bedroom. Without a story and characters you're dead.

I hope this book and the trawl through my life have been worthwhile. You might have understood that actual editing is a small part of it—though the rudiments must be learned, the actuality of the process is difficult, and cannot be taught. Experience is all. As the foregoing proves, most of the editor's time is wasted—the time taken in joining one piece of film to another is not long, and far less laborious than when we were cutting film.

It's been a good and lengthy career, very little of which could have been achieved if Laurence had not stayed by me. Sybil married David Caines, a graphic designer and artist. They produced two wonderful boys, Jackson and Dylan, who are the apples of our eye. Kate married Hart McNee, a jazz musician, and they had Lily, who is now thirty. Kate moved from San Francisco to New Orleans, where she has worked for JazzFest for many years. Hart died during 2008. David married Lucy, his childhood sweetheart, and they lived for a time in Katmandu and Greece, where their two children, Oliver and Jessica, were born. They are now in their twenties. David and Lucy eventually divorced, but we remain in touch with Lucy whom we will always regarded as our daughter-in-law.

I am retired. Laurence was right. At seventy-eight it was time. Although Mike Leigh had asked me to edit his next film in the summer of 2009, I thought I might have to let Mike down, or we'd have a *Nine* situation all over again. So I made the decision although I was sorely tempted. In any case, I don't walk that well any longer, cannot go out alone, and tend to fall down. An ideal situation for sitting and watching all the DVDs that I'd never found time to see, and reading all those books I've yet to get round to and, health willing, to enjoy the rest of my life. In Hollywood I used to watch Margaret Booth, who had begun film editing in the twenties, as she was helped from the limo that had driven her to work at Ray Stark's office. She was over ninety and crippled with arthritis, but she still worked. I didn't want to be like her.

My grandson Jackson, at fifteen, watched *The Day of the Locust* with me recently. He thought it wonderful. Laurence saw only the last sequence and said it was a masterpiece and why had Schlesinger and I not been nominated that year?

"It was not a commercial hit," I explained. "But it was a great film."

It's not always the hits that one remembers fondly. As this story has indicated, I had fun working on them all.

It did get me to thinking. Perhaps my life has not been entirely wasted after all. When I look at my family, I know it hasn't.

INDEX

400846

CPSIA information can be obtained at www.ICGtesting.com
Printed in the USA
LVOW091445280512

283599LV00002B/97/P

9 780979 718496